It may also help us realize how far we still have to go. This would be especially helpful for social workers, who, like most people in the helping professions, tend to be absorbed with the burdens of those they are trying to help. Thus, they seldom look back to learn how they arrived where they are, or to obtain perspective on the magnitude and character of the problems they are dealing with. Hopefully, this book will help them gain that knowledge. An awareness of the rich tradition behind modern social work should also add to their professional security and philosophy and help them, and others, in planning for future social action.*

In addition, a general history of social welfare in America is needed for classroom purposes, especially for students enrolled in social welfare history, social policy, and other similar courses taught at schools of social work and elsewhere. This work was written, in part, to fill that need. I have taught the history of American social welfare for several years, and, along with my students, have been frustrated at times by the lack of a text-like book that could be used for the course; this work grew, in part, from that experience.

This, then, is a history of social welfare in America. Since social welfare functions within and is determined by the larger setting of which it is a part, the book is set against the background of certain developments in American history, especially social and intellectual trends. And because so much that has happened in America in this field has been derived from or been influenced by the British experience, some attention has been given to English developments.

This is by no means a definitive or comprehensive account of the entire field; to cover all aspects of the subject would require

---

*On the role of history in social work see: Clarke A. Chambers, "The Discipline of History in a Social Welfare Curriculum," mimeographed paper prepared for the Minnesota Resource Center for Social Work Education, 1971; Karl de Schweinitz, "Social Values and Social Action—the Intellectual Base as Illustrated in the Study of History," *Social Service Review* 30 (June 1956): 119–31; Philip Seed, "The Place of History in Social Work," *Case Conference* 15 (February 1969): 407–408; and Elizabeth Wisner, "The Uses of Historical Material in the Social Work Curriculum," *Social Service Review* 34 (September 1960): 265–72. See also Merle Curti, "American Philanthropy and the National Character," *American Quarterly* 10 (Winter many volumes. Rather, it is a brief review of America's main social welfare policies and practices from the colonial period to the present—one that attempts to bridge the gap between a topical survey and a monographic study. Naturally, some developments are alluded to only briefly, such as the role of religious and ethnic groups and the whole field of corrections, and others have been omitted, particularly American social service overseas, measures for the physically handicapped, recent efforts to stimulate self-awareness, and the like. Still, the book embodies what I believe to be the essence of social welfare history and its significance in the American experience. There is little here that is new, for I have tried mainly to assemble, assimilate, and synthesize the literature that already exists in the field; I hope that the work, nevertheless, will have value.

Perhaps a word on the footnotes is in order. As stated, this book grew in part out of my classroom experience. Since it contains information accumulated from many sources (including my students) over a period of years, it would be impractical and impossible to cite all the material used. Moreover, the source of a quotation here, or a statement there, would not do justice to the associated material and the whole process of reflection that has gone into my course and into the manuscript. So I have used notes sparingly, and, for the most part, only to elaborate points made in the text. At the end of each chapter, however, I have included a bibliography in which the reader may locate sources. (Although many of the sources could have been listed in several places, for reasons of space I have listed each only once, in that place where I think it would be most useful.) These include many of the titles that my students have found helpful, as well as those I have relied on in preparing both my classroom lectures and this study.

Finally, the obvious should be mentioned—"social welfare" is a broad term that has no precise definition. Agricultural programs, for example, which were designed to provide financial help and other forms of assistance to poor farm families (but which too often have become methods of subsidizing the rich) may be considered part of our social welfare system. The same may be said of education or, to go a little afield, of political machines which, by distributing food baskets or fuel in winter, often helped the needy. In other words, almost anything can fall within its scope, as William Graham Sumner, the pioneer sociologist, indicated in an essay entitled "Sociology," written in 1881: "In truth," Sumner declared in objecting to treatment of the matter as a novel issue, "the human race has never done anything else but struggle with the problem of social welfare. That struggle constitutes history, or the life of the human race on earth." Since this book is not a history of the human race, perhaps I should define "social welfare." As used here, the term embraces those social security, social service, and health programs, activities, and organizations, public and private, intended primarily to promote the well-being of individuals who society felt needed and deserved help.

At first, the objective of those efforts was simply to care for those in need—either as individuals or in groups. Later on, it became a matter of preventing destitution and other social ills and of restoring those in need to economic and social self-sufficiency, of bringing them up to a standard of living consonant with that of others in the community. Still later, social workers fought for the creation of constructive programs aimed at ensuring a more secure and abundant life for all. Our social welfare system today, then, acts not only to support and enhance the well-being of needy individuals and groups, but also to improve community conditions and help prevent and solve social problems affecting all citizens. To use current terms, it plays an "institutional" as well as a "residual" role in society. To follow the development of these activities is to trace the evolving concept of man's responsibility to man and of the community's and the government's responsibility for the well-being of all citizens.

Far too many debts have been incurred in the preparation of this book for me to attempt to list all of them here. As indicated, much of this work rests upon the scholarship and ideas of others, including many students in my social welfare history course at the University of Wisconsin–Milwaukee. I am certain they will understand that adequate personal acknowledgment is not possible. I have attempted, however, to indicate in the text those authors and works from which I have borrowed most.

I do wish to acknowledge the special assistance of a number of people. Among these, I would like to express my special gratitude to Freeman Cleaves of Millburn, New Jersey, who read the entire manuscript and improved it in many ways. Another discerning critic who read the entire manuscript and suggested changes that I was happy to incorporate in the final revision is Clarke A. Chambers of the University of Minnesota. I am also heavily indebted to Charles Harbaugh, my research assistant, who did an excellent job reading and analyzing articles in various social work journals. For the funds to engage Mr. Harbaugh, and for me to spend the summer of 1971 working on the manuscript rather than in the classroom, thanks is due to the Graduate School of the University of Wisconsin–Milwaukee. My gratitude is also extended to the secretarial staff of the U.W.M. Department of History, and especially to Kathy Poplawski, for typing various drafts of the manuscript with speed, accuracy and good cheer.

Once again, I owe a special debt to my wife, Joan, who not only provided the atmosphere and the encouragement without which this book would not have been written, but who also took the time to improve its prose. Finally, I would be remiss if I did not mention my children, to whom this book is dedicated—Stephen, Anne, and David; never once did they complain about the long working hours, and irritabilities, of an author. For that I am deeply thankful.

While all of those mentioned helped me, the writer is solely responsible for any errors in fact, interpretation, and style.

W.I.T.

January 1973

Chapter 1

The Background

THE BASIC TENETS and programs of any social welfare system reflect the values of the society in which the system functions. Like all other social institutions, social welfare systems do not arise in a vacuum; they stem from the customs, statutes, and practices of the past. Therefore, one cannot understand current efforts to help the needy without first comprehending the foundations on which they were built. And since the practice of assisting people in need as we know it in America did not originate in this country but was transplanted from the Old World to the New during the colonial period, we must go back in time, perhaps even to antiquity, to begin our study of American social welfare.

Hospitality to strangers, for example, was recognized as a virtue even among primitive peoples. Hammurabi, the famed ruler of Babylonia some two thousand years before Christ, made the protection of widows and orphans, and the weak against the strong, an essential part of his code. Buddhism, founded about 400 B.C., taught that all other forms of righteousness "are not worth the sixteenth part of the emancipation of the heart through love and charity."

The ancient Greeks and Romans frequently discussed the matter. Aristotle (384–322 B.C.) spoke of man as a social animal and, as such, one who had to cooperate with and assist his fellow men. He also said it was more blessed to give than to receive. In fact, the words "philanthropy" and "charity," and the concepts for which they stand—love of mankind, love of humanity, brotherhood—are of Greek and Latin origin.[1] Then there was Cicero

---

[1]Philanthropy comes from the Greek words *philo,* or love, and *anthropos,* or mankind; charity comes from the Latin word *caritas* (or *carus*), or love (brotherly love), although there is some evidence that it may be derived from the Greek word *haris* (or *harieis*), which technically means grace but may imply brotherly love or its equivalent.

(106–43 B.C.), the famed Roman, who wrote: "Justice commands us to have mercy on all . . . , to consult the interests of the whole human race, to give everyone his due," rich and poor alike. It is not surprising, then, that the ancient Greeks, and the Romans after them, had a variety of ways of relieving distress and helping those in need. Some of those we might not recommend today, such as slavery, concubinage, and euthanasia. On the other hand, they also had such other practices as daily allowances or pensions for the crippled, public distribution of grain for the needy, and institutions for the custodial care of various unfortunates, especially youngsters orphaned as a result of fathers lost in battle.

Even more important for the history of American philanthropy and social welfare are the ancient Jewish doctrines which teach the *duty* of giving and, equally important, the *right* of those in need to receive. Throughout the Old Testament, the ancient Hebrew collection of historical books, laws, proverbs, psalms, and prophetic writings that go as far back in time as the late eleventh century B.C., one finds commandments to be charitable to the unfortunate—the sick, the old, the handicapped, and the poor.[2] Thus, the Scriptures not only state that "one might break off his iniquities" by showing mercy to the poor, but command that "thou shalt not harden thy heart nor shut thy hand" to the poor, and note that "it is forbidden to turn away a poor man . . . empty-handed." Moreover, such "charity should be given with a friendly countenance, with joy, and with a good heart."

Not only is everyone who can afford to do so obliged to contribute to charity, but according to the Old Testament, all those in need are obliged to take it. Thus, as Maimonides (1135–1204), the Jewish scholar and philosopher, put it: "Whosoever is so much in need of charity that he cannot live unless he receives it—as, for instance, a man who is old or sick or in constant pain—but takes none out of pride, is guilty of bloodshed and is responsible for his own life; so that he has nothing for his suffering, save punishment and sin."

The Talmud, a collection of Jewish law and tradition (based

---

[2]This is especially true of the Pentateuch, the first five books of the Old Testament, sometimes called the Torah. Within the Pentateuch, the book of Deuteronomy, the law book, is most important for these purposes.

upon biblical texts and rabbinical commentaries on those texts) codified around 500 A.D. and still considered the source of authority among orthodox Jews today, prescribes exactly how charitable funds are to be collected and distributed, including the appointment of *gabbaim,* or tax collectors, to administer the system.

How much should be given a poor man? The Talmud provides the answer: "Sufficient for his needs in that which he wanteth." Thus, if someone is hungry, "he should be fed; if he needs clothing, he should be clothed; if he lacks household utensils, they should be purchased for him . . . . [E]ach and every one should be supplied with what he needs."

Christianity carried on this tradition. Its emphasis upon good deeds, love of one's enemies, and entry into heaven through mercy and charity stemmed, of course, from Old Testament doctrine and Hebraic law and custom. Since Jesus, Peter, Paul, and the other founding fathers of the Christian church—including the first fifteen bishops in Jerusalem—were Jews, it is not surprising that the New Testament no less than the Old contains many verses that stress charity.[3] The text that perhaps more than any other weaves together the threads of early Christian–New Testament teaching on charity is the description of the Day of Judgment in St. Matthew, especially: "And the King shall answer and say unto them, Verily, I say unto you, Inasmuch as ye have done it unto one of the least of these my brethren, ye have done *it* unto me."

The Decretum, a compilation of papal decrees, canons of church councils, and commentaries of church lawyers codified in the twelfth century which, along with subsequent decrees and writings, is considered the authoritative source of law for Christians, contains an elaborate discussion of the theory and practice of charity. Study of the Decretum reveals that the leading principle underlying early Christian social welfare policy was similar to

[3]It should also be mentioned that the seventh-century Koran, the sacred text of Islam, or Mohammedanism, exhorts the believer to show charity to widows, orphans, wayfarers, and the unfortunate, and specifies various "right" ways of giving. Almsgiving is one of the Five Pillars of Islam (along with confession of faith, prayer, pilgrimage, and fasting during the holy month of Ramadan), and those who perform such good deeds are promised paradise.

the Hebrew idea that preceded it—poverty was not considered a crime. And while discretion was to be observed in bestowing assistance, and careful rules were elaborated for discriminating among the various classes of needy people,[4] generally speaking, evidence of need overrode all else. It was assumed that need arose as a result of misfortune for which society, in an act of justice, not charity or mercy, had to assume responsibility. In short, the needy had a right to assistance, and those who were better off had a duty to provide it.

In practice, these ideas operated in a variety of ways. At the outset, when the church was small and its early followers owned no private property, there was little need to establish any formal social services. While there was some poverty, it was not a social problem. Those suffering misfortune were among close friends and associates who came to their assistance as a matter of course; mutual aid, in other words, sufficed to meet the needs of the faithful.

With the passage of time, the end of persecution (as marked by Emperor Constantine's conversion to Christianity in the fourth century), an increase in members and wealth, and greater ease of travel, church fathers found it more and more necessary to establish a formal system of charities. Beginning in the sixth century, the monasteries that emerged served as basic agencies of relief, especially in rural areas. Some monastic orders, in fact, were organized to help the needy. Receiving income from their lands and from donations, legacies, and collections, they not only gave generously to those who came to their doors, but carried food and other provisions to the poor in the community.

By the eleventh century, with the evolution of feudalism, a system of government in which those who possessed landed estates also held political power, there was little uncared-for distress, at least in theory. Most people lived on feudal manors as serfs, protected by their liege lords or masters against such hazards as sickness, unemployment, and old age. In return for imposing a strong measure of constraint on individual freedom, feudalism, in

---

[4]A man's first responsibility was to his family, especially his parents, then to his neighbors, and after that, to strangers. Even among strangers, however, a rather elaborate hierarchy existed.

other words, provided a form of social insurance against the exigencies of life.

Those who received no such protection, especially in the rapidly emerging cities, were often helped by social, craft, and merchant guilds. While for the most part the guilds provided benefits for their own members (who, because of their craft or trade, were somewhat removed from the immediate threat of poverty), they also provided assistance to others. Thus, many maintained "works of charity" for the town poor—they distributed corn and barley yearly, fed the needy on feast days, provided free lodgings for destitute travelers, and engaged in other kinds of intermittent and incidental help.

A more important source of aid to the needy during the Middle Ages was the hospital. Medieval hospitals did not merely provide medical assistance to the ill; rather, they housed and cared for weary travelers, for orphans, the aged, and the destitute, and in general provided a variety of services for all those in need. Most early hospitals were attached to monasteries or were found along main routes of travel. Soon they appeared in cities and later were taken over by municipal authorities, thus forming a link between ecclesiastical and secular charity. By the middle of the fourteenth century, there were hundreds of such institutions in England alone. They varied in size from those caring for a dozen or so people, to others accommodating up to several hundred.

Most important in terms of administering medieval poor relief was the aid dispensed by ecclesiastical or church authorities at the diocese or parish level. The bishop of each diocese was charged with the duty of feeding and protecting the poor within his district. He was directed to divide the total revenue of the diocese, which came from the church tithe, and distribute a fixed portion—from a third to a fourth—to those in need. In most cases, though, the diocese was divided into several parishes and, in practice, it was the parish priest who became directly responsible for relieving distress.

Most priests were diligent in carrying out their duties, and the money available for care of the poor was sufficient for the need. By the "high" Middle Ages, then, a highly developed and effective system of poor relief had been established. Because the church was a *public* institution and the tithe a *compulsory* tax, it could be argued that the system as regulated by the church was the prototype of the one that arose under the famous English Poor Law of 1601. With the rise of the modern state, which in the middle of the sixteenth century absorbed the church, civil authorities naturally became responsible for administering the system of poor relief conducted earlier by church officials.

In any case, medieval poor relief, it must be remembered, was governed by the time-honored belief that the better off were obliged to share some of their riches with their poorer brethren. Furthermore, it was practiced in an environment of social stability in which mass destitution was absent; relief, for the most part, had to be provided only for unusual cases of poverty occasioned by accident, illness, death, or some other calamity that strained the resources of families, landlords, and voluntary associations.

In the meantime, however, certain social and economic upheavals occurred that altered the situation greatly. The general dissolution of feudalism and the manorial system resulted, on the one hand, in an increase of individual freedom but, on the other hand, in social disorder, uncertainty, and serious hardship for many, especially agricultural laborers forced from the land. The growth of commerce and international trade and the rise of a money economy with its elements of capital investment, credit, interest, rent, and wages also affected the incidence and nature of poverty. So too did the industrial revolution and development of the factory system, which, in urban centers, gave rise to masses of persons with specialized skills who experienced not only seasonal but also cyclical unemployment and other social and economic hazards over which they had no control. Subsistence, in other words, now depended not on work itself, as on the farm, but on employment by those who owned the resources—and on the state of the market.

In England, conditions were made worse by the so-called enclosure movement, which resulted from the growth of the woolens industry. As the demand for wool increased, and with it the price, it became extremely profitable for landowners to turn their fields into pastures and to raise sheep. Since sheep-raising could not be done on small fields, this upset the earlier feudal system of tillage, which rested on landlords dividing their estates into small tracts and parceling them out to tenants (or serfs) in return for certain specified services. Thus, enclosure led to the further destruction of rural homesteads, the scattering of many more cottagers, and a sizable increase in the number of unattached persons without the traditional means of support and therefore forced into wage labor in search of a livelihood.

Then a series of natural calamities—crop failures, famine, pestilence, and especially the dread Black Death (or bubonic plague), which occurred in 1348–49 and killed almost a third of England's population—produced further suffering and hardship for many. Finally, the growth of corruption and the general decay of the church in England and elsewhere ultimately led to the Protestant Reformation and, in 1536, to the dissolution of the monasteries and other church property by Henry VIII; many of those who had lived or had been employed in ecclesiastical institutions were turned out and forced to join the ranks of poor wanderers.

Taken together, these developments—the breakdown of the medieval economy, the social structure with its relatively fixed order of things, and the church with its entire framework of charity—meant for many people the loss of the economic security given to a serf by his master, and the social, economic, and spiritual security given by the church to its members during the Middle Ages. This, in turn, resulted in a tremendous increase in unemployment, poverty, vagabondage, begging, and thievery, especially in the growing commercial centers to which many of the needy gravitated. New social arrangements were required to mitigate these hardships, to reduce uncertainty, and to stabilize community life. It was in this context that the modern institution of social welfare emerged.

As early as the mid-fourteenth century, the state began to intervene where the church had no dominion. Kings, lords, and rising businessmen perceived mendicancy, widespread population movement, and labor shortages as problems. In an effort to do something about these conditions, especially to suppress the restless wandering of the landless and to keep laborers in the state of servitude from which they were just emerging, Edward III, as early as the mid-fourteenth century, initiated a series of restrictive measures. Although sometimes considered the beginning of parliamentary involvement in welfare policy, they were basically repressive statutes aimed more at regulating labor than at assisting the needy. Among these, the most important was the Statute of Laborers. Proclaimed in 1349 (a year after the Black Death, which had caused labor shortages and demands for higher wages among the poorer classes), the measure fixed maximum wages, placed travel restrictions on impotent and unemployed persons, and in effect compelled the jobless to work for any employer willing to hire them. The law also forbade the giving of charity to "sturdy" and "valiant" alms-seekers, a practice which allegedly induced mobility or laziness and unemployment; all able-bodied persons would be forced to work in their place of residence at a rate of wages fixed by law—and hence would be unable to exploit the more favorable labor market conditions resulting from the Black Death.

The social and economic changes that occasioned the statute however, were far more powerful than the law designed to stop them. The progress from feudalism toward a capitalistic-democratic society continued, not always peaceably. As a result, in the sixteenth century, other measures were enacted which further attempted to repress vagrancy and mobility. In 1531, Parliament passed a statute that provided severe punishment for able-bodied beggars. They were to be brought to the market place and "there to be tyed to the end of a carte naked and be beten with whyppes throughe out ... tyll [their bodies] ... be blody by reason of suche whypping."

The act, however, also contained constructive features concerning relief of the poor; it decreed that mayors, justices of the peace, and other local officals "shall make diligent search and inquiry of all aged poor and impotent persons which live or of necessity be compelled to live by alms of the charity of the people," and assign such people areas where they may beg. While still primarily a punitive and repressive measure designed to limit begging, by making a distinction between the able-bodied who refused to seek work and the poor who could not work and thus needed relief, and authorizing the latter to beg, and even setting aside areas where they might do so, the state took the first step toward administering an organized network of relief.

In 1536, with the passage of the Act for the Punishment of Sturdy Vagabonds and Beggars—the Henrician Poor Law—the government exercised further responsibility for the relief of persons in economic distress. While the measure made the penalties for begging even more severe (including an elaborate schedule of branding, enslavement, and execution for repeated offenses), it also ordered local public officials to obtain resources, through voluntary contributions collected in churches, to care for the poor, the lame, the sick, and the aged. Instead of merely setting up machinery for legalizing begging and confining it to the impotent poor, as the previous statute had done, this measure attempted to eliminate the need for alms-seeking, making the parish the unit of local government for poor relief.

Furthermore, the act permitted local officials to use the funds they collected to provide work for "such as be lusty or having their limbs strong enough to labor." A perceptive and novel feature of the measure, then, was its recognition of the fact that the able-bodied were not always able to find jobs. In such cases, parish officials could furnish work for those in need. They were also given the authority "to take ... children under the age of fourteen years and above the age of five years, in begging or in idleness, and to appoint them to masters of husbandry or other crafts or labors to be taught, by which they may get their living when they shall come of age." Another important feature of the statute was the provision for compensating alms collectors, anticipating by many years the development of paid public welfare workers. By the provisions of this act, then, the state, through civil and church authorities, assumed legal responsibility for the relief of *all* its poor, old and young, impotent and able-bodied alike. It was a serious attempt to cope with the economic and social problems of the age.

Although local officials—"mayors, governors and head officers of every city and the church wardens or two others of every parish"—were required to provide assistance to the destitute, funds for the purpose were to be raised through voluntary contributions in churches. The next logical step was introduction of a compulsory assessment when donations proved insufficient. This came in 1572 with the enactment of a measure stating that the justices of the peace and other local officials "shall by their good discretions tax and assess all and every the inhabitants dwelling in all and every city, borough, town, village, hamlet and place" for the care of those in economic distress. The statute also created a new public official, the overseer of the poor, who was charged with the duty of providing work relief for the able-bodied unemployed, a job more clearly defined and made mandatory by the provisions of yet another measure, enacted four years later.

By the late sixteenth century, then, the government had perceived that punitive measures directed at vagrants were insufficient to preserve order, let alone the general good of the realm, or, in the words of R. H. Tawney, that "the whip had no terror for the man who must either tramp or starve." Based on the idea that poverty was an economic rather than a personal matter and that the state should help those people who could not provide for themselves, a series of measures relating to poverty, vagrancy, and relief of the poor had been enacted that attempted to deal with the problem of economic security in light of the changing religious, social, and economic conditions of the period. The principle of relief locally financed and administered for local residents had been established. Public officials administered a system of assistance that included both direct grants-in-aid to the unemployable and a policy of apprenticeship for the young and work relief for able-bodied adults. Taken together, these measures embodied most of the principles written into the famous Poor Law of 1601.

The immediate background of the famous statute was the worsening times of the 1590s—a decade of food scarcity and widespread famine, of inflation and high prices, of insecurity and great suffering. Rioting, thievery, and social disorder again became widespread. Lawmakers, not only fearful of insurrection (especially since England had no standing army at the time), but also compelled to recognize the existence of large-scale involuntary idleness and suffering due to difficult conditions, felt the need to act.

This, too, was the age of mercantilism, an era of paternalism, and of faith in the government's capacity (and need) to arrange the affairs of mankind. The interests of the state—especially the desire to build up a strong, self-sufficient economy—were dominant. And since the means of accomplishing this were by "setting the poor to work" and turning the country into "a hive of industry," direct and active government intervention was required to overcome the threat of insecurity and the prevailing social disorder; hence, the Poor Law of 1601.[5]

Like its predecessors, the Elizabethan Poor Law, which was to stand with but minor revisions for almost 250 years, embodied the conflicting strain between the desire to reinforce the feudal structure and the increasing assumption by civil government of responsibility for the poor. Thus it had some harsh, repressive features. Parents—insofar as they had the means—were legally liable for the support of their children and grandchildren. Likewise, children were responsible for the care of their needy parents and grandparents. More important, vagrants refusing work could be committed to a house of correction; whipped, branded, or put in pillories and stoned; or even put to death. And the measure did not provide for the right of "appeal" by recipients—or potential recipients—of relief if they felt aggrieved.[6]

On the other hand, the measure had many constructive features—especially its assumption that the state had a responsibility to supplement ordinary efforts to relieve want and suffering and to insure the maintenance of life. It further conceded that there were helpless or needy people who not only deserved such assistance but who had a legal right to it. In addition, the statute defined three major categories of dependents—children, the able-bodied, and the impotent—and directed the authorities to adapt their activities to the needs of each: for needy children, apprenticeship; for the able-bodied, work; and for the incapacitated, helpless, or "worthy" poor, either home ("outdoor") or institutional ("indoor") relief.

The law firmly established the principle of local responsibility, at the lowest level, for the care of those in need. In executing the

---

[5]Although the 1601 Act is the most famous and is thought of as the most important poor law, it was in fact anticlimactic. In 1597 and 1598, a comprehensive poor law was enacted which brought together all the previous legislation on the matter; about the only thing the latter measure added to its predecessor was the extension of liability for support to grandparents. As Karl de Schweinitz has pointed out, the 1601 statute has been considered a landmark in the relief of economic distress largely because it was the last rewriting of the total law.

[6]The right of appeal against a decision made by the overseers of the poor was granted to the needy in England in 1796.

measure, the parish was to act through its church wardens and a small number of "substantial householders" who would be appointed annually by the justices of the peace to serve both as overseers of the poor and as collectors of the revenue—a wholly secular or civil position. Funds necessary for carrying the act into effect were to be raised by taxing every householder in the parish, with the threat of imprisonment for those who failed to pay such taxes.[7]

So while the basic principles of public assistance did not originate in 1601—for poor relief had been a matter of public concern long before that time—the Elizabethan Poor Law brought together, in a single coherent statute, the "inconsistent and erratic relief legislation of the previous" years, firmly placing its operation in the hands of civil authorities and establishing a definite system of obligatory financing outside of the church. According to Karl de Schweinitz, author of *England's Road to Social Security,* it culminated a development that started in 1531, or perhaps as early as 1349.[8]

Written to bring order out of chaos and with an eye toward preserving stability in case of future social and economic crises, the statute recognized the existence of involuntary unemployment and of need, and firmly established the individual's right to public assistance. For the most part it was a broad, permissive act. From what evidence we have, we can say that it was put into effect throughout England with a fair degree of efficiency and success. Although it did not eliminate all human suffering, many of the needy were helped, the able-bodied put to work, and the children apprenticed.[9] The statute also provided the pattern for

[7]The justices of the peace, who fixed the rate of assessment, also had the authority to raise revenue from other parishes should local funds prove to be insufficient and to levy fines against overseers of the poor for being negligent in their duties.

[8]Perhaps it should be pointed out that a number of statutes enacted after the Poor Law of 1601 perpetuated some of the repressive features of the Acts of 1349 and 1531, including the Law of Settlement of 1662, which restricted the movement of the poor from their parishes. Another such measure, passed in 1772, provided for the establishment of workhouses, which were to act as deterrents to home relief for the able-bodied. On the other hand, there were Gilbert's Act of 1782, which mitigated the demoralizing effects of such workhouses, and the Speenhamland system, discussed in Chapter 4.

[9]It should be mentioned that while the state gave notice (through passage of this act) that the poor were to be cared for from public funds, the state was quite

the poor laws in the American colonies, in the original thirteen states, and in the subsequent ones as they entered the Union.

Bibliography

BEER, MAX. *Social Struggles in Antiquity.* New York: International Publishers, 1925.

————. *Social Struggles in the Middle Ages.* New York: International Publishers, 1929.

BEIER, A. L. "Vagrants and the Social Order in Elizabethan England," *Past and Present* 64 (August 1974): 3–29.

BRUNO, FRANK J. "New Light on Oriental and Classical Charity in the Pre-Christian Era," *The Family* 25 (November 1944): 260–65.

CAMPBELL, ANNA M. *The Black Death and Men of Learning.* New York: Columbia University Press, 1931.

COLL, BLANCHE D. "Perspectives in Public Welfare: The English Heritage," *Welfare in Review* 4 (March 1966): 1–12.

COULTON, G. G. *The Medieval Village.* Cambridge, Mass.: Cambridge University Press, 1931.

COURTENAY, WILLIAM J. "Token Coinage and the Administration of Poor Relief During the Late Middle Ages," *Journal of Interdisciplinary History* 3 (Autumn 1972): 275–96.

DE SCHWEINITZ, KARL. *England's Road to Social Security.* Philadelphia: University of Pennsylvania Press, 1943.

FEINBERG, LOUIS, ed. *Section on Charity from the Shulhan Arukh.* New York: Charity Organization Society, 1915.

---

willing, if not anxious, to allow parishes to look after their poor through voluntary (or private) relief, if they elected to do so. The same Parliament that passed the Poor Law of 1601 encouraged private philanthropy through enactment, the same year, of the Law of Charitable Uses which, in the words of W. K. Jordan (*Philanthropy in England, 1480–1660*), "was far more important to the history of Tudor-Stuart philanthropy than the great Elizabethan Poor Law of the same year." According to Jordan, until 1660, the mainspring of the English charity system remained private, both in organization and in financing. The Trust Law directed the spirit of generosity into the founding of numerous free private schools, hospitals, almshouses, dispensaries, and the like. In short, private philanthropy at least complemented public relief at this time, providing a second cluster of institutions and services for the needy.

FLETCHER, JAMES L. "Enlightenment England: The Background and Development of Its Poor Law System," *Enlightenment Essays* 1–2 (Spring 1970–71): 1–13.

HANDS, A. R. *Charities and Social Aid in Greece and Rome*. Ithaca, N.Y.: Cornell University Press, 1968.

JORDAN, W. K. "The English Background of Modern Philanthropy," *American Historical Review* 66 (January 1961): 401–408.

———. *Philanthropy in England, 1480–1660*. New York: Russell Sage Foundation, 1959.

LEONARD, E. M. *The Early History of English Poor Relief*. Cambridge, Mass.: Cambridge University Press, 1900.

MARSHALL, DOROTHY. *The English Poor Law in the Eighteenth Century*. London: Routledge, 1926.

MARTS, ARNAUD. *The Generosity of Americans*. Englewood Cliffs, N.J.: Prentice-Hall, 1966.

———. *Man's Concern for his Fellow-man*. Geneva, N.Y.: Marts and Lundy, 1961.

MENCHER, SAMUEL. *Poor Law to Poverty Program*. Pittsburgh: University of Pittsburgh Press, 1967.

NICHOLS, SIR GEORGE. *A History of the English Poor Law*, 3 vols. London: King, 1900.

NIEBUHR, REINHOLD. *The Contribution of Religion to Social Work*. New York: Columbia University Press, 1932.

OWEN, DAVID. *English Philanthropy, 1660–1960*. Cambridge, Mass.: Harvard University Press, 1964.

"POOR LAW," *Encyclopaedia Britannica*, Vol. 18 (Chicago: Benton, 1971): 226–32.

QUEEN, STUART. *Social Work in the Light of History*. Philadelphia: Lippincott, 1922.

SALTER, FRANK R., ed. *Some Early Tracts on Poor Relief*. London: Methuen, 1926.

STILLMAN, NORMAN A. "Charity and Social Service in Medieval Islam," *Societas* 5 (Spring 1975): 105–16.

TAWNEY, RICHARD HENRY. *Religion and the Rise of Capitalism*. New York: Harcourt, Brace, 1937.

THORNDIKE, LYNN. "The Historical Background," in Ellsworth Faris et al., eds., *Intelligent Philanthropy*. Chicago: University of Chicago Press, 1930.

TIERNEY, BRIAN. *Medieval Poor Law*. Berkeley, Calif.: University of California Press, 1959.

ULLMAN, WALTER. "Public Welfare and Social Legislation in the Early Medieval Councils," in *Councils and Assemblies*. Cambridge, Mass.: Cambridge University Press, 1971.

WEBB, SIDNEY AND BEATRICE. *English Local Government: English Poor Law History, Part I, The Old Poor Law*. New York: Longmans, Green, 1927.

————. *English Poor Law Policy*. New York: Longmans, Green, 1910.

Chapter 2

Colonial America

WIDESPREAD DESTITUTION, which existed in many parts of the Old World, was not present in the New. The combination of abundant resources and a sparse population contrasted sharply with conditions in Europe, especially in England. Labor was at a premium; thus, unemployment was not a major social problem. Moreover, a liberal system of land tenure enabled many of those without property to acquire it, while commonage for grazing or tillage added to the possible sources of a livelihood. All in all, there was real opportunity for success in the New World.

Yet, the picture of America portrayed by early promoters of settlement—a land abounding in wealth and good auspices, indeed a new Paradise, a veritable Garden of Eden—was hardly true. Those who came to the colonies (land proprietors, tax-dodgers, and a handful of others excepted) were of moderate or poor means. The English practice, as authorized by Parliament and the transportation laws, of shipping to America rogues, convicts, political prisoners, beggars, vagrants, orphans, the unemployed, and other undesirables hardly helped. Then there was the trip across the Atlantic; not only a prolonged but also a debilitating experience for many. Passengers were packed into tiny ships with filthy and foul-smelling quarters, lack of adequate food and drinking water, and exposure to disease; many did not survive the wretched conditions of the voyage; those who did frequently reached shore ill or infirm.

Once in America, life was so severe, so full of hardship and deprivation, that many were forced to live in poverty or so close to it that any misfortune might reduce them to that state. As a result, despite favorable chances for acquiring land or for earning a living in other ways, in the New World they did not escape poverty and many of the other social ills that plagued them in the

Old World. Each colony soon had to deal with the problem of caring for the poor, the aged, the blind, the sick, the lame, the mentally ill, the lazy, the destitute of all kinds.

At the outset, as in all closely knit communities, especially in pioneer settings where there was no recourse to other forms of assistance, neighborly kindness, or mutual aid, sufficed; as Governor William Bradford's account *Of Plimouth Plantation* indicates, sheer survival depended upon it. As the population increased, however, and as the social life of the colonies grew more varied, the problem of dependency became more complex and the need for a permanent, carefully regulated poor relief policy and system became more acute, especially around the middle of the seventeenth century. By that time, so many indigent colonists were about—idlers, misfits, tramps, criminals, the sick, and so on—especially in growing towns such as Boston, Newport, and Philadelphia, that their care had to become a community function and responsibility. As one would expect, the colonists turned to the manners and customs, the social and legal institutions that were part of their cultural baggage, to meet the need—the English Poor Law of 1601.

Conditions in the New World seemed to invite the adoption and nurture of the relief policies of the mother country. There were neither private charitable trusts nor ecclesiastical welfare institutions in the New World. The hardships of frontier life and the isolation and self-containment of the early settlements led to the development of a strong sense of social responsibility and community solidarity which, in turn, provided a sufficient rationale for local responsibility, especially in New England where the system of local self-government prevailed.

In addition, as David and Sheila Rothman have pointed out, for seventeenth-century Americans need was in the order of things, a natural and inevitable part of the human condition. The poor, mere pawns in a divinely destined universe and hence not responsible for their condition, were always present—in America as elsewhere. This, however, was not a necessary evil, but rather a blessing, a God-given opportunity for men to do good—to serve society and their Creator.

According to God's scheme, a well ordered society was hierarchical; it had a series of ranks ranging from top to bottom. Some men, "the great ones, high and eminent in power and dignity," were at the top, others, "the poor and inferior sort," at the bottom. Each had special privileges and obligations; the poor to respect and show deference to those above them, the well-to-do to aid and care for those below them. Disparities in wealth and condition existed not to separate and alienate men from one another but to make them have more need of each other—to bind them closer together "in the bond of brotherly affection" so that they might "improve [their] . . . lives to do more service to the Lord," as John Winthrop, the noted Puritan leader, put it—or perhaps militate against class antagonism and thus maintain order, as more recent observers have suggested.

In any event, social theory and theology gave meaning to poverty in colonial America. Its presence did not indicate a flaw in society, or in the needy, something to be feared and eliminated. Its victims, permanent and integral parts of the community, were to be pitied and helped. It is not surprising, therefore, that the colonial assemblies quickly acknowledged public responsibility for those unable to care for themselves or those whose families, extending through three generations (as in England), were unable to care for them, making the taxpayers of each locality responsible for their support.

The Plymouth Colony adopted such provisions in 1642, Virginia in 1646, Connecticut in 1673, Massachusetts in 1692, and so on. The colonial poor laws not only were patterned after the Elizabethan legislation, but often retained many of its specific provisions, in some cases *in toto*. Thus, the first session of the Rhode Island colonial legislature announced that the doctrine of local care for the needy was to be implemented and that overseers of the poor were to be appointed to assess a tax and collect the money to care for the poor "according to the provisions of the law of England."

In marked contrast with the practice of applying the Elizabethan Poor Law in a simple matter-of-fact way, was the case of New Amsterdam. Settled in 1609 by the Dutch, the colony set up an ecclesiastical system of poor relief; officers of the Dutch Reformed Church were vested with the authority to raise the necessary money through voluntary collections and then to distribute it to the needy. However, when the colony came under English rule in 1664, its relief policies were transformed to conform to the English pattern—public assistance through compulsory taxation.

Colonial administration of the poor laws was left to the smallest unit of government. In New England, the town was responsible for executing the statute. The Town Meeting made the decisions, which were carried out by the selectmen, tithingmen, or overseers of the poor, civil officials. In the southern colonies where, as in England, the Anglican church was established, the parish was the administrative unit. There, the board of vestry, a group of men, usually twelve in number, chosen by the freeholders to oversee the religious affairs of the parish, was also charged with the responsibility of caring for the poor. Although the entire board assessed and collected the taxes, two vestrymen served as church wardens or the "executive arm" of the body and actually distributed the aid, which was raised through a compulsory tax designed specifically for that purpose.

The simplest method of aiding the poor, especially those unable to care for themselves, was for each family to care for a destitute person during a part of the year. Thus, in Massachusetts, the Hadley Town Meeting voted in 1687 that a certain widow should be sent "round the town" to live two weeks with each family "able to receive her." Others, particularly those who needed only temporary or partial assistance, were provided with outdoor aid. The most common seventeenth-century practice, however, was to place the poor in private homes at public expense.[1] While this usually involved the payment of a fixed sum agreed upon for each person, with the town often supplying clothing and medical care besides, it was not unusual to auction off the needy (usually at the village tavern on the Saturday evening following the Town Meeting), who went to the lowest bidder. In all cases, the family and the private home, considered to be the foundation of the social order, was the setting in which the assistance was provided.

Another form of relief was abatement of taxes or parish dues. For example, on October 29, 1656, the Boston Town Meeting agreed that a "Mr. Wales hath six shillings abated of his [tax] rate for this year in regard to his poverty." Moreover, the poor

---

[1] In some instances, the needy were so maintained for long periods of time—up to thirty years, and more.

were usually provided with free medical attention.[2] Towns and parishes employed doctors to treat those who could not afford to pay medical bills. Hence, in 1664, Boston's selectmen paid Dr. Thomas Oliver five pounds "for seven months attendance upon . . . Thomas Hawkins," a needy person. Other doctors had their taxes remitted or reduced for performing such services.

While townsmen relieved neighbors' needs rather generously, and without suspicion, they showed considerably less compassion for the plight of strangers—people who might be a source of social and political as well as financial difficulty for the community. As the number of people without means of support steadily increased, as did transiency, some communities began to restrict immigration, or the movements of strangers. As early as May 1636, Boston's selectmen prohibited citizens from entertaining strangers for more than two weeks without first securing official permission; if the visitors seemed likely to stay longer and become a public burden, such permission was denied. Those who came anyway, or perhaps were already present, were "warned away," or told to leave by the selectmen or overseers of the poor; those who did not go willingly were forcibly removed by the constable.[3] Three years later, Boston officials required that some townsman provide security for any newcomer in order "to save the town from charge," as the ordinance read, again with the threat of warning away those not so covered.[4] The frequency of these and other regulations indicates that Boston and other communities continually faced the problem of caring for unwanted strangers who became public charges.

[2]On occasion, towns and parishes even paid for the sick poor to visit health spas. Thus, one Virginia record reads: "Ordered that the Church Wardens Agree with some person on the best terms they can to carry Rich Sentale to the Spring on New River for the Recovery of his health."

[3]In "warning out" those likely to become public dependents, the town was merely exercising a right that existed because of the English theory of inhabitancy, or right to live in a certain settlement. Each town was considered a corporation established by free consent; its residents, therefore (so the reasoning went), had the sovereignty to admit or exclude their own inhabitants. "Warning out," or banishment, was perceived to be especially necessary because towns had no police forces to maintain control over such "dangerous" people.

[4]The practice of requiring strangers to post bond before being allowed to settle in a community continued until the time of the American Revolution and was revived again during the era of restrictive legislation in the late nineteenth century.

Establishment of residency requirements to determine eligibility for—or "entitlement" to—public assistance originated in the Plymouth Colony. There, as elsewhere, each town was obliged to support its resident poor, but, by the provisions of an act of 1642, the status of an "inhabitant" or "resident" was defined to apply only to those who remained in a community for three months without being asked to leave.[5] Another safeguard against the influx of needy persons was a statute that prohibited the sale of land to strangers without first obtaining official approval. Also, residents who brought servants into a town had to agree to maintain them if the latter became ill, lame, or impotent.

In New York, no stranger could be harbored in a private home or in a tavern for more than one night without first registering with the town recorder. Constables in each ward were instructed to seek out strangers and present a list of their names and addresses to the mayor.

The Rhode Island Assembly empowered town councils to expel all nonresident vagrants and indigents and to accept or reject bonds from strangers. Those who returned after having been expelled were subject to heavy fines and severe whipping. These and similar restrictions were carried out, as the frequency of town disputes concerning the care of dependents and the great deal of time and money spent in litigation over such matters indicate.

[5]Residency as a factor in determining eligibility for public assistance was declared illegal by the U.S. Supreme Court on April 21, 1969, in the case of *Shapiro v. Thompson.* Earlier, a number of states had abolished the requirement. The first to do so was Rhode Island, which acted in 1944, during World War II, when manpower shortages meant that laborers had to be more mobile and welfare administrators could not spend as much time verifying settlement and residency requirements—a time-consuming and costly venture. The Rhode Island experience indicated: (1) that people do not move in order to secure public assistance; they move in order to secure a better life for themselves, to be with relatives and friends, etc.; and (2) that the cost of assisting the needy is usually less than the administrative costs of implementing residency requirements.

As mentioned earlier, residency as a requirement for eligibility for public assistance formally began in England in 1662 with enactment of "The Law of Settlement and Removal." Paterned after the fourteenth-century Statute of Laborers, the measure prohibited parish relief to any but official parish residents—those who had obtained a legal "settlement." Such status might be acquired by birth, land ownership, taxpaying, or apprenticeship. In part, at least, this measure was a reflection of the English Revolution of 1660, which weakened the central power of the state and thus brought about less national attention to social problems.

Related was the problem of seaborne paupers entering large port towns such as Newport, Boston, and New York. In Boston, the sea was watched by a special official who warned away poor newcomers. Forty-nine of these newcomers were not permitted to disembark from the ship *Elizabeth,* which arrived in Boston Harbor from Ireland in November 1719.

The Massachusetts General Court and other colonial legislatures even required masters of all vessels to post a bond for each person they brought to the colonies. In 1721, the New York Assembly passed a similar measure requiring ship captains to file passenger lists with the town recorder within twenty-four hours after docking. Then they had to post fifty pounds security for each passenger who might become a public charge or else return that person to his port of embarkation. Again, in most places, ship captains were required to post bonds for sick mariners left in port.

Finally, the influx of impoverished refugees from frontier settlements during times of trouble, such as Indian wars (or from small inland towns as a result of being warned away), created a stubborn problem in some areas, especially in wealthy seaport towns. These victims of misfortune (often widows and orphans) posed more of a problem for some coastal communities than did aliens. Early during King Philip's War (1675–77), Boston officials reported that sixty-two people who had come to town were public charges and should be warned away, and no doubt many others escaped detection. Officials asked the legislature for more power to prevent such from residing in Boston, for those who came "thither for relief and shelter in time of war . . . had already proved a great expense to the town" and should be removed.

Fugitives from the frontier pouring into Newport at this time exhausted that town's charitable resources. More than 500 such persons arrived there in 1675 alone, and some 800 pounds had to be spent on their care. It was this problem of the "unsettled poor" in times of trouble that led to the first important change in the practice of local responsibility.

Faced with the prospect of having to care for large numbers of those driven from their homes during King Philip's War, Boston authorities appealed urgently to the General Court which provided funds from the colonial treasury to succor the nonresidents. Such was the beginning of state aid, in whole or in part, for the needy, a practice that gradually expanded. Thus, beginning in

1701, local communities were reimbursed by the colonial treasury for the relief of "unsettled persons" with contagious diseases—people who, if sent away, would endanger other communities. In thé meantime, other colonies began assigning funds to localities for the care of certain nonresidents.

As Englishmen with a poor law heritage, and as religious people for whom the injunctions about the sacredness of human life had sense and meaning, most colonists felt an obligation to help those members of their community who were unable to care for themselves. At the same time, their Calvinistic ideas about the virtue of hard work and the sin of idleness—their concept of the "calling" made work sacred—their desire to avoid an unduly heavy burden of taxes, and, perhaps more important, the existing need for labor in the colonies convinced many that all able-bodied persons should and could work. Thus, powerful religious and economic forces converged to see to it that there would be little sympathy for "sturdy beggars." As the Puritan divine Cotton Mather put it: "For those who indulge themselves in idleness, the express command of God unto us is, that we should let them starve."

In this spirit, the Virginia Assembly, as early as 1619, ordered the apparent slothful bound over to compulsory labor. A few years later, the Massachusetts Bay settlers told Governor John Endicott that "no idle drone [should] be permitted to live amongst us." The General Court followed that, in 1633, with a decree inflicting harsh punishment on those who spent their time "idly or unprofitably." So, in the American colonies (as in England), voluntary idleness was regarded as a vice, and the able-bodied unemployed were either bound out as indentured servants, whipped and run out of town, or put in jail; in short, they were viewed not only as odious but also as criminal, threats to themselves as well as to the entire community. Later, toward the latter seventeenth and early eighteenth century, many were placed in workhouses as they began to appear.[6] The great era of

[6]As time passed and some people began to prosper, philanthropic citizens began to make bequests to towns for various charitable purposes, including the building of workhouses. In Boston, between 1656 and 1662 at least three, and probably more, probated wills included bequests to the town for the relief of the poor; these were combined and a workhouse was built with the funds. Before long, other communities did the same. This trend resulted in part from developments in England, where it was believed that putting the poor to work was both morally therapeutic and beneficial to the economy.

institution building, however, did not come until the following century.

Having red skin was also considered a vice by most of the colonists, who did not really understand the Indians, especially their love of nature, their communal life, and their concept of collective land ownership. Although the Indians had attained a high level of civilization long before the Europeans came to the New World, they were assumed to be savages, especially by the property-conscious and land-hungry English settlers. When efforts to "civilize" the Indians failed, a policy of extermination followed, usually justified on moral and religious grounds. Cotton Mather, in his major work, *Magnalia Christi Americana* (1702), described what happened to one Indian tribe that repudiated Christianity and the white man's ways:

> The Nation of Narragansetts was one of the most populous among the Indians, and once filled this mighty wilderness. Unto that woeful nation the gospel of our Lord Jesus Christ was freely rendered, but they with much affront and contempt, rejected it.... The glorious Lord Jesus Christ, whom they had slighted, was with our army.... Their city was laid in ashes. Above twenty of their chief captains were killed; a proportionable desolation cut off the inferior savages, mortal sickness and horrid famine pursued the remainders of them, so that we can hardly tell where any of them are left alive on the face of the earth.

Needless to say, there was little social welfare for native Americans during the colonial period—or later on, for that matter; most of those who survived were forced onto the nation's worst lands where, out of sight, they were either ignored despite their poor plight, or placed on federal reservations administered by corrupt and uncaring officials.

Then there were blacks, who were also viewed by most colonists as uncivilized and inferior—children of Satan not entitled to the same rights as white people and hence excluded from the social welfare system. Black slaves were the responsibility of their masters and could not receive aid under the poor laws; free blacks, for the most part, were simply denied assistance and forced to develop their own informal self-help mechanisms.

For pauper, illegitimate, and orphaned white children, the colonies enacted typical Elizabethan legislation—apprenticeship. Indeed, the town had the authority to remove children from their parents and apprentice them out if they were not being taught a trade, as this inscription in the Boston records for November 25, 1656, indicates: "It is agreed upon the complaint against the son of Goodwife Samon, living without a calling, that if she dispose not of him in some way of employ before the next [town] meeting, that then the townsmen will dispose of him to some service according to law."

Apprenticeship was widely used at home and abroad for a number of reasons. As mentioned, it was commonly believed that all people should be attached to a family. Also, it was argued that it was a good method of disciplining children. In addition, the practice relieved the town fathers of the burden of caring for needy youngsters, keeping public outlays and the poor rate down. And, finally, the system provided a sound means of social and economic control—it reduced idleness and unemployment and it trained workers for the needs of a growing town or colony.

Finally, there were the mentally ill. Although there is no way to know the exact number of such persons during the colonial era, it is evident from scattered references that many were present in the colonies. They did not cause widespread public concern, nor were they accorded much special treatment. With the exception of the separate "mental section" in the newly established Pennsylvania Hospital, opened in 1756, and a state hospital at Williamsburg, Virginia, founded in 1773, no special facilities were provided for the mentally ill prior to the American Revolution.

Because insanity and dependency were intimately related—it often disrupted family relationships and undermined the means of support—and because specific therapies were lacking, mental disease was viewed primarily as an economic and social rather than as a medical problem.[7] Its victims came under the jurisdiction of the local community as a result of the poor laws. And except for those who were especially troublesome and deemed threats to public safety, who were usually confined to quarters, the mentally ill were regarded simply as other needy people un-

[7]The responsibility for determining insanity was always placed with civil officers—governors, selectmen, church wardens, vestrymen, etc., depending upon the political structure of the colony—never with medical men; so, too, was guardianship of estates.

able to care for themselves.[8] Residents were boarded, at public expense, in the homes of relatives or others, or housed in public institutions as they began to appear. Nonresident insane indigents were warned away or, on occasion, returned home, as a note in John Winthrop's *Journal,* dated December 11, 1634, indicates: "One Abigail Gifford, widow, being kept at the charge of the parish Weldsen in Middlesex near London, was sent by Mr. Ball's ship to this country, and being found to be somewhat distracted and a very burdensome woman, the governor and assistants returned her back by warrant . . . to the same parish in the ship *Rebecca. . . .* "

The first statute concerned specifically with providing special care for the insane was enacted in Massachusetts, in 1676, when the General Court noted a rise in the number of "distracted persons" and problems stemming from their behavior. It read:

> Whereas there are distracted persons in some towns that are unruly, whereby not only the families wherein they are, but others suffer much damage by them, it is ordered by this Court that the Selectmen in all towns where such persons are, are hereby empowered and enjoined to take care of all such persons that they do not damnify others.

The act recognized that the mentally ill, at least those who were seriously disturbed, needed to be treated in a special way—less for their own good than to prevent them from annoying or "damnifying" others. The care provided at least some of the insane poor under the provisions of this statute was revealed in a vote of the residents of Braintree, Massachusetts, who, in 1689, agreed to pay for the construction of a house seven feet long and five feet wide in which one member of the community could "secure his sister and goodwife Wittey, [both] being distracted." However poor the care provided under its provisions, the statute was at least a beginning. Its principle that some kind of special care

[8]To quote from the most recently published work on the subject: "There is little evidence . . . to substantiate the oft-repeated allegation that the insane were singled out for harsh and inhumane treatment. Given the living standards in the colonial period, the limited resources and the lack of medical knowledge and facilities, there is no reason for believing that the condition of the insane was appreciably worse than that of other dependent groups within colonial society." See Gerald Grob, *Mental Institutions in America: Social Policy to 1875* (New York: Free Press, 1973), p. 12.

should be provided for the mentally ill was important; eventually, the care provided under this and similar statutes would improve.

By the end of the seventeenth century, it was quite evident not only that poverty was a natural product of the human situation and an inevitable concomitant of urban growth, but also that it would get worse. Yet, for the most part, the American colonists were attacking the problem seriously. Although the poor increased in number and skilled administration was lacking, most communities expressed genuine sympathy for the needy and tried to improve their methods and facilities for helping them. One should not dwell on the shortcomings or the harsher aspects of their efforts. Most localities had so many of their own poor to maintain and were forced to spend so much money for their aid that it is understandable that they denied assistance to those who clearly were able-bodied but lazy and that they pursued a vigorous policy of attempting to exclude poor strangers. Recent scholarship has suggested that there was a clear connection between the public response to poverty and the factor of age—at least in seventeenth-century Massachusetts. In general, those who received aid tended to be older, while those who were not given assistance tended to be younger. This, though, should not be surprising, for older persons were more likely to become dependent through no fault of their own than were younger ones. The most noteworthy fact is the apparent readiness with which the colonists accepted responsibility for so many of their indigent; they did not allocate blame for poverty nor, for the most part, did they punish or isolate the needy.

Most communities attacked the problem of poverty with a high degree of civic responsibility. The large amount of money spent on public relief (and, as time passed, the philanthropies of private individuals and voluntary associations) is evidence of a consciousness of the problem and a real attempt to meet it. In the American colonies, where natural resources were abundant and labor was scarce, human life was held in esteem; the wisdom of providing for the poor was rarely, if ever, seriously challenged. On the contrary, the colonials were more interested in providing good treatment for the poor than they were in economizing on welfare costs. And what evidence we have indicates that they were fairly successful in doing so; while they did not design programs to eradicate poverty, there was little suffering for lack of support.

By the eighteenth century, then, the problem of poverty had been defined and the lines of attack against it were marked out. In many areas, selectmen, county justices, overseers of the poor, constables, church wardens, or whoever the authority happened to be, made regular surveys of their areas to determine the condition of the population and to call attention to those who needed assistance. (Failure to do so was punishable by a fine, the proceeds of which went to the support of the poor). The care provided those individuals was beginning to become more sophisticated, in some cases taking on an element of rehabilitation and prevention. By and large, the poor—at least the white poor—were dealt with humanely and often wisely, even when measured by English standards, and especially when compared to later developments. Furthermore, the needy were quite conscious of their rights within the law and were not merely pawns, or powerless victims, of the system and its administrators; they actively used it to meet their needs. Yet the vicissitudes of colonial life, especially in the larger towns, made the problem appear to be permanent, one likely to grow rather than diminish in the years ahead.

Bibliography

BERNHARD, VIRGINIA. "Poverty and the Social Order in Seventeenth-Century Virginia," *Virginia Magazine of History and Biography* 85 April 1977): 141–55.

BRADFORD, WILLIAM. *Of Plimouth Plantation.* New York: Capricorn Books, 1962.

BROWN, ROY M. *Public Poor Relief in North Carolina.* Chapel Hill, N.C.: University of North Carolina Press, 1928.

CREECH, MARGARET. "Some Colonial Case Histories," *Social Service Review* 9 (December 1935): 699–730.

———. *Three Centuries of Poor Law Administration: A Study of Legislation in Rhode Island.* Chicago: University of Chicago Press, 1936.

DAIN, NORMAN. *Disordered Minds: The First Century of Eastern State*

Hospital in Williamsburg, Virginia, 1766–1866. Williamsburg, Va.: Colonial Williamsburg Foundation, 1971.

DEUTSCH, ALBERT. "Public Provision for the Mentally Ill in Colonial America," *Social Service Review* 10 (December 1936): 606–22.

GROB, GERALD. *Mental Institutions in America: Social Policy to 1875.* New York: Free Press, 1973.

HALL, PETER. "A Model of Boston Charitable Benevolence and Class Development," *Science and Society* 38 (Winter 1974–75): 464–77.

HEFFNER, WILLIAM C. *History of Poor Relief Legislation in Pennsylvania, 1682–1913.* Cleona, Pa.: Holzapfel, 1913.

HOSMER, JAMES KENDALL, ed. [Governor John] *Winthrop's Journal "History of New England" 1630–1649.* New York: Scribner's, 1908.

JERNEGAN, MARCUS W. "The Development of Poor Relief in Colonial America," *Social Service Review* 5 (June 1931): 175–98.

———. *Laboring and Dependent Classes in Colonial America, 1607–1783.* Chicago: University of Chicago Press, 1931.

———. "Poor Relief in Colonial Virginia," *Social Service Review* 3 (March 1929): 1–18.

JONES, DOUGLAS. "The Strolling Poor: Transiency in Eighteenth-Century Massachusetts," *Journal of Social History* 8 (Spring 1975): 28–54.

KELSO, ROBERT. *The History of Public Poor Relief in Massachusetts, 1620–1920.* Boston: Houghton Mifflin, 1922.

KLEBANER, BENJAMIN J. "Pauper Auctions: The 'New England Method' of Public Poor Relief," *Essex Institute Historical Collection* 91 (1955): 195–210.

KLEIN, RANDOLPH S. "Medical Expenses and the Poor in Virginia," *Journal of the History of Medicine* 30 (July 1975): 260–66.

LEE, CHARLES R. "The Poor People: Seventeenth-Century Massachusetts and the Poor," *Historical Journal of Massachusetts* 9 (January 1981): 41–50.

LEET, GLEN. "Rhode Island Abolishes Settlement," *Social Service Review* 18 (September 1944): 281–87.

McCAMIC, CHARLES. "Administration of Poor Relief in the Virginias," *West Virginia History* 1 (April 1940): 171–91.

MACKEY, HOWARD. "The Operation of the English Old Poor Law in Colonial Virginia," *Virginia Magazine of History and Biography* 73 (January 1965): 29–40.

MOHL, RAYMOND. "Poverty in Early America, A Reappraisal: The

Case of Eighteenth-Century New York City," *New York History* 50 (January 1969): 5–27.

MORGAN, EDMUND. *The Puritan Dilemma: The Story of John Winthrop.* Boston: Little, Brown, 1958.

MORRIS, RICHARD. *Government and Labor in Early America.* New York: Columbia University Press, 1946.

MURDOCK, KENNETH B., ed. *Selections from Cotton Mather.* New York: Harcourt, Brace, 1926.

PARKHURST, ELEANOR. "Poor Relief in a Massachusetts Village in the Eighteenth Century," *Social Service Review* 11 (September 1937): 446–64.

PUMPHREY, RALPH AND MURIEL, eds. *The Heritage of American Social Work.* New York: Columbia University Press, 1961.

RIESENFELD, STEFAN. "The Formative Era of American Assistance Law," *California Law Review* 43 (May 1955): 175–233.

ROTHMAN, DAVID AND SHEILA, eds. *On Their Own: The Poor in Modern America.* Reading, Mass.: Addison-Wesley, 1972.

SCHNEIDER, DAVID M. *A History of Public Welfare in New York State, 1607–1867.* Chicago: University of Chicago Press, 1938.

———. "The Patchwork of Relief in Provincial New York, 1664–1775," *Social Service Review* 12 (September 1938): 464–94.

SMITH, ABBOTT E. *Colonists in Bondage: White Servitude and Convict Labor in America, 1607–1776.* Chapel Hill, N.C.: University of North Carolina Press, 1947.

WATSON, ALAN D. "Public Poor Relief in Colonial North Carolina," *North Carolina Historical Review* 54 (October 1977): 347–66.

WINTHROP, JOHN. "A Model of Christian Charity," in Perry Miller, ed., *The American Puritans.* New York: Doubleday, 1956.

WISNER, ELIZABETH. "The Puritan Background of the New England Poor Laws," *Social Service Review* 19 (September 1945): 381–90.

———. *Social Welfare in the South.* Baton Rouge, La.: Louisiana State University Press, 1970.

Chapter 3

The Era of
the American Revolution

IT IS IMPOSSIBLE to determine exactly how many people received public assistance during the late seventeenth and early eighteenth centuries. The number, however, was large. By 1691, the care of the poor consumed so much of the selectmen's time in Boston, for example, that they turned the work over to four full-time officers—the town's first overseers of the poor. The number of sermons delivered on "doing good" rose dramatically during these years. And in 1712, the Reverend Cotton Mather noted in his diary: "The distressed Families of the Poor [in my congregation] are now so many, and of such daily occurrence, that it is needless for me to . . . mention them."

Not only was the number large but each year it increased, as did relief expenditures and taxes. In 1700, the residents of Boston spent about 500 pounds on public relief; by 1715, the annual expenditure was more than 2000 pounds, half of what it would be some twenty years later. By 1753, poor relief expenditures in Boston climbed to 10,000 pounds per year, and the figure continued to increase even more rapidly each year thereafter through the 1770s, even though the population was relatively static by that time.

The same was true for New York. By 1752, the needy so burdened that city's residents that in order to care for them, poor law officials had to borrow 150 pounds against the following year's taxes. So it went elsewhere. Gary Nash, in an article on "Poverty and Poor Relief in Pre-Revolutionary Philadelphia," concluded that on the eve of the war "poverty . . . blighted the lives of a large part of the population." In 1772, for example, one out of every four free men in that city could be "classified as having been poor or near poor by the standards of that time." Nash and others have suggested that widespread poverty in the late colonial period— when most large cities were spending on poor relief about three times per capita (after inflation) the amount they had spent thirty years earlier and when, in the North and the South alike, poor relief consumed on the average anywhere from 10 to 35 percent of all municipal funds, the single largest annual outlay—may have been a major cause of the American Revolution: widespread poverty probably "eroded the allegiance of many urban dwellers to the British mercantilistic system and also to their own internal social systems." Poverty and the charitable impulse it fostered also helped break down localism and proved to be a spur to national unity in that way as well, according to these observers.[1]

In any case, many factors contributed to the rising rate of indigency during these years. A number of needy immigrants continued to come to America each year. Frequent wars or military skirmishes, especially with the French and Indians, added disabled soldiers and refugees from the frontier and from Canada to the multitude of others—the aged, the ill, the improvident, and so on—for whom care had to be provided. For example, about 1,000 Acadians, after being expelled from Nova Scotia during the French and Indian Wars (1754–63), settled in Massachusetts, where for a long time they were dependent upon public support.

Another very real problem, particularly in New England, was the large number of widows and orphans bereft by husbands and fathers lost at sea. Then there was the seasonal nature of many jobs. Fisherman, seamen, longshoremen, craftsmen who worked out of doors, and others went without pay several months each year. A steady rise in the number of illegitimate children—many of whom had to be cared for at public expense—contributed to swollen poor lists. Colonel Lawrence Smith, a Virginian, complained in 1699 of the "excessive charge" that was brought to the parishes "by means of bastards. . . . " This, however, was not a regional problem; the North had its share of illegitimacy as well.

---

[1]See Gary Nash, "Urban Wealth and Poverty in Pre-Revolutionary America," *Journal of Interdisciplinary History* 6 (Spring 1976): 582, and *The Urban Crucible: Social Change, Political Consciousness, and the Origins of the American Revolution* (Cambridge, Mass.: Harvard University Press, 1979); Peter Virgadamo, "Charity for a City in Crisis: Boston, 1740–1775," *Historical Journal of Western Massachusetts* 10 (January 1982): 22–33.

In fact, it has been estimated that during the Revolutionary era one-third to one-half of *all* recorded first births were the result of pre-marital sexual intercourse.

Economic depressions disrupted trade and caused financial hardship for many. Destructive fires further increased the ranks of the distressed, as did recurring illnesses, diseases, and epidemics of all kinds—smallpox, dysentery, measles, and the like. Thus, in 1749, the village of Waterbury, Connecticut, lost 130 people in a single dysentery epidemic while 800 to 900 residents of Charleston, South Carolina, died from measles in 1772. These and other accumulated misfortunes caused poverty to be an ever present and even alarming problem at times in the eighteenth century. So, too, did growing overcrowdedness in the colonies' major cities, which, with the passage of time, became more stratified and contained an increasing proportion of propertyless and impoverished persons.

Although the towns and parishes spent a good deal of money to care for the needy, the problem was so large that it demanded (and received) assistance from private sources as well. Private charity began early in American history, as a notation in John Winthrop's *Journal,* dated August 16, 1635, indicates: "In the tempest a bark was cast away.... None were saved but one Mr. Thatcher and his wife.... The General Court gave Mr. Thatcher £26.13.4 towards his losses and divers good people gave him besides." In the seventeenth century, though, private charity was rather limited in scope; donors with great resources to distribute in philanthropic ventures were few and far between. By the eighteenth century, however, as wealth increased in general and a growing number of people began to accumulate sizable fortunes, individuals and private groups proved of enormous service. Sometimes they supplemented public relief activities, at other times assisted individuals or families whose need had not yet been recognized as a public responsibility, and on occasion even attacked some of the causes of poverty.

In the North, the names of Benjamin Franklin,[2] Thomas Bond,

---

[2]Perhaps a few words about Franklin are in order. Certainly, he did not like public assistance or the poor laws. He believed that economic want was necessary to prevent sloth, wastefulness, and dissipation, and that industry and thrift were sufficient to meet the economic needs of life. Rather than aiding the needy finan-

founder of the Pennsylvania Hospital, Benjamin Rush, physician
and reformer, Stephen Girard, merchant, banker, and philan-
thropist, and others became synonymous with "doing good." In
the Anglican South, private efforts, especially large-scale giving,
were even more sustained. There, Calvinist principles of hard
work were less pressing than in the North and many large land-
holders, imbued with a spirit of noblesse oblige and trying to
maintain a social system not unlike that of feudalism, felt that aiding the needy was more a personal than a civic responsibility.

Typical in this respect was George Washington who, even
while leading the military struggle against Great Britian, could
not neglect that obligation. In November 1775, he wrote a letter
to the agent of his estate at Mt. Vernon that stressed, in effect,
open house:

> Let the hospitality of the house, with respect to the poor, be kept up.
> Let no one go away hungry. If any of this kind of people shall be in
> want . . . supply their necessities . . . ; and I have no objection to your
> giving my money in charity to the amount of forty or fifty pounds a
> year. . . . What I mean by having no objection is that it is my desire that
> it should be done.[3]

Not only individuals, but private groups of all kinds, aided the
needy. Churches frequently took up collections for their own
needy members, and others. Thus Boston's South Church raised
some 260 pounds for the relief of sufferers from a great fire of
1711, and an equally large amount for those afflicted during a
smallpox epidemic of 1752. Other churches did likewise.

Then there were the Quakers, who spent an enormous amount
of time, effort, and money aiding the needy. Looking upon themselves as bound together through love and fellowship, and believing that whatever the differences among people all were children

---

cially or materially, then, he helped them in other ways—by working for social
betterment in order "to establish conditions in which all people would be able to
care for themselves," as he put it. In his preventive approach and in other
ways—he was an astute student of community organization, for example—he was
quite farsighted and even modern in his approach to matters of social welfare.

[3]Letter from George Washington to Lund Washington, November 26, 1775, in
Worthington Chauncey Ford, ed., *The Writings of George Washington,* Vol. 3
(New York: Putnam's, 1889), pp. 236–37.

of God, carriers of his seed and spiritually equal in his sight, Quakers were concerned about the problem of need the world over, extending help first to their own, but then to others as well. Thus, each Quaker meetinghouse or congregation had a permanent poor fund for the use of its members, but in time of general calamity or widespread suffering of any kind, they were among the first to raise additional funds for the unfortunate, whoever or wherever they happened to be.

It may well be, as Sydney James has suggested, that the Quakers were motivated less by humanitarianism than by other goals—self-interest, a desire to avoid giving up their place in society. As a result of various eighteenth-century developments —social, political, and religious—the sect was thrown on the defensive; it was vulnerable to a "challenge by power, votes and competitive religiosity," to use James's words. Humanitarianism was the Quaker response to this attack by colonial society. Benevolence helped solidify the church and give it a place in American society:

> By benevolent activities ... [Quakers] found a way to win a place for themselves in American society without either sacrificing their strict fidelity to their distinctive code of behavior or compromising with worldliness.... They purified their own conduct, maintained the solidarity of their church, and by offering examples of philanthropic action for the national welfare in ways which they believed it their special duty to do, showed the way in virtue and public policy to fellow Americans.

Be that as it may, the Quakers (and many other "private" groups), whatever their motives, proved enormously helpful in times of stress. Of all their relief work, perhaps the most notable Quaker effort came during the British siege of Boston in 1775. Their belief in the divinity or sacredness of each individual led them to insist that no man could remain a Friend if he participated "in the spirit of war." Most members of the group, therefore, refused to bear arms in the struggle, a practice that did not endear them to many of their fellow countrymen. Persecuted as a result, they nevertheless contributed to the cause—in peaceful ways. Even before the war broke out, New England Friends had organized "The Meeting of Sufferings," composed of Quaker delegates from all the colonies and designed to deal with the hardships likely to arise from the impending struggle. The group raised several thousand pounds which, when the fighting began, its members distributed to those in need, in and out of Boston, without respect to religious or political belief.

In addition to religious bodies, numerous other private organizations—nationality groups, fraternal societies, social organizations, and the like—aided the unfortunate. Appealing to common sense and self-interest as well as compassion, these bodies gave their members a sense of economic security through mutual aid while performing charitable services for others as well.

The first, and in some ways the most important, of these "friendly societies" was the Scots Charitable Society, organized in 1657 by twenty-seven Scotsmen living in Boston. The group was founded, according to its charter, for the "relief of ourselves and any other for which [sic] we may see cause." By 1690, it had 180 members, including several wealthy merchants in Boston and elsewhere. Largely based on ties of common nationality in a strange land, the society aided its poor, provided for its sick, and buried its dead, reducing the number of public dependents at a time when official agencies were heavily burdened.

More important, the society, still functioning today, became the model for countless similar bodies that sprang up throughout America in the eighteenth and succeeding centuries. In 1754, fifty-four Boston Anglicans founded the Episcopal Charitable Society of Boston, distributing private charity to needy members of the Church of England in that city. Thirteen years later, the Charitable Irish Society of Boston was born. Soon the German Society of New York came into existence, as did the French Benevolent Society, and so on.

Clearly then, at this time, social welfare was a partnership. Private philanthropy complemented public aid; both were part of the American response to poverty. While, from the outset, the public was responsible for providing aid to the needy who, in turn, had a right to such assistance, as soon as they could afford to do so, private citizens and a host of voluntary associations also gave generously to those in distress—orphans, widows, debtors, needy mariners, the religiously oppressed, new residents of communities who were not covered by the poor laws, and others who could not care for themselves. In view of the antagonism later thought to exist between public assistance and private charity, this cooperative approach to the problem is one of the more noteworthy aspects of American colonial history.

The men and women who took part in these philanthropic activities were moved, no doubt, by a variety of impulses—to prove to themselves and to others that they were worthy of respect and admiration, to rub shoulders with distinguished citizens, or to control the poor. Clearly, however, many possessed a genuine concern for others, for this was an age of humanitarianism, not only in America but in much of the western world. In America, the urge to help the distressed was particularly strong because of certain social phenomena, such as the Great Awakening, the Enlightenment, and the American Revolution.

Briefly, the Great Awakening was a series of emotional, religious revivals which began in the late 1720s and reached a climax about fifteen years later. Put in its simplest terms, it rested upon a rejection of the Calvinistic doctrine of predestination, postulating in its place the idea that anyone could achieve salvation through faith, repentance, and conversion. Christ died not for the elect alone, but for all people, its adherents claimed. The movement not only strengthened individual piety but also encouraged a spirit of religious independence to such an extent that it weakened the authority of the established churches; thousands upon thousands of adherents flocked to great outdoor meetings to hear itinerant preachers.

At the same time, by stressing the potential salvation of all human beings, the Great Awakening, a mass movement, fostered humane attitudes and popularized philanthropy at all levels of society, especially among the poorer classes. In the words of the social welfare historian Robert Bremner, it transformed "dogoodism from a predominatly upper- and middle-class activity—half responsibility, half recreation—into a broadly shared, genuinely popular avocation." As another student of the period, Raymond Mohl, put it, "Pious men everywhere seemed to transcend interest in their own souls in an aggressive concern for the salvation of others"—or perhaps to exhibit their own Christian spirit. Whatever, the result was the same—benevolent efforts to improve and purify the human condition.

The humanitarian impulse found in the Great Awakening was

personified by its leading figure, George Whitefield, who constantly spoke about the misery of the poor as well as the suffering of the damned and made the collection plate as important as the mourner's bench. Wherever he preached, Whitefield, who had a tremendous ability to move the purses as well as the hearts of his listeners, took up collections for poor debtors, for victims of disaster, for hard-pressed colonial colleges, and for a variety of other good causes, including his pet project, an orphanage in Georgia.[4] Even Benjamin Franklin, the author of *Poor Richard's Almanac* and other writings on economic individualism, who was never noted for being careless with his money, fell before Whitefield's spell as he heard the revivalist speak, and he emptied his pockets, "gold and all" for the cause.[5]

The so-called Enlightenment, which resulted mainly from the growth of science, especially Sir Isaac Newton's studies of the planets (which established the notion of a mechanical, harmonious, law-governed universe that could be understood by man through the use of his reason), and John Locke's treatises on psychology (which held that man is born without any innate ideas, original sin, or anything else—he is a blank, plastic being who will be molded by his environment), also challenged the public to alleviate the lot of the poor; its belief in boundless progress wore away the rather grim determinism of Calvinism and the notion that misery and want were inevitable.

Advocates of the Enlightenment argued that all people possess reason and therefore are, or can be, equal; that there is no need for supernatural revelation, for man, through the use of his

[4]Georgia, the last of the American colonies to be settled (in the 1730s), was itself a unique experiment in philanthropy. Besides serving as a buffer to the other colonies against Spanish, French, and Indian attacks, it was created to serve as a haven for English debtors and ex-prisoners.

[5]In his autobiography, Franklin wrote:

I happened . . . to attend one of [Whitefield's] . . sermons, in the course of which I perceived he intended to finish with a collection, and I silently resolved he should get nothing from me. I had in my pocket a handful of copper money, three or four silver dollars, and five pistoles in gold. As he proceeded I began to soften, and concluded to give the coppers. Another stroke of his oratory made me ashamed of that, and determined to give the silver; and he finished so admirably, that I emptied my pockets wholly in the collector's dish, gold and all.

reason, can comprehend the universe; and that since man was not evil but good (or had the capacity for being good) and could test social institutions by virtue of his reason and reform them according to its light, man can attain salvation here on earth. Poverty was not natural and incapable of being eradicated, something to be tolerated with stoicism and resignation. On the contrary, its elimination, along with that of other injustices and inequities, was both right and just, for the poor had human qualities comparable to those of the more privileged, and had the right to share more adequately in the resources of the nation.

Social reform and humanitarianism followed naturally from these ideas. To quote Mohl again, groups "were formed for every imaginable ... purpose: to assist widows and orphans, immigrants and Negroes, debtors and prisoners, aged females and young prostitutes; to supply the poor with food, fuel, medicine, [and] employment ... ; to promote morality, temperance, thrift, and industrious habits; to educate poor children in free schools, Sunday schools, and charity schools; to reform gamblers," drunkards, and juvenile delinquents.

In Boston, the Society for Encouraging Industry and Employing the Poor was created. A society to relieve "every poor person without distinction" was founded in South Carolina in 1764. The Society for Inoculating [and providing medical care for] the Poor Gratis was organized in 1774 by Philadelphia doctors. Marine societies to aid disabled seamen and their families were created throughout the land.

Finally, the American Revolution intensified the sense of humanitarianism and reform that had already gripped many Americans. The Declaration of Independence, with its emphasis upon reason and human equality, naturally tended to call attention to the need to improve the common person's lot. Independence in the New World, where resources were abundant, offered Americans the opportunity, if not the obligation, to root out old errors and vices and erect a society which would be a beacon to the world. At the very least, if the independent republic and democratic rule were to endure, American citizens had to be exempt from such impediments as illiteracy, poverty, and distress to cast their ballots freely and rationally.

And so, even the state became an instrument for advancing the welfare of the entire population, resulting in many reforms, including the separation of church and state. There were widespread attacks on slavery, which came to be banned in the northern states. Imprisonment for debt was attacked and the criminal codes revised. Public and private groups associated with these and countless other reforms multiplied.[6]

At the same time, the social and economic dislocations caused by the Revolution created special problems, including an increase in need and the breakdown of poor law measures in many communities. The relief of refugees from the invaded and wasted areas of some of the colonies proved difficult to handle on a local basis. It became necessary for the state to take the reins as a financial and in some cases, even as an administrative agency.

In New York, for example, a state body—the Committee on Superintendence of the Poor—was appointed to administer emergency relief to persons removed from their places of settlement because of the war. The principle of settlement was thereby relaxed as a prerequisite for public aid. There arose then, in New York and elsewhere, what had occurred earlier in Massachusetts when Boston was flooded with victims of Indian skirmishes on the frontier—the category of dependents known as the "state poor," who were not chargeable to any local unit; while individual towns did "subsist them," they were reimbursed by the colonial treasury.

To be sure, such special state provision was not a reaction against or a repudiation of the concept of local responsibility. Rather, it was a recognition of the inadequacy of the care, if any, given by local authorities in certain difficult times. So it was that the state began to assume added responsibility for public relief; in

---

[6]Two quite interesting bodies were the humane societies of Boston and Philadelphia. Their main concern was the rescuing and reviving of those suffering from "suspended animation"; i.e., people who appeared to be dead but were not. While there were various causes of the condition, the primary cause was drowning. The societies provided special life-saving equipment and stored it at wharves and taverns near the waterfront. Such equipment included bellows for inflating and deflating the lungs, drag hooks, and medicines. Long a favorite with these humane societies was the fumigator, an instrument for pumping tobacco smoke into the rectum of someone supposedly drowned but who, it was believed, was really in a state of suspended animation. Regardless of the results, the intention was good and it was typical of the age.

1796, it allocated funds to New York City (and then other municipalities) "for the maintenance and support of such persons as shall not have gained settlement in the state." Before long, it provided special facilities and services for the blind, the deaf, the mentally ill, and other needy groups with special problems.

National independence brought few immediate changes in the public welfare system. The poor laws had not been an issue in the Revolution, so they were not only retained by the original states but passed on to the western territories and to the new states that were carved from them. In the North, then, as people migrated from the eastern seaboard to the areas west of the Appalachian Mountains, they reenacted amidst the difficulties of frontier life the poor laws they had brought with them, just as their forefathers had enacted similar statutes carried from England to the New World. Thus, in 1790, only three years after its establishment, a poor law based on those of the northeastern states was enacted in the Northwest Territory; the township was made the administrative unit and overseers of the poor were appointed to implement the statute. Ohio, the first of the northwestern territories to enter the Union (in 1803), duplicated those provisions. Ohio's poor law served as a model for the new states of Indiana and Illinois, which in turn influenced the statutes in Michigan and Wisconsin, and so on.[7]

In the South, however, a significant change occurred—a switch from parish and quasi-ecclesiastical to county and completely civil jurisdiction. The southern system of parish administration of poor relief had become unsatisfactory even before the Revolution. The addition of new parishes had not kept pace with the westward migration of population, causing some distress and discontent. Then came the Revolution and the separation of church and state and, with it, the dissolution of the parishes and their vestries.

As the southern states drew up new constitutions, between 1780 and 1785, they created the position of county overseer of the poor, elected by the freeholders within the county to collect and administer relief funds raised through a compulsory tax. Thereafter, in the South as in the North, public poor relief was

---

[7]Likewise, the settlement laws of these new states were influenced by the northern colonies.

entirely a secular matter, but on a county rather than a township basis. And beginning with Kentucky in 1793, as new states came into the Union from the Southwest, they followed this pattern.

While the Revolution and its aftermath brought few immediate changes in the social welfare system, many important long-range effects may be traced. The establishment of a federal system of government, for example, gave American social welfare some of its most distinctive hallmarks. Unlike Great Britian, Germany, and other European countries, the United States has had no single legal code affecting social welfare matters throughout the nation. Instead, it has had various state laws and court decisions which, on the one hand, have made for confusion, uncertainty, inefficiency, and tardiness in matters of social welfare, but on the other, have permitted flexibility.

More important, by stressing states' rights and limited central government, the federal system, until recently, tended to minimize the role of the national government in assuming responsibility for aiding the needy. This is not to say that it assumed no responsibility, but that less was assumed in America than elsewhere. And since the states themselves also supported relatively few measures designed to aid the unfortunate, the town or other local units, with their relatively limited resources, and private citizens continued to take on most of the welfare burden, in marked contrast to the Old World practice.

The separation of church and state also had a significant effect. The absence of a state church meant that in America many sects would flourish. And since most churches and religious groups have been interested in maintaining their own orphanages, hospitals, aid societies, and other welfare institutions, these have abounded in America. Furthermore, the long experience of promoting social welfare through these and other voluntary associations may have led Americans to feel that there was unique value in such private operations.

The tendency to assume that voluntary associations and institutions were superior in a sense to public ones was furthered by the process of relatively free and unlimited immigration after the Revolution. Just as in prior years, during the nineteenth and early twentieth century numerous ethnic and nationality groups, no less than religious organizations, aided their compatriots in need, and thus served to strengthen the concepts of self-help, mutual aid, and private philanthropy. Perhaps it was this that prompted Lord Bryce, the noted student of American affairs, to write in 1888:

> In the works of active benevolence no country has surpassed, perhaps none has equalled, the United States. Not only are the sums collected for all sorts of philanthropic purposes larger relatively to the wealth of Americans than in any European country, but the amount of personal effort devoted to them seem to a European visitor to exceed what he knows at home.

The opening of the West for settlement after the Revolution had an effect on American social welfare. To begin with, the frontier, with its creed of individual responsibility and personal achievement, further emphasized the idea of self-help. The frontier stimulated private charity in another way: many of our early philanthropic efforts were motivated by fears of irreligion or loose morality in the West.

The frontier also fostered personal mobility, making it difficult for anyone on the rise to be certain of social success. In addition, an abundance of free land and a liberal land policy meant that America could not have a landed aristocracy. Taken together, these conditions encouraged many people to engage in charitable or philanthropic activities (and other voluntary programs of civic concern) in order to win social recognition—or to exhibit the fact that they had the wherewithal to deserve such recognition. Charity work became an index of social status, especially in the late nineteenth century when metropolitan newspapers, entering their great age, celebrated the activities of "Society."[8]

And finally, the frontier, with its abundant resources, meant that the nation would be a land of plenty. Many Americans, therefore, have rejected the Old World's belief in the inevitability of poverty which, in turn, has had a variety of results. It has at times led Americans to act as though distress would cure itself, or

---

[8]Observing America in the 1830s, Alexis de Tocqueville, the noted Frenchman, made much of the "principal of association," as he called it, which drove Americans to establish voluntary organizations of all kinds. Such organizations, he stated, were America's substitutes for the more stable institutions and status relationships of Europe.

that it could be treated by spiritual (rather than by economic) means. At other times, it has been a dynamic force for reform. We have never lacked critics who have taken us to task for our shortcomings; each generation has had its fair share of people who have reminded us that in a land of affluence poverty is shameful, not only to those who suffer from it, but also to the society that allows it to exist.

This is not to say that Americans have always agreed on the best way to eliminate poverty, or even to help the poor. Indeed, immigration and rapid urbanization along with higher taxes and changing economic attitudes generated new ideas concerning poverty and dependency during the early nineteenth century.

Bibliography

ABBOTT, EDITH. *Some American Pioneers in Social Welfare*. Chicago: University of Chicago Press, 1937.

ALEXANDER, JOHN K. *Render Them Submissive: Responses to Poverty in Philadelphia, 1760–1800*. Amherst, Mass.: University of Massachusetts Press, 1980.

BERNHARD, VIRGINIA. "Cotton Mather and the Doing of Good: A Puritan Gospel of Wealth," *New England Quarterly* 49 (June 1976): 225–41.

BOORSTIN, DANIEL J. *The Americans: The Colonial Experience*. New York: Knopf, 1964.

———. *The Americans: The National Experience*. New York: Knopf, 1965.

BREMNER, ROBERT H. *American Philanthropy*. Chicago: University of Chicago Press, 1960.

BRIDENBAUGH, CARL. *Cities in Revolt: Urban Life in America, 1743–1746*. New York: Knopf, 1955.

———. *Cities in the Wilderness: The First Century of Urban Life in America*. New York: Knopf, 1955.

———. *Rebels and Gentlemen: Philadelphia in the Age of Franklin*. New York: Oxford University Press, 1962.

BRYCE, JAMES. *The American Commonwealth*, 2 Vols. New York: Macmillan, 1889.

COLL, BLANCHE D. "Perspectives in Public Welfare: Colonial Times to 1860, Part I," *Welfare in Review* 5 (November-December 1967): 1–9.

CORNER, GEORGE W., ed. *The Autobiography of Benjamin Rush.* Princeton, N.J.: Princeton University Press, 1948.

COWING, CEDRIC B. *The Great Awakening and the American Revolution.* Chicago: Rand McNally, 1971.

CURTI, MERLE. *The Growth of American Thought.* New York: Harper, 1964.

DE TOCQUEVILLE, ALEXIS. *Democracy in America,* 2 Vols. New York: Vintage Books, 1957.

JAMES, SYDNEY V. *A People Among Peoples: Quaker Benevolence in Eighteenth Century America.* Cambridge, Mass.: Harvard University Press, 1963.

JAMESON, J. FRANKLIN. *The American Revolution Considered as a Social Movement.* Boston: Beacon Press, 1956.

JORNS, AUGUSTE. *The Quakers as Pioneers in Social Work.* New York: Macmillan, 1931.

KOCH, ADRIENNE, ed. *The American Enlightenment.* New York: Braziller, 1965.

LEMISCH, JESSE, ed. *Benjamin Franklin: The Autobiography and Other Writings.* New York: New American Library, 1961.

MCMASTER, JOHN B. *The Life and Times of Stephen Girard.* Philadelphia: Lippincott, 1918.

MAIN, JACKSON TURNER. *The Social Structure of Revolutionary America.* Princeton, N.J.: Princeton University Press, 1965.

MOHL, RAYMOND A. "Poverty in Early America, A Reappraisal: The Case of Eighteenth-Century New York City," *New York History* 50 (January 1969): 5–27.

NASH, GARY. "Poverty and Poor Relief in Pre-Revolutionary Philadelphia," *William and Mary Quarterly* 33 (January 1976): 3–30.

———. *The Urban Crucible: Social Change, Political Consciousness, and the Origins of the American Revolution.* Cambridge, Mass.: Harvard University Press, 1979.

———. "Urban Wealth and Poverty in Pre-Revolutionary America," *Journal of Interdisciplinary History* 6 (Spring 1976): 545–84.

O'CONNELL, NEIL J. "George Whitefield and Bethesda Orphan House," *Georgia Historical Quarterly* 54 (Spring 1970): 41–62.

SAVELLE, MAX. *Seeds of Liberty.* Seattle: University of Washington Press, 1968.

SMITH, BRADFORD. *A Dangerous Freedom*. Philadelphia: Lippincott, 1954.

SMITH, DANIEL S., AND MICHAEL S. HINDUS. "Premarital Pregnancy in America, 1640–1971: An Overview and Interpretation," *Journal of Interdisciplinary History* 5 (Spring 1975): 537–71.

SMYTH, ALBERT H., ed. *The Writings of Benjamin Franklin*. New York: American, 1907.

SWEET, WILLIAM WARREN. *Religion in Colonial America*. New York: Harper, 1942.

VIRGADAMO, PETER R. "Charity for a City in Crisis: Boston, 1740–1775," *Historical Journal of Western Massachusetts* 10 (January 1982): 22–33.

WALCH, TIMOTHY. "Catholic Social Institutions and Urban Development," *Catholic Historical Review* 64 (January 1978): 16–32.

WILLIAMS, HOWELL V. "Benjamin Franklin and the Poor Laws," *Social Service Review* 18 (March 1944): 77–91.

WILLIAMS, WILLIAM H. "The 'Industrious Poor' and the Founding of the Pennsylvania Hospital," *Pennsylvania Magazine of History and Biography* 97 (October 1973): 431–43.

Chapter 4

The Trend Toward Indoor Relief

WHILE, AS A MATTER of course, the poor laws spread westward as new lands were opened up after the American Revolution, in the coastal cities they were being questioned for the first time. There, the forces of change—large-scale immigration, rapid industrialization, and widespread urbanization—tended to alter the relatively stable and well-ordered society of the colonial years and to bring with them a rising incidence of poverty that caused public relief spending to rise to ever higher levels; year after year, outlays for poor relief continued to top all other items in town and city budgets. This, along with heightened social tensions and general disarray,[1] aroused not only a great deal of concern about poverty but attempts to ferret out its causes and efforts to eliminate it—a clear departure from colonial practice.

The same was true in England, which was also undergoing pronounced and disturbing changes. There, as in America, concern over the poor laws was widespread. First of all, the system's effectiveness and equity were questioned. Local responsibility often led to inadequate and unequal standards, on the one hand, and inefficient and sometimes corrupt administration, on the other. Thousands of untrained and often incompetent overseers of the poor, many of whom were employed on only a part-time basis, did not make for effective administration. More important,

---

[1]Religious denominations and congregations were separating. Deism and secularism appeared to be spreading. The French Revolution threatened to undermine the established classes. The West attracted restless families, stirring mobility and further upsetting settled communities, etc.

because many of the poorer districts had a higher proportion of needy residents and less money to spend on relief than the more prosperous ones, not only was treatment of the poor unequal, but the communities that could least afford it usually had the highest poor rates. Everywhere, however, taxes went up. Between 1760 and 1818, poor relief expenditures throughout England increased sixfold while the population about doubled.

One of the reasons, it was thought, for the higher tax rates was what amounted to an assured annual income, popularly known as the Speenhamland system or rate-in-aid of wages. Low wages and high prices had caused much distress in late eighteenth-century England. As a result, in 1795, after several unsuccessful attempts at regulating wages, the district of Speenhamland (and others later) adopted a system by which all laborers paid less than a certain amount, which varied according to the price of wheat, were granted relief allowances. "Every poor and industrious man and his family," the legislation read, "was to have a certain weekly income produced by his own or his family's labor," the cost of which was "to be borne from the poor rates."

As the system spread, it seemed to bring with it higher prices, higher taxes, and the belief that, since the poor were guaranteed a minimum income, they not only were becoming lazy but were encouraged to multiply. Furthermore, it was alleged that since employers, who never paid higher salaries than they were forced to, knew that their workers would not starve, the system invited low wages and perpetuated poverty.

A general subsidy of wages, in which employers paid low salaries and the public footed the bill and which encouraged early marriages and large families certainly would have left a great deal to be desired. But the system did not operate that way. Wages were below standard before the program was implemented. To attribute substandard wages to Speenhamland, therefore, was not accurate. Furthermore, those who bore the burden of the system—that is, who paid the taxes to finance it—were, for the most part, employers of agricultural and industrial labor who therefore had little to gain by cutting wages. Nor, in practice, was it true that the system promoted population growth; at best, it led to a reduction in infant mortality although, as one historian has recently concluded, "not substantially enough to affect the general death-rate or . . . the rate of population growth."

In short, Speenhamland was not responsible for the evils attributed to it. If anything, it was a forward-looking measure that provided financial aid to the destitute according to need as determined by the cost of living. Increased relief expenditures and higher taxes resulted not from Speenhamland but from other factors, especially chronic technological unemployment. Abolition of the system in itself had no salutary effect on the national economy or the condition of the poor. (The drop in relief expenditures after its termination was largely due to good harvests, a boom in railroad building, and a substantial increase in private charity.) Nevertheless, it was widely believed that the poor laws were responsible for these and other evils.

In the meantime, the poor laws had come under attack from another source—the so-called classical economists, who believed that poverty was the natural state of the wage-earning classes. The possession and accumulation of property and wealth, they argued, was a "natural right" with which the state must not interfere; the poor law, an artificial creation of the state which taxed the well-to-do for the maintenance and care of the needy, violated that right and was morally wrong.

Dissatisfaction with the poor law on these grounds and evolution of the laissez-faire philosphy resulted from major social and economic changes that occurred between the seventeenth and nineteenth centuries, changes which had profound consequences for social welfare policy. The dominance of the old landed aristocracy, with its sense of social responsibility and its assumption that the stability of the state required public action to regulate the affairs of mankind, was waning rapidly under the competitive pressure of the rising business classes, the emergence of a capitalist economy that substituted the price mechanism for the state in determining the status of labor, and the disintegrating relationship between employer and employee caused by industrialization and urbanization. It was held that interference with normal market operations—a fluid national labor force controlled by supply and demand—would threaten, if not overturn, the economic order. In short, the mercantilist philosophy underlying the Elizabethan

Poor Law was being replaced by the idea of free and unlimited exchange—a self-regulating market economy, or laissez-faire. All of the restrictions on trade and industry had to be removed. The poor laws and other anachronistic measures would have to undergo major change.[2]

Thus, the sytem was not only morally wrong, according to economists Adam Smith, David Ricardo, and others, but it was also economically unsound. Residency rules, an inevitable concomitant of the poor law, interfered with the labor mobility required in a free market. In addition, the poor law was socially bad. According to Thomas Malthus (whose famous *Essay on the Principle of Population* was first published in 1798), one of the severest opponents of the poor law and a firm advocate of its abolition, it caused overpopulation, already a serious problem, lowering wages and living standards, causing more misery than it alleviated. Adhering to the "wage-fund" theory—the idea that there existed at any one time a certain fixed sum of money to be used for the wages of *all* workers—the classical economists argued that the money spent to support paupers comprised wages withheld (in the form of taxes) from industrious workers. Public assistance, then, lowered the standard of living; rugged individualism was not only natural, but ideal.

As a result, immediately after the manufacturing interests gained power from the landed mercantile classes through the electoral reforms of 1832, Parliament created a Royal Poor Law Commission for Inquiring into the Administration and Practical Operation of the Poor Laws. The commission, dominated by the laissez-faire philosophy and intent upon altering the welfare system to meet the requirements of industrial capitalism—that is, the existence of a national pool of laborers who would work in factories for long hours and low wages—approached its investigation

[2]Denying the organic concept of society in favor of "natural law" and a belief in the harmony of the universe, the dominant philosophy of the nineteenth century was individualism and laissez-faire. Human happiness, or rather the greatest happiness for the greatest number, was the purpose of life and the goal of society. Society, it was believed, was composed of isolated individuals, each of whom was the best judge of his or her own interest. The sum of each individual's good led to the good of the whole. As a result, any interference with the individual was a blow or an impediment, to the social good or welfare. Since wealth was a primary source of happiness, unfettered self-interest and the accumulation of wealth (and property) was the ideal; the economic welfare of the nation was not a matter of predetermined policy, but one of free and natural growth.

with an a priori attitude and thus found exactly what it was looking for—that the prevailing poor law system (especially wage supplementation), and the way in which it was being administered, was responsible for debasing the character and energy of the English laboring classes.

Based, then, upon faulty history, gross exaggeration, contemporary social philosophy, and the fears of the day, the commission's report, written by its secretary, Sir Edwin Chadwick, together with some classical economists, and published in 1834, contained two recommendations which were immediately enacted into law.

Recognizing that the problem of relief was larger than that of any single unit, the first called for a national supervisory body with the authority to combine parishes in order to coordinate and thus improve poor law services throughout the land. Within three years, 90 percent of Great Britain's parishes (some 13,264 of them) were combined into 568 units, poor law districts presided over by boards of guardians, which effected some improvement in the public welfare system.

The second recommendation was for an end to public assistance for able-bodied persons, except in public institutions. While the framers of the report did not intend for the principle to be applied to the helpless poor, by implying, among other things, that the reduction of public relief and the cutting of taxes were the ideal, it was carried out indiscriminately. Most of those on public relief—the young and the old, the sick and the disabled, the unemployed and the underpaid, as well as the lazy—would be deprived of outdoor assistance.

Curtailment of home relief also resulted from what was perhaps the most important aspect of the report—its general tone, which implied that poverty was an individual moral matter. An essential corollary to this, written into the report and its subsequent legislation, was the doctrine of "less eligibility"—the notion that the status of those dependent on public assistance "shall not be made really or apparently so eligible [satisfactory] as the situation of the independent laborer of the lowest class." In other words, the condition of all welfare recipients, regardless of need or cause, should be worse than that of the lowest paid self-supporting laborer. While relief should not be denied the poor, life should be made so miserable for them that they would rather work than accept public aid.

Passage of the Poor Law Reform Bill of 1834, which implemented these recommendations, epitomized the punitive attitude toward the poor. Thenceforth, it was publicly known, to use the words of Prime Minister Benjamin Disraeli, that it was "a crime to be poor" in England. Poor relief was redesigned to increase fear of insecurity, rather than to check its causes or even to alleviate its problems. At best, it would prevent starvation or death from exposure, but it would do so as economically and unpleasantly as possible. The measure of the system's soundness would be its deterrent effect—or, to quote Karl Polanyi, a more recent critic, its ability to oil "the wheels of the labor mill."

The trip, then, from the Middle Ages to 1834 brought with it a vast change in the public attitude toward the poor and the way in which they should be cared for. During the Middle Ages, evidence of need overrode all else. It was generally assumed that need arose from misfortune for which society, in all justice, should assume responsibility. The individual's right to public assistance was firmly established. The Elizabethan Poor Law of 1601 endorsed that right, placing the ultimate charge for implementing it upon secular authorities. It also distinguished between the impotent and the able-bodied poor and acknowledged the existence of involuntary unemployment.

By the early nineteenth century, conditions had changed. Industrial capitalism, urbanization, greater poverty, higher taxes, and the laissez-faire philosophy had made the pursuit and accumulation of wealth a moral virtue and dependency a vice. It was assumed that destitution was the individual's fault, and since most of the needy were recipients of help from the public treasury, it followed that public aid was a cause of pauperism and thus inherently bad. If bestowed at all, it should be done so as carefully and as stringently as possible, hence in public institutions where, it was felt, the costs would be lower, the opportunity for control better, the chances for propagation fewer and the deterrent power greater.

In America, where land was abundant and labor scarce, the Malthusian population theory, one of the most telling arguments used against the British poor laws, had little relevance. Nevertheless, the influence of the classical economists and the laissez-faire philosophy in general, and the idea that public relief tended to pauperize and demoralize recipients and depress the standard of living in particular, had even more rigid acceptance in the United States than in England. The reasons for this may be of interest.

First of all, some of the very influences that led to reform and efforts to help those in need, especially the Enlightenment and the American Revolution, also stimulated distrust of the poor. The Enlightenment, by helping to wear away the notion that misery and want were endemic to society, made it appear as though the poor were personally responsible for their condition. The same was true for the American Revolution; by fostering the belief that poverty need not exist, it encouraged a harsh and suspicious view of the poor. God's will was no longer a satisfactory explanation for defective social conditions, especially in America, a land of abundance and virtually unlimited resources where work was more plentiful than elsewhere, especially crowded England. Observers concluded that no one ought to be poor, and there was little tolerance for the able-bodied pauper. The only cause of such poverty, it was assumed, was individual weakness. As Nathanial Ware, a social philosopher of the early nineteenth century, saw it, the able-bodied man who begged or received public assistance was beyond redemption, having sunk to the level of a mere eating brute. "Humanity aside," reported Ware, "it would be to the best interest of society to kill all such drones." Thus, whereas colonials had accepted the notion that the poor must always be present and citizens are obliged to do whatever is necessary to help them, by the late eighteenth and the early nineteenth century, Americans began to believe that poverty could be obliterated—in part, by allowing the poor to perish.

Unconcerned about the inadequacy or uncertainty of wages, such detractors accepted uncritically the prevailing economic doctrines of Adam Smith and his followers. It was assumed that anyone who wanted to could work, and that all those working received or invariably would receive enough wages to support themselves and their families. They failed to recognize that even in America some people could not find jobs, that even in the best of times some branches of industry were depressed and opportunities were limited or below-standard wages prevailed, that seasonal and technological unemployment was inevitable, and that nothing could be done about these ills. Thus, the New York Society for the Prevention of Pauperism, in the midst of the nation's worst depression to date (1821), contended: "No man who is temperate, frugal, and willing to work need suffer or become a pauper for want of employment." Or, in the words of one reformer, the "sober and able-bodied, if industriously disposed, cannot long want employment. They cannot, but in their own folly and vices, long remain indigent."

Stereotypes rather than individuals in need dominated the public mind. Although, on occasion, a verbal distinction was made between the "worthy" and the "unworthy" poor, between those willing to work but who, for one reason or another, were unable to and the voluntarily unemployed, most people tended to regard all the needy with contempt. The "worthy" poor soon discovered that no matter how hard they struggled they still were condemned as moral failures. Thus, a New York Humane Society report on the "sources of vice and misery" nowhere mentioned economic causes. "By a just and inflexible law of Providence," the report stated, "misery is ordained to be the companion and the punishment of vice." Pauperism obviously resulted from laziness, extravagance, immorality, or some other moral defect.

The Protestant ethic, which, as Raymond Mohl has observed, demanded benevolence of the rich but also hard work and morality of the poor, complemented the belief that the individual had the power to achieve economic success through his or her own efforts.[3] So, too, did the Second Great Awakening and the growth of revivalism at this time, which preached that salvation depended on personal factors—diligence, frugality, virtue, and conversion. If a person failed, then, in the religious or the secular realm, it was his or her own fault; idleness, bad habits, and other human frailties were responsible. Poverty and damnation were personal matters; only the individual could overcome them.

This outlook appeared to be borne out by the large number of

---

[3]For many of the ideas in this (and in the previous) chapter, I am heavily indebted to the works of Raymond Mohl, some of which are listed in the bibliographies.

immigrants entering the country at the time, another reason for the change in attitude toward the poor in America. Some six million foreigners came to the United States between 1800 and 1860, mainly impoverished German and Irish Catholics who landed at entry points between Baltimore and Boston. For the most part, they remained in the North, where they congregated in cities. From the outset, these newcomers, alien to the dominant Protestant middle-class culture, aroused concern. In fact, as early as 1796, the commissioners of New York City's poorhouse complained of the "enormous and growing expense . . . not so much from the increase of our own poor, as from the prodigious influx of indigent foreigners in this city." With time, the situation grew even worse. In 1820, the annual report of New York's Society for the Prevention of Pauperism listed "emigrants to this city from foreign countries" as the largest source of pauperism.

Making matters worse, the Irish and German immigrants, who could hardly enjoy life in their cramped and stuffy tenements, often congregated in neighborhood bars, even on holidays and Sundays. Their drinking habits, observance of the Sabbath, and other customs differed from those of the dominant and alarmed Protestant majority intent upon maintaining order in an increasingly chaotic society. That many of the immigrants were victims of malnutrition, exploitation, the Irish potato famine, the cruel voyage across the sea, thieves and swindlers waiting to fleece them as soon as they stepped off the boat, vile slums and substandard wages, and other wretched living and working conditions, was ignored by the dominant majority who "found it difficult to apply Christian benevolence to [these] ragged, uncouth, 'different,' [unChristian,] and seemingly immoral newcomers."

Outdoor aid, especially public relief, only aggravated the problem. "The more paupers you support, the more you will have to support," claimed one citizen. To another, public aid was like a drug and was as dangerous: "Very often it creates an appetite which is more harmful than the pain it is intended to relieve," he asserted. "Of all the modes of providing for the poor," declared Boston's Mayor Josiah Quincy, who in 1821 chaired a state commission that investigated public outdoor relief, "the most wasteful, the most expensive, and the most injurious to their morals and destructive to their industrious habits is that of supply in their own families." By encouraging the poor to rely upon the public dole rather than upon their own energies, and by removing the dread of want, considered by many to be the prime mover of the needy, the poor laws destroyed the incentive to work, causing the poor to become even more idle and improvident.

Equally galling was the attitude it fostered among the needy, the idea that relief was a right; thus, there was no gratitude for those who provided it. Public assistance, then, deprived the giver of the pleasure of observing the supplicant's joy when his plea was granted. Moreover, by compelling people to pay taxes for relief, public assistance dried up (or would inevitably dry up) private charity. Hence, it was un-Christian, for charity was a Christian virtue.

So, for these reasons, the abolition of public assistance had many proponents. Its elimination, they contended, would end pauperism. Those who could not contribute labor to the market-place and thus remained in need would be helped by private charity, which would not lead to the willful lack of productivity; the poor could not interpret such assistance as a right for they had no statutory claim to it. Similarly, the private sector would prove less susceptible to political pressures for liberalization of benefits. Too, agents of voluntary agencies were better equipped to exert those moral and religious influences that would prevent relief from degenerating into a mechanical pauperizing dole. And final-ly, private giving also bound the poor to the well-to-do and had such other desirable characteristics as precariousness and uncer-tainty.

The system of public aid, however, was too deeply ingrained in the culture to be abolished. As J. V. N. Yates, New York's Secre-tary of State, who would have liked to abolish it, remarked: "The total want of a pauper system would be inconsistent with a humane, liberal, and enlightened policy," and perhaps domestic peace and tranquility as well. It was up to the private citizen to exercise vigilance to see to it that it was administered as economi-cally and, therefore, as efficiently as possible. To this end, empha-sis was placed on the widespread use of institutions—almshouses and workhouses. A sort of division of labor arose. Public assis-tance would be confined to institutional care, mainly for the "worthy" or hard-core poor, the permanently disabled, and others who clearly could not care for themselves. Also, the able-bodied or "unworthy" poor who sought public aid would be institutionalized in workhouses where their behavior not only could be controlled but where, removed from society and its tempting vices, they presumably would acquire habits of industry and labor and thus prepare themselves for better (i.e., self-sufficient) lives. The institution, in other words, would have a therapeutic as well as a wholesome economic effect. For the remainder, home relief of a new kind—mainly, moral relief administered by private benevolent agencies—would be available.

The greater emphasis on the use of almshouses resulted, in part, from the English experience. More important, however, was a similar, and even earlier, development in America—the Yates Report, one of the most influential documents in American social welfare history. New York's Secretary of State, J. V. N. Yates, was commissioned by the legislature to conduct a survey of public poor relief throughout the state. His report, based mainly upon the replies to questionnaires sent to poor law officials throughout the state, was presented to the lawmakers in February 1824.

Widely received and considered to be a progressive document during its time, the Yates Report offered an excellent account of prevailing poor relief practices. Yates cited four main methods of public assistance that were used throughout the state—institutional relief, home relief, the contract system, and the auction system—and outlined what he felt to be the cruelty, waste, and inefficiency arising from this chaotic situation. Where the poor were "farmed out," either through the contract or auction system, they were often treated cruelly, even inhumanely. Moreover, the "education and the morals of children were almost wholly neglected" and, according to Yates, "they grow up in filth, idleness, and disease, becoming early candidates for the prison or the grave." The able-bodied poor were rarely employed; home relief encouraged idleness, and "vice, dissipation, disease and crime" resulted.

For Yates (and others who conducted similar studies in Boston, Baltimore, Philadelphia, Providence, and elsewhere), the ending of home relief and the building of institutions was the solution, especially for dependent youngsters. In public institutions, he argued, children's "health and morals" would be improved and "they would receive an education to fit them for future usefulness." Not content with merely evaluating the system, he made three recommendations for its improvement: that no able-bodied person between the ages of eighteen and fifty be given public assistance; that for the old, the young, and the disabled, institutional relief be supplied; and that the *county,* rather than the town, become the administrative unit.

So it was, that in 1824, that same year, the New York State legislature enacted the County Poorhouse Act, a measure that called for one or more poorhouses to be erected in each county of the state. Thenceforth, all recipients of public assistance were to be sent to that institution (unless sickness or infirmity rendered their removal from home dangerous). All expenses for building and maintaining the institution and supporting its inmates were to be defrayed by the county out of tax funds. The act also created a new body of relief officials—County Superintendents of the Poor—whose principal function was to manage the almshouse. The measure, then, marked two significant nineteenth-century trends in American social welfare: the transfer of responsibility for public assistance from towns to counties (in the North), and the general trend toward indoor relief.

While it may be true, as Blanche Coll (the author of an earlier history of public assistance) has suggested, that, contrary to popular belief, institutional relief did not monopolize public assistance—it did not become the sole method of providing for the poor—it did increase significantly during this period. In fact, it became fundamental. To use David Rothman's words, "to an extraordinary degree [indoor relief] dominate[d] the public response to poverty."[4] For example, in 1824 Massachusetts had 83 almshouses; fifteen years later the number had increased to 180, and by 1860 the total had risen to 219. Although public officials continued to dispense some outdoor assistance to meet emergencies, by the end of the Civil War "four out of every five persons in Massachusetts who received extended relief remained within an institution," and the situation was similar elsewhere. Whereas the

[4]David Rothman, *The Discovery of the Asylum* (Boston: Little, Brown, 1971), p. 185, but see pp. 180–205.

family and the private home were the setting in which assistance was provided to the needy in the preindustrial era, during the nineteenth century social welfare functions were transferred, for the most part, to institutions in the larger community.

Not only was there a greater use of county institutions, but the state began to build its own institutions at this time as well. The growth of state participation resulted from a greater nonresident population, as well as from the evils of county almshouse care.

With regard to the first, the changes in the nation's socioeconomic life—the influx of immigrants, the expansion of an industrial economy, the growth of cities and a vast network of canals, railroads, and highways, the increase in travel and mobility, the westward movement, and so on—made it impossible to maintain a completely local and insular poor relief system. Local officials, continually occupied with nonresident indigents, from home as well as from abroad, naturally demanded state aid to relieve their communities of that burden; as you recall, there was a precedent for such action. (Once the sentiment of local responsibility weakened and the poor lost their status as "neighbors" and became members of the "lower classes" instead, it was much easier to reprimand and institutionalize them.)

Equally important were the faulty results of the county institution system. While for the most part the public accepted its responsibility for erecting such institutions, oftentimes little or no regard was paid to the type of care provided within their walls. Into many were herded the old and the young, the sick and the well, the sane and the insane, the epileptic and the feebleminded, the blind and the alcoholic, the juvenile delinquent and the hardened criminal, male and female, all thrown together in haphazard fashion. Nakedness and filth, hunger and vice, and other abuses such as beatings by cruel keepers were not uncommon in many of these wretched places, vile catchalls for everyone in need, defined by one contemporary as "living tombs" and by another as "social cemeteries."

Blaming an indifferent public for the foul conditions, a New York State legislative committee in the 1850s said the following about many of New York's rural almshouses:

It is much to be regretted that our citizens manifest so little interest in the condition even of those in their immediate neighborhood. Individuals who take great interest in human suffering whenever it is brought to their notice, never visit them, and are entirely uninformed, that in a county house almost at their own doors, may be found the lunatic suffering for years in a dark and suffocating cell, in summer, and almost freezing the winter—where a score of children are poorly fed, poorly clothed, and quite untaught—where the poor idiot is half starved and beaten with rods because he is too dull to do his master's bidding—where the aged mother is lying in perhaps her last sickness, unattended by a physician, and with no one to minister to her wants—where the lunatic, and that lunatic, too, a *woman* is made to feel the lash in the hands of a brutal underkeeper—yet these are all to be found—*they all exist in our State.*

It must be pointed out, however, conditions varied among county poorhouses. While many were like those described above—houses of degradation, disease, near-starvation, and the like—others were not. Some, in fact, provided reasonably good care for their inmates, including adequate medical services, administered in a fairly personal and caring way. Furthermore, recent demographic studies of county poorhouses in Buffalo, New York, and elsewhere show that for many people such institutions were not places of permanent residence; rather, they were temporary refuges during times of personal crisis and widespread social and economic distress. They were places in which the poor stayed for a while during the cold winter months; temporary shelters for the jobless during times of depression and widespread unemployment; maternity homes for young, unmarried pregnant women; and places of last resort for sick, helpless, elderly persons. In other words, whatever the official purposes of such institutions, the poor sometimes put them to their own use; they served as key life supports amidst the harshness and uncertainty of existence in early industrial America. Later on, however, more and more of them became long-term custodial institutions, mainly for the aged.

There is an ongoing intellectual debate about the effectiveness or the possible effectiveness of such institutions—of all residential institutions, in fact. Scholars like David Rothman and Gerald Grob assert that county poorhouses, mental institutions, and other "asylums" that were created at the time failed—that is, they did not reform or cure their inmates or patients, they were very expensive to maintain, and they quickly degenerated from therapeutic to custodial establishments—because of external factors, including lack of adequate funds, improper training of staff, and poor management. Other commentators, however, such as Erving Goffman and Christopher Lasch, have argued that such institutions were and are flawed from the start and hence doomed to failure. The institution itself, rather than inmates' or patients' needs, is the crucial determinant of life within its walls: the administrators' desire to maintain order and insure a smooth daily routine is at odds with the therapeutic goals that supposedly justify operation of the facility, yet the former always take precedence.

Whether successful or not, and in most cases they were not, whether useful way stations for temporarily distressed citizens or wretched places of long-term confinement for the older poor, and they soon became the latter, these institutions persisted. Before long, humanitarians, journalists, and others (in England as well as in the United States, as some of Charles Dickens's works indicate) began writing shocking accounts of life within those institutions, especially the worst ones. Under such circumstances, it was inevitable that reformers would turn to the state to step in and improve the situation, especially by establishing, and then running, its own institutions for people in need of specialized care or treatment—the young, the delinquent, the defective, the mentally ill, and so on. Thus, the period also witnessed the beginning of the classification and segregation of different types of dependents in state institutions. The institutional ideal, then, was not confined to county poorhouses; the founding of houses of refuge, or orphanages, penitentiaries, and mental hospitals during this period was part of the same movement.

One of the earliest developments along these lines was in the area of child welfare. In 1824, the House of Refuge for Juvenile Delinquents, the first juvenile reformatory in America, supported by state funds, was established in New York City. In 1847, the Massachusetts legislature enacted a law for the founding of a state reformatory, and two years later another was opened in New York. Five years later Ohio followed suit, and so on. In the meantime, many state orphanages were founded, especially after the 1860s when laws were enacted in many states calling for the mandatory removal of all children from county almshouses. Meanwhile, state institutions for the mentally ill and the physically handicapped, as well as for the feebleminded and the deaf and dumb, had come into existence.

Not only did social reformers seek and obtain state aid at this time, but many also turned to Washington for help. That they did so should not be surprising. Population expansion coast to coast and improvements in transportation and communication highlighted the obvious—that the grave problems and malfunctions of sorts that overwhelm people are not matters merely of local or even state concern but are national in scope and, therefore, within the province of the federal government.

Moreover, many social projects were already receiving federal aid of one kind or another. Such aid could be traced back to the eighteenth century. Upon passage of the Northwest Ordinance in 1787, Congress, under the Articles of Confederation, decreed that a portion of the public domain in the Northwest Territory be set aside for the financial support of public education, the first of a long history of federal grants-in-aid. In 1803, when Ohio entered the Union, it received such aid, as did most of the other states that later came into the Union. Proceeds from the sale of public lands given the states by the federal government were used not only for public education, but also for land reclamation, railroad building, and other internal improvements, such as canals and roads.

Then, too, in 1818 Congress had enacted the Revolutionary War Pension Act—the nation's first military pension program, one that combined features of a pension plan with poor law principles to provide assistance to impoverished Continental army veterans. In addition, the federal government on occasion had made funds and other forms of direct aid available to civilian victims of fires, floods, and cyclones. Finally, and perhaps most important, some public and private welfare institutions had appealed for and received federal aid, chiefly on the grounds that they provided educational as well as custodial services, and that they cared for out-of-state as well as in-state residents. Thus, in the spring of 1819, the Connecticut Asylum for the Deaf and Dumb (a private institution) was granted 23,000 acres of public land which, when sold, brought the institution some $300,000.

And, in 1826, Congress granted a township of public land to the Kentucky Deaf and Dumb Asylum (a state institution).[5] So it was that social reformers began to look for more help from the U.S. government.

The high-water mark in the nineteenth-century drive to get the national government to assume added responsibility in the area of social welfare centered around the attempt to get federal aid for the care and treatment of the mentally ill, a movement synonymous with the name of Dorothea Dix. A great figure in the field of social welfare, Dix's career offers an excellent example of sustained constructive action for the downtrodden. Her method of fact-gathering, preparing memorials and bills, and then rallying public opinion behind them, is still of value today.

Dorothea Lynde Dix was born in Hampden, Maine, in April 1802. At age twelve, she moved to Boston where, living with her grandparents, she received a good education and then turned to teaching. First, she opened a fashionable private school for girls, and then a free school for paupers. She also found time to write several children's books. But her heavy schedule proved too great a strain, and in 1836 she collapsed. She remained in retirement until 1841, when she heeded a call for a Sunday school teacher for women inmates of the East Cambridge jail. There she witnessed the crude and barbaric treatment of prisoners and the degradation to which they were subjected, especially those mentally disturbed. Horrified by what she saw, she apparently experienced a tremendous emotional reaction which led her to embark upon one of the most remarkable crusades of the century—an effort to obtain better care and treatment of the mentally ill.

Dorothea Dix was not among the first to work for better treatment of the insane who, like the poor, had fallen victim to the institutionalization movement of the early nineteenth century; they, too, had become odd and even menacing figures no longer accepted in society merely as one group among others whose incapacitating ailment made them dependent upon relatives or the community. Ironically, this opened the door to constructive change. Just as reformers had come to perceive poverty as abnor-

[5]See Walter I. Trattner, "The Federal Government and Social Welfare in Early Nineteenth-Century America," *Social Service Review* 50 (June 1976): 243–55.

mal and had moved to end it by eliminating home relief and confining the needy to almshouses, so physicians now insisted that
insanity was not the inevitable result of God's will and that it
could be cured—through kind and gentle treatment in an institution. Much had been accomplished along these lines when
Dorothea Dix began her work. Several good private hospitals for
the mentally ill had been founded by incorporated bodies, and a
number of states and municipalities had opened public institutions as well. Private hospitals, however, were small in size, extremely expensive, and selective in their admissions policies;
hence they catered to a small and affluent clientele. Public institutions were few in number and, like almshouses, tended to deterio-
rate quickly into wretched places. As a result, the overwhelming
majority of mentally ill persons, especially the indigent insane
(particularly members of ethnic minorities), were either placed in
inadequate public mental institutions or, more likely, confined to
jails, almshouses, or other institutions where their care and treatment was faulty, to say the least.

Such was the case when Dorothea Dix began her fight for the
insane in Massachusetts, where the number of dependent insane
was more than twice as large as the total capacity of the three
mental institutions—one state, one municipal, one private—in
the state. Visiting numerous jails, houses of correction, dreary
almshouses, and other places where the bulk of the mentally ill
were housed, she set down in detail all she had seen. She
described vividly how many of the unfortunate crazed were im-
pounded in cabins, cages, closets, stalls, and other pens of one
kind or another, often chained and then abandoned to filth and
neglect, or else brutally beaten—a horrifying picture. Having
decided that neither private philanthropy nor local responsibility
could effectively remedy the situation, she embarked upon a
crusade for more and better state care. Possessing a keen sense of
political strategy, she embodied her findings in a memorial to the
state legislature, which in part read:

> I come to present the strong claim of suffering humanity.... I come as
> the advocate of the helpless, forgotten, insane and idiotic men and
> women, beings sunk to a condition from which the most unconcerned
> should stare with real horror. If my pictures are displeasing, coarse,

and severe [she continued], it must be remembered [that] . . . the conditions of beings reduced to the extremest states of degradation and misery cannot be exhibited in softened language and adorn a polished page.

After pleading passionately for its adoption, she eventually won her point—that the state should enlarge its facilities for poor mental patients.

Dorothea Dix did not stop there. Convinced that the issue transcended geographical boundaries, that mental illness was no respecter of persons or places, and that the public had a responsibility to provide adequate care for the sick and suffering, she carried her crusade into a dozen other states, including six in the South—Kentucky, Mississippi, Louisiana, South Carolina, Georgia, and Virginia—where tensions over the slavery issue were high and where it was extremely dangerous for a Yankee (especially a woman) to be traveling about. Still, she went on. Journeying by train, stagecoach, lumber wagon, and foot over muddy roads and across swollen rivers to visit places far removed and difficult to get to, she operated throughout on the assumption that proved successful in her home state—that reform comes from patient, factual research. Before starting out, she read widely on the subject and then, wherever she went, studied antiquated and impractical commitment laws, inspected buildings, talked with and observed the patients and their overseers, and so on, confining her thoughts and the harsh facts to writing. Thus armed with numerous case studies and statistics depicting the extent and nature of the problem, she made her appeal. And between 1843 and 1853, the "decade of victory," as her biographer has called it, she became personally reponsible for the founding of state hospitals for mental patients in nine states, North and South alike (and quite a few others around the world, it might be added).

Still, the naturally timid and diffident crusader was not satisfied, for she had failed in some instances. She was convinced that her defeats resulted less from an unwillingness of legislators to help the mentally ill than from their inability to do so because of the high costs involved. So, at a time when the government had already allocated some 135 million acres of land for the purposes mentioned (and when not more than one-twelfth of the insane population in America could be accommodated in existing hospitals and asylums), she appealed to Congress to appropriate ten million more acres to the states to help pay for the construction and maintenance of mental hospitals.

A bill based upon research that had taken her some 60,000 miles to visit jails, poorhouses, and mental institutions throughout the country, was introduced in Congress in 1848. After the lawmakers adjourned without acting on the measure, Miss Dix had it reintroduced at the next session. Numerous clergymen, prominent citizens, newspapers, public and private organizations, including the Association of Medical Superintendents for the Insane, and some government officials wrote or acted in support of the measure. Still the bill was not acted upon, for most congressmen were more interested in using the public domain for their own and for land speculators' purposes than for the mentally ill. Undaunted, she kept up the fight, spending the next five years in and out of congressional corridors promoting the measure. Finally, in 1854, it was passed by both houses of Congress.

The promise of a continued, and perhaps expanded, social welfare program stimulated by federal funds was shattered by a veto from the pen of President Franklin Pierce. While expressing "the deep sympathies in [his] . . . heart" for "the humane purposes sought to be accomplished by the bill," Pierce felt compelled to veto it because it was illegal: "If Congress has the power to make provision for the indigent insane . . . it has the same power for the indigent who are not insane," and thus all the nation's needy. He continued: "I cannot find any authority in the Constitution for making the Federal Government the great almoner of public charity throughout the United States." To do so "would be contrary to the letter and spirit of the Constitution, and subversive of the whole theory upon which the union of these states is founded." As for previous acts of Congress which furnished precedents for the bill, particularly the land grants to the Connecticut and Kentucky institutions, Congress, in his opinion, had simply erred—it had transcended its power. Those examples, declared the President, generally conceded to be a "strict constructionist" and a wily northern politician courting southern favor in the midst of the states' rights controversy, should "serve . . . as a warning [rather] than as an inducement to tread in the same path." For the most part, Pierce's reasoning was followed; the veto was upheld and federal involvement in social welfare, while not eliminated, was retarded for years to come.

Meanwhile, private benevolent societies—which aimed not at providing material aid to the needy but at uplifting them through improving their character—grew in number.[6] Most Americans continued to believe that, since the nation offered unlimited natural resources and opportunities for success, poverty resulted from individual moral failure—idleness, intemperance, immorality, and irreligion. Such shortcomings could be countered only by bringing contrary forces to bear, "by inculcating religion, morality, sobriety, and industry" into the poor. If malign influences could be eliminated and beneficent ones substituted, the better nature of the needy would assert itself and the problem would be solved. As a result, many middle-class Americans engaged in a crusade for moral enlightenment. In urban areas throughout the country, agencies sprang up that emphasized godliness and the salvation of character as a prerequisite to improvement in the condition of the poor—and as a means to minimize discontent and social instability among a highly mobile and discordant population.[7]

Probably the most important of these was the New York Association for Improving the Condition of the Poor; to describe it is to describe all the others. Ironically, the immediate background of this and similar groups was the financial panic of 1837 and the depression that followed, which caused great hardship among the working classes of New York City and elsewhere. Existing relief agencies, both public and private, proved inadequate to the task

---

[6]With public assistance frowned upon, private aid necessarily increased. In part, however, private charity also was an obvious consequence of heavy immigration and a mixed population; each ethnic and sectarian group established its own charitable agencies.

[7]As Clifford Griffin has suggested in his work on religious benevolence and social control in early nineteenth-century America, in a sense, leaders of these benevolent societies were transmitting and enlarging the heritage from their forebears—the idea, first from the colonial theocrats and then from the Federalists, that the upper classes, a small number of people of particular attainments, should shape, govern, and lead society, which included not only caring for the unfortunate but also dictating their conduct and behavior.

of relieving the thousands of needy families. Destitution was widespread; beggars and vagrants stalked the streets.

In an attempt to improve the situation, in the winter of 1842–43, some New Yorkers came together to examine the city's charities. Their report portrayed a situation that undoubtedly existed in other cities and which, it was felt, constituted a serious menace. Public institutions were badly overcrowded and their resources seriously strained. More important, a lack of discrimination in the giving of private aid was seen; voluntary agencies, acting independently of each other, not only gave too much to insistent beggars, but at times duplicated their efforts. And, finally, there was inadequate contact between the donors and the recipients of welfare. The New York Association for Improving the Condition of the Poor, a citywide organization, was created in 1843 to remedy the situation; it would repress pauperism and aid the poor through the influence of male volunteers, "paternal guardians"—for the most part, the woman's place, it was still widely believed, was in the home—who would lead the dependent to self-support through instruction in the basic virtues of religious observance, thrift, hard work, and temperance. Through skillful leadership, it evolved into a leading spokesman for an urban middle class bewildered by the rapid spread of poverty and anxious over its possible effects.

Like most people working to ameliorate poverty, members of the A.I.C.P. were mainly white middle-class Protestants—merchants, professional people, real estate developers, shopkeepers, artisans, and so on, the very people responsible for the conditions whose consequences they so emphatically deplored. They were concerned with the problem because, as Christians, they could not ignore the distress suffered by the needy, because the financial drain for supporting the poor fell largely on their shoulders, and because the growing number of dependents (mainly Catholic immigrants) seemed to menace the virtues they so dearly cherished. Motivated then by a number of impulses—sometimes contradictory—they approached the poor in a spirit of Christian benevolence tempered by fear and perhaps a pang of guilt. On the one hand, they felt a moral obligation to help the needy, while on the other they feared, and perhaps even despised, them for the moral faults and imperfections which were supposedly responsible for their pauperism. How it was possible to love those who were, by all standards of wealth, education, and virtue, so obviously inferior, they did not say.

In the final analysis, members of the A.I.C.P. probably loved the poor less than they feared or perhaps even hated them. Their object was not so much to help the poor as to remold them into good middle-class citizens, to make them "respectable." Unless steps were taken to do this, the A.I.C.P. warned, the poor would "over-run the city as thieves and beggars and endanger the security of property and life—tax the community for their support and entail upon it an inheritance of vice and pauperism." Self-interest and social justice, in other words, went hand in hand.

In effect, then, the A.I.C.P. was no more a charitable agency than an instrument for reducing relief costs and keeping society orderly, stable, and quiet. Indeed, according to its constitution, the organization looked to "the *elevation* of the moral and physical condition of the indigent; and so far as compatible with these objects, the relief of their necessities" (italics added). Its goal—self-support and the permanent improvement of the condition of the poor—could best be achieved not through "indiscriminate charity," but through the uplifting of character. "The most effectual encouragement of [paupers] ... is not alms ... or any other form of charity as a substitute for alms, but that *sympathy* and *counsel* which re-kindles hope and that expression of respect for character which such individuals never fail to appreciate," stated an early A.I.C.P. manual.

Charity, it was maintained, only softened the moral fiber of the poor and intensified the problem. Reeducation, moral suasion, and individual counseling, not relief-giving, were the objectives. As a result, the poor were constantly told by their "protectors" that if they but worked hard, that if they were economical and good Christians, that if they gave up that glass of beer on the way home from the factory, everything would be all right.

The most important, or leading, causes of poverty in the A.I.C.P.'s view were extravagance, improvidence, indolence, and, above all, intemperance—all noneconomic factors. Drink was clearly the leading cause of want and woe: "We may consider intemperance as the most prolific source of degradation," declared one member. Or, in the words of Robert Hartley, the agency's long-time chief executive, who never tired of denouncing the pernicious evil, "intemperance is the master vice, exerting above all other evil influences a steady and determined opposition to every good word and work."

The A.I.C.P.'s concern with character building led inevitably to what it termed "incidental labors"—activities that later came to be regarded by many as the most important element in social work—an examination of environmental causes of poverty. Entering the homes of the poor, association members quickly discovered that in the slums, where most of the needy were forced to live, all those features of poverty that middle-class citizens found most reprehensible were concentrated and intensified—filth, crime, sexual promiscuity, drunkenness, disease, improvidence, and indolence—serious obstacles to morality. It was difficult to inculcate the virtues of thrift, temperance, diligence, and cleanliness into the unfortunate victims of such wretched living conditions. It was also found that despite all their hints on household management or admonitions on waste, intemperance, idleness, and the virtues of self-help, many persons could not maintain themselves for lack of jobs or a living wage. Recognizing that the material welfare of the poor was, under such circumstances, of primary concern, the A.I.C.P. began to seek jobs for the unemployed. Before long, it even distributed financial aid to the needy. It also engaged in surveys to ascertain mortality rates in slum areas. It built "model tenements" and sought municipal legislation to clean up the slums and to improve the construction of new housing. It strove to prevent adulteration of milk, to establish free medical dispensaries, public baths and washhouses, and, in general, it became a leading advocate of social reform.

The early history of the A.I.C.P. is important, then, less for the problems it solved than for at least defining those problems and, in the process, laying the path for others to follow. Insisting at the outset that poverty was basically a moral problem, the group became concerned with the relationship between dependency and the environment, turning eventually to the state for the regulation of behavior. It also insisted that assistance must be well planned, that relief methods can be defined and transmitted, and that personal service has value. In so doing, it set important precedents for later generations to follow; it had great impact on the later charity organization movement and, indeed, on the eventual emergence of a social work profession.

In the meantime, most people continued to accept the belief that poverty was an individual moral matter. To be sure, there were some in Great Britain, as well as in the United States, who, preaching the virtues of an altogether new society, dissented from that view. Robert Owen and other believers in socialist utopias did not subscribe to that idea. Nor, of course, did Karl Marx, who, living then in London, was close to issuing his manifesto for economic and political revolution. Then there were others such as Mathew Carey, a young Philadelphia bookseller, pamphleteer, and economist, and Sarah Josepha Hale, well known editor of *Godey's Lady's Book,* who also founded and headed the Boston Seamen's Aid Society; both Carey and Hale saw the intimate relationship between poverty and low wages and hence the need for public assistance.

The Reverend Joseph Tuckerman, a Unitarian "minister to the poor" in Boston, preferred preventive measures to both public relief and private charity. Recognizing the economic causes of poverty, he became a leading champion of social reform. Dr. John H. Griscom, a New York City health officer, also shifted the concept of fault away from the unfortunate sufferer and attached it instead to other things, not only to "physical disability and premature mortality among the lower classes" which were "in a great degree the results of causes which are removable," but also to greedy landlords and to the system under which they operated. Both the landlord and the system, he believed, should be subject to regulation.

Very little was accomplished along these lines. Rather, in an attempt to cope with the disturbing social and economic conditions and to restore a sense of community to urban America, moralism superseded humanism; public aid and private charity were transformed from acts of justice and benevolence into mechanisms for bringing order and stability to a new and unsettling social environment.

This, of course, raises the question of social control, at least the way in which it has come to be used during the past twenty years or so. Whereas originally the term "social control" had benign connotations—it was used approvingly by progressives to describe those processes in a society that supported a level of social cohesiveness sufficient for its survival, including measures that enabled the needy and helpless to function within the social order—more recently it has come to symbolize sinister activities —efforts by the middle and upper classes to manipulate and regulate the behavior of the lower classes in order to promote the former groups' own interests, often through enhancing the capitalist system.

Were these antebellum "reformers," philanthropists, and charity workers so motivated? Were they, in other words, evil people deliberately seeking to promote or protect their own and their class's interests at the expense of others? That, of course, is a difficult question to answer. Human motives, with regard to social welfare or any other matter, usually are complex and difficult to discern; in fact, they may not always be discernible to the individuals involved, let alone to historians many years later. No doubt, however, as some critics now charge, some middle and upper class Americans "gave" to the poor or supported efforts at that time and later to uplift them, for reasons of social control; they feared that allowing pauperism to grow or continuing to treat it through the older, more generous welfare system would endanger society and their place (and property) within it. In addition, as Paul Boyer has argued in *Urban Masses and Moral Order in America, 1820–1920,* others participated in philanthropic activities not to safeguard their position in the community but to alter it—to advance by demonstrating to themselves and to others that they had "made it" and thus were worthy of increased admiration and respect.

On the other hand, the evidence also suggests that many people helped the poor because they viewed such activity as the handmaiden of religion; they "gave," in other words, to please God. Clearly, for some a sense of civic duty, not self-interest or religion, was the motivating factor. Others possessed a real humanitarian concern for the needy. Some simply enjoyed giving or got involved because a particular appeal touched their hearts or because they were genuinely convinced that their actions would be in the best interest of all. Yet others were moved by cultural nationalism: they wished to fulfill their dream of an enlightened republic free from the evils and inequities that contaminated European society. No doubt other factors operated as well; motives were mixed and many. Whatever the motive or motives, the Civil War brought changes in the nation's social welfare needs and practices.

Bibliography

BECKER, DOROTHY G. "The Visitor to the New York City Poor, 1843–1920," *Social Service Review* 35 (December 1961): 382–96.

BLAUG, MARK. "The Myth of the Old Poor Law and the Making of the New," *Journal of Economic History* 23 (June 1963): 151–84.

————. "The Poor Law Report Reexamined," *Journal of Economic History* 24 (June 1964): 229–45.

BOYER, PAUL. *Urban Masses and Moral Order in America, 1820–1920.* Cambridge, Mass.: Harvard University Press, 1978.

BROWN, ELIZABETH G. "Poor Relief in a Wisconsin County, 1846–1866: Administration and Recipients," *American Journal of Legal History* 20 (April 1976): 79–117.

CARROLL, DOUGLAS G., AND BLANCHE D. COLL. "The Baltimore Almshouse: An Early History," *Maryland Historical Magazine* 66 (Summer 1971): 135–52.

CHADWICK, EDWIN. *Report for Inquiring into the Administration and Practical Operation of the Poor Laws,* reprinted in Roy Lubove, ed., *Social Welfare in Transition.* Pittsburgh: University of Pittsburgh Press, 1966.

CLEMENT, PRISCILLA F. "The Philadelphia Welfare Crisis of the 1820s," *Pennsylvania Magazine of History and Biography* 55 (April 1981): 150–65.

COLL, BLANCHE D. "The Baltimore Society for the Prevention of Pauperism, 1820–1860," *American Historical Review* 61 (October 1955): 77–87.

————. *Perspectives in Public Welfare.* Washington, D.C.: Government Printing Office, 1969.

DAIN, NORMAN. *Concepts of Insanity in the United States.* New Brunswick, N.J.: Rutgers University Press, 1964.

DOYLE, DON H. "The Social Functions of Voluntary Associations in a Nineteenth-Century American Town," *Social Science History* 1 (Spring 1977): 333–35.

ELDER, WALTER. "Speenhamland Revisited," *Social Service Review* 38 (September 1964): 294–302.

GALPER, JEFFREY. "The Speenhamland Scales: Political, Social or Economic Disaster?" *Social Service Review* 44 (March 1970): 54–62.

GOFFMAN, ERVING. *Asylums: Essays on the Social Situation of Mental Patients and Other Inmates.* Garden City, N.Y.: Doubleday, 1961.

GRIFFIN, CLIFFORD S. "Religious Benevolence and Social Control, 1815–1860," *Mississippi Valley Historical Review* 44 (December 1957): 423–44.

————. *Their Brothers' Keepers: Moral Stewardship in the United States, 1800–1865.* New Brunswick, N.J.: Rutgers University Press, 1965.

HEALE, M. J. "Humanitarianism in the Early Republic: The Moral Reformers of New York, 1776–1825," *Journal of American Studies* 2 (October 1968): 161–75.

————. "The New York Society for the Prevention of Pauperism, 1817–1823," *New-York Historical Society Quarterly* 55 (April 1917): 153–72.

————. "Patterns of Benevolence: Associated Philanthropy in the Cities of New York, 1830–1860," *New York History* 57 (January 1976): 53–80.

HUZEL, JAMES P. "Malthus, the Poor Law, and Population in Early Nineteenth-Century England," *Economic History Review* 22 (December 1969): 430–51.

KLEBANER, BENJAMIN J. "Poverty and Its Relief in American Thought, 1815–61," *Social Service Review* 38 (December 1964): 382–99.

————. "Public Poor Relief in America, 1790–1860," Ph.D. dissertation, Columbia University, 1952.

LASCH, CHRISTOPHER. "Origins of the Asylum," in *The World of Nations: Reflections on American History, Politics, and Culture.* New York: Knopf, 1974.

LUBOVE, ROY. "The New York Association for Improving the Condition of the Poor," *New-York Historical Society Quarterly* 43 (July 1959): 307–28.

McCLOSKEY, DONALD N. "New Perspectives on the Old Poor Law," *Explorations in Economic History* 10 (Summer 1973): 419–36.

MALTHUS, THOMAS. *An Essay on the Principle of Population.* London: Dent, 1914.

MARSHALL, HELEN. *Dorothea Dix: Forgotten Samaritan.* Chapel Hill, N.C.: University of North Carolina Press, 1937.

MELDER, KEITH. "Lady Bountiful: Organized Women's Benevolence in Early 19th Century America," *New York History* 48 (July 1967): 231–54.

MOHL, RAYMOND A. *Poverty in New York, 1783–1825.* New York: Oxford University Press, 1971.

POLANYI, KARL. *The Great Transformation.* Boston: Beacon Press, 1957.

POYNTER, J. R. *Society and Pauperism: English Ideas on Poor Relief, 1795–1834.* Toronto: University of Toronto Press, 1969.

RESCH, JOHN P. "Federal Welfare for Revolutionary War Veterans," *Social Service Review* 56 (June 1982): 171–95.

RIMLINGER, GASTON V. "Welfare Policy and Economic Development," *Journal of Economic History* 26 (December 1966): 556–76.

ROSE, MICHAEL E. "The Allowance System Under the New Poor Law," *Economic History Review* 19 (December 1966): 607–20.

———, ed. *The English Poor Law, 1780–1930.* New York: Barnes and Noble, 1971.

ROSENKRANTZ, BARBARA, AND MARIS A. VINOVSKIS. "Caring for the Insane in Ante-Bellum Massachusetts," in Allan Lichtman and Joan Challinor, eds., *Kin and Communities: Families in America.* Washington, D.C.: Smithsonian Institution, 1979.

ROTHMAN, DAVID J. *The Discovery of the Asylum: Social Order and Disorder in the New Republic.* Boston: Little, Brown, 1971.

SCHWARTZ, HAROLD. *Samuel Gridley Howe: Social Reformer, 1801–1876.* Cambridge, Mass.: Harvard University Press, 1956.

SPEIZMAN, MILTON. "Speenhamland: An Experiment in Guaranteed Income," *Social Service Review* 11 (March 1966): 44–55.

TRATTNER, WALTER I. "The Federal Government and Social Welfare in Early Nineteenth-Century America," *Social Service Review* 50 (June 1976): 243–55.

YATES, J. V. N. *Report of the Secretary of State in 1824 on the Relief and Settlement of the Poor*, in *Assembly Journal*, Appendix B (January 1824): 386–99.

YOUNG, A. F., AND E. T. ASHTON. *British Social Work in the Nineteenth Century*. London: Routledge and Kegan Paul, 1956.

ZAINALDEN, JAMIL S., AND PETER TYOR. "Asylum and Society: An Approach to Institutional Change," *Journal of Social History* 13 (Fall 1979): 23–48.

Chapter 5

The Civil War and After — Scientific Charity

LIKE ALL WARS, the War between the States created enormous relief problems—problems which could not be blamed on the individuals or families involved.[1] As a result, public officials and private citizens responded accordingly; in fact, the war aroused the charitable energies of the American people as never before. Warnings of unwise giving were forgotten as public and private agencies showered assistance on the needy throughout the conflict.

Methods of distributing such assistance varied. Laws were enacted enabling localities to raise funds for the relief of sick, destitute, and wounded soldiers and their families and, in some instances, for the founding of homes for disabled veterans. Beginning in 1862, state legislatures, North and South alike, appropriated large sums of money for the same purposes. Thus, the war brought a temporary reversal of charitable practices; direct public aid, on a grand scale, became available once again.

The war had other effects on social welfare. To begin with, when the fighting broke out, the first contingents of northern troops had to be hurried into battle so quickly that little provision was made for their sanitary or medical care. Consequently, at the outset, the mortality rate from disease alone was so great that it appeared as though the horrors of the Crimean War (1853–56), in which thousands of men died unnecessarily simply for lack of

---

[1]The Confederacy may have suffered even more than the Union in this regard. One scholar has gone so far as to suggest that the welfare problem was so great in the region that it contributed to desertion in the army and disaffection with the war. See Paul D. Escott, "The Cry of the Sufferers: The Problem of Welfare in the Confederacy," *Civil War History* 23 (September 1977): 228–40.

medical supplies and attention, would be reenacted in America; some observers predicted the loss of 50 percent of the fighting force by the end of the first summer. As a result, a group of people—the most important of whom were Dr. Henry W. Bellows, a New York Unitarian minister, Louisa Lee Schuyler, a scion of a wealthy and distinguished New York family and a member of Bellows' congregation, and Dr. Elisha Harris, a well known sanitary reformer—saw the need to do something about it.

Appalled by the stories of filth and disease in army camps and hospitals and the lack of trained nurses and adequate transportation facilities for the wounded, they sought to establish some sort of voluntary citizen effort to remedy the situation. They organized the U.S. Sanitary Commission, the nation's first important national public health group.

Organized in 1861 and composed chiefly of women, the commission was solely financed and directed by private means.[2] Its chief aim, which was largely realized, was to unite numerous local voluntary relief societies into a national organization that would supplement the work of governmental agencies in meeting the physical and spiritual needs of the men in uniform. At the outset, its work was mainly preventive—to educate inexperienced troops in proper personal hygiene and to inspect and supervise living arrangements in army camps and field hospitals. By so doing, it prevented much needless suffering and death through disease and illness; thousands of lives were saved each year.

Soon it expanded its work in a variety of ways. It distributed bandages, food, and clothing to the army. It recruited and supplied a corps of nurses, maintained special relief lodges and houses for soldiers in transit, and set up channels of communication between the men on the battlefield and the people at home. In short, it undertook most of the wartime duties later as-

[2]Dr. Bellows drafted the constitution and served as president of the commission. Other prominent members who took part were George Templeton Strong, its treasurer, and Frederick Law Olmsted, its executive secretary. Bellows and others wanted the government to empower the commission with official authority to carry on its work. The army medical department would not hear of this, however, so the U.S. Sanitary Commission was organized without any power to enforce its recommendations. Later, after it had proved its worth, the commission was able to influence the selection of a new surgeon general more in sympathy with its aims and purposes, and thenceforth it enjoyed the respect and close cooperation of the medical corps and other federal officials.

sumed by the Red Cross, winning universal acclaim. John Stuart Mill said of it: "History afforded no other example of so great a work of usefulness extemporized by the spontaneous self-devotion and organizing genius of a people altogether independent of the government."

Aside from its material contributions to welfare, the Sanitary Commission (which ultimately had about five hundred people working for it and performed approximately $25 million "worth" of services) helped lay the groundwork for progress in public health that followed the war. Among other things, the training in sanitary science and surgical procedures provided young army physicians tended to further medical progress later on. Also, by awakening public opinion to preventive sanitary practices that could save thousands of lives each year, and the ease with which they could be implemented, the work of the commission stimulated public health reform in later periods. Thus, four years after the war ended, the first state board of health came into existence, followed by similar boards in most populous states. Ten years later, in 1879, the federal government recognized the importance of public health activities by creating a National Board of Health which, while short lived, was nevertheless instrumental in setting precedents for future federal activities in the area of health and welfare.[3]

Moreover, the Sanitary Commission demonstrated that a well organized and coordinated effort by small voluntary groups or committees supported by a central association can educate masses of people, influence public opinion, and effect important reforms; its success confirmed in many persons' minds the value and power of voluntary organizations in promoting the public welfare, and many such organizations were created in the postwar years. To cite just one example, in 1872, Louisa Lee Schuyler organized the New York State Charities Aid Association, a voluntary organization patterned after the U.S. Sanitary Commission, which to this day works for improved public health and social welfare legislation throughout New York State—and the nation.

[3]While the founding of the U.S. Public Health Service (the federal agency traditionally responsible for promoting good health) dates back to 1798, the U.S. government assumed almost no interest in public health matters until the 1870s and the creation of the National Board of Health.

The wartime demonstration of private philanthropy's usefulness, especially the part played by civilians in financing and staffing the U.S. Sanitary Commission and similar organizations, also aided the cause of social welfare. Never before had the nation seen such wholehearted, generous, and sustained sacrifices from the people, and the lesson would be remembered.

So, too, were the efforts of women, who during the war worked valiantly side by side with men in hospitals and even on the battlefield. President Abraham Lincoln, who, along with Secretary of War Edward Stanton, was not particularly happy over the prospect of having members of the Sanitary Commission, especially women, in the vicinity of the war zone, later remarked:

> I am not accustomed to the language of eulogy and have never studied the art of paying compliments to women, but I must say that if all that has been said by the orators and poets since the creation of the world in praise of women were applied to the women of America, it would not do them justice for their conduct during the war.

Their participation in wartime activities and the recognition they won for it, in turn, gave women not only a new self-image but also rising expectations, what William O'Neill, the historian of feminism, has referred to as a "heroic myth"—a claim on the nation, one that, unfortunately, was not fulfilled. Some women, though, did make progress, winning for themselves a stronger voice in public affairs. Finding themselves in service to others, they could not relapse into total domesticity; thus, they got involved in a variety of postwar reform movements. The war, in other words, launched some women on lifelong careers of service.[4]

The political decision settled by the war—that the national government was supreme and the state governments subordinate to it—also had an important effect upon sanitary and social

---

[4]In an 1888 Memorial Day address, a quarter-century after Gettysburg, Clara Barton, head of the American Red Cross, an organization she had created seven years earlier, recalled women's work in the Civil War and declared that because of it the American woman "was at least fifty years in advance of the normal position which continued peace . . . would have assigned." Clara Barton herself, who began her career nursing sick and wounded soldiers during the Civil War, was perhaps the best example of what she was talking about.

reform. Social welfare, especially public health, is a matter that transcends village, city, and even state boundaries. It flourishes best under strong central authority. So, by establishing, once and for all, the supremacy of the federal government, the Civil War ultimately drew the states together and introduced a greater amount of coordination among them. A health program in one state, as a consequence, was less likely to be jettisoned by the unrestrained acts or negligence of another, and vice versa—a reform in one state usually resulted in many others following suit.

In these and other ways, the Civil War had a constructive impact upon social welfare in America. The same could not be said for the immediate postwar years.

Between the years 1865 and 1900, America underwent a spectacular expansion of productive facilities and output that was without parallel in the history of the world. Statistics tell part of the story. In 1860, approximately $1 billion was invested in manufacturing plants; the annual value of manufactured products was $1,885,000,000; and 1,300,000 workers were employed in American factories. By the turn of the century, the amount of capital invested had risen to more than $12 billion, the yearly value of products to over $11 billion, and the number of workers to 5,500,000. But as Charles and Mary Beard, historians of American civilization, have indicated, statistics barely reflect the developments of the era:

> With a stride that astonished statisticians, the conquering hosts of business enterprise swept over the continent; twenty-five years after the death of Lincoln, America had become in the quantity and value of her products, the first manufacturing nation in the world. What England had once accomplished in a hundred years, the United States had achieved in half the time.

The consequences of this experience, so pervasive as to be referred to as an "economic revolution," were enormous. On the one hand, it enhanced the national wealth, raised the general standard of living, encouraged immigration, speeded up urbanization, and had many other constructive effects. On the other hand, it produced, among other things, periodic cycles of depression and unemployment, a small group of men who controlled the nation's resources and modes of production, wretched living and working conditions, a high incidence of industrial accidents and fatalities, and numerous other very unfortunate results that affected every segment of American society.

It was primarily in industry that the effects of this revolution were most apparent. The swift and enormous growth of the factory system, with its simple, repetitive processes, not only eroded the instinct of craftsmanship and a sense of pride in one's work, but also swept more and more people—men, women, and children—into industrial occupations where they were reduced to a mere part in a mechanical process, automata performing the same monotonous operation hundreds of times a day, usually under noisy and exceedingly unhealthy conditions, with long hours and low pay, over which they and the other "hired hands" in the factory had little or no control. Upton Sinclair described the situation this way in *The Jungle,* published in 1905:

> Each one of the hundreds of parts of a mowing machine was made separately, and sometimes handled by hundreds of men. Where [one man] . . . worked there was a machine which cut and stamped a certain piece of steel about two square inches in size; the pieces came tumbling out upon a tray and all that human hands had to do was to pile them in regular rows and change the trays at intervals. This was done by a single [person]. . . . Thirty thousand of these pieces he handled every day, nine or ten millions every year. Nearby him sat men bending over whirling grind-stones, putting the finishing touches to the steel knives of the reaper; picking them out of a basket with the right hand, pressing first one side and then the other against the stone, and finally dropping them with the left hand into another basket. One of these men . . . sharpened three thousand pieces of steel a day for thirteen years.

Many of the unfortunate victims of these cruel, and in some cases even inhumane, conditions would need help. First, however, as the Civil War was coming to an end, an acute but different problem of relief faced the nation—that of aiding the freedmen, several million of whom, largely uneducated, unskilled, and unprepared for their abrupt change in status, would shortly be roaming the South in search of employment and assistance.[5] To

[5]Ironically, the first real casualties of emancipation and the new labor system were those freedmen who could not work for one reason or another—old age, illness, infirmity, etc. Since slaveowners were responsible for their property, they

meet the problem—clearly a national problem since it was one that, for the most part, the southern communities and states had neither the resources nor the desire to deal with—in March 1865, two months before the conflict ended, Congress established in the U.S. War Department the Bureau of Refugees, Freedmen, and Abandoned Lands, the nation's first federal welfare agency. Usually referred to as the Freedmen's Bureau, it was authorized to administer a program of temporary relief for the duration of the war and one year thereafter, a time of unusual stress. However, after a bitter struggle between President Andrew Johnson, who hoped to terminate the bureau and hence vetoed a measure to prolong its life, and Congress, which sought to continue it indefinitely and overrode the President's veto, the life of the Freedmen's Bureau was extended for six years.[6]

Under the able direction of General Oliver O. Howard, a West Point graduate who was extremely sensitive to the feelings and needs of the freedmen, the bureau undertook a wide variety of tasks in its effort to aid blacks in the transition from slavery to freedom. It served as a relief agency on an unprecedented scale, distributing twenty-two million rations to needy persons in the devastated South. It served as an employment agency, helping many blacks to obtain jobs and supervising the writing of contracts between them and their employers.

In addition, it served as a settlement agency, leasing certain abandoned properties to black cultivators. In the field of health, it employed doctors and maintained hospitals, reducing the mortality rate among the freedmen. As an educational agency, it encouraged the founding of black schools and then provided them with financial aid. And finally, it served as a legal agency, maintaining courts in which both civil and criminal cases involving ex-slaves were dealt with in an informal and just manner. Despite many problems—financial, bureaucratic, and political—all in all

---

had been "cared for" earlier by their masters and by other slaves on the plantation. The question was, who would assume responsibility for their welfare now, and on what basis?

[6]Just as Pierce had done earlier with the Dix bill, President Johnson, a southerner who had no love for blacks, vetoed the measure on constitutional grounds: "A system for the support of indigent persons in the United States," he wrote, "was never contemplated by the authors of the Constitution...." Recovery from slavery was, in his opinion, the freedmen's own responsibility.

the bureau provided a variety of welfare services that were unavailable from any other source and saved untold numbers of needy blacks (and some poor whites) from additional pain and hardship.

Finally liquidated in 1872, the Freedmen's Bureau had shown that the federal government could provide for the welfare of people on a broad scale when poverty and hardship could (or would) not be treated locally. The bureau, however, was ahead of its time; its impact on the social welfare policies of the era—public and private—was nil. Not until the twentieth century did the federal government again become involved in social welfare in any significant way. And as Victoria Olds, a historian of the agency, has pointed out, the bureau had little impact on private charity as well. As an emergency relief program concerned primarily with ex-slaves, it seemed to have little relevance or importance for private philanthropy. Since most of the important private charitable agencies were located in the Northeast or Midwest, where they had a predominantly white clientele, most northerners failed to recognize the importance of the bureau, which, centered in the South, had served mostly blacks.[7]

While the Freedmen's Bureau was the major source of public welfare for blacks in the South after the Civil War, the counties and states did make some strides, at least during the period of so-called Radical, or Congressional, Reconstruction (1867–76). For the most part, though, blacks were treated separately from the white poor and in an inferior manner. Thus, while the new state constitutions generally included sections that required the provision of aid to all the needy on an equal basis, usually in state or county institutions, integration rarely occurred in the provision of such assistance.

In 1867, for example, the state of Tennessee made special provision for the black mentally ill when the legislature authorized the Tennessee Hospital for the Insane to construct quarters

---

[7]The oversight persisted well into the twentieth century. Despite the similarities between the Freedmen's Bureau and the Federal Emergency Relief Administration, which was created during the early years of the Great Depression when it was generally recognized that the resources of voluntary agencies and local government were inadequate to meet mass needs, few references to the bureau were found in the literature of social welfare until recently.

for Negroes "so as to keep them secure and safe and yet separate from the white patients." More often than not, however, completely separate facilities were provided, usually fewer in number and poorer in quality. In Richmond, Virginia, for example, where the situation was typical, the white almshouse was a three-story brick building while the black institution, which normally contained far more residents, was a much smaller, rickety wooden structure. Nevertheless, opening the doors of public institutions to blacks in the South was a significant break with the past, though it proved to be rather temporary.

With the termination of Reconstruction, southerners continued to give verbal support to a segregated (but allegedly equal) welfare program, but in practice they generally reverted to the policy of complete exclusion. As a result, by the late nineteenth century deprived blacks were once again left to fend for themselves. Consequently, they were forced to turn to self-help, or mutual aid.

At the core of these efforts were Negro benevolent societies of one kind or another, many of which were connected to local churches.[8] In return for small monthly dues, members were often entitled to some assistance, usually sick benefits, and, when necessary, burial fees. While the number of these societies was not great and their resources were limited, collectively they did help to soften the impact of the exclusionary practices. On the whole, however, black Americans continued to suffer throughout this period, just as they had done earlier.

So, too, perhaps it should be added, did many whites who resided in the region, which by far had the highest incidence of poverty in America. Hard times after 1865 perpetuated a deeply depressed lower class of white farmers and farm laborers, who, like their black counterparts in the South, suffered greatly from hookworm, pellagra, malnutrition, and a variety of other ailments and problems. They eventually would straggle into mill villages, where working and living conditions would be only slightly better.

---

[8]One of the first such organizations was the Nashville (Tennessee) Colored Benevolent Society. Another, located in Atlanta, Ga., had as its motto: "We assist the needy: we relieve our sick; we bury our dead."

In the meantime, with the liquidation of the Freedmen's Bureau, the federal government removed itself from the social welfare scene. For the time being, at least, the state would be responsible for public dependents removed from the jurisdiction of local overseers of the poor and from county almshouses. As a result, state-supported institutions continued to multiply. For the most part, such institutions were administered by separate, independent, unsalaried boards, composed chiefly of prominent citizens and state officeholders appointed by the governors. In theory, the governors and the state legislatures were supposed to supervise and coordinate their efforts. In practice, it did not work that way. The various public officials usually had so many other duties that they had little time, let alone knowledge, to supervise these institutions. Policies were not uniform; extravagance and waste prevailed. Abuses often went unattended.

The situation in Massachusetts was typical. In 1859, the commonwealth had three state mental institutions, a reform school for boys, an industrial school for girls, a hospital, and three almshouses for the state or nonresident poor. In addition, four private charitable institutions—schools for the blind, the deaf and dumb, the feebleminded, and an eye and ear infirmary—received state aid. Each of these was managed by its own board of trustees. So uncoordinated a system not only increased the cost of operation, but did not provide for a channel of communication between institutions; a reform in one, then, might not be implemented in the others. The situation obviously called for some method of state supervision, as a report of the state legislature's Joint Standing Committee on Public Charitable Institutions indicated:

> If ever there was a system at loose ends [the report stated] it is the present pauper system.... There is a fatal want of harmony between the administrative elements.... In truth, there is an evident feeling of jealousy prevalent, and a want of centralized authority injurious to the interests of the state. Unison, cooperation, oneness, is eminently desirable.

The legislature responded by creating, in 1863, a Board of State Charities (later called the State Board of Charities) which was charged with the responsibility of investigating and supervising all of the state's charitable and correctional institutions and recommending changes that would bring about their more efficient and economical operation. Thus, Massachusetts was the first state to coordinate and centralize its state welfare activities. Its example was followed by Ohio, New York, Illinois, Wisconsin, Michigan, Kansas, and Connecticut. By 1886 twelve states had such bodies, and four more added them within another decade.

The various boards were similar in purpose in that they sought to bring the supervised institutions directly under the aegis of the state—to see to it that they were operated as economically and as humanely as was possible. Although most had some executive power (especially the authority to transfer inmates from one institution to another), their duties were largely supervisory in nature. Nevertheless, they had a profound effect upon social welfare at the state level. And because many of the boards had the authority to recommend whether or not their legislatures should provide aid to county and municipal institutions and, in some cases, even to private agencies, they affected local social welfare as well. Of particular significance were their studies and written documents, such as annual reports to their legislatures. These studies, which dealt with almost every aspect of public relief and institutional treatment, served to educate not only officeholders but also the general public to conditions that required remedial action in the form of corrective legislation and improved standards of care.[9] As Robert Bremner has pointed out, in an age not noted for the excellence of its public servants, the members and secretaries of these boards—Samuel Gridley Howe, Franklin B. Sanborn, Frederick H. Wines, to cite only a few—set high standards of integrity and competence.

Public welfare, however, again played second fiddle, so to speak, to private charity where, as we shall shortly see, there was also a trend toward coordinating administration and supervision in a single agency. The idea that distress was an individual moral matter was not only revived but strengthened as the wounds of the Civil War were healed and the nation grew and prospered. The

---

[9]This was especially true with regard to the mentally ill. The boards not only resumed the struggle to obtain state care for the indigent insane but were largely responsible for getting Congress, in 1882, to make it unlawful for the mentally ill to enter the country.

poor were held in contempt in an acquisitive society in which
wealth became almost an end in itself. It was not difficult to
believe that indigence was simply punishment of the improvident
for their lack of industry and morality—the direct consequence of
sloth and sinfulness.

This interpretation, which confined the poor to a purgatory of
personal failure and made them mere outcasts of society, was
strengthened by the pseudoscientific teaching of Herbert
Spencer, the English civil engineer turned philosopher, who coined
the phrase "survival of the fittest," and others who applied the
Darwinian theory of evolution to social conditions and thought.
Social Darwinism, as it was called, a happy union of laissez-faire
economics and the doctrine of the struggle for existence and survival of the fittest, became the prevailing philosophy of the era.

It was argued that government should confine itself to insuring
liberty for individual citizens by protecting them from assault
upon their persons and property. Orthodox social Darwinists
found no place in their general scheme of things for public support of education, or for sanitary regulation, a public mail system,
regulation of business or trade, or, least of all, for public assistance to the needy.

If, as the Spencerians claimed, competition was the law of life,
there was no remedy for poverty other than self-help. Those who
remained poor were the unfit, who had to pay the price exacted
by "the decrees of a large far-seeing benevolence." Any interference in their behalf, whether undertaken by the state or by unwise
philanthropists, was not only pointless but hazardous. Protecting
the ill favored in the struggle for existence would only permit
them to multiply and could lead to no other result than a disastrous weakening of the species; it would thwart nature's plan of
evolutionary progress toward higher forms of social life. "If we
do not like the survival of the fittest," declared Spencer, "we have
only one possible alternative, and that is the survival of the unfit-
test. The former is the law of civilization, the latter is the law of
anticivilization." "The unfit must be eliminated as nature intended," he opined on another occasion, "for the principle of natural selection must not be violated by the artificial preservation of
those least able to take care of themselves." Or as another social
Darwinist maintained, "society is constantly excreting its un-

healthy, imbecile, slow, vacillating, faithless members to leave room for the deserving. A maudlin impulse to prolong the lives of the unfit stands in the way of this beneficent purging of the social organism." Thus, as one writer in the *Nation* put it in 1894, the only solution to poverty is "nature's remedy—work or starve."

Although these arguments—advanced to justify inequality and, in effect, to condone misery—never went completely unchallenged, the theory that poverty was caused by personal frailty was not easily supplanted; endowed with this new aura of authority, it retained a loyal following for a long time. Nevertheless, most Americans did not carry the idea to its logical extreme. Only a few read Spencer and/or understood the full implications of social Darwinism. More important, America was a Christian nation with a charitable impulse and tradition that was too strong to be eliminated. Even Herbert Spencer, when accused of hardness of heart because of his attitude toward the poor or ill privileged, retreated to the position that voluntary charity could be tolerated in that it encouraged the development of altruism, a Christian virtue. What resulted therefore was further denigration of public assistance.

Those who opposed public relief had a new and potent weapon in political graft and corruption. This was the so-called Gilded Age, when political scandals and raids on the public treasury were common. Legislators and other public officials expected, as a matter of course, to be paid for the "favors" they performed and, unfortunately, departments of public charities were not exempt from the venality. Chicanery linked with public aid came to light in several cities in the 1870s and 1880s. Was it possible for public relief, especially home relief, to be handled honestly, efficiently, and economically?

For most, the answer was no. A system of well coordinated voluntary organizations staffed by people who would keep accurate records of applicants, distribute aid honestly and carefully, and at the same time help uplift the needy appeared to be the better way to meet the problem. It would insure that welfare remained a charity rather than an entitlement, a political plum, or a source of demoralization. It also would bind the lower to the upper classes and thus avoid potential conflict. As Robert W. deForest, an influential lawyer-philanthropist, contended: "Public outdoor relief makes for class separation and the enmity of classes. Private charity makes for the brotherhood of man."

So, the informal division of labor that arose earlier in the century but was set aside temporarily during the Civil War was put back into effect. Indeed, it was strengthened considerably. Beginning in the 1870s, cities all across America abolished municipal home relief. By 1900, public outdoor assistance had been abandoned in New York, Baltimore, St. Louis, Washington, D.C., San Francisco, Kansas City, New Orleans, Louisville, Denver, Atlanta, Memphis, Charleston, S.C., Cincinnati, Indianapolis, Pittsburgh, and elsewhere. A year later, *Cooperation,* the official organ of the Chicago Bureau of Charities, a private agency, reported with great satisfaction that virtually all of the nation's large cities had taken such steps and lamented that Chicago was the exception to the rule. Public authorities, then, cared for dependents and defectives who required (or consented to) confinement in asylums, almshouses, and other such institutions.

Those in need who remained outside public institutions—the vast majority, for whom "the county" was the last resort—looked first to family, kin, and neighbors for aid, including the landlord, who sometimes deferred the rent; the local businessman, who frequently carried them for a while by allowing bills to go unpaid; and the local saloonkeeper, who often came to their aid by providing loans and outright gifts, including free meals, and, on occasion, temporary jobs. Next, the needy sought assistance from various agencies in the community—those of their own devising, such as churches and religious groups, social and fraternal associations, mutual aid societies, and local ethnic groups. Only when these resources were either exhausted or unavailable, as was the case for marginal inhabitants of the neighborhood or immigrants without friends or relatives in the area, did the needy turn to the "official" private charitable agencies in the community—and then with reluctance and anxiety. Nevertheless, such agencies continued to proliferate as the nation grew—and its economy witnessed a number of severe dips. So rapidly did private agencies multiply that before long America's larger cities had what to many people was an embarrassing number of them. Charity directories took as many as 100 pages to list and describe the numerous voluntary agencies that alleviated misery, combated pauperism, and met every other imaginable emergency. In Philadelphia alone, in 1878, there were some 800 such groups of one kind or another in existence.

It was inevitable that charity workers and others should become concerned over the magnitude of benevolent work. William Graham Sumner, the Yale professor and social Darwinist, was appalled by the "unlimited supply of reformers and would-be managers of society" he saw all around him. Such conditions, he and others were certain, only led to waste, inefficiency, and, above all, demoralization of the needy.

The hardship and destitution created by the severe depression of the 1870s seemed to confirm these feelings. With some three million men thrown out of work, apprehension gripped industrial and commercial centers throughout the country, especially in 1877, when in state after state the militia and even federal troops were mobilized to put down rioting resulting, in part, from unsuccessful efforts by the unemployed in many large cities to get public works programs and other forms of assistance from local and state authorities. The threat of revolution seemed imminent. Private citizens, charitable bodies, and public authorities responded to the crisis by setting up soup kitchens, breadlines, and free lodging houses, and by distributing coal, food, clothing, and even cash to the poor. Little attention was paid to investigation of need, to tests of destitution, to safeguards against duplicity, or to provision of counsel. In time of such social and economic distress, separation of material relief from spiritual relief was inevitable; naturally, the former took precedence over the latter.

Many charity workers, however, were horrified by this "excess" of relief and the chaotic way in which it was distributed. As one put it, "Next to alcohol, and perhaps alongside it, the most pernicious fluid is indiscriminate soup." Or, in the words of another, "It is not bread the poor need, it is soul; it is not soup, it is spirit." They argued not only for the cessation of all public outdoor aid but also for the improvement of all relief operations, especially by paying more attention to the individual needs of those helped. Charity work, they argued, needed to be organized along scientific lines—made more rational and efficient—giving rise to the so-called charity organization movement, or "scientific charity."

The new era in philanthropy dawned in Buffalo, New York, in December 1877, when the Reverend Stephen Humphreys Gurteen, an Englishman by birth, proposed the creation of an agency patterned after the London Charity Organization Society, which he had studied while on a visit to his native land during the previous summer. He assured the residents of Buffalo that such an agency would bring order to their charitable work by combating the indiscriminate relief policies of overlapping private agencies and a municipal relief system which presumably encouraged indolence, pauperism, and fraud.

The promotion of cooperation and higher standards of efficiency among the older relief-dispensing societies was one of the basic aims of the movement, which spread so rapidly that within six years twenty-five cities had such organizations and by the turn of the century there were some 138 of them in existence.[10] The new charity organization societies did not themselves grant relief; there were already too many relief-granting agencies to suit them. Instead they served as clearing houses for all the operating charitable bodies in the community. They maintained registries of relief applicants, kept detailed records of the aid given to them, and referred to the proper relief-dispensing agency the "helpable" or "worthy" poor.

The organized charity movement aimed not only at eliminating fraud, inefficiency, and duplicity in the field but also at devising a constructive method of dealing with or treating poverty. "We sought to organize the charitable impulses and resources of the community" in order to "develop the special capacities of each [needy] individual," a worker related. In part, the movement hoped to treat poverty by guarding against overlapping, but more important, by having "friendly visitors" look into each case so as to diagnose the cause of destitution. Investigation was the keystone of treatment; granting relief without investigation was analogous to prescribing medicine without diagnosis. Friendly visit-

---

[10]The organizations went under a number of different names. In some instances they were called Societies for Organizing Charity (Philadelphia); in others they were referred to as Bureaus of Charities (Chicago, Brooklyn) or Associated Charities (Boston). Regardless of title, their function was the same—namely, to organize the sources of relief in the community and to provide moral relief to their clients.

ing, then, or personal contact between the rich and the poor as a substitute for alms, was the second basic aim of the movement. Along with registration, cooperation, and coordination, it formed the basis of this "science" of social therapeutics that was supposed to relieve philanthropy of sentimentality and indiscriminate almsgiving—to make it a matter of the head as well as the heart—and thereby to eradicate pauperism and, in the words of the Reverend D. O. Kellogg, a tireless C.O.S. propagandist, make "the socialistic and communistic theories now being energetically taught to the people" specters of the past. Or, as the movement's founder put it, if friendly visitors did their job well, "all avoidable pauperism would soon be a thing of the past, and an age of good will would be ushered in, when the poor would regard the rich as their natural friends and not, as now, fair object of their deceit and imposition."

For all their self-proclamation as new or scientific, the charity organization societies were patterned after such earlier bodies as the New York Association for Improving the Condition of the Poor, which were created to coordinate private charitable agencies, to investigate relief applicants, and, if possible, to make the needy self-sufficient. The newer bodies did, however, spend more time organizing and coordinating the charitable resources of a given community and engaging in consultation with the needy. And, in contrast to their predecessors, most agents of the organized charities were women, thanks in large part to their "emancipation" during and after the Civil War.[11] And finally, the older organizations had succumbed to the great evil of becoming relief-giving agencies, something, of course, the organized charities were intent upon avoiding.

In addition, charity organization societies reflected the spirit of their times, the broad developments affecting all aspects of Amer-

[11]These women were less authoritarian than their male counterparts and perhaps a bit more disposed toward humanistic concerns, at least according to John Cumbler. In a recent article, he suggested that as women moved into positions of control in private charitable agencies, they altered the policies and orientation of those agencies; they paid less attention, for example, to welfare cheaters and more to reforms affecting women and children. More work, however, needs to be done on this subject before one can affirm or deny the proposition. Meanwhile, see Cumbler's "The Politics of Charity: Gender and Class in Late Nineteenth Century Charity Policy," *Journal of Social History* 14 (Fall 1980): 99–111.

ican life during the late nineteenth century.[12] Rationality, efficiency, foresight, and planning were middle-class virtues applied not only to charity but to business enterprise as well. Scientific charity, in its attempt to organize the philanthropic resources of the community and to relieve suffering in as efficient and economic a manner as possible, was similar to the monopolization and trustification of big business. In fact, as one leader of the movement stated, the "same wisdom which has given this generation its wonderful industrial capacity will preside over the administration of charity." (The state boards also reflected an attempt to apply business methods to charities—in the public realm.) No wonder scientific charity found its main support in the business and professional classes.[13] It also had a good deal of support, at least initially, in the academic community; its emphasis on the need for hard data for the resolution of social problems was related to the emergence of the social sciences in American higher education at this time.

Furthermore, the charity organization philosophy rested upon a series of preconceived moral judgments and presuppositions about the poor which were embodied in the "self-help" cult of the

[12]The charity organization movement also had deep roots overseas. Early in the nineteenth century, the influential Scotsman Thomas Chalmers had made a plea for the individual and organized approach in his famous work entitled "The Parochial System Without a Poor Rate, the Christian and Economic Policy of a Nation." Chalmers believed that almost every kind of help was deleterious because it interfered with the "natural operation" of the incentive to work, thus making the poor less industrious and resourceful. He was adamantly against public assistance. Like Spencer, he consented grudgingly to private charity because it stimulated altruism on the part of the giver. Another early exponent of this view was Octavia Hill, who thought that the best way to treat the needy was to encourage them, to provide "help without alms," as she stated it, a motto borrowed by the advocates of scientific charity. Then, as mentioned, there was the London Charity Organization Society, under the leadership of Charles Loch, the prototype on which Gurteen based his agency in Buffalo, New York.

[13]Too, as big businessmen increasingly came under attack from "reform Darwinists" and others in the late nineteenth century, they attempted to refurbish their image by demonstrating that their wealth was an inextricable part of the economic system—that it had social as well as personal value. They not only sat on boards of trustees of charity organization societies but also organized their own private philanthropies, usually large foundations that bore their names, and staffed them with "experts" who helped them decide how best to grant their funds—another effort by private charity to be "scientific" and businesslike in a corporate-technological age.

Gilded Age. Leaders of the movement believed in the individual-moral concept of poverty; they accepted the prevailing economic and sociological philosophy that attributed poverty and distress to personal defects and evil acts—sinfulness, failure in the struggle for survival, excessive relief-giving, and so on. After all, the road from rags to riches was open to all, wasn't it?

And, finally, scientific charity was based upon a rather pessimistic view of human nature, at least the poor's—the notion that no members of the lower class would exert themselves if they felt secure. Josephine Shaw Lowell, founder of the New York Charity Organization Society and a leader of the movement, spoke for many when she declared:

> Human nature is so constituted that no [working] man can receive as a gift what he should earn by his own labor without a moral deterioration. No human being . . . will work to provide the means of living for himself if he can get a living in any other manner agreeable to himself.

For the stern Mrs. Lowell and her colleagues, the poor had to be forced to endure deprivation in order to be kept at work; deprivation was the essential incentive. When a contributor to the New York C.O.S. asked Mrs. Lowell how much of her money would go to the poor, she replied proudly, "Not one cent!" "NO RELIEF GIVEN HERE," announced signs posted on both sides of the entrance to the Buffalo C.O.S.

The fallacy of relief-giving, for Josephine Shaw Lowell and her colleagues, was "that it is material, that it seeks material ends by material means and therefore must fail. . . . For man is a spiritual being, and if he is to be helped, it must be by spiritual means." Rather than alms, therefore, the poor needed supervision to help them combat or overcome intemperance, indolence, and improvidence. The C.O.S. provided, ideally at least, as its motto indicated, "not alms but a friend" (although critics of the movement charged that its motto should be, "neither alms nor a friend").[14]

---

[14]At best, relief was a necessary evil, the "final resort" for those who could not compete in the ceaseless struggle for survival—the aged, the infirm, the sick, the orphaned, perhaps the widowed with dependent children. Under any circumstances, it had to be given discriminately and sparingly, in public institutions, for it "should be surrounded by circumstances that shall repel everyone from accepting it," said Mrs. Lowell.

In carrying out their work, the charity organization societies relied on their corps of friendly visitors. These agents were to investigate appeals for assistance, distinguish between the worthy and unworthy poor, and above all provide the needy with the proper amount of moral exhortation. In the words of the Reverend Mr. Gurteen:

> The basic axiom, the cardinal principle of the charity organization society is diametrically opposed to all systems, all institutions, all charities, all forms of relief whatsoever.... The fundamental law of its operation is expressed in one word. "INVESTIGATE." Its motto is "No relief (except in extreme cases of despair or imminent death) without previous and searching examination."

The Reverend R. E. Thompson, in his *Manual for Visitors Among the Poor,* employed similar terms: "The best means of doing the poor good is found in friendly intercourse and personal influence." Gifts or alms, he maintained, are not needed but rather "sympathy, encouragement, and hopefulness." In fact, he added, "Nothing will so much interfere with ... proper work as to be recognized as an ... almoner." Mary Richmond agreed: "If you are going to be a *friend,* fertile in helpful suggestions, sympathetic and kind, you cannot be an almoner too," she contended.

Some people, especially more reform-minded individuals, were severely critical of the charity organization societies, comprised, as they were, of the "better classes," emphasizing painstaking investigation and individual treatment. Jane Addams, the founder of Hull-House in Chicago, felt that C.O.S. agents were cold and unemotional, too impersonal and stingy, that they were pervaded by a negative pseudoscientific spirit. Their vocabulary, she argued, was one of "don't give," "don't act," "don't do this or that"; all they gave the poor was advice—and for that they probably sent the Almighty a bill.

Boston's famed Irish-American poet-reformer, John Boyle O'Reilley, noted scathingly: "The organized charity scrimped and iced, In the name of a cautious, statistical Christ." The Reverend James O. S. Huntington of New York condemned the movement for its predilection to judge individual worthiness by business standards, and for establishing standards of truthfulness and labor for the poor which were not applied to the well-to-do.

Another clergyman reminded the Cleveland Charity Organization Society:

> Your society, with its Board of Trustees made up of steel magnates, coal operators, and employers, is not really interested in charity. If it were, it would stop the twelve hour day; it would increase wages and put an end to the cruel killing and maiming of man. I doubt as I read the New Testament whether the twelve disciples would have been able to qualify as worthy according to your system. And Christ himself might have been turned over by you to the police department as a vagrant without visible means of support.

Even political bosses, who often provided the needy with aid without the paternalism—or maternalism—and humiliation that often accompanied the charity organization societies' efforts, scorned the efforts of the societies. As George Washington Plunkitt, the "Sage" of Tammany Hall, put it:

> What tells in holdin your grip on your district is to go right down among the poor families and help them in different ways they need help. I've got a regular system for this.... If a family is burned out I don't ask whether they are Republicans or Democrats, and I don't refer them to the charity organization society, which would investigate their case in a month or two and decide that they were worthy of help about the same time they are dead from starvation. I just get quarters for them, buy clothes for them if their clothes are burned up, and fix them up till they get things runnin again. Its philanthropy, but its politics too—mighty good politics.... The poor are the most grateful people in the world.

The charity organization societies remained undaunted by these attacks. They saw no incompatibility between their profession of being scientific and their reliance upon voluntary service. On the contrary, the ultimate goal—self-sufficiency or the cure and prevention of poverty—depended wholly upon the enlistment and use of the volunteer. It was the volunteer's personal service that not only differentiated scientific benevolence from mere almsgiving or public relief, but made it superior; it was the "heart and soul" of the movement, for charity, like love, could not be purchased. To work, it had to regenerate character, which involved the direct influence of kind and concerned, successful and cultured, middle- and upper-class people upon the dependent.

Friendly visiting, then, assumed the right and the duty of intervention in the lives of the poor by their social and economic betters. Sensitive to charges of meddling, Mary Richmond wrote: "Some question our right to go among the poor with the object of doing good, regarding it as an impertinent interference with the rights of the individual. But... [we] *must* interfere when confronted by human suffering and need. Why not interfere effectively?" However much they distrusted the poor and believed that poverty was mainly a consequence of moral failing, many charity organizers felt a sincere responsibility to serve the needy. To them, the question was not whether to provide aid but how to do so and by whom.

The poor were not inherently vicious or mean. Rather, they were wayward children who drifted astray or who were incapable of discerning their own self-interest. They required no resource so desperately, therefore, as the advice of an intelligent friend who would offer sympathy, tact, patience, cheer, and wise counsel. The visitor's job was to discern the moral lapse responsible for the problem and then supply the appropriate guidance—something, of course, they were certain they could do.

There was, however, a great deal of ambiguity in this approach, and, in the long run, the work of the friendly visitors undermined their own deeply cherished beliefs. To begin with, it was assumed that the poor wanted the moral guidance, which was seldom the case (although, as Jane Addams observed, despite feelings to the contrary, desperate clients would "laud temperance,... thrift and religious observance" when the friendly visitor would appear, in order to receive aid). Too, friendly visitors intervened in the lives of the poor by virtue of a presumed wisdom and superiority while, at the same time, professing to conceive of their charges as personal friends—an impossibility, for moral uplift is far from friendship. Friendly visitors did not really consider their clients as equals, or even potential equals, but as objects of character reformation whose lowly condition resulted from ignorance or other deviations from middle-class norms—intemperance, indolence, improvidence, or whatnot. And while it was possible to create a satisfactory *professional* relationship between nonequals (doctor-patient, lawyer-client), it was impossible to establish satisfactory *personal* relationships between "superior" volunteers and "inferior" dependents.

In addition, the charity organization societies and their agents hoped to discourage pauperism and vagrancy by stringent relief policies—another impossibility. Poverty and dependence were not largely expressions of individual moral perversity. Rather, they were manifestations of other things, especially accidents, ill health, low wages, technological (and cyclical) unemployment, and premature loss of the family breadwinner. Poverty rooted in ill health, unemployment, substandard wages, and structural changes in the economy was too deep-rooted and complex to be affected very much by *any* relief policy, let alone one of benevolent stinginess.

Friendly visitors (like paternal guardians before them) began to see this, not because they wanted to, but because it was inevitable. They began to see the difficulty, for example, in trying to distinguish between the worthy and the unworthy poor when no amount of verbal effort could raise the income of a family to a subsistence level, or when a depression, which occurred like clockwork in nineteenth- and early twentieth-century America, threw several million people out of work.

More important, since the organized charities had insisted upon gathering the facts, records were kept and preserved in order to evaluate progress and insure continuity. As a result, the friendly visitors compiled comprehensive data on the social and economic problems of the poor, the real poverty-producing factors that had little to do with the sufferers' character. Their investigations uncovered information on involuntary unemployment, industrial accidents, and low wages, not on intemperance, improvidence, and the like. It became quite clear, then, that preconceived notions about the poor had to be discarded, or at least seriously reconsidered; the needy were not all alike, members of the "dangerous" or "depraved" classes.

George Buzelle, general secretary of the Brooklyn Bureau of Charities, was one of the first to see and publicly admit this. At the 1886 National Conference, he offered friendly criticism of his colleagues in the organized charity movement, especially their proneness to categorize: "Once, some of us would have undertaken to arrange all the human family according to intellect, development, merit, and demerit, in accurate divisions and subdivisions, each with a label, ready for indexing and filing away," he told his audience. But he and others were learning that "the poor . . . have not in common any type of physical, intellectual, or moral development which would warrant an attempt to group them as a class."

Three years later and then again in 1894, with the appearance of his influential *American Charities,* Amos G. Warner, Stanford University professor and former general agent of the Baltimore C.O.S., published studies of the causes of poverty that became landmarks both because of their content and their attempt to be systematic and empirical in reaching conclusions about the needy, conclusions which indicated that social factors were more important than personal ones in causing dependency. Other studies did the same—with interesting results. One was conducted by the New York C.O.S. in cooperation with a number of Columbia University professors and students. Based upon the agency's records for the years 1890–97, a period of sharp depression and hard times, it indicated that lack of employment was the most frequent cause of poverty, sickness and accident second, while shiftlessness and intemperance were causes in only about 10 percent of the cases. Even Josephine Shaw Lowell, that remarkable bellwether of C.O.S. opinion, could conclude from the report only that, for most, the causes of distress are "as much beyond their power to avert as if they . . . [are] natural calamities of fire, flood, or storm." Such studies also indicated that the C.O.S. approach did not work; it neither prevented nor relieved mass poverty. According to Robert Hunter, whose classic work *Poverty* was the most careful and objective study to date when it was published in 1904, at least ten million Americans, or one out of every eight, were poor. They lived below a standard of normal existence that was necessary for industrial efficiency, according to Hunter, through no fault of their own: "Poverty was bred of miserable and unjust social conditions," he wrote. The environment had to be reformed!

Beginning, then, with a narrow, moralistic, and individualistic attitude toward poverty and its causes, the charity organization movement ultimately fostered the development of a broader point of view. The knowledge of misfortune experienced by hundreds of different families and thousands of individuals eventually induced many representatives of these agencies to regard the social and economic causes of poverty as more pressing than personal inadequacy. In 1895, Robert Treat Paine, president of the Boston Associated Charities, asked whether the charity organization movement had not for too long been content to relieve single cases of distress without asking whether there were "prolific causes permanently at work" to create want, vice, crime, disease, and death which could be eradicated. "If such causes of pauperism exist," he declared, "how vain to waste our energies on single cases of relief when society should aim at removing the prolific sources of all the woe."

Even notions about home relief underwent scrutiny and change, for they rested upon a conception of pauperism that was no longer credible. Brooklyn Bureau of Charities secretary Samuel Bishop pointed out that, while the slogan of the movement was "not alms but a friend," there was no reason "why a friend may got give alms." Indeed, by 1907, the Buffalo C.O.S., America's first, had become a relief-giving agency. By that time, Edward T. Devine, general secretary of the New York C.O.S. and editor of its publication, *Charities,* had pretty well summed up the distance the movement had traveled when he declared: "We may quite safely throw overboard, once and for all, the idea that the dependent poor are our moral inferiors, that there is any necessary connection between wealth and virtue, or between poverty and guilt."

Finally, in addition to gathering specific information on the real causes of poverty and dependency and fostering new concepts of treating them, organized charity agents contributed to the development of a technique of social service and research—casework—and with it, the growth of a profession. The inevitable tendency of scientific charity, with its individualistic orientation, the very thing so many critics deplored, was to emphasize the objective and factual rather than the deductive and discretionary approach to social questions. This, in turn, made the use of volunteer visitors, however "friendly," harder and harder, for it was increasingly difficult to reconcile untrained, part-time service with sustained individual treatment based on scientific knowledge. It became increasingly clear that the gathering and interpreting of factual material, the technical character of many of the services that had to be performed, and the consistency of effort required in case treatment—really putting the "scientific" into scientific philanthropy, in other words—could be achieved only by full-time workers with education, experience, and professional discipline. This led to the creation of training schools for charity workers, the demise of volunteer service, and the rise of a social work profession.[15]

The devaluation of volunteers did not take the form of outright rejection, largely because of the long tradition of voluntarism in social welfare and because profession social workers needed the power, influence, and financial help of volunteers. What occurred, then, was a reversal of roles. Whereas earlier the real work of the agency was conducted by volunteers and the menial labor by paid staff members, by the turn of the century, the opposite was beginning to occur; volunteers did the office work or, by serving as trustees helped shape policy and raise funds, while the work in the field, casework, was in the hands of paid professional agents. Viewed earlier as a civic duty, voluntarism became, instead, a privilege granted by agencies to those who accepted their authority and discipline.

By the turn of the century, the organized charities were establishing training schools for charity workers. In addition, they were taking part in other activities which, if not aimed at altering the social order, at least sought to mitigate some of its worst effects—housing reform, antituberculosis work, publication of reform-oriented journals, and the like, including juvenile court, probation work, and other measures for child welfare. Most Americans realized that the nation's future depended upon the health and welfare of its young people. Interest in child welfare, therefore, was strong.

---

[15]Along with their insistence that charity work had or should have a scientific base and thus required intellectual discipline and professional training, the organized charities' demands that social services be efficiently administered and that inter-agency cooperation take place also were significant influences on modern social work practice.

Bibliography

ADAMS, GEORGE W. *Doctors in Blue: The Medical History of the Union Army in the Civil War*. New York: Schuman, 1952.

AUSTIN, ANNE L. *The Woolsey Sisters of New York, 1860–1900: A Family's Involvement in the Civil War and a New Profession*. Philadelphia: American Philosophical Society, 1971.

BECKER, DOROTHY G. "Exit Lady Bountiful: The Volunteer and the Professional Social Worker," *Social Service Review* 38 (March 1964): 57–72.

———. "Social Welfare Leaders as Spokesmen for the Poor," *Social Casework* 49 (February 1968): 82–89.

BLASSINGAME, JOHN W. *The Slave Community: Plantation Life in the Antebellum South*. New York: Oxford University Press, 1972.

BOSANQUET, HELEN. *Social Work in London, 1869–1912: A History of the Charity Organization Society*. London: Murray, 1914.

BRANDT, LILLIAN. *Growth and Development of the AICP and COS*. New York: Community Service Society of New York, 1942.

BREMNER, ROBERT. *From the Depths: The Discovery of Poverty in the United States*. New York: New York University Press, 1956.

———. "The Impact of the Civil War on Philanthropy and Social Welfare," *Civil War History* 12 (December 1966): 293–303.

———. "The Prelude: Philanthropic Rivalries in the Civil War," *Social Casework* 49 (February 1968): 77–81.

———. *The Public Good: Philanthropy and Welfare in the Civil War Era*. New York: Knopf, 1980.

———. "Scientific Philanthropy," *Social Service Review* 30 (June 1956): 168–73.

CLARK, CLIFFORD. "Religious Beliefs and Social Reforms in the Gilded Age: The Case of Henry Whitney Bellows," *New England Quarterly* 43 (March 1970): 59–78.

COLCORD, JOANNA, AND RUTH MANN, eds. *The Long View: Papers and Addresses by Mary E. Richmond*. New York: Russell Sage Foundation, 1930.

CROSS, ROBERT D. "The Philanthropic Contributions of Louisa Lee Schuyler," *Social Service Review* 35 (September 1961): 290–301.

CUMBLER, JOHN T. "The Politics of Charity: Gender and Class in Late Nineteenth Century Charity Policy," *Journal of Social History* 14 (Fall 1980): 99–111.

DEVINE, EDWARD T. *The Principles of Relief.* New York: Macmillan, 1904.

ESCOTT, PAUL D. "The Cry of the Sufferers: The Problem of Welfare in the Confederacy," *Civil War History* 23 (September 1977): 228–40.

FINE, SIDNEY. *Laissez-Faire and the General Welfare State.* Ann Arbor, Mich.: University of Michigan Press, 1964.

FLEMING, DONALD H. "Social Darwinism," in Arthur M. Schlesinger, Jr., and Morton White, eds., *Paths of American Thought.* Boston: Houghton Mifflin, 1963.

FRANKLIN, JOHN HOPE. "Public Welfare in the South During the Reconstruction Era, 1865–1880," *Social Service Review* 44 (December 1970): 379–92.

GETTLEMAN, MARVIN E. "Charity and Social Classes in the United States, 1874–1900," *American Journal of Economics and Sociology* 22 (April 1963): 313–30; 22 (July 1963): 417–26.

———. "Philanthropy as Social Control in Late Nineteenth Century America," *Societas* 5 (Winter 1975): 49–59.

GILMAN, DANIEL C., ed. *The Organization of Charities.* Chicago: International Congress of Charities and Correction, 1893.

GREENBIE, MARJORIE B. *Lincoln's Daughters of Mercy.* New York: Putnam, 1944.

GURTEEN, S. HUMPHREYS. *A Handbook of Charity Organization.* Buffalo: Charity Organization Society, 1879.

GUTMAN, HERBERT C. "The Failure of the Movement by the Unemployed for Public Works in 1873," *Political Science Quarterly* 80 (June 1965): 254–77.

Hand-Book for Friendly Visitors Among the Poor. New York: Charity Organization Society, 1883.

HASSON, GAIL S. "Health and Welfare of Freedmen in Reconstruction Alabama," *Alabama Review* 35 (April 1982): 94–111.

HOFSTADTER, RICHARD. *Social Darwinism in American Thought, 1860–1915.* Boston: Beacon Press, 1959.

HUGGINS, NATHAN. *Protestants Against Poverty.* Westport, Conn.: Greenwood, 1971.

JACKSON, PHILIP. "Black Charity in Progressive Era Chicago," *Social Service Review* 52 (September 1978): 400–417.

JOHNSON, ALEXANDER. *Adventures in Social Welfare.* Fort Wayne, Ind.: Fort Wayne Printing, 1923.

KAPLAN, BARRY J. "Reformers and Charity: The Abolition of Public Outdoor Relief in New York City, 1870–1898," *Social Service Review* 52 (June 1978): 202–14.

KOGUT, ALVIN B. "The Negro and the Charity Organization Society in the Progressive Era," *Social Service Review* 44 (March 1970): 11–21.

KRAMER, HOWARD D. "Effect of the Civil War on the Public Health Movement," *Mississippi Valley Historical Review* 35 (December 1948): 449–62.

KUSMER, KENNETH L. "The Functions of Organized Charity in the Progressive Era: Chicago as a Case Study," *Journal of American History* 60 (December 1973): 657–78.

LANE, JAMES B. "Jacob A. Riis and Scientific Philanthropy During the Progressive Era," *Social Service Review* 47 (March 1973): 32–48.

LEIBY, JAMES. "Amos Warner's *American Charities,* 1894–1930," *Social Service Review* 37 (December 1963): 441–55.

———. "State Welfare Institutions and the Poor," *Social Casework* 49 (February 1968): 90–95.

LEWIS, VERL S. "The Development of the Charity Organization Movement in the United States, 1875–1900," Ph.D. dissertation, Western Reserve University, 1954.

———. "Stephen Humphreys Gurteen and the American Origins of Charity Organization," *Social Service Review* 40 (June 1966): 190–201.

LLOYD, GARY A. *Charities, Settlements, and Social Work: An Inquiry into Philosophy and Method, 1890–1915.* New Orleans: Tulane University School of Social Welfare, 1971.

LOWELL, JOSEPHINE SHAW. *Public Relief and Private Charity.* New York: Putnam, 1884.

MAXWELL, WILLIAM Q. *Lincoln's Fifth Wheel: The Political History of the United States Sanitary Commission.* New York: Longmans, Green, 1956.

MAY, J. THOMAS. "A Nineteenth Century Medical Care Program for Blacks: The Case of the Freedmen's Bureau," *Anthropological Quarterly* 46 (July 1973): 160–71.

MOWAT, C. L. "Charity and Casework in Late Victorian London: The Work of the Charity Organization Society," *Social Service Review* 31 (September 1957): 258–70.

———. *The Charity Organization Society, 1869–1913.* London: Methuen, 1961.

OLDS, VICTORIA. "The Freedmen's Bureau: A Nineteenth Century Federal Welfare Agency," *Social Casework* 44 (May 1963): 247–54.

PLECK, ELIZABETH H. *Black Migration and Poverty in Boston, 1865–1900.* New York: Academic Press, 1979.

RABINOWITZ, HOWARD. "From Exclusion to Segregation: Health and Welfare Services for Southern Blacks, 1865–1890," *Social Service Review* 48 (September 1974): 327–54.

RAUCH, JULIA. "The Charity Organization Movement in Philadelphia," *Social Work* 21 (January 1976): 55–62.

———. "Women in Social Work: Friendly Visitors in Philadelphia, 1880," *Social Service Review* 49 (June 1975): 241–59.

RICH, MARGARET. *Josephine Shaw Lowell.* New York: Family Service Association of America, 1954.

RICHMOND, MARY E. *Friendly Visiting Among the Poor.* New York: Macmillan, 1899.

SANBORN, FRANKLIN B. *Recollections of Seventy Years.* Boston: Badger, 1909.

Sanitary Commission of the United States Army, The. New York: n.p., 1864.

SAVETH, EDWARD N. "Patrician Philanthropy in America: The Late Nineteenth and Early Twentieth Centuries," *Social Service Review* 54 (March 1980): 76–91.

SAVITT, TODD L. "Politics and Medicine: The Georgia Freedmen's Bureau and the Organization of Health Care, 1865–1866," *Civil War History* 28 (March 1982): 45–64.

SCHNEIDER, DAVID M., AND ALBERT DEUTSCH. "The Public Charities of New York: The Rise of State Supervision After the Civil War," *Social Service Review* 15 (March 1941): 1–23.

SHRYOCK, RICHARD H. "A Medical Perspective of the Civil War," *American Quarterly* 14 (Summer 1962): 161–73.

SPEIZMAN, MILTON. "Poverty, Pauperism and Their Causes: Some Charity Organization Views," *Social Casework* 46 (March 1965): 142–49.

STEWART, WILLIAM R. *The Philanthropic Work of Josephine Shaw Lowell.* New York: Macmillan, 1911.

SUMNER, WILLIAM GRAHAM. *What the Social Classes Owe Each Other.* Caldwell, Idaho: Caxton, 1963.

TAYLOR, LLOYD C. "Josephine Shaw Lowell and American Philanthropy," *New York History* 44 (October 1963): 336–64.

TRATTNER, WALTER I. "Louisa Lee Schuyler and the Founding of the State Charities Aid Association," *New-York Historical Society Quarterly* 51 (July 1967): 233–48.

WARNER, AMOS G. *American Charities*. New York: Crowell, 1894.

WATSON, FRANK D. *The Charity Organization Movement in the United States*. New York: Macmillan, 1922.

Chapter 6

Child Welfare

OF ALL SOCIAL WELFARE ACTIVITIES, none was deemed more important than those dealing with children. Early nineteenth-century reformers, A.I.C.P. agents, charity organization society friendly visitors, settlement house residents, and almost every other agency or individual working for social betterment saw in children the possibility for constructive altruism. As a result, a broad child welfare movement swept through America from the mid-nineteenth century through the twentieth.[1]

The movement took many forms, including the removal of dependent, neglected, and delinquent children from almshouses and other institutions and their placement in private homes. Also, the creation of juvenile courts and probation systems, the provision of mothers' or widows' pensions, the passage of compulsory school attendance laws, crusades against child labor, and a host of other activities were initiated or pursued.

This great interest in child welfare is easy to understand. Aside from the fact that a child in trouble generally makes a strong appeal, a real need for social work on behalf of the nation's young citizens existed. Being more numerous than adults in an age when large families were the rule, children formed one of the largest groups among the ranks of the neglected and needy. In many ways their sufferings were the most grievous, and it was difficult to argue that they were responsible for their condition. Of all those who required help, then, children seemed the most deserving.

Moreover, the social upheaval resulting from large-scale immigration and rapid industrial and urban growth was especially

[1]Child welfare includes all those activities and services by individuals and public and private agencies for the benefit of dependent, neglected, or delinquent children.

hard on children. Casualties in industry frequently deprived them, often early in life, of a parent—or sometimes two. And the mobility and anonymity of a swiftly changing urban-industrial society meant that many of these deprived youngsters were left in a strange and sometimes hostile environment.

Low wages, especially those paid immigrants, and simplified industrial processes resulting from technology and mass production, also drew large numbers of children as well as their mothers into factories, where the accident rates for both were shockingly high and where they worked long hours for a pittance to help supplement the family's meager earnings. Children lucky enough to stay out of industry but whose mothers went to work were deprived of parental supervision and a normal home life, and this resulted in an alarming increase in juvenile delinquency.

A growing concern with child welfare, however, resulted above all else from the fact that many citizens viewed the child as the key to social control. If future generations were to possess the strength of mind, body, and character to become good self-supporting citizens, able to assume the responsibilities and burdens of democratic rule, they had to be protected as children; safeguarding them was considered essential to society. As one reformer argued:

> The fate of the world is determined by the influences which prevail with the child from birth to seven years of age. . . . All our problems go back to the child—corrupt politics, dishonesty and greed in commerce, war, anarchism, drunkenness, incompetence, and criminality. We know that much of our labor for the radical betterment of society is costly and fruitless. It is because we are working against nature. We take the twig after it is bent and has stiffened into a tree. We take the brook after it has become a torrent.

Or, as Robert Hunter put it in his classic *Poverty,* published in 1904: "Poverty degrades all men who struggle under its yoke, but the poverty which oppresses childhood is a monstrous and unnatural thing, for it denies the child growth, development, strength; it robs the child of the present and curses the man of the future." Some thirty years later, President Franklin D. Roosevelt expressed the same idea when he remarked: "The destiny of American youth is the destiny of America."

For a long time—from the colonial period until well into the nineteenth century—childhood was not considered a special phase of human development. For the most part, children were considered to be more or less alike, essentially miniature adults who were inherently aggressive and sinful, and hence prone to all sorts of vices, including idleness.[2] Therefore, they required close supervision and stern treatment so that they would grow up to lead industrious, upright, godly lives. As the Pilgrim minister John Robinson put it, "There is in all children . . . a stubbornness and stoutness of mind arising from natural pride" which "must be broken and beaten down. . . ." Or, in the words of Cotton Mather, "Better whipt than Damn'd." That "whipping" and "breaking and beating down," or oversight and restraint essential for proper development, could best be provided, it was believed, by the family, the basic economic as well as social institution in preindustrial America.

By the mid-eighteenth century, this concept of childhood and childrearing was undergoing significant change. By that time, Enlightenment notions of free will and human progress had begun to challenge the harsh earlier doctrines. Americans had come to accept the theories of John Locke, who, as we have seen, speculated that children were not depraved but that the "souls of the newly born are just empty tablets afterwards to be filled in by observation and reasoning." By the middle of the next century, some Americans—Ralph Waldo Emerson, Henry David Thoreau, and other Transcendentalists, for example—had gone beyond Locke's *tabula rasa* theory to proclaim that children were innately pure and good, corrupted only by an overbearing society. At the same time, thanks in part to the wave of evangelical religious revivals and humanitarian sentiment that swept across America in the decades prior to the Civil War, the idea of "Christian nurture" emerged, a concept popularized by Horace Bushnell, the liberal minister whose book entitled *Christian Nurture* first appeared in 1846. According to Bushnell, children were plastic creatures who could attain salvation through a healthful (or

---

[2]Although some historians are now beginning to challenge the notion that colonial Americans treated their children as "miniature adults," I adhere to the older and still prevalent view. For the revisionist interpretation, see the Ross Beales article cited in the bibliography.

nurturing) environment, especially a family that provided affection, good example, and gentle guidance as opposed to strict discipline and hard work.

In addition, the need of children to exercise their minds and bodies was recognized, thanks largely to Friedrich Froebel, whose ideas began filtering through to the United States by mid-century. The German educator, founder of the kindergarten movement, argued that children were not little grownups but special beings with their own needs, especially the need for recreation and play.

Scientific developments in the second half of the nineteenth century, including the theory of evolution, strengthened these ideas, especially the conviction that children were basically innocent and malleable creatures who needed special treatment, particularly a relaxed and healthy home life. While Darwinism bolstered the idea of inherited traits and capacities, it also presented a developmental view of human growth and behavior, stressing the power of the environment to modify both. Thus it lent support to those who claimed that children's flexible characters, if carefully and gently nurtured, would develop in accordance with proper Christian and American ideals. Then, too, there was Sigmund Freud, the famed Austrian neurologist and founder of psychoanalysis, who stressed the vital importance of sound nurturance in infancy and childhood for the formation of a good character and a healthy personality. And, finally, there was the work of the psychologist G. Stanley Hall, the "father of the child study movement" in America, who began to look closely at what follows the onset of puberty and whose important book *Adolescence,* published in 1904, not only contained a vast amount of information on human development but was a milestone in child study, contributing greatly to the growing tendency to raise the status of children in society. All of these developments had an impact on the field of child welfare.

In the earlier period in American history, however, destitute and neglected children, as we have seen, were placed in private families and put to work or bound out as apprentices. As in England, the practice was designed to teach them occupations and trades and to inculcate in them the habits of industry and thrift so that they would become self-supporting citizens. The system also helped to relieve the community of their support and, at the same time, to provide the handicrafts with a cheap source of labor—a neat admixture of private and public economics, one that coincided perfectly with the prevailing concept of childhood as a brief, unimportant prelude to adulthood and the real business of living. For the children, however (since there were few if any provisions for inspection and supervision), the system was full of abuses. The master's obligation to his young charge was rarely carried out. All too often, the children received little or no training in the trades and their education was ignored; poorly fed and clothed, they performed menial tasks and grew up in ignorance.

A reaction set in, especially during the antislavery period, for the similarities between apprenticeship and forced bondage were great in the minds of many. As a result, while apprenticeship was still used on occasion in the nineteenth century (especially in the South after the Civil War, when whites sought to use it as a means of virtually re-enslaving black youngsters and thus securing a cheap supply of labor), most needy children were cared for in the same way as other dependents—in institutions. In the county almshouse, it was widely believed, their "health and morals would be improved," and they "would receive an education to fit them for future usefulness," as New York's Secretary of State Yates put it in his influential report, written at a time when there were still few public schools in America.

Before long, it became evident that these hopes would not be realized. Many almshouses, as we have seen, were vile catchalls for victims of every sort of misery, misfortune, and misconduct who were herded together and badly mistreated. The tales of uneducated, half-starved, tear-stained young outcasts in these wretched institutions—where, due to inadequate diet and lack of proper sanitary facilities, the mortality rates were extremely high—were sorrowful ones.

As a result, again, as we have seen, concerned citizens began to demand reform of these vile places, especially through the segregation or removal of certain types of inmates. Children were the first beneficiaries of these successful pleas: various groups of disadvantaged children were removed from county almshouses and placed, instead, in separate children's institutions; the institutional ideal, in other words, still dominated the thinking of reformers. Founders of child care institutions shared fully with the proponents of other caretaker institutions—almshouses and mental hospitals, for example—the notion that only careful and diligent training within an institution to cope with the open, freewheeling, and often disordered life of the community would prevent their charges from falling victim to ignorance, vice, and crime.[3]

Actually, the first separate children's institution predated the American Revolution. As early as 1727, a unit was set up at the Ursuline Convent in New Orleans for children whose parents had been slain in an Indian raid. The first permanent orphanage created for the purpose was Bethesda, the noteworthy institution founded in Savannah, Georgia, in 1740 by the Reverend George Whitefield of Great Awakening fame (and still in operation today—as a modern child care center for emotionally disturbed children). To Charleston, South Carolina, goes credit for the first public institution solely for children, established in 1790. It was only after the 1830s, however, when people began to demand the removal of children from almshouses, that the number of such places multiplied. By 1861, when Ohio passed the first statute calling for the mandatory removal of all children from county almshouses, there were some seventy-five separate children's institutions in existence. By 1890, they had increased in number to 600.

Although these separate institutions were on the whole superior to the almshouses as places for child care, they too had many defects. Most were large, congregate institutions which brought together under a single roof anywhere from fifty to as many as 2000 children. Managers of such institutions put a premium on order, obedience, and precision. The poor wards commonly slept and ate together in large dormitories or barracks. Their lives were governed by extremely rigid schedules; individuality was sup-

---

[3]At the same time, however (thanks to the changing concept of childhood), they felt themselves to be singularly fortunate, for their clientele was young, impressionable, and not fixed in deviant or dependent behavior. If the young were vulnerable to corruption, they were also eminently teachable. "Youth," said one reformer, "is particularly susceptible to reform. . . . It has not yet felt the long continued pressure which distorts its natural growth. . . . No habit can be rooted so firmly as to refuse a cure," especially under the tutelage of a kind caretaker.

pressed, and the atmosphere was one of monotonous routine. Practice had not yet caught up with changing theory. The institutions were properly named orphan "asylums."

Making matters worse was the so-called subsidy system—the practice of the states providing funds for private institutions, either in a lump sum on an annual basis, or periodically on a per capita basis. While it was cheaper for the states to do this than to build and maintain their own institutions, they seldom had the power of supervision or control over the appropriations or the agencies to which they were granted. The result was that the private institutions operated independently on public funds and, as in the county almshouses, abuses abounded.

They often provided poor and protracted care. The retention of children in these overcrowded institutions was in the hands of their managers who ran them as business or profit-making ventures. As many youngsters as possible were brought in, fed and cared for as inexpensively as possible, and retained for as long as possible. The story was often told of the manager of one such place who, each night before going to bed, would pray for more orphans so that he could build a new wing to his institution.

The growth of these child care institutions therefore turned out to be a doubtful blessing. Again, concerned citizens and reformers moved in, this time to displace the asylum or children's institution. A system of placing needy children in private homes gradually developed. Family care, in other words, began to replace institutional treatment. By this time, many of the states were beginning to establish public school systems and even to enact compulsory school attendance laws; the chances of children receiving an education outside an institution, therefore, were far greater than they had been earlier.

The first children's organization in America to adopt family care, or placing-out, as its policy was the New York Children's Aid Society, founded in 1853 by the Reverend Charles Loring Brace, a twenty-seven-year-old missionary in New York's notorious Five Points District. For the next third of a century, he and the N.Y.C.A.S. were synonymous.

While not insensitive to the plight of needy children, Charles Loring Brace was as impelled by other motives as by the suffering of the youngsters with whom he concerned himself. To begin with, he was not very fond of the city. He was particularly alarmed, however, over increasing juvenile delinquency and crime among the young poor of New York and was fearful of what might happen to the property, morality, and political life of the city if nothing was done to relieve the area of its homeless, vagrant, and delinquent children, menaces to society, or the "dangerous classes," as he referred to them in his autobiography, *The Dangerous Classes of New York and Twenty Years Work Among Them,* published in 1872. Indeed, his appeals for funds for the C.A.S., which he described as a "moral and physical disinfectant," aroused more popular anxiety over the situation than they did pity for the unfortunate youngsters. The founding of the agency, he thus wrote in the opening sentence of his first annual report, reflected "the increasing sense among our citizens of the evils of the city," especially the "outcast, vicious, reckless, multitude of . . . boys swarming now in every foul alley and low street" who might "come to know their power and *use* it."

A pragmatist who worked through trial and error, Brace made use of several approaches in his efforts to help needy children, combat delinquency, and safeguard the property of the well-to-do. The program included evening schools, sheltered workshops, industrial education classes (for boys), training schools for sewing machine operators and household servants (for girls), lodging houses for newsboys and bootblacks, penny savings banks, and outings and vacations. But, above, all, he pinned his hopes on foster home placement.[4]

More and more, Brace became convinced of the futility of helping dependent and delinquent children save by transplanting them (while still saplings) to new environments; removal from society became the only answer. Unlike many of his contemporaries, however, who advocated locking up the needy behind the walls of an institution, Brace contrived a way of both securing their removal and capitalizing on the beneficial influences of home life. While this was not entirely new—for it bore resemblances to the

---

[4]Brace disliked institutional care because, as he put it, "asylum life is not the best training for outcast children in preparing them for practical life. In large buildings, where a multitude of children are gathered together, the bad corrupt the good, and the good are not educated in the virtues of real life."

apprenticeship system—Brace injected a novel element: the promise of the expanding West. For a long time in American history, "the West" was the medicine prescribed for all those who wished to better their lot. Like many nineteenth-century Americans, Brace took comfort in the belief that the rich and relatively unpeopled area would provide a new opportunity for the disadvantaged and needy, especially young children.

Brace subscribed to two other related ideas widely held at the time, the so-called agrarian myth and the individualistic social philosophy—the notions that the farmer was the ideal individual and citizen; that agriculture, as a calling, was uniquely productive and important to society; that rural life was inherently more moral and virtuous than urban living; that the fewer restraining forces on the individual the better. (He would read Charles Darwin's *Origin of Species* thirteen times and praise the theory of natural selection as "one of the great intellectual" achievements of the age, one that would prove profoundly relevant to the moral and physical history of mankind.) For Brace, the best of all asylums was the home of the farmer, "our most solid and intelligent citizen." He was convinced that the availability of such homes, especially in the West, where youngsters could nurture their freedom, their creativity, and their "go-gettedness," was almost unlimited.

The language of the Children's Aid Society's first circular detailed, and again betrayed, the purpose of its work:

> The Society has taken its origin in the deeply settled feeling of our citizens that something must be done to meet the increasing crime and poverty among the destitute children of New York. Its objects are to help this class. . . . We hope . . . especially to be the means of *draining the city* of these children by communicating with farmers, manufacturers, or families in the country who may need such employment. When homeless boys are found by our agents, we mean to get them homes in the families of respectable persons, and to put them in the way of an honest living (italics added).

The success of the plan to "drain the city" of destitute children depended, of course, upon the demand for unpaid farm labor. To Brace, that did not lessen the charity of those who gave the children homes. The best charity, he felt, was the opportunity to work, especially in good Christian farm homes. Boys and girls were better off there than in any institution or on the streets of New York City.

The C.A.S. began its "emigrant parties" in 1854 when forty-six boys and girls were taken by train from New York City to a small town in Michigan, where they were disposed of by methods suggested in the following excerpt from an early C.A.S. journal:

> At the close of the sermon the people were informed of the object of the Children's Aid Society. It met with cordial approval of all present and several promised to take children.... Monday morning the boys held themselves in readiness to receive application from the farmers ... and before Saturday they were all gone.

The process was always the same. Despite his conviction that family life was best for the needy child, Brace bypassed the natural family, the child's own parents. Instead, he flooded the western countryside with wayward youths. Operating in a rather casual way, he rarely took the time to investigate the quality of the substitute family and the way in which it cared for the foster child. More often than not, he never heard from the youngsters again; most of them were under fourteen years of age, but some were beyond their teens. After twenty-five years of such practice, Charles Loring Brace and the Children's Aid Society removed more than 50,000 children from New York City. It is not surprising, therefore, that the city—and the state—subsidized their operation.

Nor is it surprising that such a system, or lack of one, should have met firm opposition. With the absence of any care and supervision in placement and the lack of any followup, all the abuses of the apprenticeship system reappeared. Families commonly overworked the children, failed to educate them, fed and clothed them poorly, and in general mistreated them. As a result, despite the possible advantages of family care (and the recognized faults of children's institutions, especially their blighting effects), charity workers, who sometimes referred to the program as "the wolf of indentured labor in the sheep's clothing of Christian charity," took up arms against home placement.

Opposition came also from the poor themselves, many of whom did not want their children sent so far from home. In addition, many of the western states became quite unhappy with the scattering of thousands of needy children each year within their borders, where many of them—close to 60 percent, according to a study conducted by the secretary of Minnesota's State Board of Charities, Hastings H. Hart—became sources of trouble and public expenditures. Mistreated and overworked in their new homes, many of the youngsters ran away and became public charges. Soon, many of the western states began passing legislation either prohibiting the practice or requiring that the C.A.S. post bond for each child in the event he or she became a public burden.

And finally, Brace's practices set off a heated controversy with the Catholic Church. Right or wrong, the Church charged that the C.A.S. was a Protestant device to proselytize the Catholic children of the city. Throughout the period, the Church sought to keep its dependent children within the shelter of its own institutions rather than distribute them in faraway homes, especially in Protestant rural areas where they were likely to lose their faith.

Still, whatever his shortcomings, Brace was an important figure in the history of child welfare, having done much to popularize foster home care. And, as Robert Bremner has pointed out, his "preventive 'child-saving' approach, adopted at a time when so much emphasis was placed on correctional or reformatory methods, exercised a wholesome influence on later developments" in the field.

Indeed it did. Toward the end of the nineteenth century when several child welfare workers—John Finley of the New York State Charities Aid Association, Charles Birtwell of the Boston Children's Aid Society, and Homer Folks of the Children's Aid Society of Pennsylvania—began to develop sound administrative procedures, the placing-out of children spread rapidly. By the turn of the century, it had replaced institutional treatment in a number of cities.

By that time, however, the practice was far different from the "emigrant parties" of the 1850s. Since the family was considered a unit and its importance in molding the life of the child was once again recognized, whenever possible home ties were preserved. When this was not possible, children were placed in private homes, but by licensed authorities and only after being studied by a social worker and a physician, and later by a psychologist and, on occasion, even by a psychiatrist as well. Prospective homes were studied carefully by paid full-time agents in order to guide the agency in making a proper placement; that is, to see to it that the child was placed in a home that was both emotionally and financially able to meet his or her needs. Even then, the placement was probationary until it could be determined whether or not the child and the foster home were suited to each other. Because of the supervision involved, placements were made within the immediate community whenever feasible. In short, the emphasis was on individual treatment, on understanding each child's needs so that the child would be placed in a home where he or she would be happy and would develop soundly.

While legal adoption was the ultimate ideal, this occurred rarely and only after a long waiting period.[5] Furthermore, it was recognized that in some cases adoption was undesirable or unfeasible, giving rise to the "boarding-out" system—which involved the payment of a fee (weekly, monthly, or yearly) for the rearing of a child—a plan justified on economic as well as on altruistic grounds. Welfare workers found, for example, that as children grew in years, the likelihood of their being adopted decreased. Many were unsuitable for adoption because of a physical or mental handicap; few families would adopt such children. And finally, whenever a living parent might want to reclaim the child, it was impractical or impossible for the youngster to be adopted by others. Boarding-out secured for the child the benefits of home life without depriving surviving (although perhaps destitute) parents of the opportunity to visit their children and even to reclaim them if and when circumstances permitted.

In addition, it was argued that a family reluctant to open its home to a needy child free of charge might do so when paid for it,

[5]Adoption was unknown to the Common Law of England; as a result, such measures developed in America largely by means of state statutes. Primarily, they were intended to provide a procedure whereby the custody of a child could be legally transferred from the natural parent to the adopting parent. However, as was characteristic of the methods used throughout most of the nineteenth century, little attempt was made to understand the child's needs or the character of the adoptive parents until Michigan, in 1891, recognized the need for a preadoptive investigation. This marked the beginning of child legislation that emphasized the human elements in adoption.

and then grow to love the youngster and eventually to adopt him or her. Moreover, it was less costly to care for dependent children by boarding them out than it was to house and maintain them in institutions. The practice therefore grew in popularity—and was used even with delinquent children.

Through study and investigation, especially at Dr. William Healy's Juvenile Psychopathic Institute, created in 1909, child welfare workers and others found that delinquents were not necessarily from the pauper classes, as was widely assumed, but from a cross-section of the population. The causes of delinquency, which could be determined only through careful, individual study, were many, including physical defects. The most prevalent cause was lack of parental discipline, usually due to the loss of one or both parents.[6] Home care, therefore, rather than confinement in a penal or correctional institution, was the best hope of preventing repetition of the delinquent act.

That the long controversy over the best method of caring for children in need was being resolved by the turn of the century was epitomized by a statement of approved methods and principles issued by the National Conference of Charities and Correction's Committee on Children. Read before the 1899 National Conference by Chairman Thomas M. Mulry, head of the Catholic Society of St. Vincent de Paul, long the leading advocate of institutional care for dependent children, the report urged the preservation of the home wherever and whenever possible. Where that was impossible, the committee recommended placing- or boarding-out of children—after careful investigation and with constant supervision. The nineteenth century, which began with attempts to get needy children into institutions, ended with attempts to get them out of those institutions.

Efforts to remove or keep children from entering almshouses

[6]Many studies of the problem came out of the careful research conducted at the Juvenile Psychopathic Institute, which was located at Hull-House in Chicago. Among the most important of these was Dr. Healy's *The Individual Delinquent* (1915), which rejected the theory that delinquency and crime were caused primarily by heredity and instead emphasized environmental or social factors in a multicausal approach. Thus sociologist Charles H. Cooley could say with confidence, "The criminal [or delinquent] class is largely the result of society's bad workmanship upon fairly good material."

and then other institutions aided the development, late in the nineteenth and early in the twentieth century, of houses of correction, juvenile courts, and probation systems. Earlier, there were few institutions in the United States for the reformation of juvenile delinquents. Children convicted of crimes were either sent to almshouses or, more often, committed along with adult offenders to prisons, most of which were in wretched condition—antiquated, unsanitary, and regulated by brutal officials who cared little and knew less about penal matters. Alexis de Tocqueville, the French prison reformer who visited the United States in the 1830s, was aghast at the "vile nature of American jails"—"schools of crime," as he called them.

Juvenile reformation in America during the nineteenth century can be summarized in a single sentence: Youthful offenders were removed from harsh surroundings and from association with adult criminals and placed in special institutions or private homes where they were treated from an educational and constructive rather than a punitive point of view—as changing concepts of childhood and childrearing dictated.

This did not happen overnight. Early special institutions for juvenile delinquents, usually state reform schools, were, like jails, pretty gruesome. According to Dr. Hastings Hart, an authority on the subject, most "of the juvenile reformatories were, at first, in reality juvenile prisons, with prison bars, prison cells, prison garb, prison labor, prison punishment, and prison discipline." Based on the prevailing nineteenth-century belief that the roots of delinquency were in the individual, who freely chose to act in a deviant manner and thus needed to be "reformed," severe punishment was considered not only a legitimate part of such institutions but also their very function.

As time passed, it was realized that punishment did not act as a deterrent to crime. Nor did it return the offender to society in any way improved as a result of his or her sentence. On the contrary, he or she usually returned to the community bitter and vengeful. Moreover, because a large proportion of those who left such institutions usually wound up back inside them within a rather short period of time, such treatment was not only unwise but uneconomic. An awareness of these factors eventually led to a number of changes, including the development of houses of correction (which emphasized education and training), the use of indeterminate sentences, the introduction of parole and probation, the creation of detention homes and diagnostic centers; and, in more recent years, such methods of treatment as group therapy, counseling, and the like. In short, correctional institutions began to make serious efforts to rehabilitate rather than to punish offenders.

Some of these new ideas were first put into effect with the opening of the New York State Reformatory at Elmira, in 1876. Under the dynamic leadership of Zebulon R. Brockway, a noted corrections reformer and founder of the newly created National Prison Association, Elmira was the first correctional home for young men to adopt the indeterminate sentence. There, free from association with hardened criminals, the inmates helped to determine the length of stay (up to an imposed maximum) through their performance and progress as determined by a professional authority.[7]

When released, they were usually sent to places of employment which had been arranged for them, and for which they had been trained. Also, they remained on parole until their discharge became final; thus, their reentrance into community life was supervised and controlled. After ten years of trial, it was found that four of every five Elmira "graduates" showed complete reformation—or at least did not return to a penal institution. The merits of the system were so obvious that by 1898 eight other states—Massachusetts, Pennsylvania, Ohio, Michigan, Illinois, Minnesota, South Dakota, and Indiana—had established similar juvenile homes.

With the growth of special institutions for youthful offenders, the breaking down of the prison atmosphere, and the growing emphasis on the environmental causes of crime, juvenile delinquency came to be recognized as a social problem that required improved legal as well as correctional machinery. There arose

[7]Similar institutions for girls developed less rapidly. Here again, New York led the way when it opened the Western House of Refuge at Albion, in 1893. One might argue, however (as has Harold Helfman in his article cited in the bibliography), that the first female reformatory in America was established in August 1861, when, under the leadership of Zebulon Brockway, the newly created Detroit House of Correction opened a separate women's wing.

then, especially among enlightened judges, lawyers, public-spirited citizens, and child welfare workers, a demand that children no longer be subjected to the Common Law definition of criminal behavior and the harsh procedure of the criminal court—that they be tried differently and apart from adult offenders.

Massachusetts had pioneered in special court procedures for juveniles charged with crimes; in the 1870s it enacted legislation requiring separate hearings for children's cases—although the same judges and courtrooms were used. The world's first full-fledged juvenile court, however, was created in Cook County (Chicago) in July 1899, after an eight-year battle led by the Illinois State Conference of Charities, the Chicago Bar Association, and the city's settlement house residents.[8] Located across the street from Hull-House, the court was presided over superbly during its early, precarious years by Judge Merritt Pinckney. The famous children's court in Denver, Colorado, that Judge Ben B. Lindsey served so well for so long was created a year later.

The object of the juvenile court was to avoid the stigma of crime by creating a new mechanism for dealing with child offenders. Criminal procedure was abolished and replaced by nonadversary or chancery court proceedings, a legal device that went back to medieval England and that was based on the theory that a youngster who commits an illegal act should be considered someone whose social development has been so faulty that the state is warranted in intervening as an authority in order to bring to bear such corrective influences as will compensate for his or her previous upbringing. Instead of a courtroom trial, hearings were held in an informal atmosphere in the judge's private chamber; no lawyers, oaths, or robes were used.

The role of the judge was supposed to be that of a parental guide. As the statute creating the first such court worded it:

---

[8]According to one student of the subject, Joseph Hawes, the measure that created that court—An Act to Regulate the Treatment and Control of Dependent, Neglected, and Delinquent Children—was "the single most influential law concerning juvenile delinquents in the United States," one that "marked the end of the essentially penal official approach to juvenile delinquency and the beginning of the flexible 'scientific' and preventive approach."

The care, custody, and discipline of the children brought before the court shall approximate as nearly as possible that which they should receive from their parents, and ... as far as practicable they shall be treated not as criminals but as children in need of aid, encouragement, and guidance.

Reeducation rather than retribution was the aim of the court; it was not to punish offenders but to enlighten and save them. "The State," the long-remembered Judge Ben Lindsey declared, "has come to help and not to hurt, to uplift and not to downgrade, to love and not hate." In effect, the court was the child's defender, and its petition was changed from "The People Against ..." to "The People in the Interest of. ... "[9]

Despite the emphasis on individual treatment and reformation (or perhaps because of it), considerable concern arose over the years regarding the question of due process in such courts. All too often, children—especially if members of a minority group—were apprehended by police, detained, questioned, given a closed hearing by a juvenile court judge, and then either placed on probation or committed to an institution without regard for their rights or those of their parents.[10] The pretext of reformation, or "the good of the child," sometimes, perhaps even often, proved to be a substitute for justice. In fact, there was some question as to whether or not the legal safeguards embodied in the U.S.

[9]Just as the stern parent of the Victorian era was being superseded by the more lenient parent of the so-called Progressive era, the harsh court of the nineteenth century was being replaced by the more humane court of the twentieth. Moreover, the absolute authority of the father, which came from the Common Law, was being restricted at this time by legislation and judicial action as the state, charged with the obligation of protecting its future citizens, assumed a degree of parental authority—*parens patriae*. Reformers also worked for, and generally secured at this time, contributory negligence laws giving the court jurisdiction over parents who did not provide proper guidance for their children.

[10]The fact that black youngsters and members of other minority groups as well received harsher treatment than white children in such courts has been well documented. See, for example, T. N. Ferdinand and E. G. Luchterhand, "Inner-City Youth, the Police, the Juvenile Court, and Justice," *Social Problems* 17 (Spring 1970): 510–27, and Sidney Axelrod, "Negro and White Institutionalized Delinquents," *American Journal of Sociology* 57 (May 1952): 569–74. Perhaps it should be added that along with the attack on the children's court came an attack on the indeterminate sentence, for the same reason—it allowed for too much administrative discretion.

Constitution were as applicable to the child as to the adult offender.

In May 1967, the U.S. Supreme Court settled the question, at least with regard to procedural safeguards in cases that might result in commitment to an institution. In the momentous *Gault* decision, it asserted that "neither the Fourteenth Amendment nor the Bill of Rights is for adults alone" and then ruled that timely notice of all charges against a juvenile must be given; that the child has the right to be represented by legal counsel (which must be appointed by the court if the family cannot afford one); that the child has the right to confront and cross-examine complainants; and that the child has protection against self-incrimination.[11]

Pointing to these and other developments at the time, some scholars, most notably Anthony Platt, have argued that the "child savers" of the late nineteenth and early twentieth centuries, especially those middle class women who worked to create the juvenile court, were influenced less by concern with child welfare than by other motives, principally a desire to control the children of the "dangerous classes" and to carve out more meaningful lives (including perhaps professional careers) for themselves.

A useful corrective, or at least counterpoint, to the Platt view and to the entire "social control" thesis in this regard is Ellen Ryerson's *The Best-Laid Plans: America's Juvenile Court Experiment,* published in 1978. Ryerson argues, and I think demonstrates, that the children's court (and the entire child welfare movement) represented a sincere, humane effort by dedicated, well-meaning reformers to establish an agency that would make the law and the judicial system constructive influences in the lives of young offenders. In other words, the children's court was a product of the progressive era, an institution that its proponents really believed would benefit both the individuals involved and all of society. Although they may have been wrong or in the long run their efforts failed, these reformers were altruists attempting to do good; the origin of the court and the motivations of its originators should not be judged by those later failures.

---

[11]See *In re Gault,* 387 U.S. 1 (1967). Two years later, in *Tinker v. Des Moines Independent Community School District,* 393 U.S. 503 (1969), the Court opened the door to even wider rights for children by declaring them "persons" under the Constitution.

In any event, if in the past the court sometimes ignored the rights of children (and their families), it no longer could do so after the *Gault* decision, at least in theory. As it stood, the juvenile court was a forum for children in difficulty and a service different in character from other courts (i.e., more flexible and service oriented), but still one in which due process of law provided fully as much protection to the parties involved as was provided to litigants in other courts.

Along with the aim of treatment and education rather than punishment and retribution, the principle of prevention was implicit in the juvenile court movement. One of it major objectives was to check adult crimes by giving a constructive direction to the life of the potential criminal while he or she was still in the formative stage of life. In other words, proponents of the court realized that measures for the protection of individual children were measures for the protection of society. It was no accident, therefore, that the movement occurred during the time of the settlement house movement and the period of preventive social work, when the work of G. Stanley Hall and other child study experts was becoming increasingly popular.

Since at the base of the juvenile court was the theory that the individual child and his or her needs should be considered rather than the offense and its legal penalty, the resort to such legal procedure was naturally part of, and gave added impetus to, the child home care movement. In theory at least, whenever possible children's court judges would hand down suspended sentences and permit offenders to remain in their own homes, where they would receive treatment. Therefore, a necessary adjunct of the court—in fact, its single most important component—was an effective system of probation, the instrument through which the court would apply that treatment. Probation represented, in the words of one children's court judge, "the keystone which supports the arch" of the system and, according to another, "the cord upon which all the pearls are strung.... Without it," he added, "the court could not exist."

Probation was not considered by its advocates to be an act of clemency by the judge. Rather, it was a positive measure for individual and community welfare. It was argued that since individuals were largely products of their environment—for the most part, in other words, they were not free moral agents who willingly chose to break the law, as had been believed previously—when someone was charged with committing an illegal act it was not merely a personal, but also a community, matter.[12] The misdeed was probably brought on by many influences and factors, both personal and social, that had exercised an unfavorable influence upon the offender. The juvenile delinquent (or, for that matter, the adult criminal as well) was someone who needed help in adjusting to community life.

To provide this help, it was deemed best not to remove the child from his or her home and place him (or her) in the artificial environment of an insitution. On the contrary, inquiring into the home conditions and helping the offender adapt to them, or changing those conditions to meet his or her needs, was essential. Unfortunately, the more traditional method of dealing with erring children—locking them up—failed to do this; it took into consideration only the individual element in wrongdoing. Probation took into account both the individual and the surroundings, regarded the offense as the product of both, and sought to influence both so that in the future they would work for the good rather than the harm of the child.

This assumed that probation would not be haphazardly administered. Unfortunately, for a long time it was. The Chicago situation was typical. There the court was authorized to appoint "one or more discreet persons of good character" to serve as probation officers. No money, however, was authorized for the position. Early proponents of the court feared that the cost involved in paying probation officers might defeat the legislation and thus prevent the courts themselves from coming into existence. Too, it was feared that well-paying probation posts might become political plums for those responsible for the appointments—usually the justices.

As a result, at the outset probation was administered on a vol-

---

[12]Regarding the "social" causes of crime and delinquency, Edward T. Devine wrote: "One may understand crime and the criminal precisely in the degree in which [one] . . . comprehends that it is not the individual standing there at whom stones are to be thrown, but literally the community itself . . . which is responsible for this thing we call crime."

unteer basis or paid for, sparingly, by private sources such as the Woman's Club in Chicago. Most officers were untrained citizens, court clerks, or, paradoxically, policemen. However, the precedent at least had been set, and over the years probation made headway. Eventually, especially after the creation of state probation commissions in most places, beginning in New York in 1907, probation was placed under civil service, so that appointments were made on the basis of personality, training, and experience. As pay levels increased and professional standards gained ground, more competent people were attracted to the field.

Meanwhile, the promise of the *Gault* decision regarding the rights of children in difficulty with the law (and the rights of their parents as well) was not fulfilled. Priority remained with "rehabilitation" rather than with justice, despite the paucity of resources, which undermined the quality of the facilities and the services that were supposed to rehabilitate the troubled children.

In addition, juvenile delinquency increased significantly, especially in the years following World War II. As a result, whereas earlier child welfare enthusiasts and psychiatric social workers had dominated the field, more and more sociologists turned their attention to it. Beginning with Robert Park and Clifford Shaw at the University of Chicago in the 1930s, who were particularly interested in neighborhood disorganization and street gangs, a succession of scholars—Sheldon and Eleanor Glueck, William F. Whyte, Albert Cohen, Lloyd Ohlin, and Richard Cloward—researched and wrote about juvenile delinquency and its apparent causes. By the 1960s, prevailing opinion among those studying the subject was that delinquency was largely a response to frustration, which in turn was caused by lack of opportunity.[13] The means of prevention, then, lay in opening up legitimate avenues of success for deprived youngsters. Thus was born Mobilization for Youth, a pioneer delinquency control project on New York City's Lower East Side.

Funded initially in 1958 by the National Institute of Mental Health, Mobilization for Youth consisted of employment bureaus, manpower training programs, remedial educational

---

[13]See Richard Cloward and Lloyd Ohlin, *Delinquency and Opportunity: A Theory of Delinquent Gangs* (Gencoe, Ill.: Free Press, 1960).

work, anti-discrimination activities, and neighborhood service centers, designed to provide greater opportunities for young people in slum neighborhoods. The program's results were mixed, at best.

At the same time, however, benevolent action was becoming increasingly suspect: a growing number of people were beginning to question the consequences of social welfare policy, whatever the motivations of the reformers, vis-à-vis children and others. They even went so far as to suggest that the juvenile justice system might be more harmful than helpful both to the offender and to society, even under the best of circumstances, something Sheldon and Eleanor Glueck had hinted at back in the 1930s, when they published *One Thousand Delinquents: Their Treatment by Court and Clinic.* Summarizing the available research for a presidential commission in 1967, sociologist Edwin Lemert pointed out that youth who come under court jurisdiction commit more, rather than fewer, crimes later in life: "The conclusion that the court processing rather than the [youth's] behavior in some way helps to fix and perpetuate delinquency in many cases is hard to escape," Lemert testified. No wonder, then, that some lawyers, civil libertarians, scholars, and even a handful of social workers placed "children's rights" as the next item on the social policy agenda. Children, they argued, need fewer benefactors, not more; they need fewer child welfare services and facilities, not more; they need, above all, the chance to make decisions about their lives free from parental and state interference.[14] Whether or not society will move in that direction remains to be seen.

To go back to the earlier period, however, the placing- and boarding-out of dependent, neglected, and deliquent children, and the establishment of true houses of correction, juvenile courts, and probation systems, were only part of the large nineteenth- and twentieth-century concern for the problems of childhood. The growing emphasis on the prevention of need and the desire to conserve human as well as physical resources make it increas-

---

[14]Ironically, at the same time the rising crime rate, the urban disorders of 1964–67, and the various disruptive demonstrations made "law and order" a popular slogan—and a new emphasis on punishment and imprisonment followed, at least among many working class Americans.

ingly apparent that every effort to achieve what was termed social and industrial justice (indeed, all movements for social betterment) was directly related to child welfare. What was for the welfare of the community was for the welfare of the family and for the welfare of its children—and vice versa.

Thus, the fight for the regulation of child labor was part of the child welfare movement. At one reformer put it: "Effective and adequate child-caring work must include the enforcement of proper child labor laws; they are an essential part of the child caring system." So, too, were the movements for widows' pensions and numerous other reforms, including enactment of the Social Security Act. Clearly, by the early twentieth century there was increasing awareness of the needs of all children and of the necessity to provide a range of services that would afford them the opportunity for full development. Among the most urgent of those services was the need to curtail illness and death—not only of children, but of their parents as well—resulting from preventable disease.

Bibliography

ABBOTT, GRACE, ed. *The Child and the State,* 2 Vols. Chicago: University of Chicago Press, 1938.

BEALES, ROSS W. "In Search of the Historical Child: Miniature Adulthood and Youth in Colonial New England," *American Quarterly* 27 (October 1975): 379–98.

BEARD, BELLE B. *Juvenile Probation.* New York: American, 1934.

BLOCK, HERBERT A., AND FRANK T. FLYNN. *Delinquency: The Juvenile Offender in America Today.* New York: Random House, 1956.

BRACE, CHARLES LORING. *The Dangerous Classes of New York and Twenty Years Work Among Them.* New York: Wynkoop and Hallenbeck, 1872.

BRECKINRIDGE, SOPHONISBA, AND EDITH ABBOTT. *The Delinquent Child and the Home.* New York: Survey Associates, 1912.

BREMNER, ROBERT H., ed. *Children and Youth in America,* 3 Vols. Cambridge, Mass.: Harvard University Press, 1970–74.

BROWN, JAMES. "Child Welfare Classics," *Social Service Review* 34 (June 1960): 195–202.

BRYANT, KEITH. "The Juvenile Court Movement," *Social Science Quarterly* 49 (September 1968): 368–76.

BUCKINGHAM, CLYDE. "Early American Orphanages: Ebenezar and Bethesda," *Social Forces* 26 (March 1948): 311–22.

CABLE, MARY. *The Little Darlings: A History of Child Rearing in America.* New York: Scribner's, 1975.

CAMPBELL, D. ANN. "Judge Ben Lindsey and the Juvenile Court Movement, 1901–04," *Arizona and the West* 18 (Spring 1976): 5–20.

CAVALLO, DOMINICK. *Muscles and Morals: Organized Playgrounds and Urban Reform, 1880–1920.* Philadelphia: University of Pennsylvania Press, 1981.

CLEMENT, PRISCILLA F. "Families and Foster Care: Philadelphia in the Late Nineteenth Century," *Social Service Review* 53 (September 1979): 406–20.

CLOWARD, RICHARD, AND LLOYD OHLIN. *Delinquency and Opportunity: A Theory of Delinquent Gangs.* Glencoe, Ill.: Free Press, 1960.

CORDSACO, FRANCESCO. "Charles Loring Brace and the Dangerous Classes: Historical Analogues of the Urban Black Poor," *Journal of Human Relations* 20 (Third Quarter 1972): 379–86.

Crusade for Children, The. New York: Children's Aid Society, 1928.

DEUTSCH, ALBERT. *Our Rejected Children.* Boston: Little, Brown, 1950.

EARLE, ALICE M. *Child Life in Colonial Days.* New York: Macmillan, 1927.

FLEXNER, BERNARD, AND ROGER BALDWIN. *Juvenile Courts and Probation.* New York: Century, 1941.

FLYNN, FRANK T. "Judge Merritt W. Pinckney and the Early Days of the Juvenile Court in Chicago," *Social Service Review* 28 (March 1954): 20–30.

FOLKS, HOMER. *The Care of Destitute, Neglected and Delinquent Children.* New York: Macmillan, 1902.

FOX, SANFORD J. "Juvenile Justice Reform: An Historical Perspective," *Stanford Law Review* 22 (1970): 1187–1239.

FREY, CECILE P. "The House of Refuge for Colored Children," *Journal of Negro History* 66 (Spring 1981): 10–25.

GLUECK, SHELDON AND ELEANOR. *One Thousand Delinquents: Their*

Treatment by Court and Clinic. Cambridge, Mass.: Harvard University Press, 1934.

HALL, G. STANLEY. *Adolescence: Its Psychology and its Relation to Physiology, Anthropology, Sociology, Sex, Crime, Religion, and Education.* New York: Appleton, 1904.

HART, HASTINGS. *Cottage and Congregate Institutions for Children.* New York: Charities Publication Committee, 1910.

————. *Juvenile Court Laws in the United States.* New York: Charities Publication Committee, 1910.

————. *Preventive Treatment for Neglected Children.* New York: Charities Publication Committee, 1910.

HAWES, JOSEPH. *Children in Urban Society: Juvenile Delinquency in Nineteenth Century America.* New York: Oxford University Press, 1971.

HEALY, WILLIAM. *The Individual Delinquent.* Boston: Little, Brown, 1915.

HELFMAN, HAROLD M. "The Detroit House of Correction, 1861–74," *Michigan History* 34 (December 1950): 299–308.

JACOBY, GEORGE P. *Catholic Child Care in Nineteenth Century New York.* Washington, D.C.: Catholic University, 1941.

JAMES, ARTHUR W. "Foster Care in Virginia, 1676–1796," *Public Welfare* 8 (March 1950): 60–64.

JONES, MARSHALL. "Foster-Home Care of Delinquent Children," *Social Service Review* 10 (September 1936): 450–63.

KADUSHIN, ALFRED. *Child Welfare Services.* New York: Crowell Collier and Macmillan, 1967.

KAHN, ALFRED. *A Court for Children.* New York: Columbia University Press, 1953.

————. *Planning Community Services for Children in Trouble.* New York: Columbia University Press, 1963.

LANGSAM, MIRIAM. *Children West: A History of the Placing-Out of the New York Children's Aid Society.* Madison, Wis.: State Historical Society, 1964.

LARNED, J. N. *The Life and Work of William P. Letchworth.* Boston: Houghton Mifflin, 1912.

LARSEN, CHARLES. *The Good Fight: The Life and Times of Ben B. Lindsey.* Chicago: Quadrangle Books. 1972.

LINDSEY, BENJAMIN B. *The Dangerous Life.* New York: Liveright, 1931.

————. *Twenty-Five Years of the Juvenile and Family Court of Denver.* Denver: Ben B. Lindsey, 1925.

LOU, H. H. *Juvenile Courts in the United States.* Chapel Hill, N.C.: University of North Carolina Press, 1927.

LUNDBERG, EMMA. *Unto the Least of These: Social Services for Children.* New York: Appleton-Century, 1947.

MANGOLD, GEORGE. *Problems of Child Welfare.* New York: Macmillan, 1936.

MERGEN, BERNARD. "The Discovery of Children's Play," *American Quarterly* 27 (October 1975): 399–420.

NEIGHER, ALAN. "The *Gault* Decision: Due Process and the Juvenile Court," *Federal Probation* 31 (December 1967): 8–18.

PICKETT, ROBERT S. *House of Refuge: Origins of Juvenile Reform in New York State, 1815–1857.* Syracuse, N.Y.: Syracuse University Press, 1969.

PLATT, ANTHONY M. *The Child Savers: The Invention of Delinquency.* Chicago: University of Chicago Press, 1969.

————. "The Rise of the Child-Saving Movement," *Annals of the American Academy of Political and Social Science* 381 (January 1969): 21–38.

ROMANOFSKY, PETER. "Infant Mortality, Dr. Henry Dwight Chapin, and the Speedwell Society," *Journal of the Medical Society of New Jersey* 73 (January 1976): 33–38.

————. "Saving the Lives of the City's Foundlings: The Joint Committee and New York City Child Care Methods, 1860–1907," *New-York Historical Society Quarterly* 61 (January-April 1977): 49–68.

————. "'To Save . . . Their Souls': The Care of Dependent Children in New York City, 1900–1905," *Jewish Social Studies* 36 (July-October 1974): 253–61.

ROSENHEIM, MARGARET K., ed. *Justice for the Child.* New York: Free Press, 1962.

————, ed. *Pursuing Justice for the Child.* Chicago: University of Chicago Press, 1976.

ROSS, DOROTHY. *G. Stanley Hall: The Psychologist as Prophet.* Chicago: University of Chicago Press, 1972.

RUBIN, SOL. "Trends in Juvenile Court Philosophy," *Social Service Review* 7 (April 1962): 53–57.

RUBIN, TED, AND JACK SMITH. *The Future of the Juvenile Court.* Washington, D.C.: Government Printing Office, 1968.

RYERSON, ELLEN. *The Best-Laid Plans: America's Juvenile Court Experiment*. New York: Hill and Wang, 1978.

SCHLOSSMAN, STEVEN L. *Love and the American Delinquent: The Theory and Practice of "Progressive" Juvenile Justice, 1825–1920*. Chicago: University of Chicago Press, 1977.

SCOTT, REBECCA. "The Battle over the Child: Child Apprenticeship and the Freedmen's Bureau in North Carolina," *Prologue* 10 (Summer 1978): 101–113.

SILVERMAN, MARVIN. "Children's Rights and Social Work," *Social Service Review* 51 (March 1957): 171–78.

SLATER, PETER G. "Ben Lindsey and the Denver Juvenile Court," *American Quarterly* 20 (Summer 1968): 211–23.

SPARGO, JOHN. *The Bitter Cry of the Children*. New York: Macmillan, 1906.

SPEIZMAN, MILTON D. "Child Care: A Mirror of Human History," *Children and Youth Services Review* 3 (1981): 213–32.

TEETERS, NEGLEY K. "The Early Days of the Philadelphia House of Refuge," *Pennsylvania History* 27 (April 1960): 165–87.

THURSTON, HENRY W. *The Dependent Child*. New York: Columbia University Press, 1930.

TRATTNER, WALTER I. *Homer Folks: Pioneer in Social Welfare*. New York: Columbia University Press, 1968.

———. *Crusade for the Children: A History of the National Child Labor Committee and Child Labor Reform in America*. Chicago: Quadrangle Books, 1970.

VAN WATERS, MIRIAM. *Parents on Probation*. New York: New Republic, 1927.

WHITTAKER, JAMES K. "Colonial Child Care Institutions: Our Heritage of Care," *Child Welfare* 50 (July 1971): 396–400.

———. "Nineteenth Century Innovations in Delinquency Institutions," *Child Care Quarterly* 2 (Spring 1973): 14–24.

WINSTON, ELLEN. "The Shape of Things to Come in Child Welfare—The Broad Outline," *Child Welfare* 45 (January 1966): 5–11.

ZIETZ, DOROTHY. *Child Welfare: Principles and Methods*. New York: Wiley, 1959.

Chapter 7

The Public Health Movement

BY THE MIDDLE of the nineteenth century, American cities were disorderly, filthy, foul-smelling, disease-ridden places. Narrow, unpaved streets became transformed into quagmires when it rained. Rickety tenements, swarming with unwashed humanity, leaned upon one another for support. Inadequate drainage systems failed to carry away sewage. Pigs roamed streets that were cluttered with manure, years of accumulated garbage, and other litter. Outside privies bordered almost every thoroughfare. Slaughterhouses and fertilizing plants contaminated the air with an indescribable stench. Ancient plagues like smallpox, cholera, and typhus threw the population into a state of terror from time to time while less sensational but equally deadly killers like tuberculosis, diphtheria, and scarlet fever were ceaselessly at work. Thus, at a time when the general death rate for the nation was around twenty per thousand inhabitants, that of New York and other large cities averaged over twenty-five. In the poorer quarters of most large cities, however, the rate often ranged between thirty and forty per thousand, and was as high as 135 per thousand for children under five years of age. A horrified humanity was forced by such conditions to recognize not only that a sanitary problem existed, but also that the very life of the city was at stake, for if it was to survive the city had to be made a safe and healthy place in which to live. Beginning around the middle of the nineteenth century, then, the nation's first major sanitation program began.

Public health activities were not new.[1] Laws and regulations to

[1]According to a widely used definition, public health is "the science and art of preventing disease, prolonging life, and promoting physical health and efficiency

135

prevent the spread of disease go far back in history. Whenever and wherever people gathered together in communities, they felt a need for some kind of regulation to protect the public health; thus, the Massachusetts Poor Law of 1692 gave local authorities the power to remove and isolate infected members of the community. The organized public health movement, however, which included both the improved treatment and the prevention of disease, did not begin in the United States until around the middle of the nineteenth century, nor did it amount to much until after the 1870s, when Drs. Louis Pasteur and Robert Koch discovered the true etiology of disease—germs.

Earlier in the nineteenth century there were two widely held views of disease. The first, held by most people, including many physicians and public health enthusiasts, was that disease, like poverty and disaster (earthquakes, floods, and so on), was a providential matter, usually the visitation of a just God upon a frail and erring person (or people), a direct consequence of undesirable personal or social behavior. The second, held by many others, was that disease resulted from environmental factors, namely dirt and filth—or, in some cases, the odors given off by Irish ditch diggers. If disease was the result of God's wrath, the inescapable consequence of sin, the answer was improved or better behavior. If it resulted chiefly from dirt, filth, and foul air, then by changing the environment through amending or eliminating those factors, one could improve the public health. By engaging in a vast moral crusade and by improving the water supply, building sewers, initiating better street cleaning and garbage removal, draining bogs and swamps, and planting trees (which served as "ventilators" that absorbed pernicious odors in the air and gave off oxygen instead), most problems of public health would be solved. It was on the basis of these beliefs—especially the latter—that Americans began their first crusade for good health.

As in so many other areas, the influence of England was important. As a consequence of her advanced industrialization,

---

through organized community efforts for the sanitation of the environment, the control of community infections, the education of individual principles of personal hygiene, the organization of medical and nursing services for the early diagnosis and treatment of diseases. . . ."

England's sooty cities in the 1830s and 1840s were even more squalid than America's, giving rise there to busy social reformers who began to wage war against disease. The most important among them was Edwin Chadwick, author of the Royal Poor Law Commission *Report of 1834,* who, shortly thereafter, began to see that ill health—the result of deplorable environmental conditions, not moral ones—was the major cause of poverty and dependency.

Chadwick spent several years studying urban conditions and gathering material from all over Britain. It all led to the same conclusion: Surrounded by foul miasmas, deprived of fresh air and water, living in the midst of overflowing cesspools and privies, even those people who tried could scarcely abide by the rules of cleanliness and health. The more Chadwick studied the situation, the more he became convinced of the need for far-reaching sanitary reform.

In 1842, he published his famous report on *The Sanitary Condition of the Labouring Population of Great Britain*. Probably no single document so profoundly affected the development of public health as did this grim, detailed account of the squalid filth and its consequences in England's slums. This remarkable study not only awakened the public conscience to the sanitation needs of a growing urban population but also led to enactment of the Public Health Act of 1848, which marked the legal birth of modern sanitation reform and set the pattern, both in Europe and in America, for the war against disease.

Passage of the English Public Health Act of 1848, which created the world's first modern board of health, encouraged concerned American sanitarians to press for similar reforms on this side of the Atlantic. By that time, the unsanitary and wretched living conditions prevalent in America's older communities not only duplicated, but in some cases surpassed, those in England; indeed, the mortality rate in most Atlantic seaboard cities exceeded that of London.

First to be encouraged by the English example was a small group of public-spirited citizens in Massachusetts who, alarmed by the distressing state of the nation's health, persuaded the state legislature to finance a sanitary survey of the Bay State. The resulting report and its recommendations for change (written by

Lemuel Shattuck, a Boston city councilman and public health en-
thusiast, and published in 1850) was the first plan for an integrated health program in the United States.

The Shattuck proposals were short-lived, however, in part
because of medical indifference, but more important, because the
slavery issue preoccupied the public mind. Then, of course, came
the Civil War and its important influence on public health reform.
Not only did the health problems created by large armies give
supporters of sanitation reform a chance to substantiate their
claims,[2] but a growing number of laymen gained some apprecia-
tion of the purposes of sanitation and the benefits to be derived
from the practice of public hygiene.

When the war came to an end, concerned citizens sought to
take advantage of the situation. Thus, when sanitarians, public-
spirited persons, magazine writers, and some physicians voiced
alarm over the distressing state of America's health and urged
hygienic measures for its improvement, some notable advances
were achieved. In 1866, the New York Metropolitan Health Law
was enacted, creating the nation's first real municipal board of
health; other major cities soon followed suit. In 1869, Massachusetts created the first state board of health; again, the example was widely followed. In 1872, the American Public Health
Association was founded. The federal government passed the
National Quarantine Act of 1878, and a year later created the
National Board of Health.

Yet these developments did not produce the results that the
public had been led to expect. First, most of the new municipal
boards of health were not much better than their predecessors—
poor, makeshift, ineffective bodies that either took a do-nothing
attitude or else did as much harm as good. (New York's new
board, it should be said, was better than its predecessor, a body
that prompted Mayor C. Godfrey Gunther in the fall of 1865 to

---

[2]Here was another example of where the British experience affected American
developments, in this case the Crimean War, which had been waged several years
earlier. Many sanitarians, doctors, and concerned citizens had studied the reports
of the British Sanitary Commission, or excerpts from that report which were
printed in American journals, which related the medical history of the campaign,
and they were determined to make good use of the sanitary knowledge purchased
at such sad cost in the Crimea.

reply to a delegation of medical men who pleaded with him to summon it into session in view of an approaching cholera epidemic: "I will not call the Board, for I consider it more dangerous to the city than cholera.")

For the most part, the boards were composed of the mayor and a group of political hacks, sometimes the most crooked and least knowledgeable members of the municipal legislature. Of the seven men on Cincinnati's board, for example, six were saloonkeepers. They convened only when compelled to do so, usually during an emergency; seldom, if ever, did they pay due attention to the conditions responsible for endemic disease.

Another reason for the lack of success in improving the public health at this time was that reform met a great deal of opposition, both from the public in general and from certain interested groups in particular. Such improvements as the construction of municipal drains and sewers, for example, cost a good deal of money, which meant higher taxes. And many people, still not yet aware that public health saves money in the long run, objected.

Moreover, public health reform often meant the destruction of slum dwellings and other profitable private property, so that tenement owners and others objected. And in an age of individualism, of laissez-faire and social Darwinism, these objections carried weight. Then, too, the medical profession often stood in the way of meaningful reforms.

The most important reason for the failure of the early public health program however, was lack of medical knowledge concerning the true cause of disease. As Pasteur, Koch, and others demonstrated, it was germs, not the wrath of God or dirt and filth, that caused disease; bacteria were not the end product of disease, as was widely believed, but rather its causative agent. Specific microorganisms which could be discovered, tracked down, avoided, and destroyed, were responsible for specific diseases. Neither corruption of morals nor putrification and filth (in themselves) could cause epidemics. However clean a city was, it could still be subject to widespread illness. Taste and smell could not be relied upon as judges of purity. Laboratories and microscopes, scientific specialists and their instruments were more important than cleaning the street. When this was understood, discovery of the origin of most of man's most ancient scourges followed rapidly: typhoid, leprosy, and malaria in 1880; tuberculosis in 1882; cholera in 1883; diphtheria, tetanus, and bubonic plague in 1884; dysentery in 1898; and so on.

Although the knowledge that specific illnesses were caused by specific germs allowed health officers quickly to identify disorders, the "germ theory" of disease and preventive medicine remained in a relatively primitive stage until the importance of the personal factor in contagion was discovered; only after the role of the infected individual in spreading disease was understood did sanitation control operate effectively. This came near the close of the nineteenth century with elaboration of the concept of the "human carrier." Disease germs, it was discovered, are parasites that reside in the human body. The major mode of transmission, then, is contact with an infected person. As a result, personal cleanliness, inoculation, serums, antitoxins, antidotes, the segregation of "carriers" of disease, and the enactment of effective hygienic laws replaced environmental sanitation (and exhortations to conscience) as the basis for reform, resulting in what has been described as the "golden age of public health."

During this period (approximately 1890–1910), municipal and state boards of health began to attract better personnel and to set up diagnostic laboratories to apply the new medical discoveries to the prevention and cure of disease. Medical education was improved and research work was better organized. And, equally important, campaigns were initiated to educate the public in the ways of modern hygiene and persuade it to support change.

In other words, preventive medicine was not merely a matter of pathological research and laboratory diagnosis conducted by medical experts. It also contained social instruments, the most important of which was a well organized program of public health education, essential for success, for despite the great medical and scientific advances, the movement needed popular support to succeed. The public had to be made aware of the new discoveries and the advantages of their application, however costly and inconvenient. Here, charity workers (or social workers, as they were beginning to be called) and others made an enormous contribution to the movement for improved health, for prior to 1900 the war against disease was mainly the business of professional sanitarians, health officials, and medical men. Early in the twentieth century, when social workers and others began to understand the relationship between dependence and ill health, they opened a new line of attack on disease—the mobilization of the lay forces of the community for its control.[3]

Although perhaps not immediately realized, social workers especially had a large stake in medical progress; social work and public health had much in common. They were concerned with essentially the same problem—relieving the home of distress that often resulted from death or illness caused by some preventable disease. As one reformer pointed out, "Social workers and health officers met because their work brought them to the same place, namely, the home in which there was both communicable disease and poverty." Or, in Robert Hunter's words, "Poverty and sickness form a vicious partnership." Broadly speaking, then, social work embraced health work; the interests of social workers overlapped those of physicians. It was no accident that medical social work officially began at this time when, in 1905, Dr. Richard C. Cabot placed a social worker, Miss Garnet Pelton, on the staff of the Massachusetts General Hospital in order "to study the conditions under which patients lived and to assist those patient in carrying out the treatment recommended by the medical staff."[4]

In any event, by the turn of the century, convinced that the conditions making for charity work must themselves be eradi-

---

[3]One of the first physicians to advocate "social medicine" was the great German pathologist Rudolph Virchon, who as early as 1848 argued that "medicine is a social science." He developed the basic principles that health is a matter of direct social concern, that social and economic conditions have an important effect on health and disease, and that therefore social as well as medical steps must be taken to promote health and combat disease.

[4]Medical social work is a form of casework, the study and treatment of a sick person in light of the social factors that influence recovery. The function of the medical social worker is to aid the physician in the treatment of the ill. He or she does not treat the disease but the person, trying to discover and interpret the social and economic factors involved in the illness and then to regulate them so that they will favorably influence the outcome of the illness. Since a good deal of medical research depends on surveys involving interviewing techniques, an area in which social workers have considerable expertise, the medical social worker also serves as a member of the doctor's research team. Along with Dr. Cabot, the person most responsible for the early growth and development of medical social work was Miss Ida Cannon, who for many years served as chief of the Social Service Department of Massachusetts General Hospital.

cated, reformers studied the sources of dependency. They discovered that, in most cases, acute need resulted from the breakdown of family life, which in turn was caused by poverty—
poverty rooted not in immorality and personal failure but in social
and economic conditions, especially illness, invalidity, and the
premature death of the family breadwinner. "Even the most cur-
sory examination of the causes of destitution," wrote Homer
Folks, the noted child welfare worker turned public health crusader, "shows that sickness is always one of the leading causes,
and is usually the leading cause of dependency." Or, as another
reformer put it: "The relationship between health and dependency is well known. Illness causes poverty by creating economic
burdens, and social and economic insecurity in turn increase ill
health—a vicious circle which brings self-supporting families to
the dependency level and keeps them there." Focusing upon the
medical rather than the moral roots of poverty and dependency,
social workers began to wage war on injustice through promoting
good health. Sanitation science and social reform went together;
despite becoming a science with professional methods and objectives, public health work remained, in part at least, reformist in
nature.

Tuberculosis was the first disease attacked. The chief cause of
death throughout the world, tuberculosis took its greatest toll of
persons between the ages of fifteen and forty-four. In that age
span, about one-third of all deaths were caused by this one
disease, creating havoc among those in their most productive
years; it had the highest "social mortality" rate of all the contagious diseases. Since its victims either died or needed medical
care precisely at the time their illness deprived them and their
dependents of an income, it caused more suffering and greater
economic loss than any other affliction. It was, according to
Samuel Hopkins Adams, the noted journalist, "The Real Race
Suicide."[5]

Earlier, because members of the same families tended to
become infected, it was assumed that tuberculosis was hereditary
and that therefore not a great deal could be done about it. When it

[5]The situation was far worse for the nation's Negroes than for its white citizens;
in 1900, the annual mortality rate from tuberculosis was three times higher for
blacks than for whites.

was proven to be a communicable disease, the attitude of medical and lay leaders changed. As the members of one early anti-tuberculosis society put it, "To know that it is *not* an inherited disease should bring hope and gladness to thousands of tuberculous parents, and to the children of such parents"—and it did.

Still, controlling the disease was no simple matter, for despite the fact that doctors knew the pathology and etiology of tuberculosis, they could not induce any active or passive immunization to it, nor was there any specific therapy other than a healthy diet, fresh air, and rest, and these were helpful only in incipient cases. These limitations, as well as the high costs of medical treatment and the lack of financial support for patient's dependents, highlighted the need for avoiding exposure to the infection—or acting immediately after contracting it.

The general public was more concerned with therapy than with prevention. Treatment appealed to those most immediately concerned, while preventive measures seemed vague, impractical, or of uncertain value. In any event, since there were only a few hospitals available to care for the tubercular, the prospects for controlling the disease appeared dim.

The first comprehensive analysis of tuberculosis in the United States was made by social workers. Undertaken in 1903, it was carried out by the Committee on the Prevention of Tuberculosis of the Charity Organization Society of New York—an agency that had come a long way since the days of "scientific charity." Under the leadership of secretary Edward T. Devine, the committee investigated the social and other nontechnical aspects of the disease. It set out to broadcast the seriousness, incidence, and symptoms of tuberculosis, and to explain how it could be arrested or prevented. In short, the committee sought to arouse the public; its aim was not the enactment of any legislation.

Similarly, in 1904, the National Association for the Study and Prevention of Tuberculosis was organized by a number of socially minded physicians and laymen in order to intensify and coordinate popular knowledge of the disease in the hope that education would lead to its ultimate control. The National Association's functions were chiefly promotional and advisory; it did not locate cases, provide relief, or found hospitals. Instead, it aided in the formation of other volunteer bodies which it hoped would perform those functions. As a result of these activities, the anti-tuberculosis movement began to expand, affiliated bodies were formed, state and local societies and sanitarium facilities multiplied, and, in state after state, organized campaigns against the dread disease were initiated.

The fight against tuberculosis in New York State provides a case study of similar work elsewhere. Beginning in 1907, the New York State Charities Aid Association (the voluntary organization patterned after the U.S. Sanitary Commission that was founded in the 1870s by Louisa Lee Schuyler) led the movement to curtail the disease.

As a start, the group hired John A. Kingsbury, a young Columbia University graduate student of sociology, as a full-time field agent in charge of antituberculosis work. When he hired several assistants, New York became the first state in America which, in effect, had a field staff engaged in antituberculosis work. Next, the S.C.A.A. created a Committee on the Prevention of Tuberculosis, composed of laymen and physicians noted for their public health work. The S.C.A.A. then began its work—a statewide educational campaign emphasizing the prevention of tuberculosis.

To be sure, a program of public enlightenment had to rest upon complete and accurate information. Accordingly, Kingsbury and his assistants went from city to city probing the prevalence of the disease and the measures, if any, in operation for the relief of the ill and the protection of those not yet infected. These facts served as the basis of the committee's educational efforts, which were aimed at securing in each locality of the state the most effective means of prevention, including, among other things, free bacteriological examination of sputum, free dispensaries and visiting nurse services, and early registration of cases.

The campaign began in Utica, New York, and from there it was carried to most other large cities throughout the state. An exhibit comprising photographs, statistical tables, charts, and slides showing comparative death rates, symptoms of the disease, unsanitary dwellings, and preventive measures was carried about. The committee also distributed thousands of leaflets and pamphlets, sponsored lectures, and held meetings for doctors, nurses, teachers, and concerned citizens. Also in attendance were such dignitaries as Governor Charles E. Hughes, Joseph H. Choate,

S.C.A.A. board member and Ambassador to Great Britain, Dr. William H. Welch, "dean" of the nation's medical profession, state legislators, and mayors of surrounding communities. The campaign was also endorsed by President Theodore Roosevelt, whose supporting message was read at each of the gatherings, giving a tremendous impetus to the antituberculosis work.

The reformers were committed to the proposition that saving and prolonging lives was socially desirable—the antithesis of the view held by social Darwinists. They did not repudiate the evolutionary theory, they merely reinterpreted it in a way that made it useful to them. They argued that they were not simply allowing the unfit to exist, but were reviving them and restoring their fitness to serve. They were substituting "rational selection" for natural selection.

They also believed that good health was attainable and that a healthy populace would lead to a sounder society, a more just and humane social order. They sought to utilize the new scientific knowledge and the increasing store of defensive and preventive medicine to battle disease, especially tuberculosis, by making the public aware of its dangers in the hope that people would begin to take the necessary steps to avoid the infection. In a sense, they were propagandists, or medical muckrakers, in their efforts to overcome public ignorance or apathy, an obvious barrier in the way of improved public health.

Thanks to this educational campaign, within a year six tuberculosis dispensaries were opened in New York State, visiting nurse services for consumptives were provided in six cities, and two large hospitals were being built.

Despite this progress, public health reformers knew that statistics and information alone would not solve the problem. It became increasingly evident that however widely disseminated, knowledge alone would not prevent the spread of tuberculosis; contacts within the family were so intimate and prolonged that, even with an awareness of communicability, infection spread to an alarming degree.

Another factor that greatly retarded control of tuberculosis was an unwillingness by the public and the medical profession to report cases. In many communities, tuberculosis was regarded as a disgrace and a public menace; to avoid the stigma attached to it, victims frequently went unattended. To protect the sensibilities of those patients who did seek medical help, physicians often reported cases of tuberculosis as bronchitis or pneumonia. In fact, so untrustworthy were physicians' death reports for tuberculosis (and other communicable diseases), that Chicago's Board of Health began to look to the city's undertakers for information on the causes of death; and it was on the morticians' rather than the physicians' reports that the health authorities relied.

Many doctors also believed that because the disease was so contagious many of its victims might commit suicide if they knew they had it in order to prevent other members of their family from becoming infected. Thus, they had another reason for refusing to report cases. Some physicians justified their reticence on other grounds: "We aren't paid for reporting cases," one doctor admitted bluntly, "why should we be required to work for nothing?"

Yet efficient public health work depended above all upon prompt discovery and registration, and then segregation, of all carriers of the disease. So the next battle in the campaign was to obtain legislation that would bring this about. In 1908, the New York State reformers succeeded in getting a statute through the legislature providing for the mandatory reporting of tuberculosis by physicians, with prosecution for willful violation. It also made local health boards responsible for home supervision of reported cases, free sputum analysis, and the disinfection and renovation of apartments occupied or vacated by consumptives.

About a year later, an equally important measure was enacted—the County Tuberculosis Hospital Law. This statute resulted from an International Congress on Tuberculosis which met in Washington, D.C., in 1908. Attended by leading figures in this country as well as by notable foreign delegates, the congress produced several significant papers which emphasized the futility of home treatment. Most important was a paper read by Dr. Arthur Newsholme, Chief Medical Officer of England's Local Government Board and an authority on vital statistics.

Newsholme demonstrated that the tuberculosis death rate declined directly in proportion to the adequacy of hospital or institutional care. Since the carrier was necessarily a radiating center of infection, treatment of the infected and protection for the uninfected were related; proper hospital care of the sick was the best protection from contagion for those who were well. Many reformers left the congress convinced that, both on humanitarian grounds and in the interest of public safety, no substitute could be found for institutional care.

Like all other states, New York had an appalling lack of proper accommodations for its victims of the "white plague." Most of the afflicted were either in general wards of hospitals (where they spread the disease to other patients), in almshouses, or in their miserable slum flats. In the words of A. S. Knopf, a renowned authority on the subject, "the majority of America's tubercular are going to die, not because they are incurable, but because there is no place to cure them." One investigator estimated that "no city in the whole country has public institutions available for consumptives which would accommodate one in twenty of its citizens actually perishing for the lack of the simplest treatment," and "no state has institutions which could house one in fifty of its tuberculosis victims."

Public health workers realized that it was too costly for private sources to build and maintain the broad network of badly needed hospitals. In any event, it was a public matter; for an individual or a needy family to bear the financial burden of the treatment for tuberculosis or any other deadly disease was, in their minds, the height of social injustice. Moreover, such hospitals would be preventive as well as curative forces in the community; clearly, they were a public responsibility. Thus, in New York, and later in other states, public health crusaders met with legislators to discuss the need for such hospitals.

While humanitarian interests were uppermost in their minds, they also appealed to self-interest, always making the lawmakers aware of the economics of the situation. It was argued that, in view of the loss of a patient's earning power and the enormous cost of relief to the dependent, it was economical to eliminate tuberculosis. The building of public tuberculosis hospitals, then, was neither extravagant nor paternalistic. Rather, it was a prudent and wise course, a matter of self-interest.

While at first the lawmakers did not see it that way, they eventually passed a statute permitting the counties to tax their citizens for the erection and maintenance of public tuberculosis hospitals. Seven years later, another law made such hospitals (open to all on a first-come, first-served basis) mandatory for all counties within the state that had a population of more than 35,000. And finally, a few years after that, the state erected three tuberculosis hospitals to provide for the needs of those counties too small to build and operate their own institutions. Thus, every resident of New York State had easy access to a public tuberculosis hospital.

But conditions were not quite the same for black and white residents of the Empire State, or elsewhere. At first, most anti-tuberculosis societies, North and South alike, simply ignored blacks. Eventually, however, it became obvious that self-interest—or the public health—demanded an effort to cure blacks, especially in those areas where members of the two races came into frequent contact with one another. Yet, on the whole, blacks were encouraged to take care of themselves. Their efforts proved ineffective. The lack of black physicians and adequately trained nurses, as well as the fact that the black community was too poor to support enough institutions to meet the problem proved to be a major stumbling block. When public facilities were provided, they tended to be inferior and segregated. Thus the disparity in the tuberculosis mortality rate of the two races remained great throughout the period—about three to one.

Nevertheless, the general effectiveness of the antituberculosis campaign in New York may be readily summed up by a quick glance at some statistics. In 1907, there was no tuberculosis legislation in the state outside New York City; ten years later, it had the most advanced tuberculosis laws in the nation. In 1907, the disease was the greatest single cause of death in the state; the mortality rate per 100,000 population was 152.18. Twenty-five years later, it ranked as far down as seventh in causes of death; the mortality rate per 100,000 people was 59.2, a decline of 61 percent. Thus, the antituberculosis campaign in New York State alone saved thousands of lives each year. It also prevented thousands of people from becoming severely ill, it saved many wives from becoming widowed, and many children from becoming orphaned; and through lower relief costs and higher tax revenues, it made a substantial contribution to the economic life of the state—and the nation. The movement, in New York and elsewhere, provided vivid testimony to the contention of Dr. C. E. A. Winslow, a public health authority and leader in the movement, that

> the discovery of the possibilities of widespread social organization as a means of controlling disease was one which may almost be placed alongside the discovery of the germ theory of disease itself as a factor in the evolution of the modern public health campaign.

Next, public health crusaders and social workers attacked diphtheria and the venereal diseases, all of which also had relatively high "social mortality" rates and, in view of the knowledge of how to control them, presented good prospects of achieving success, another important factor in the minds of those engaged in the work.

In the 1920s, physicians had a better knowledge of and power over diphtheria than over any other communicable disease; through the use of antitoxin and toxin-antitoxin they had the weapons needed to prevent and treat it, yet diphtheria still occupied third place among the dread communicable diseases, killing thousands of people each year. Syphilis, like tuberculosis and diphtheria, was another communicable disease that could be both prevented and cured. Similar to the "white plague" in certain respects, its early recognition and adequate treatment were major factors in its prevention as well as in its cure; cure was slow and costly while prevention was easy and inexpensive. Yet it, too, continued to victimize many citizens every year.

The story of the battle against diphtheria and syphilis need not be told here. Suffice it to say that the organized attacks upon these diseases were also successful, again demonstrating the effectiveness of modern administrative and educational methods in combating disease.

In the long run, however, the success or failure of the public health movement depended upon the work of public health officials. All the reforms and legislation in the world would be useless if they were not administered properly, as too often was the case—at least at the start.

In general, at the turn of the century, public health officers were incompetent; most were political appointees with little knowledge of the fields. Also, most states had an uncoordinated array of health districts and authorities. In New York alone, for example, health legislation was implemented by some 1400 health officers attached to 500 or 600 separate boards in various towns, villages, and cities throughout the state. Something had to be done to improve and bring order to so faulty and inefficient a system.

Once again, as in so many other health and welfare matters, New York State led the way when in 1913, by means of a Public Health Law, it revamped its entire Health Department and all of its services. Other than certain minor changes, the statute was responsible for some major revisions in the state's health program. First, and most important, was the creation of a Public Health Council, composed of the State Commissioner of Health and six other members appointed by the Governor. The council had two unique powers—to enact and amend a sanitation code for the entire state, and to fix eligibility rules for all public health positions.

Since the subjects of sanitation laws were so complex and technical that they could not be handled properly by politicians in a legislative session, the delegation of ordinance-making power to a small expert administrative body was an enormous advance in public health work.[6] And when the council provided for the appointment and tenure of all public health personnel to be determined solely on the basis of merit (proven experience as well as education and a high mark on an examination), public health work in New York was removed from politics.

The Public Health Council also ordered a satisfactory minimum wage for the State Commissioner of Health and other health officers so that people of merit would be attracted to and remain in the service. Finally, the new body gave direct control over most aspects of local health work, including the power to enforce both the public health law and the state sanitary code, to the State Department of Health and its commissioner, bringing health work throughout the state under the control of a centralized authority.

[6]The council had only quasi-legislative power. Its decrees and resolutions were not necessarily or immediately acts of law. To achieve legal status they had to be promulgated by the State Commissioner of Health and filed by the Secretary of State, neither of whom was obligated to do so. Furthermore, the statutory acts of the council were subject to review by the courts. Since its creation, however, no State Commissioner of Health ever failed or refused to file any of the council's recommendations, and no court has ever overruled any of its acts.

Speaking of the statute responsible for these changes, Dr. C. E. A. Winslow said that it "unquestionably marked the most important landmark in the history of state health administration in the United States since the creation of the first health department by Massachusetts in 1869." Although amended in its details several times, the 1913 Public Health Law remains the basis of public health work not only in New York, but in most other states, all of which reorganized their own procedures according to its provisions.

The remarkable reduction in the morbidity and mortality rates of tuberculosis, diphtheria, syphilis, and other communicable diseases cannot be attributed solely to improved and better administered sanitation laws, health education, hospitals, public health nursing, and the like. New scientific discoveries, improved services by private medical practitioners, better social and economic conditions, free school lunches and better diet, and numerous other developments related elsewhere all contributed to the saving of lives. Nevertheless, a large share of the extraordinary progress may be credited to the organized public health movement of the late nineteenth and early twentieth centuries.

Social workers and other laymen whose devotion to public service was great, played an important part in that movement. They left as a permanent legacy to the nation not so much the principle that a great many lives could be saved through the prevention of communicable diseases, but that it was practical to do so. Their technical skill, political resourcefulness, and executive abilities helped transform scientific knowledge into legislation, ideas into public policy, that not only saved many lives and prolonged countless others but also improved the quality of life for all Americans.

Another element, and perhaps these citizens' greatest contribution to the struggle for health and welfare at this time, was their recognition of the vital importance of mobilizing the entire community—public officials and private citizens, health officers and social workers, physicians and ordinary citizens—in the war against illness and insecurity. And, as a result of their ability to do so, to fuse all these elements into a working team—to engage in successful community organization long before it became an important method among professional social workers—they helped to make the fruits of scientific advance the common knowledge of all, to bring preventive medicine into the organized social welfare crusade of the era, and to extend the scope of social work, thereby making it a more valuable and welcome addition to organized efforts for the improvement of the community. Other developments, meanwhile, including the appearance of settlement houses in the nation's larger cities, were heading in the same direction.

Bibliography

ADAMS, SAMUEL HOPKINS. "Guardians of the Public Health," *McClure's Magazine* 31 (July 1908): 241:52.

———. "Tuberculosis: The Real Race Suicide," *McClure's Magazine* 24 (January 1905): 234–49.

BARTLETT, HARRIET M. *Fifty Years of Social Work in the Medical Setting.* New York: National Association of Social Workers, 1957.

———. "Ida M. Cannon: Pioneer in Medical Social Work," *Social Service Review* 49 (June 1975): 208–29.

———. *Social Work Practice in the Health Field.* New York: National Association of Social Workers, 1961.

BELL, MOBERLY E. *The Story of the Hospital Almoners: The Birth of a Profession.* London: Faber and Faber, 1961.

BOAS, ERNST. "The Contribution of Medical Social Work to Medical Care," *Social Service Review* 13 (December 1939): 626–33.

BRAINARD, ANNIE M. *The Evolution of Public Health Nursing.* Philadelphia: Saunders, 1922.

CANNON, IDA. *On the Social Frontier of Medicine: Pioneering in Medical Social Service.* Cambridge, Mass.: Harvard University Press, 1952.

———. *Social Work in Hospitals: A Contribution to Progressive Medicine.* New York: Russell Sage Foundation, 1913.

CANNON, M. A. "History and Development of Hospital Social Work," *The Family* 4 (February 1924): 250–55.

CASSEDY, JAMES H. *Charles V. Chapin and the Public Health Movement.* Cambridge, Mass.: Harvard University Press, 1962.

———. "The Roots of American Sanitary Reform, 1843–47: Seven Letters from John R. Griscom to Lemuel Shattuck," *Journal of the History of Medicine and Allied Sciences* 30 (April 1975): 136–41.

CHADWICK, EDWIN. *The Sanitary Condition of the Labouring Population of Great Britain,* in Roy Lubove ed., *Social Welfare in Transition.* Pittsburgh: University of Pittsburgh Press, 1966.

CHADWICK, H. D., AND A. S. POPE. *The Modern Attack on Tuberculosis.* New York: Commonwealth Fund, 1946.

DUBLIN, LOUIS I. *Twenty-five Years of Health Progress.* New York: Metropolitan Life Insurance, 1937.

DUFFY, JOHN. *A History of Public Health in New York City, 1625–1966,* 2 Vols. New York: Russell Sage Foundation, 1968–74.

ELIOT, MARTHA M. "New Frontiers of Health and Welfare," *Social Service Review* 15 (December 1941): 636–50.

FLEMING, DONALD H. *William H. Welch and the Rise of Modern Medicine.* Boston: Little, Brown, 1954.

FOX, DANIEL. "Social Policy and City Politics: Tuberculosis Reporting in New York, 1889–1900," *Bulletin of the History of Medicine* 49 (Summer 1975): 169–95.

GALISHOFF, STUART. *Safeguarding the Public Health: Newark, 1895–1918.* Westport, Conn.: Greenwood Press, 1975.

GUNN, S., AND P. PLATT. *Voluntary Health Agencies.* New York: Ronald Press, 1945.

Handbook on the Prevention of Tuberculosis. New York: Charity Organization Society, 1903.

KRAMER, HOWARD D. "The Beginnings of the Public Health Movement in the United States," *Bulletin of the History of Medicine* 21 (May-June 1947): 352–76.

———. "Early Municipal and State Boards of Health," *Bulletin of the History of Medicine* 24 (November-December 1950): 503–29.

———. "The Germ Theory and the Early Public Health Program in the United States," *Bulletin of the History of Medicine* 22 (May-June 1948): 233–47.

LARSEN, LAWRENCE H. "Nineteenth-Century Street Sanitation: A Study of Filth and Frustration," *Wisconsin Magazine of History* 52 (Spring 1969): 239–47.

MEEKER, EDWARD. "The Improving Health of the United States, 1850–1915," *Explorations in Economic History* 9 (Summer 1972): 353–73.

PUMPHREY, RALPH. "Michael Davis and the Transformation of the Boston Dispensary, 1910–1920," *Bulletin of the History of Medicine* 49 (Winter 1975): 451–65.

RAVENEL, MAZYCK P., ed. *A Half Century of Public Health.* New York: American Public Health Association, 1921.

ROSENBERG, CHARLES. "Social Class and Medical Care in Nineteenth-Century America: The Rise and Fall of the Dispensary," *Journal of the History of Medicine and Allied Sciences* 29 (January 1974): 32–54.

ROSENKRANTZ, BARBARA GUTMANN. *Public Health and the State: Changing Views in Massachusetts, 1842–1936.* Cambridge, Mass.: Harvard University Press, 1972.

SHATTUCK, LEMUEL. *Report of a General Plan for the Promotion of Public and Personnel Health . . . Relating to a Sanitary Survey of the State.* Boston, 1850; facsimile edition, Cambridge, Mass.: Harvard University Press, 1948.

SHRYOCK, RICHARD H. *The Development of Modern Medicine.* New York: Knopf, 1947.

———. *National Tuberculosis Association, 1904–1954.* New York: National Tuberculosis Association, 1957.

———. "The Origins and Significance of the Public Health Movement in the United States," *Annals of Medical History* 1 (November 1929): 645–65.

SMILLIE, WILSON G. *Public Health: Its Promise for the Future.* New York: Macmillan, 1955.

TERRIS, MILTON. "Concepts of Social Medicine," *Social Service Review* 31 (June 1957): 164–78.

TOBEY, JAMES A. *Public Health Law.* New York: Commonwealth Fund, 1947.

TORCHIA, MARION. "The Tuberculosis Movement and the Race Question, 1890–1950," *Bulletin of the History of Medicine* 49 (Summer 1975): 152–68.

TRATTNER, WALTER I. "Homer Folks and the Public Health Movement," *Social Service Review* 40 (December 1966): 410–28.

WASSERMAN, MANFRED. "The Quest for a National Health Department in the Progressive Era," *Bulletin of the History of Medicine* 49 (Fall 1975): 353–80.

WINSLOW, C. E. A. *The Conquest of Epidemic Disease.* Princeton, N.J.: Princeton University Press, 1943.

———. *The Evolution and Significance of the Modern Public Health Campaign.* New Haven, Conn.: Yale University Press, 1935.

———. *The Life of Hermann M. Biggs.* Philadelphia: Lea and Febiger, 1929.

Chapter 8

The Settlement House Movement

UNTIL LATE in the nineteenth century, most social welfare efforts were aimed at alleviating distress. Poor law officials and charity workers administered public assistance and private philanthropy, moral or material, to the destitute. For the most part, they overlooked the actual causes of need. In the late 1880s, however, a new approach developed—the settlement ideal. Largely a reaction to organized charity work, which for a long time did little to improve urban living and working conditions, settlement house residents regarded themselves as social reformers rather than charity workers.[1] They were not interested in doling out relief, either financial or verbal. Rather, their goal was to bridge the gap between the classes and races, to eliminate the sources of distress, and to improve urban living and working conditions. Like the public health reformers, with whom they frequently cooperated, theirs was the preventive approach.

American cities, which contained a bewildering number of people—mainly immigrants who lived crowded together in wretched tenements—needed improving. They had grown enormously in the late nineteenth and early twentieth centuries. In 1860, one-sixth of the American people lived in cities; by 1900,

[1]In fact, settlement workers tried desperately to disassociate themselves from the charity organization societies in the public mind, and there was a great deal of antagonism between the two movements. A typical encounter occurred at a meeting in the 1890s, when a charity organization society speaker made the usual allusions to the failings of the urban poor and the need for "moral force" to lift them up. The next speaker, a settlement house resident, said she could not bring herself to criticize a filthy tenement apartment when she knew that smoke and soot were pouring into it from unregulated factories nearby. Only in the twentieth century did they come together and cooperate.

155

the proportion of city dwellers had grown to one-third; and by 1920, it was one-half. New York City's population increased by four times between 1860 and 1910, rising from 1,174,779 to 4,766,883. Philadelphia's population increased threefold between 1870 and 1910, and the same was true for Boston. Yet the most dramatic growth occurred in the Midwest. Chicago was eighth among American cities with 109,260 inhabitants in 1860; by 1910, it was the nation's second largest city with a population of 2,185,283, a twentyfold increase. Growing almost as rapidly were St. Louis, Cleveland, Detroit, and other midwestern cities.

While a large proportion of the urban population came from Americans leaving farms, the major share of it came from Europeans migrating to the United States. Between 1860 and 1900, some fourteen million immigrants came to America, and about another nine million, mainly from southern and eastern Europe —Austrians, Hungarians, Bohemians, Poles, Serbs, Italians, Russians, and so on—arrived between 1900 and 1910. Too poor to buy a farm or invest in the machinery and stock necessary for agriculture, and lacking the skill needed to strike out for themselves in a new country in farming or in any other occupation in the modern age, most of the immigrants settled in cities where they became unskilled laborers in the nation's factories.

Thus, in America's eight largest cities in 1910—all having 500,000 inhabitants or more—more than one-third of the population was foreign born, and considerably more than another third was of second-generation immigrant stock. By 1900, three-fourths of Chicago's population was foreign born, and the proportion in New York City was even higher. The number of Italians living in New York in the 1890s, even before the wave of "new immigrants" engulfed the nation in the following decade, equaled that of Naples, while the number of Germans equaled that of Hamburg. Twice as many Irish lived in New York as in Dublin, and so it went.

Nowhere in the world were people as crowded as in the poorer quarters of America's larger cities. By 1893, 1.5 million human beings, of whom five out of every six huddled together in cramped tenements, lived in the congested neighborhood of New York's Lower East Side, described by observers as the home of push-carts, paupers, and consumptives. While the densest crowding in

London never got beyond 175,000 people per square mile, New York's Lower East Side contained 330,000 inhabitants per square mile. And although New York's conditions were the worst in the nation, similar conditions existed elsewhere, creating all sorts of problems.

Housing, already desperate by the time of the Civil War, was among the most serious of those problems. Most of the newcomers were forced to live in the cluttered, filth-ridden tenements described so well by Jacob Riis—breeding places for vice, crime, and disease. Life in the sordid, dark, damp structures, in which the inhabitants underwent a process of decay which they themselves termed "tenant house rot," was made worse by overcrowding. Within the two or three rooms which comprised each of the so-called dwellings, there often lived a household composed not only of man, wife, and several children, but of other relatives and lodgers as well.

Sanitary facilities were scarcely endurable. Several families used a common sink and a common toilet, rarely cleaned by anyone. Bathtubs were luxuries most tenement dwellers never enjoyed. Even drinking water was scarce, for the pressure often was too low to lift the water above the first floor of the buildings which, like the streets they were on, were covered with mounds of matted debris. "Look up, look down," wrote one observer, "turn this way, turn that way—here is no prospect but the unkempt and disorderly, the slovenly and the grim; filth everywhere, trampled on the sidewalks, lying in the windows, collected in the eddies of doorsteps." While most immigrants found life in the New World, even under these conditions, sweeter than what they had known in the Old, many nevertheless realized that the famed American entrepreneurial ethic—the notion that with hard work, morality, and perhaps a bit of luck, anyone could prosper—was becoming less a realistic ideal than a fantasy. Thus, they sometimes concluded, as did one Rumanian immigrant: "This was the boasted American freedom and opportunity—the freedom for respectable citizens to sell cabbages from hideous carts, the opportunity to live in those monstrous dirty caves [tenements] that shut out the sunshine."

Settlement house residents sought to improve these conditions, to promote social and economic reform so that those who had dreams about getting ahead would have the opportunity to do so. Where their predecessors had emphasized the individual and moral causes of destitution, drawing distinctions between the worthy and unworthy poor, settlement house workers looked upon all the indigent alike, stressing the social and economic conditions that made and kept them poor. While the charity workers were interested in dependency, settlement house residents were concerned with poverty. Whereas the philosophy of the charity organization movement led to private charity and spiritual uplift, the philosophy of the settlement house movement led to social and economic change. While charity organization society agents constantly said "don't, don't," settlement house residents would say "do, do."

There were some similarities between the two movements. Both believed that the urban poor had been hurt by the circumstances of city life, including the separation of the classes, and both relied heavily on the use of volunteers, especially well motivated people of the privileged classes who, for one reason or another, felt impelled to do something about the class divisiveness. Friendly visitors and settlement house residents, in other words, had similar conceptions of individual duty and class relationships; both Josephine Shaw Lowell, spokeswoman for the organized charities, and Jane Addams, leader and philosopher of the settlement house movement in America, emphasized sacrifice and human fellowship, the need to bring the rich and the poor together, to reduce social disintegration and class divisiveness.

Both movements were "romantic" in that they were as interested in people's "spiritual" conditions as in their material conditions; that both had a religious tone to them is not surprising. And finally, both the organized charities and the settlement houses believed in the need for investigation; each demanded the facts before acting.

On the other hand, the settlement and charity organization movements were in many ways the very antithesis of each other. While not all social settlements were alike, most exemplified the democratic ideal in principle and in action, while the organized charities were the very opposite—the embodiment of inequality in theory and in practice. It should be pointed out, however, that some scholars would take issue with this statement. In their opinion, concentration by historians on such nationally known settlements as Hull-House "has created a distorted picture of the entire movement." While it is true that such people as Jane Addams, Graham Taylor (of Chicago Commons), Lillian Wald (of the Henry Street Settlement), and others "were genuinely progressive or even radical in their political and social orientation," accepting "the immigrants on their own terms" and practicing "some degree of cultural pluralism," these people and their institutions were not typical of the movement, according to these critics. Rather, in the words of Raymond Mohl and Neil Betten, "most settlements were religious missions" that "reflected, acted upon, and transmitted the values and attitudes of the larger society; beyond their proselytizing activities, they adopted a derogatory view of ethnic traditions and assumed that their proper role was that of Americanizing the immigrant with all possible speed." Settlement house residents, too, equated human betterment with middle class values and supported Americanization, voluntarism, and anti-radicalism, although, according to Paul Boyer, they did so by more subtle means than their predecessors had used; they tended to mute "their negative . . . judgments [of their working class neighbors] or place them within a larger framework of positive comment," as opposed to the louder, more "aggressive[ly] moralistic" pronouncements of C.O.S. members. Also, more responsive than the older C.O.S. leaders to the newer social thought, with its emphasis on the role of the environment in shaping behavior and morals, settlement house residents relied on technical skills and social "reform"—such as tenement house legislation and the building of parks—to regulate the poor, while friendly visitors utilized the older class dominance and moral uplift. In any case, settlement houses, no less than charity organization societies, were conservative responses to cultural diversity and social fragmentation.[2]

[2]For the revisionist view, see Raymond A. Mohl and Neil Betten, "Paternalism and Pluralism: Immigrants and Social Welfare in Gary, Indiana, 1906–1940," *American Studies* 15 (Spring 1974): 5–30; Paul Boyer, *Urban Masses and Moral Order in America, 1820–1920* (Cambridge, Mass.: Harvard University Press, 1978), pp. 156–58; Edward A. Shapiro, "Robert A. Woods and the Settlement House Impulse," *Social Service Review* 52 (June 1978): 215–26; Dominick Cavello, *Muscles and Morals: Organized Playgrounds and Urban Reform, 1880–1920* (Philadelphia: University of Pennsylvania Press, 1981); John F. McClymer, *War and Welfare: Social Engineering in America* (Westport, Conn.: Greenwood Press, 1980).

It is possible, then, that the settlement house movement may not have been quite as democratic and progressive a force for social change as I have portrayed it here. Certainly, additional research on the subject is needed, especially from the vantage point of the present. Until that research is completed, however, I remain convinced that, despite some similarities, the settlements were far different from the organized charities and that for the most part they were mechanisms for reform that made invaluable contributions to the movement for social welfare and justice in late nineteenth- and early twentieth-century America. To the extent that settlement house residents advocated or practiced social control, it was because they realized that social cohesion and justice in modern society depended upon purposeful planning and the curtailment of some individual liberty. The two were neither contradictory nor antagonistic; rather, they were entwined and inseparable. Suffering could be alleviated and justice achieved only through some measure of social control, as E. A. Ross, the famed sociologist who coined the term (and used it benevolently), pointed out in his classic study, *Social Control* (1901). Many settlement house residents regarded themselves, and were regarded by others, as friends and neighbors of the poor, not as dispensers of charity; they were more fraternalistic than paternalistic, more objective than judgmental. Their work was based upon the needs and desires of those with whom they were working, not upon a pattern of behavior prescribed by donors of moral enlightenment. Rather than look down upon the poor or seek to impose their way of life upon them, they preserved and bolstered their self-respect and accepted them for who they were. Among the first social workers to realize that cultural differences were important for welfare work and the nation, an idea in sharp contrast to prevailing views during the period, they even encouraged immigrants to retain and be proud of their Old World heritage. They also taught second-generation immigrants to be proud of their parents' traditional ways and values—"gifts" they brought to America, as Jane Addams put it in her autobiography, *Twenty Years at Hull-House*.

Too, while charity workers were concerned only with paupers—those dependent upon others for their livelihood—settlement house residents felt that their task included all people, the employed as well as the unemployed, those above the poverty line as well as those below it. The settlements, explained Jane Addams, were designed "to aid in the solution of the social and industrial problems which are engendered by the modern conditions of life," which affect all people. Their services, therefore, were directed toward others besides the antisocial, the ill, the dependent, or the like. They believed in the concept that later came to be known as "social engineering," the notion that constructive workers (reformers) or "engineers" were needed all the time, not just when there was something wrong.

And finally, while settlement house residents did not lose sight of the individual, they saw him or her as a member of a group and not as an isolated human being. Thus, they worked for group rather than individual improvement; they concentrated on the problems of an entire area and neighborhood. In the words of Stanton Coit, who in 1886 opened America's first settlement house, Neighborhood Guild:

> The fundamental idea which the settlement embodies is this: that, irrespective of religious belief or non-belief, all the people, men, women, and children, in any one street, on any small number of streets in every working-class district . . . shall be organized into a set of clubs which are by themselves, or in alliance with those of other neighborhoods, to carry out, or induce others to carry out, the reforms—domestic, industrial, educational, provident or recreative—which the social ideal demands. It is an expression of the family idea of cooperation.

The settlements, then, embodied the neighborhood ideal—the desire to create an organic community among the people and institutions of a specific location. Rejecting the prevalent idea that society would benefit while all men pursued their own self-interest, they stressed instead the interdependence of social groups (and the state) in an organically structured society.

This view of society, in turn, led to the conclusion that action to help some would in the end help all. It was a misfortune for all people, the well-to-do as well as the needy, if the different classes lived in complete isolation from each other—physically and intellectually. Settlement house residents sought to bridge the gap between the classes: "What a blessing it would be to the residents of Fifth Avenue to have a settlement of mechanics there," pioneer resident Robert Woods said in all seriousness. "Living among the poor," said another, "my sense of values changed, for the better. Whereas I was brought up to cherish frugality and thrift, I learned from the needy that other things were more important—patience, amiability, sharing, and the like."

The gulf between the classes, however, was usually bridged the other way—by members of the middle or upper classes moving into the nation's poorest neighborhoods for the purpose of getting to know local living and working conditions at first hand, and then helping to improve those conditions. The settlements, therefore, had no well defined method or specific goal. In fact, the residents took great pride in being opportunistic and pragmatic—in program and in philosophy—something for which they were criticized by charity organization society leaders.

C.O.S. agents dismissed settlement house residents as too sentimental and unscientific, too vague to be useful. One friendly visitor compared the settlement house worker to a man who found a drunkard lying in the gutter and said to him, "I can't help you, my friend, but I will sit down in the gutter beside you." Another told of the elderly society matron who inspected a settlement house from top to bottom and when finished said, "Well, I do think you people down here are doing magnificent work—whatever it is you are doing."

What the organized charities people did not understand was that the settlements did not seek to do any one thing but, rather, to provide an atmosphere for ties of understanding and sympathy between people of different backgrounds and positions in life. Full of optimism and zeal, the settlement house residents were confident that if the more fortunate members of society were to live among the less fortunate they would learn to know the real problems of the poor and how to meet them.

Interested in people rather than doctrine, in action rather than theory, Residence, Research, and Reform were the "3 Rs" of the movement. And in attaining their goals, the settlements had an enviable record. Accepting the forces of urbanization and industrialization, they went about their task of eliminating the causes of poverty and making the city a better place in which to live. Because they had a realistic understanding of the social forces and the political structure of the city, and nation, and because they battled in legislative halls as well as in urban slums, they became successful initiators and organizers of reform.

Who were these idealistic men and women, conscious of real problems in urban-industrial America, confident that they could be solved, and certain that the settlement ideal was the key to the solution? As a group they were quite young, averaging only about twenty-five years of age. They were single and fairly well-to-do native Americans who had graduated from college. Most had been born and brought up in the Northeast or Midwest in an environment far removed from the slums.

What was it, then, that impelled them to postpone or abandon a comfortable way of life for one of social reform in some of America's most wretched neighborhoods? For one thing, they were members of the first sizable generation of American college graduates, men and women, who came to maturity in an industrial or commercial society in which there was no clearly defined place for them. With big business at the top and organized labor at the bottom, many felt alienated from the society into which they had been born.[3] The complexity and challenge of the large city, however, offered them opportunities to create meaningful careers for themselves and, at the same time, to rescue society from the social ills resulting from rapid industrial and urban change. Instead of pulling up stakes and heading west, as they might have done a half-century earlier, these young people became "settlers" in the slums in order to help discover solutions to the social and economic problems of the new frontier—the wilderness of the modern city, or perhaps "the jungle," as Upton Sinclair would call it. This was especially true for many young women, who, if they wished to embark upon a career, had few other useful activities open to them.

By the late nineteenth century, the higher education of American women was an established fact; as early as 1880, about one-third of all students enrolled in institutions of higher learning were

[3]Basically, this is the so-called Hofstadter or status thesis, the idea that the reform spirit derived less from external changes or conditions in American society than from the alienation of the professional classes, those with learning and skills; their security and status threatened by industrialists at the top and political bosses and labor union leaders at the bottom, they became reformers. See Richard Hofstadter, *The Age of Reform* (New York: Knopf, 1956), esp. pp. 131–72.

women, and the percentage would increase over the next few decades. The chief difficulty facing American women, then, was not
securing a college degree but using it. Those graduates who were
unwilling or unable either to return home, get married, and settle
down as wives and mothers or to perform work for which they
were vastly overqualified had difficulty finding suitable employment, especially in the professions. Either the difficulties and
social disapproval facing them were sufficient to keep many from
seeking such work, or most professions barred their admission.
Nursing, which by now had been elevated to a profession, was
open to women, as was teaching, especially at the lower grades.
Most of the other professions, however, including law and medicine, were still largely closed to them. As a result, America had a
sizable group of educated women searching for self-satisfaction
and a way to play a more important role in society than custom
permitted. For many of these women, social service, especially
settlement house work, proved to be an acceptable solution to the
problem. Not only did it provide opportunities for them to utilize
their college educations but also it furnished a supportive atmosphere in an often otherwise hostile environment, one that allowed
them to develop their talents and enjoy ties of companionship and
sociability like those they had nurtured and come to cherish while
at college, especially at female institutions.

Many of these people, men and women alike, had discovered
the city and its problems firsthand, either while at college or during the depression of 1893. Others read about it in the muckraking magazines and books that came from the nation's presses at
the time, works that depicted in lurid detail many of the nation's
urban problems and social injustices. But it was more than a loss
in status and hostile feelings toward those who possessed power,
or the discovery and challenge of the city, or the desire for some
avenue of satisfaction or advancement, that made many settlement workers want to serve. As Allen Davis, the historian of the
movement, has demonstrated, most residents took their religion
seriously, and religious feeling was an important factor in the conversion to settlement work and social reform. Jane Addams, in
describing her own motivating "impulse to share the lives of the
poor," spoke for many when she indicated that it came from a
desire "to make social service ... express the spirit of Christ."
Influenced by the militant Social Gospel movement of the day, an

attempt by liberal Protestant ministers in the late nineteenth century to revitalize the Church and recapture the militant spirit of Christ by concerning it with matters of poverty and social justice and by aligning it with the working rather than the employing classes, these neophytes found in settlement work a sense of mission to God and to mankind that had been aroused and nurtured by the religion of their youth. Instead of entering the ministry, which for the most part was closed to women (or becoming teachers as so many of their parents had done and as they might have done otherwise), they chose a life of practical helpfulness to the poor, one that was devoid of theological doctrines and ritualistic practices, one that would give them more satisfaction than was afforded by the cloth (or the classroom). Settlement house work, then, was for many a practical substitute for a religious (or educational) vocation, one that allowed them to translate theory into action, to practice rather than preach (or teach).

In addition, many of the women who became residents—well over 40 percent—had fathers or other male family members who were, or had been, active in some way in "politics," another field that was closed to women at the time. Settlement house work, then, no doubt was for many of these women an alternative to that form of service as well.[4]

Others—journalists, novelists, and graduate students in sociology, political science, economics, and the other social sciences —were attracted to settlement house work for different reasons. For journalists writing muckraking articles, novelists in the new naturalistic school, or graduate students in search of material for doctoral dissertations, the settlements offered the perfect vantage point from which to observe and study the teeming city and to collect the necessary data for studies on child labor, crowded tenements, workers' strikes, racial strife, and other topics of human interest. The settlements, then, not only carried on the struggle for social justice and a more tolerable and humane urban environment, but they were intellectually stimulating places in which to live. An early Russian revolutionist who had

---

[4]For that insight, I am indebted to Kathryn Kish Sklar, who is writing a biography of Florence Kelley and who, on May 2, 1983, delivered a paper at the University of Wisconsin-Milwaukee on Kelley and the Chicago settlement house workers in which she stressed that point.

escaped from Siberia and gone to Hull-House testified that she enjoyed her stay there, especially because of the interesting conversations and discussions; she had not felt so much at home, she declared, since joining the Terrorists.

Like the charity organization societies, the American social settlements had English predecessors. In fact, the movement originated in England among British intellectuals such as John Ruskin and Thomas Carlyle, and among Christian Socialists such as Frederic Maurice and Charles Kingsley. More immediately, settlements in the United States were patterned after Toynbee Hall, established in 1884 in East London, which many pioneer residents knew firsthand.

Stanton Coit, a young Amherst graduate engaged in further study in Europe, visited Toynbee Hall and then served as a resident there for several months. In 1889, two of Coit's assistants, both Smith College graduates, joined a Wellesley College instructor, Vida Scudder, who had also visited Toynbee Hall, in opening America's second settlement house—the College Settlement. In Chicago, Hull-House, which would become the most famous, was founded that same year by yet another visitor to Toynbee Hall, Jane Addams. Although only four settlements were founded before 1890, their number increased rapidly thereafter; by 1900 there were about 100 in existence (already far more than in England), and by 1910 roughly 400 were in operation.

Needless to say, these highly educated, well-dressed young men and women were at first quite conspicuous in their new surroundings. Soon after Graham Taylor opened his settlement house, Chicago Commons (in 1894), a friend who visited him pointed out that "a missionary in the heart of Africa could hardly present a greater contrast with his surroundings" than did the cultured and refined Dr. Taylor among the many poor immigrants on the city's West Side. So striking was the contrast between the new residents and their surroundings that neighbors questioned their motives. For instance, shortly after opening her University of Chicago Settlement, Mary McDowell, who had come from Hull-House, was confronted by a suspicious citizen who asked: "Why should you come here, why should you want such a place? Does Mr. Rockefeller furnish the money?"

At most settlements, then, the residents' first task was to establish good relations with their neighbors so that, together, they could work to improve the neighborhood. The initial step in the program usually called for a kindergarten, in large part to gain rapport with the parents, but also because of the desperate need for play space in the slums. (Perhaps, too, it was a consequence of the preponderance of women staff members.) Soon, nurseries and day care centers were created, so that working mothers had a safe place to leave their children.

As mutual understanding and trust were gained, the settlements broadened their activities. They added such things as men's clubs, courses in arts and crafts, libraries, gymnasiums, penny savings banks, employment bureaus, kitchens, music halls with orchestras, art galleries, and other services, such as dispensaries in which low-cost medicines could be purchased. When Mary McDowell, the first kindergarten teacher at Hull-House, opened the University of Chicago Settlement she developed not only these programs but also a school in citizenship for recent immigrants. Lillian Wald made a visiting nurse service a major feature of the settlement house she opened on Henry Street in New York's Lower East Side.

In addition to the programs and services offered by the residents, the facilities were made available to various groups and clubs in the neighborhood. Ethnic and religious groups, trade unions, and others partook of the hospitality of these new social centers. Certainly, the problems did not disappear, nor did easy long-lasting solutions usually emerge, but by providing these and other everyday needs of slum dwellers at least a spirit of helpful cooperation and warm friendliness developed. And, if nothing else, that spirit helped to restore a sense of neighborliness and community in many of the nation's most depressed urban areas.

But the settlements did more than that. Most residents did not merely want to live in the city and work with its people. They wished to understand, explain, and write about the slum dwellers and their needs. By means of speeches, magazine articles, and books full of human interest, they produced a whole body of literature on urban ills and tenement life.[5] As a result, many citizens

---

[5]They wrote not only about the problems of the city but about their hopes as well. Thus, as one settlement house worker phrased it: "The city historically and inherently is the most important and permanent political unit," the source of civili-

not identified with the movement, and perhaps unaware of the seamy side of life, were made cognizant of how the other half lived. Long before the discovery (or rediscovery) of the "other America" in the 1960s, settlement house residents were concerned about the invisibility of the poor—and they did something about it.

Too, residents were convinced from the very beginning that research was an integral part of their work; many had gone to the settlements for that very reason. This, along with their personal relationships with their neighbors, with whose problems and needs they became well acquainted, enabled them to lay bare the true causes of poverty. They did not visit tenement families only in times of trouble but, living among them as they did, they saw all sides of slum life and did not consider their neighbors as miserable wretches in need of moral uplift, but as underprivileged or oppressed human beings.

Never losing sight of the fact that research should lead to action—even a rough count of bathtubs in a neighborhood was translated into petitions demanding public bathhouses—the settlements became, in Allen Davis's words, "spearheads for reform." Whereas the agents of the organized charities felt that poverty could be obliterated by moral virtue alone, settlement house residents turned to social change. Through their clubs, lectures, and other activities, they sought to encourage cooperative efforts toward community betterment. And while they did not initiate the widespread reform movement that swept through America in the late nineteenth and early twentieth centuries, they did contribute significantly to it. By providing meeting places, discussion centers, and clearing houses for urban reform, and by wrestling with the social and economic problems facing many Americans, they played a vital part in what historians have called the Progressive or "social justice" movement.

In the struggle for Negro freedom, as in their effort to preserve the cultural heritage that foreigners were bringing to America, settlement house residents stood far above most other so-called

---

zation's highest achievements. "From the city," he predicted, "will come the humanity, opportunity, and justice that will bless the individual . . . and make more glorious the nation."

Progressives. As indicated earlier, as a group blacks received little or no attention from the public or private sector in the late nineteenth century. In the South, where the overwhelming majority of the nation's Negroes resided and where their lot was extremely difficult, they were excluded from the welfare system. In the North, where black poverty was as pervasive, racial discrimination and neglect also prevailed. It was easier to ignore the plight of northern Negroes because, until they migrated from the South in large numbers during the era of World War I, they were relatively few in number.[6] In any event, since charity workers stressed the individual-moral causes of poverty, they could be of little assistance to destitute blacks, even had they chosen not to be indifferent to their problems.

Settlement house workers, however—Jane Addams, Lillian Wald, Frances Kellor, Florence Kelley, Mary White Ovington, Louise de Koven Bowen, Sophonisba Breckinridge, William E. Walling, Henry Moscowitz, and many others—were exceptions to the rule. In an age of widespread racism and bigotry, many—although certainly not all—advocated the unpopular cause of equality for all Americans, blacks included; they were among the few outstanding pioneers in the fight against racial discrimination. As one of the few groups that had at least some direct contact with urban Negroes, settlement house residents were aware of the unique problems that blacks faced as a result of racial discrimination. They understood the stresses and strains to which blacks were exposed in a hostile environment and were aware of the deep gulf that separated most blacks from the larger society in which they lived but to which they did not belong. Thus, they not only had greater sympathy for their lot than did most Americans, but by their many efforts to improve the nation's living and working conditions and by engaging in careful research and speaking out on the problem, they sought to combat

---

[6]In New York City, blacks constituted only 2 percent of the population in 1900 while members of various foreign-born white groups comprised about 40 percent of the city's inhabitants. Likewise, in Chicago at the turn of the century, there were fewer than 100,000 Negroes in a population of close to two million, or less than 5 percent of the total; blacks ranked tenth among the city's various racial or ethnic groups. The same thing was true throughout the North at this time. It was easy, therefore, to argue that blacks should receive no special attention.

prejudice and do battle against Jim Crowism.[7] Long before it was popular to do so, at least some settlement house workers helped foster black pride and Afro-American culture. They played an important part (in 1909) in the creation of the National Association for the Advancement of Colored People and in the establishment, two years later, of the National Urban League, the nation's leading black welfare agency. They also served as delegates to the 1921 Pan-African Congress held in London, Brussels, and Paris, under the leadership of the noted black American educator and writer, William E. B. DuBois. In these and in yet other ways, they sought to aid blacks in their struggle for a better life.

Still, these years produced little social or economic progress for the oppressed minority. The general public did not share the settlement house workers' perceptions of and concern for the problem, and racism continued to permeate American society. Most blacks were unaffected by the reform activities and social advances that characterized the era, for these benefits applied largely to those who lived in white rather than black ghettos and worked in industries in which Negro participation was minimal. As the authors of a recent study on the subject have indicated, in "an era marked by economic progress and social mobility, this group [the nation's black citizens] remained poor and powerless."

In any event, whether working with blacks, with whites, or with both, settlement house residents first sought to improve the neighborhood by means of building more public parks and playgrounds, establishing more and better public health facilities and services, and supporting improved garbage collection. Better tenement house laws and their strict enforcement, a more practical curriculum in the schools, and political reform through the election of honest and more responsive local officials were also matters of prime concern.

Soon, settlement workers became active in broader fields.

---

[7]Thus, in 1913 Louise de Koven Bowen and some fellow settlement house workers published the well researched *The Colored People of Chicago,* which in no uncertain terms documented wholesale discrimination against blacks in business, employment, labor unions, the criminal justice system, education, housing, and recreational facilities. Two years earlier, Mary White Ovington authored *Half a Man,* a study of the New York City Negro, which also documented widespread discrimination against blacks and the massive difficulties they faced as a result. She also was one of the major organizers of the National Association for the Advancement of Colored People.

Beginning their drive for reform in the neighborhood, they soon found that they had to get involved in municipal, state, and even national affairs. Thus, Jane Addams and other settlement house residents played a prominent role in the Chicago Civic Federation, an influential citywide political reform group. Julia Lathrop, a Hull-House resident, led the fight for the founding of the Cook County Juvenile Court, the first of its kind in the world. She and others also campaigned for a progressive state child labor law, which was enacted in 1903.

Beginning to see the connection between justice and the struggling labor movement, concerned residents toiled not only for improved working conditions but also for recognition of trade unions and the opportunity to organize, for women as well as for men. Thus, some, including "Fighting Mary" McDowell, cooperated with nonsettlement house reformers in helping to create the National Consumers' League in 1899, the National Women's Trade Union League in 1903, and similar groups later on.

Their research and the support of others' also had wide ramifications. Jane Addams and other residents were influential in persuading President Theodore Roosevelt and Congress to launch the important federal investigation of women and child laborers in America which ultimately resulted in the enactment of federal child labor legislation. Equally important was the creation, in 1905, by settlement workers and others, of the Charities Publication Committee. Organized specifically to sponsor social investigations, the committee immediately began two studies, one on the lot of blacks in northern cities, the other on the conditions of life, labor, and education in Washington, D.C. The success of these investigations and financial support from the newly founded Russell Sage Foundation (which made the project its first extensive investment in social research) inspired a much larger endeavor—the Pittsburgh Survey.

The Pittsburgh Survey, directed by Paul Kellogg (a young man who came to New York from a small town in Michigan to edit various publications for the New York C.O.S.), was designed to study the entire life of one industrial city as carefully and as exhaustively as possible—the first major attempt to do so by team research. Published in six volumes between 1909 and 1914, the survey revealed the cost and consequences of low wages, preventable diseases, industrial accidents, ramshackle housing, and lack of urban planning. With page after page of statistics and other factual material, the investigators documented the appalling human waste and misery, driving home the need for reform, regulation, and planning. The Pittsburgh Survey, which was read, summarized, and discussed around the country, inspired many similar investigations. Thus, the Russell Sage Foundation immediately sponsored similar surveys in six other cities from Atlanta, Georgia, to Topeka, Kansas, and numerous other communities organized their own self-study programs, all of which fed the fires of reform.

In addition, Lillian Wald and Florence Kelley (avowed socialists, or "slowcialists," who put aside their radicalism to push for social reform) worked with James West and others interested in child welfare to prepare the way for the historic White House Conference on Dependent Children in 1909, and were primarily responsible for the creation, three years later, of the U.S. Children's Bureau. Also in 1912, a number of settlement house residents participated in the drafting of a program of "national minimums" for well-being in an industrial society—an eight-hour workday and a six-day workweek, the abolition of tenement homework, the prohibition of child labor, and so on—that became part of the Progressive Party's 1912 presidential platform—one of the most advanced major party platforms in American history.

Sometimes the lessons learned in the settlement neighborhood led even further afield—to the international scene. The involvement of Jane Addams and other residents in the organized peace movement stemmed in part from the realization that men and women of different backgrounds got along well on Chicago's Halsted Street, New York's Henry Street, and numerous other American working-class neighborhoods.

By the early twentieth century, then, as the settlements and the organized charities were beginning to cooperate, indeed merge, into "social work" (in 1905, Graham Taylor's settlement house journal, *The Commons,* merged with the New York Charity Organization Society's *Charities* into *Charities and The Commons,* and four years later, Jane Addams was elected president of the National Conference of Charities and Correction, the first woman and settlement house resident to be accorded that honor), the theory that if an individual depended upon others for his or her maintenance it was due to some inherent personal defect or weakness was being reexamined. Settlement house residents and others, including charity organization society agents, did not deny that personal frailties and shortcomings contributed materially to want and insecurity, but they considered a poor environment or other adverse social or economic factors as the basic causes of poverty. Actually, some went even further, such as Edward T. Devine, who declared: "Personal depravity is as foreign to any sound theory of the hardships of our modern poor as witchcraft or demonic possession . . . these hardships are economic, social, transitional, measurable, [and] manageable."

Since in most cases need resulted from circumstances outside and beyond the control of the individual, he or she, therefore, ought not be held responsible for dependency—or locked up in an institution because of it. Unemployment, low wages and high living costs, overwork, unsanitary and unhealthful living conditions, dangerous working conditions and industrial accidents, poor health, lack of security in old age, child labor, and other shortcomings in the social and economic order took precedence over the idleness, improvidence, and intemperance considered primary by earlier advocates of the moralistic view of poverty. ("Many, many thousand families," wrote Robert Hunter in *Poverty,* "receive wages so inadequate that no care in spending . . . will make them suffice for the family needs.") Poor people were no longer considered a social burden, but an oppressed lot. Social reform was more important than the elevation of personal morality; anything short of that was only a "down payment" toward justice.

In view of the business at hand, reformers turned to two solutions to the problem as they saw it—preventive legislation and social insurance, or replacing charity with social justice. As for the first, their research and experience convinced them that the social evils had to be eradicated, that the forces breeding poverty and degrading living and working conditions had to be, and could be, eliminated. To discover the evils, to draft bills aimed at eliminating them, and then to arouse the public to support the proposed measures comprised the basic task. State intervention was not only permissible but essential. As Jane Addams phrased it: since the "very existence of the State depends upon the character of its citizens, . . . if certain industrial conditions are forcing the workers below the standard of decency, it becomes . . . [necessary to have] State regulation."

Specifically, legislation to establish and maintain fair standards of wages, hours, and housing, to prohibit child labor and regulate the dangerous trades, to establish more vigorous and effective public health programs, and to institute a more practical system of public education was proposed. And, in respect to the passage of this protective legislation, the reformers were highly successful.

They were far less successful, however, in achieving their second proposal—the enactment of a comprehensive system of compulsory social insurance against the hazards of sickness, unemployment, physical disability, old age, and the death of the family breadwinner. If dependency was primarily a problem of the social system rather than one of personal fault for which the needy should be blamed, to spread its burden more rationally, to regularize financing, and to assure recipients (or eligible recipients) of their benefits on the basis of objective qualifications, rather than official discretion, made sense. Despite that logic and the many European precedents for such action, the reformers were, at best, only partially successful in their efforts to substitute social cooperation for individual provision of losses and thus make life more secure for all. While they succeeded in getting widows' pensions, workmen's compensation, and some old-age pension programs, they were rebuffed in their attempts to secure health insurance and unemployment compensation; those efforts—the successful and the unsuccessful ones—will be discussed in Chapter 10.

Still, the reformers should be applauded for their efforts. Taken separately, the proposals for preventive legislation or those for distributing the costs of uncontrollable social and economic hazards were neither novel nor drastic. Taken together, however, they did imply a new attitude in America toward politics and economics. Nearly all the proposals involved, in one way or another and in varying degrees, limitations on private property rights and the extension of public authority into areas previously regarded as the exclusive preserve of the individual. Collectively, they demonstrated a strong tendency to substitute public benefit for private profit, to place human rights above property rights. At the time they were formulated, supporters of the measures referred to them as "preventive social work."[8] Since the Great Depression and the New Deal, when most of them were adopted, we have referred to them as the "welfare state."[9]

In the meantime, the settlements had declined in importance. They had been doing so since World War I, which had an adverse effect on them. While many residents supported the war, looking upon it as an opportunity to unite the nation in reform and reconstruction, many others—including Jane Addams, Grace Abbott, Lillian Wald, and other leaders—became preoccupied with international affairs, especially with efforts to keep America out of the struggle, and then, after its entrance, with attempts to bring a halt to the fighting. The less-than-enthusiastic support by these people of America's decision to enter the war and the efforts to bring the conflict to a quick end through negotiations were not particularly appreciated by a people intent upon destroying the "Hun." Public suspicion and distrust grew, and the settlements suffered; financial support was more difficult to obtain and people began to look elsewhere for leadership.

The immediate postwar recession made matters worse, as did the conservative reaction that set in with the return of prosperity. As Grace Abbott remarked, reform and social justice lost their

[8]Perhaps it should be noted that the same developments were occurring in England, where for some time there had been a great deal of dissatisfaction with the Poor Law Reform Act of 1834. In December 1905, a Royal Commission on the Poor Laws and the Relief of Distress was appointed to study the situation. After thirty-eight months of investigation and deliberation and the writing of fifty volumes, the commission completed its work and returned a report that departed drastically from the principles of 1834 and the idea of "less eligibility," namely, that the needy should be provided only bare maintenance under deterrent conditions. While there were majority and minority reports, members of both groups agreed on the need for more administrative centralization of the public welfare system, a public assistance program geared to prevention and rehabilitation, and creation of a compulsory universal tax-supported system of social services, including health care; in short, a positive rather than a negative approach, a constructive rather than an ameliorative one.

[9]It has been argued that these reformers laid the basis for the New Deal and the welfare state not only through their ideas and programs but through their organizations as well—"proto-bureaucratic associations" that were vital for the modern era. See Robert L. Buroker, "From Voluntary Association to Welfare State," *Journal of American History* 58 (December 1971): 643–60.

appeal in the Jazz Age: it was "a long, hard struggle . . . uphill all the way," she noted. The general public, keeping cool with Coolidge or relishing Herbert Hoover's "two chickens in every pot," became indifferent to the plight of the poor—or denied their existence.

Furthermore, there seemed to be less need for social settlements in the 1920s and thereafter. The growth of night and summer school programs, neighborhood youth centers, the Y.M.C.A., summer camps, and so on seemed to make their presence less imperative.

Of importance, too, were the population changes that occurred at the time. Not only did many members of the professional classes (including social workers) move out of the cities and into the suburbs, but so did the newly rich. The central city increasingly became the home of various minority groups that few people really cared about—Latin Americans, Puerto Ricans, Indians, and especially blacks migrating in large numbers from the rural South to northern cities. It was very difficult to raise money or to sustain interest in programs aimed at helping these people.

The settlements were also hurt by their inability to continue to attract the dedicated young reformers who had done so much to make them "spearheads for reform" early in the century. Aside from the changing nature of the urban population and the increased opportunities for women to enter the male work world, living in the slums of New York City was no longer as attractive as previously when compared to teaching school in Africa, working with the Red Cross in war-ravaged Europe, or even just living in Greenwich Village. In any event, for the most part, the postwar charity workers were not reformers; rather, they were professional social workers, graduates of training schools, experts in casework which, perhaps more than anything else, hastened the decline of the settlement movement.

Beginning in the second decade of the twentieth century, social workers became preoccupied with professionalization, resulting in an emphasis on specialization, technique, and expertise, especially in casework, including psychiatric casework. Casework, with its concern for the individual and emotional and personality problems, became not only fashionable but virtually synonymous with "social work." Settlement house residents, generalists without a well defined method who engaged in reform rather than in personality adjustment, were "old fashioned." As such, they were regarded as a threat by most of their "professional" colleagues, who spoke of clients rather than of neighbors in need. Thus, while not completely dead, the settlement house movement was seriously injured in the postwar years. In addition, those settlements that survived into the 1920s and after became, for the most part, institutions to serve the neighborhood rather than to alter it. Concentrating on "group work," they engaged largely in educational and recreational programs. While on occasion they cooperated with others in agitating for reform, they no longer led or initiated it. In 1928, Paul Kellogg referred to them as "convents and monasteries" rather than the "missionary outposts of yesteryear."

In the long run, these developments had many drawbacks. Among other things, participation by untrained volunteers was curtailed almost completely. Thus, social workers lost potential allies, interpreters, and sources of revenue, all of which they needed.

Too, social workers lost interest in research and reform. As a result, badly needed social legislation was either ignored or drafted by politicians who usually knew little and cared less about the needy than about creating the jobs and contracts on which the spoils system and staying in office rested.

The decline of the settlements also brought the demise of the principle of residence. Few social workers continued to communicate with the poor and the public as earlier residents had done. The new breed of social workers talked to their colleagues in their own jargon, at annual meetings or through professional journals. They lost touch with neighborhood leaders, local politicians, union organizers, and others speaking for the poor, especially for the new groups rapidly moving into the inner city.[10] As events in the 1960s all too clearly demonstrated, social

[10]Because these groups had no indigenous leaders and, for a variety of reasons, did not develop the array of voluntary associations—social, cultural, and philanthropic—which other immigrant groups had, they were really at the mercy of unconcerned politicians and were in a poorer position than their predecessors to meet hardship.

workers isolated themselves from the mainstream of American reform and were no longer friends of the poor.

The interest in casework and psychological, emotional, and mental problems was not entirely new to the "prosperity decade." Since that which affects a part, or parts, of the physical body also affects the mind, and vice versa, social workers and others realized long before that it was essential to concern themselves with mental as well as physical health.

Bibliography

ABBOTT, EDITH. "The Hull House of Jane Addams," *Social Service Review* 26 (September 1952): 334–38.

ADDAMS, JANE. "Charity and Social Justice," *North American Review* 192 (July 1910): 68–81.

———. "Function of the Social Settlements and the Labor Movement," *Annals of the American Academy of Political and Social Science* 13 (May 1899): 323–45.

———. *The Second Twenty Years at Hull-House*. New York: Macmillan, 1930.

———. *Twenty Years at Hull-House*. New York: Macmillan, 1910.

AMSTERDAM, SUSAN. "The National Women's Trade Union League," *Social Service Review* 56 (June 1982): 259–72.

APTHEKER, HERBERT. "DuBois on Florence Kelley," *Social Work* 11 (October 1966): 98–100.

ATHEY, LOUIS L. "Florence Kelley and the Quest for Negro Equality," *Journal of Negro History* 54 (October 1971): 249–61.

BLUMBERG, DOROTHY M. *Florence Kelley: The Making of a Social Pioneer*. New York: Kelley, 1967.

BUROKER, ROBERT L. "From Voluntary Association to Welfare State: The Illinois Immigrants' Protective League, 1908–1926," *Journal of American History* 58 (December 1971): 643–60.

CANDELA, JOSEPH L. "The Struggle to Limit the Hours and Raise the Wages of Working Women in Illinois, 1893–1917," *Social Service Review* 53 (March 1979): 15–34.

CHAMBERS, CLARKE A. *Paul U. Kellogg and the Survey*. Minneapolis: University of Minnesota Press, 1972.

————, AND ANDREA HINDING. "Charity Workers, the Settlements, and the Poor," *Social Casework* 49 (February 1968): 96–101.

COIT, STANTON. *Neighborhood Guilds, an Instrument of Social Reform.* London: Sonnenschein, 1891.

DAVIS, ALLEN F. *American Heroine: The Life and Legend of Jane Addams.* New York: Oxford University Press, 1973.

————. "The Social Workers and the Progressive Party, 1912–1916," *American Historical Review* 69 (April 1964): 671–88.

————. *Spearheads For Reform: The Social Settlements and the Progressive Movement, 1890–1914.* New York: Oxford University Press, 1967.

DEVINE, EDWARD T. *Misery and Its Causes.* New York: Macmillan, 1924.

————. *The Spirit of Social Work.* New York: Macmillan, 1911.

————. *When Social Work Was Young.* New York: Macmillan, 1939.

DINER, STEVEN J. "Chicago Social Workers and Blacks in the Progressive Era," *Social Service Review* 44 (December 1970): 393–410.

DUFFUS, ROBERT. *Lillian Wald, Neighbor and Crusader.* New York: Macmillan, 1938.

GANS, HERBERT J. "Redefining the Settlement's Function for the War on Poverty," *Social Work* 9 (October 1964): 3–12.

GILBERT, BENTLEY B. *The Evolution of National Insurance in Great Britain: The Origins of the Welfare State.* London: Joseph, 1966.

HAMILTON, ALICE. *Exploring the Dangerous Trades.* Boston: Little, Brown, 1943.

HARMON, SANDAR D. "Florence Kelley in Illinois," *Journal of the Illinois State Historical Society* 74 (Autumn 1981): 163–78.

HOPKINS, CHARLES H. *The Rise of the Social Gospel in American Protestantism, 1865–1915.* New Haven: Yale University Press, 1940.

HUNTER, ROBERT. *Poverty.* New York: Macmillan, 1904.

————. "The Relation Between Social Settlements and Charity Organization," *Proceedings* of the National Conference of Charities and Correction (Boston: Ellis, 1902): 302–14.

JACKSON, PHILIP. "Black Charity in Progressive Era Chicago," *Social Service Review* 52 (September 1978): 400–417.

KALBERG, STEPHEN. "The Commitment to Career Reform: The Settlement Movement Leaders," *Social Service Review* 49 (December 1975): 608–28.

KELLEY, FLORENCE. *Some Ethical Gains Through Legislation.* New York: Macmillan, 1905.

KIRSCHNER, DON S. "The Ambiguous Legacy: Social Justice and Social Control in the Progressive Era," *Historical Reflections* 2 (June 1975): 69–88.

KOGUT, ALVIN. "The Settlements and Ethnicity, 1890–1914," *Social Work* 17 (May 1972): 22–31.

LEIBY, JAMES. "How Social Workers Viewed the Immigration Problem—1880–1930," in *Current Issues in Social Work Seen in Historical Perspective*. New York: Council on Social Work Education, 1962.

———. "Social Welfare Institutions and the Poor," *Social Casework* 49 (February 1968): 90–95.

LEVINE, DANIEL. *Jane Addams and the Liberal Tradition*. Madison, Wis.: State Historical Society, 1971.

LUBOVE, ROY. *The Progressives and the Slums*. Pittsburgh: University of Pittsburgh Press, 1962.

McCLYMER, JOHN F. *War and Welfare: Social Engineering in America*. Westport, Conn.: Greenwood, 1980.

MAY, HENRY F. *Protestant Churches and Industrial America*. New York: Harper, 1949.

MENCHER, SAMUEL. "The Influence of Romanticism on Nineteenth Century British Social Work," *Social Service Review* 38 (June 1964): 174–90.

MOHL, RAYMOND, AND NEIL BETTEN. "Paternalism and Pluralism: Immigrants and Social Welfare in Gary, Indiana, 1906–1940," *American Studies* 15 (Spring 1974): 5–30.

NATHAN, MAUD. *The Story of an Epoch Making Movement*. Garden City, N.Y.: Doubleday, 1926.

OVINGTON, MARY W. *The Walls Came Tumbling Down*. New York: Harcourt, Brace, 1947.

PACEY, LORENE M., ed. *Readings in the Development of Settlement Work*. New York: Association Press, 1950.

PICHT, WERNER. *Toynbee Hall and the English Settlement Movement*. New York: Macmillan, 1914.

REINDERS, ROBERT C. "Toynbee Hall and the American Settlement Movement," *Social Service Review* 56 (March 1982): 39–54.

Report of the Royal Commission on the Poor Laws and Relief of Distress (1909), in Roy Lubove, ed., *Social Welfare in Transition*. Pittsburgh: University of Pittsburgh Press, 1966.

REYNOLDS, JAMES B. "The Settlement and Municipal Reform," *Proceedings* of the National Conference of Charities and Correction (Boston: Ellis, 1896): 138–42.

RIIS, JACOB. *How the Other Half Lives*. New York: Scribner's, 1890.

Ross, Edward A. *Social Control: A Survey of the Foundation of Social Order*. New York: Macmillan, 1901.

Rousmaniere, John P. "Cultural Hybrid in the Slums: The College Woman and the Settlement House, 1889–1894," *American Quarterly* 22 (Spring 1970): 45–66.

Scott, Anne F. "Jane Addams and the City," *Virginia Quarterly Review* 43 (Winter 1967): 53–60.

Scudder, Vida. *On Journey*. New York: Dutton, 1937.

Shapiro, Edward A. "Robert A. Woods and the Settlement House Impulse," *Social Service Review* 52 (June 1978): 215–26.

Simkhovitch, Mary K. *Neighborhood: My Story of Greenwich House*. New York: Norton, 1938.

———. *Twenty-Five Years of Greenwich House, 1902–1927*. New York: Greenwich House, 1927.

Taylor, Graham. *Chicago Commons Through Forty Years*. Chicago: University of Chicago Press, 1936.

———. *Pioneering on Social Frontiers*. Chicago: University of Chicago Press, 1930.

Taylor, Lea D. "The Social Settlement and Civic Responsibility—The Life Work of Mary McDowell and Graham Taylor," *Social Service Review* 28 (March 1954): 31–40.

Wade, Louise C. *Graham Taylor: Pioneer for Social Justice*. Chicago: University of Chicago Press, 1964.

———. "The Heritage from Chicago's Early Settlement Houses," *Illinois State Historical Society Journal* 60 (Winter 1967): 411–41.

Wald, Lillian D. *The House on Henry Street*. New York: Holt, 1915.

———. *Windows on Henry Street*. Boston: Little, Brown, 1934.

White, George C. "Social Settlements and Immigrant Neighbors, 1886–1914," *Social Service Review* 33 (March 1959): 55–66.

Wilson, Howard E. *Mary McDowell: Neighbor*. Chicago: University of Chicago Press, 1928.

Woods, Eleanor. *Robert A. Woods: Champion of Democracy*. Boston: Houghton Mifflin, 1929.

Woods, Robert. *The City Wilderness*. Boston: Houghton Mifflin, 1918.

———. *The Neighborhood in Nation-Building*. Boston: Houghton Mifflin, 1923.

———, and Albert J. Kennedy. *The Settlement Horizon: A National Estimate*. New York: Russell Sage Foundation, 1922.

Chapter 9

The Mental Health Movement

BECAUSE MENTAL HEALTH is an aspect of total health, it was essential that Americans develop a sound mental as well as public health program. The development of such a program resulted from a combination of public and private activities.

As we have seen, in the nineteenth century, the state began to assume responsibility for the care and treatment of the mentally ill, mainly by building and maintaining mental institutions. That trend, which Dorothea Dix furthered in the 1840s, continued for the next half-century, culminating in 1890 with passage of the historic New York State Care Act. Under its provisions, New York State assumed complete care of all its insane poor—chronic and acute cases alike. A milestone in the history of the care and treatment of the insane in America, the statute reached beyond the boundaries of New York in that it prompted similar action in other states.[1]

While for the most part the federal government adhered to the principles of the Pierce veto and thus, throughout the nineteenth century, did little in this as in other fields of social welfare, indirectly it took at least one significant action. Due largely to prompting by the state boards of charities, the U.S. Congress enacted legislation in 1882 making it unlawful for the mentally ill

[1]Among the fundamental provisions of the act, which swept away all local responsibility for the indigent insane, were the following: The mentally ill in all county institutions (with the exception of three) were to be removed to state hospitals as rapidly as accommodations could be accorded them; the state was to be districted, each state hospital receiving the patients in its district; the entire cost of the system was to be borne by the state (which was prohibited from requiring relatives to reimburse it for the expenses incurred in maintaining their poor kin).

to enter the country; and over the next several years it revised and stengthened that legislation.

By the turn of the century, then, the federal and state governments were participating, in one way or another, in the field of mental hygiene, still largely centered, however, in "asylums." Over the next forty or fifty years, however, private citizens—physicians and members of the laity, including social workers—led the way in developing a new mental health program, one designed to replace custodial institutions with what one analyst has called "civic medicine"—a variety of individualized community-based programs, one of which was "aftercare" work.

Aftercare of the insane, or providing temporary assistance for people discharged from mental institutions, was not a new idea when in 1905 it was mentioned for the first time at the National Conference of Charities and Correction. Although widely used in Europe, especially in London and Paris, the plan had never been tried in America. Yet within a few years it became one of the most important features of work with the mentally ill.

After hearing of the idea at the National Conference, Alexander Johnson, long-time secretary of that organization who was then head of the New York School of Philanthropy, and Homer Folks of the New York State Charities Aid Association, hired two young social work students to investigate the condition of the patients discharged from the Manhattan State (Mental) Hospital during the previous three months. To their amazement, they discovered that about one-third of the patients could not be found, although so short a time had elapsed since their discharge. Of the remaining ones, it was discovered that some were doing well, some were in danger of relapse, and some were once again seriously disturbed. It appeared certain that some of the former patients would have benefited from suitable aftercare work at the time they were discharged.

On the basis of this study and the belief that the social environment of patients could contribute to the prevention and cure of mental problems, a voluntary statewide aftercare system for the insane was launched in New York. Working under the direction and control of the New York State Charities Aid Association's central office in New York City (and in the tradition of the "friendly visitor"), volunteer aftercare committees for each of the state's mental hospitals were organized to provide "temporary [financial] assistance, employment, friendly aid and counsel for needy persons discharged recovered" from mental institutions.

Aftercare work—which looked not to the chronic patient and dependence but to the cured indigent person and independence —was a manifestation of the larger progressive social reform movement of the period, which emphasized the underprivileged individual and his or her social environment. Its essence was the recognition of a mental patient as a human being, not simply a case, and, like the juvenile court and probation, it was based on the conviction that an individual's behavior was determined to a large extent by his or her surroundings. "The process of cure is not completed when the hospital doors open and the patient leaves," explained one proponent of the system. "The opportunity and the need for treatment, advice, aid, and counsel," he continued, "are only [a] little less in the period immediately following release from the hospital than they were in the period preceding such release."

In large part, then, aftercare work was a formal recognition of the medical value of a constructive intellectual and emotional environment in the treatment of what are now called neurotic diseases. It was no accident that it paralleled not only the rise of reform in social welfare but psychotherapy in psychiatry, behaviorism in psychology, and public health work in medicine. As James V. May, an eminent New York psychiatrist, phrased it early in the century: "If the mental habits and surroundings of an individual are largely responsible for the onset [or recurrence] of a psychosis, we can look forward to accomplishments which may rival the success achieved in the crusade against tuberculosis." Science and reformism went hand in hand in this as in other areas.

In any event, by the end of the aftercare program's first year of operation in New York State (1907), interest in the subject, which received widespread publicity, was aroused and organizations in other states began to take up the work. Within a few years—beginning in 1911 in New York, by which time less emphasis was placed on economic assistance and more on psychological adjustment—trained social workers were placed on the payrolls of mental hospitals (giving birth, in effect, to psychiatric social work) and aftercare work became (and still is) an integral part of the services of all such institutions throughout the United States.[2]

Early aftercare work in New York had much broader consequences. In New Haven, Connecticut, on May 6, 1908, Clifford Beers, a former mental patient interested in and influenced by the aftercare work being carried on in New York State, organized the Connecticut Society for Mental Hygiene, the first committee of its kind, thus initiating the organized mental health movement in America.

Let us consider its background. In 1900, three years after graduating from Yale University, Clifford Beers succumbed to severe mental illness, which ran a course from mute depression to extreme excitement. After an unsuccessful suicide attempt, he was confined. During his three years in public and private institutions, he suffered not only from deprivation but from severe cruelty on the part of incompetent, callous, and even sadistic attendants and members of medical staffs. Upon his discharge, he was determined to expose the evils of the system, hoping to bring relief to the other victims of such harsh treatment in the nation's insane asylums, retreats, and sanatoriums.

Five years later, in 1908, with the help of others, including William James, the noted Harvard psychologist, and Adolf Meyer, the Swiss immigrant who became America's most influential psychiatrist, Clifford Beers published his famous *A Mind That Found Itself,* a graphic description of his mental collapse, the inhuman treatment to which he was subjected, his recovery, and his determination to effect radical changes in the system. While the book did not immediately alter the care of the mentally ill, it did stimulate interest in the subject. Beers then formed the Connecticut Society and began his lifelong crusade.

According to his plan (one that eventually came to fruition), the Connecticut Society was to be the first in a growing network of societies extending across the United States and around the

---

[2]Actually, it could be argued that psychiatric social work began in 1905 (the same year in which medical social work began) when for the first time a social worker was employed to work with mental patients in a hospital—in the neurological clinic of the Massachusetts General Hospital under the direction of Dr. James J. Putnam. The following year, a social worker was employed in the psychopathic wards of Bellevue Hospital.

world; it was to serve as a pilot effort to provide experience in organizing. As soon as feasible, he proposed to found a national society, a plan he carried out to the letter when, on February 19, 1909, he invited about a dozen people to come to New York City's Manhattan Hotel for the purpose of creating the National Committee for Mental Hygiene (later the National Association for Mental Health), a group instrumental in improving mental hospitals, in arousing public concern over the nation's unfortunate victims of mental illness, and in furthering prevention of the disease.

Most fundamental for mental health work was a knowledge of the disease and its causes, and a movement for its prevention. Despite the nineteenth-century work of physicians and lay reformers such as Dorothea Dix and others, these were still lacking, for the most part—even at the time the National Committee for Mental Hygiene was organized. While the early twentieth century presaged hopeful developments, including an increasing concern with the causes and treatment of mental illness (as opposed to the mere classification and custody of sufferers), preventive medicine had not yet really permeated the field.

Among the few who comprehended, or at least wrestled with, the true nature of mental disease, there was some agreement as to its major causes. As byproducts of such diseases as typhoid, diphtheria, and influenza, the body was sometimes so weakened that interference with the nervous system occurred and mental breakdown followed. Also, concussions, falls, and other accidents were said to cause insanity at times. There were, then, physical or somatic causes of the disease which, generally speaking (with the exception of maintaining a sound body), could not be prevented—by the patient or by the doctor; in such cases medical treatment by kind, concerned physicians was the answer.

Doctors, however, were most interested in what were considered to be the moral and psychological causes of insanity, such things as intemperance, domestic difficulties, marital problems, jealousy, pride, excessive ambitions, personal disappointments, daydreaming, brooding, fears and anxieties, and especially the pressures of an urban, industrial, and commercial civilization. These not only seemed to account for the largest number of mental cases but appeared to be preventable.

The question of heredity and mental illness was controversial.

Many felt it was an important, if not the main, cause of insanity. Foremost among those stressing the woeful results of heredity were physicians connected with the nation's institutions for the feebleminded. Others gave it only secondary importance at best. One did not inherit insanity, they claimed, although mental instability was another matter. This, though, was no cause for alarm. An unstable person, whether he or she came from a family with a history of mental illness or not, could escape the dread consequences through proper training (especially during childhood), good surroundings, healthful and temperate activities, and a suitable mental and physical regime. The most important fact with regard to heredity and insanity, they pointed out, was that most ancestors of each individual were normal. Therefore, heredity tended strongly toward mental health rather than illness.

On the basis of what facts were known, or believed (and the experience of the early aftercare work), the National Committee for Mental Hygiene, in conjunction with state and local groups—as well as some physicians, social workers, and other interested citizens—began to fill the obvious need for a widespread educational campaign on the causes, early diagnosis, prevention, and treatment of mental illness. Attempting to mold a sympathetic public opinion and convince the public that insanity could be prevented or cured—if, after all, the disease resulted from either individual shortcomings or physical breakdown, it followed that a healthy social and medical environment could reverse the tendency (providing it had not yet reached a chronic stage)—they distributed hundreds of thousands of leaflets endorsed by knowledgeable physicians, supplied newspapers and periodicals with news and information, sponsored lectures in the larger cities, and prepared exhibits for conferences and other large meetings.

Sympathy and knowledge were not enough. The reformers saw the vital importance of having resources in the community for detecting and treating the illness, especially in rural areas where such facilities were almost totally lacking; it availed little to understand the needs of the mentally ill if treatment was impossible because of a lack of facilities. For this reason, their chief goal was the founding, wherever needed, of free child guidance clinics, dispensaries, outpatient centers, and hospitals for the early detection, diagnosis, and treatment of mental disorders.

Social workers, as individuals and in their official capacities, helped develop and strengthen not only the therapeutic model but also mental health work itself through these outreach programs and facilities. They realized that efficient social services were a necessary corollary to successful clinical work. Moreover, a reduction in mental illness would not only lessen suffering, but because as much as one-sixth of the entire budget in many states went for caring for the insane, it would also release a large sum of money that might be expended on more constructive measures for social betterment. Crusaders for mental health, then, just as those working for the prevention of tuberculosis and other physical ailments, courted two natural instincts—self-interest and altruism; by helping to prevent (and cure) insanity, they served both the sick and themselves.

While the mental hygiene movement never entirely fulfilled its promise—as David Rothman has shown in *Conscience and Convenience,* many patients remained confined to overcrowded institutions, where they were ignored or mistreated, and others never were identified and helped—progress did occur. By the 1920s and 1930s, free clinics for mental patients could be found, if not in rural areas, at least in most large cities around the nation. There, the ailing could receive expert medical consultation and treatment as well as social services from field agents, trained nurses, and social workers attached to the clinics as well as to staffs of state hospitals.

In broad terms, through its efforts to create a wholesome physical and social environment as a key to mental hygiene (as well as its new way of looking at mental illness, especially the notion that it was susceptible to research and could be prevented), the mental health crusade may be interpreted as part of the larger struggle after 1900 to conserve the nation's human as well as physical resources. Like other reforms that sought to improve the social conditions of men, women, and children, the campaign to prevent mental illness represented an effort to liberate the human personality from a repressive burden—a mental rather than a physical one.

In addition to the crusade to prevent insanity, another important early twentieth-century campaign—one in which social workers again played a crucial role—was the movement for the identification, custodial care, special education, and social supervision of higher-grade defectives, the feebleminded, or retarded, as they are now called.[3] The ugly aspects of neglected feeblemindedness had been revealed many times to social workers, especially to child welfare workers who, in the course of their work, discovered entire families and even groups of families that were feebleminded.

Most early studies of the feebleminded, such as Robert Dugdale's *The Jukes* (1877) and the Reverend Oscar C. McCulloch's "The Tribe of Ishmael" (1888), supposedly supplied data to support the thesis that the feebleminded tended almost invariably to reproduce and multiply their kind in increasing number. The studies also showed, or seemed to show, an undue amount of disease, incapacity, pauperism, alcoholism, crime, and vice among the descendants of certain family groups, indicating the inheritance of mental retardation and these other "traits."[4]

The first large-scale systematic survey of the care and control of the feebleminded was undertaken by the British Royal Commission in 1904. In 1908, the commission published an eight-volume report that reaffirmed most of the stereotypes, including the hereditary nature of feeblemindedness. As a result, the mentally deficient, like the diseased and the defective, were for the most part tucked away in custodial institutions and forgotten.

Concern about the problem of feeblemindedness in this country was heightened as a result of the British study. A series of further studies, investigations, and reports on the subject by American investigators followed (including H. H. Goddard's *The Kallikak Family*, 1912), all of which agreed with the earlier findings.

---

[3]There is no generally accepted definition of feeblemindedness. However, there is agreement that the term contains three essential and interrelated concepts: (1) marked limitation or deficiency of intelligence, frequently associated with other shortcomings of personality, due to (2) lack of normal development, rather than to mental disease or deterioration, which manifests itself in (3) social and economic incompetence.

[4]The work of some Europeans in related fields seemed to verify these findings, especially the research of the influential criminologist, Cesare Lombroso. After a series of detailed studies, Lombroso concluded that criminal behavior resulted from atavistic heredity; criminals displayed the marks of savagery—oddly shaped heads, hooked noses, cleft palates, etc. The message was clear: deviant behavior was hereditary and, therefore, not susceptible to social reform.

Concerned citizens who saw the need to act pointed out the differences between the insane and the feebleminded, for, while both groups were mentally defective, they differed in significant ways. In general, feeblemindedness occurred earlier in life than insanity. Insanity was seen to arise largely from external factors while feeblemindedness appeared to be congenital. More important, much insanity seemed preventable through hygienic measures, whereas feeblemindedness appeared to be controllable only through death, sterilization, or segregation during the reproductive years.

To a few alarmists, euthanasia was the solution. Wiser counsel, however, advocated eugenics, the science of improving the human race by better breeding through the use of sterilization or segregation—another import from England. Despite its frightful implications and possible uses, eugenics actually reflected the rise of the preventive ideal among reformers. The prevention of feeblemindedness seemed to be a key in the fight against crime, pauperism, and prostitution; by preventing the birth of children condemned by defective heredity to lives of sinfulness, squalor, and vice, its advocates thought of themselves as humanitarians seeking the improvement of society. They were convinced that eugenics was a reform of major value, and no doubt many people believed them since it became public policy during the era—one usually referred to as the era of Progressivism. Beginning with Indiana in 1907, fifteen states enacted sterilization laws within a few years.

This is not to say that the matter was not controversial. Proponents of sterilization met with a great deal of opposition not only from people whose response was moral and emotional, but also from scholars and in many cases from social workers, who argued that the research behind the movement was inadequate. While they acknowledged that the problem was a serious one and a matter of public concern, they also felt that the hereditary transmission of mental and moral characteristics according to known genetic laws had not been conclusively proved. For them, the most practical and acceptable means of controlling the reproduction of the feebleminded was not with a scalpel, but through segregation in institutions during the childbearing years.

Unfortunately, there were not enough facilities to go around.

Studies of the problem demonstrated both the evils that resulted from allowing the feebleminded to remain at large, and the overcrowded conditions at existing institutions. Hence, social workers throughout the country, either individually or through the National Committee on Provision for the Feebleminded and similar groups, carried on major campaigns to remedy the situation. In response to their efforts, state after state provided funds for more institutions to care for and segregrate the feebleminded.[5]

This response failed to solve the problem. During the 1920s, it was estimated that only a fraction of the feebleminded who, most experts agreed, comprised about 3 percent of the total population, were in institutions. In New York, one of the nation's most progressive states, only about 8 percent of its feebleminded were in institutions in 1923. There were simply not enough custodial facilities to provide places for all who needed them.

As it turned out, infatuation with heredity proved to be relatively short-lived; by the 1920s, it was fading rapidly. The decline stemmed in part from an awareness of the unsavory uses to which extreme hereditarian ideas might be put, and in part from a growing knowledge of the complex relationship between heredity and environment. More meaningful experiments were conducted, both on animals and on human beings, which cast doubt on the simple assumption that mental defects (and illness) stemmed directly and inevitably from the genes. Other studies called into question the earlier findings that the feebleminded were extremely prolific and outrunning "normal stocks," that they were dangerous, and that they could not manage their own affairs.

Concurrently, the introduction of Freudian ideas and of behaviorism turned psychologists and others to the study of early childhood experiences to explain the apparently inexplicable traits that earlier had been attributed to heredity. As a result, new devices for the care of the feebleminded emerged. Such measures

[5]Eugenists, of course, could not ignore the birth control movement launched by Margaret Sanger in the second decade of the twentieth century. A minority opposed the movement out of conviction that, on the whole, persons who were prudent and farsighted would make most use of birth control; hence, those who had qualities that made them desirable parents would be influenced to refrain from parenthood. A majority of eugenists, however, supported birth control. Indeed, by the 1920s, they led the movement in the hope that proper education would lead the indigent and others to practice restraint in their breeding.

were constructive rather than repressive in that, through training, those mentally deficient who were capable of adjustment would be restored to society.

Along these lines, the parole and colony plans, long used in caring for the feebleminded in Scotland, Belgium, and Germany, were developed in America. Under the parole plan, those retarded persons deemed suitable for normal life were permitted to return to the community on a trial basis while they remained under the continuing supervision of the institution's field agent or social worker. Dr. Walter E. Fernald (of Waverly, Massachusetts) was the first in this country to prepare certain mentally deficient charges for the more normal life in the community.

The colony idea rested on the principle that it was both inhumane and uneconomical to confine to the wards of an institution many strong, able-bodied persons simply because of a mental deficiency. Dr. Charles Bernstein, superintendent of the State School for Mental Defectives at Rome, New York, was the first to establish in an extensive and practical way a colony for the feebleminded in America.

Social workers—who, as a result of their child care work had experience with both parole and placing-out—became leading advocates in a campaign to utilize these plans for the mentally deficient. They had become convinced that it was both possible and desirable to remove some inmates from institutions and to place them in a more normal environment. Living and working where they could help care for and support themselves, they could still be supervised for their own and the public's safety. Placing-out also offered the further advantage of releasing institutional beds for more serious cases, especially for those from whom society needed protection.

The wisdom and usefulness of these plans, wrote the author of *Social Control of the Mentally Deficient,* published in 1930, "have been amply demonstrated." For the patients, they provided an outlet for energies through practical vocational training and actual development, as well as an opportunity to prove their ability to return to community life. For the public at large, the parole and colony systems offered a means of segregating and training large numbers of subnormal individuals without heavy tax burdens.

Still, not all of the mentally deficient were brought under state or medical supervision; many could not be located, and others would not "surrender." Therefore, many remained at large and attended public schools. Consequently, reformers faced this problem by helping to organize special classes for the handicapped.

The first special class for the mentally deficient in an American public school was established in Providence, Rhode Island, in 1896. Few other school systems followed suit, however, even when Alfred Binet's famous psychiatric testing techniques, which suggested that intelligence could be scientifically measured and classes established on that basis, reached America in 1906. Those school systems that did set up such classes usually made them voluntary. As a result, there were few in existence when in 1917 New York (and subsequently other states) made such classes mandatory. State aid, which social workers helped to obtain, was effective in increasing their number and quality since, in order to be eligible for the aid, school systems usually required that teachers meet exacting qualifications.

In the meantime, the movement to prevent insanity continued, with disappointing results. In a sequel to his earlier study on the nineteenth-century origins of institutions for the deviant and dependent, David Rothman has told the story of their twentieth-century alternatives—the mental hygiene programs, psychopathic hospitals, and outpatient clinics discussed earlier. In that work, *Conscience and Convenience,* he argued that those measures, designed to replace custodial institutions, fell far short of their goals (just as the earlier institutions had done). According to Rothman, they failed chiefly because personnel in the field, primarily superintendents of the older institutions, "conveniently" used the reforms (including expanded state authority) to their own advantage and succeeded in more or less perpetuating the status quo.

Whatever the reason, the number of mentally ill in need of institutional treatment continued to rise. In most states, the number of mental patients equaled that of all other state dependents combined. Overcrowding in hospitals was extremely serious and interfered with proper care and treatment. Furthermore, many of the aged buildings were firetraps and in dangerous states of disrepair. Throughout the 1920s and 1930s, concerned citizens labored with some success to finance programs to repair old and to build new mental institutions.

Such programs, however, could not keep pace with the high annual increase in mental illness. New developments in the field, though, finally began to have some impact. The use of "extrainstitutional" methods of care (parole and boarding-out) for selected mental patients (as well as for retardates), the discovery of insulin shock treatment as a cure for some forms of mental illness, and the appearance (in the 1940s) of other cheaper and more easily administered forms of shock therapy—Metrazol and electric—at least slowed the rate of growth of the nation's mental institutions, for the first time in American history.

About then, one of the most outstanding examples of a private agency's contributions to mental health and national welfare was conceived of and initiated by Katharine Ecob of the New York State Charities Aid Association's Committee on Mental Hygiene. During the early stages of World War II, as during World War I, because of the large number of men drafted, the speed with which they had to be examined, and the limited number of available psychiatrists, eliminating the mentally unfit from the draft was an enormous and basically impossible task. In the hasty procedures at draft boards and induction centers, draftees took five-minute psychiatric tests to determine their mental fitness for service in the armed forces. Mistakes were costly to the military, the taxpayers, and the individuals involved.[6]

In March 1941, it became evident to Miss Ecob that voluntary mental health agencies could assist the Selective Service boards in dealing with the problem. It appeared that the screening of drafted men would be vastly more effective if, among other things, social histories of the registrants were available to the medical and psychiatric examiners at induction centers. Therefore, she prepared a program designed to implement the idea which—after a hurried trip to the nation's capital—was approved on a trial basis by Dr. L. G. Rowntree, chief of the Medical Division, National Headquarters, Selective Service System.

[6]During World War I, General Pershing, American military chief overseas, cabled: "Prevalence of mental disorders in replacement troops received suggests urgent importance of intensive efforts in eliminating the mentally unfit from organizations in new draft prior to departure from the United States."

The plan included a six-point program whereby the State Charities Aid Association's Committee on Mental Hygiene would act as an intermediary between those in need of psychiatric service and those willing to provide it, ranging from offering psychiatric review courses to a followup program for men found unfit for military service. Of more immediate importance was the social service for securing and providing social histories of all men called up for the draft.

All available information about registrants was obtained by volunteer, trained social workers attached to local boards as field agents. They canvassed the communities in which the selectees lived, including employers, welfare agencies, school reports, court and hospital records, and the like; any history indicating unfitness for military service was summarized and presented to the local draft boards and to the examining psychiatrists at induction centers.

By the close of 1942, the committee had enlisted the volunteer services of over 700 social workers, attached to every draft board in New York State. At the peak of the work, some 19,000 names were being investigated monthly by these workers. Selective Service officials found the program, first planned for the army, so helpful that it was extended to all the armed forces. In the spring of 1943, the service was made mandatory throughout the state. And in October 1943, the War Manpower Commission announced the adoption of the plan on a comprehensive nationwide scale. Before the end of the conflict, the services of several thousand social workers were utilized to obtain the personal histories of more than a million men.

In the meantime, a federal program to provide psychiatric treatment to members and former members of the armed forces, established two decades earlier, had collapsed. Immediately after World War I, the United States government initiated a program of medical care, including psychiatric services, for soldiers and veterans who needed them. The services were rendered at local and state facilities at federal expense. The arrangement proved unsatisfactory, though, as the service was costly and usually not very good.

The problem appeared to be solved when in 1920 the newly created federal Veterans Bureau (which brought together five federal agencies serving the needs of veterans and members of the armed forces and which, in turn, in 1930 merged with the Bureau of Pensions and a number of other federal agencies into the Veterans Administration) established a chain of veterans' hospitals.

While during the interwar years these hospitals did some creative work in treating "battle fatigue," or what was then called "shell shock," on the whole they proved disappointing. They, too, were very costly, and for the most part rather backward, mainly because they took little part in psychiatric research and training and, as a result of political decisions, were located in remote places. As a result, by the time World War II broke out, they had virtually collapsed.

Therefore, when World War II came to an end, there were still several important needs for future progress in the field of mental health. More and better trained psychiatrists and hospitals were badly needed, as were new methods of treatment, greater knowledge of the causes of insanity, and stronger efforts for its prevention. Through a revamping of the Veterans Administration and passage of the National Mental Health Act, signed into law by President Harry S. Truman on July 3, 1946, Congress took giant steps toward fulfilling these needs.

Both of these developments resulted from World War II, which, like previous wars, brought some major advances along with the death and destruction. When the nation sifted through its manpower to raise a fighting force for the war, some very interesting, but unpleasant, national health statistics came to light—none more startling than those on mental illness and nervous diseases. Some 1,100,000 out of 4,800,000 men—almost 25 percent—were rejected for military duty because of mental or neurological disorders, by far the largest single group deemed unfit for service. Furthermore, of those inducted into the armed forces and subsequently given medical discharges, about 40 percent, close to 400,000 men, were dismissed for psychiatric disorders. Clearly, mental illness was one of the nation's major social problems. A revitalized Veterans Administration and the National Mental Health Act were the responses of the American people and the U.S. Congress to these conditions.

Under the aegis of a reinvigorated Veterans Administration, a nationwide program of services for veterans was established, including a wide distribution of mental hospitals and community clinics, many of which were located near medical schools, from whose counsel and cooperation they profited. In addition to providing a high quality of inpatient care, the facilities extended outpatient services as well, demonstrating the value and practicability of psychiatric services at the community level. And finally, as part of its total service to all veterans, the V.A. committed the facilities to training programs in psychiatry, clinical psychology, and psychiatric social work.

The National Mental Health Act, which created a Mental Hygiene Division within the United States Public Health Service, and a center for information and research that later became the National Institute of Mental Health, was designed mainly to develop preventive health measures. It provided for an extensive mental health program by enabling the states and private institutions to obtain federal funds for research, professional training, and community mental health programs. In short, it authorized a broad national program to combat mental illness and, more than any other development, represented a repudiation of the position taken by President Pierce in his veto message of 1854. The campaign to correct abuses in the institutional care of the mentally ill, begun in the first half of the nineteenth century by Dorothea Dix and others, had by the mid-twentieth century developed into a broad movement for mental health.

Still, conditions did not improve dramatically after passage of the National Mental Health Act. Mental illness remained a serious problem and state institutions continued to be overcrowded, in bad repair, and costly to operate. In addition, as in the area of juvenile corrections and elsewhere, critics were claiming that professional services and facilities, especially "institutions," tended to worsen rather than improve the situation for their clients. In 1954 Alfred Stanton and Morris Schwartz published *The Mental Hospital: A Study of Institutional Participation in Psychiatric Illness and Treatment,* which argued that the organization and milieu of the traditional state mental hospital made patients worse. Then came the real breakthrough— tranquilizing drugs. Introduced on a large scale that same year, they not only improved life on the wards but also, and perhaps more important, made it possible to discharge many patients who, with the help of such drugs (which decrease emotional agitation without impairing alertness), and sometimes with other assistance, could function in the community.[7] As a result, by 1957 most states had stabilized or reduced their mental hospital populations despite a continued rise in first admissions. The real problem, thereafter, was (and is still) to locate the large number of psychologically ill or maladjusted people in the community who never sought or received help and to establish adequate community mental health facilities to meet their needs.[8] In the meantime, some notable advances in public welfare occurred.

Bibliography

ACKERKNECHT, ERWIN H. *A Short History of Psychiatry*. New York: Hafner, 1959.

ALTSCHULE, MARK D. *Roots of Modern Psychiatry*. New York: Grune and Stratton, 1957.

BASSETT, CLARA. *The School and Mental Health*. New York: Macmillan, 1931.

BEERS, CLIFFORD. *A Mind That Found Itself*. New York: Longmans, Green, 1909.

BROMBERG, WALTER. *The Mind of Man: A History of Psychotherapy and Psychoanalysis*. New York: Harper, 1959.

BURNHAM, JOHN C. "Psychiatry, Psychology, and the Progressive Movement," *American Quarterly* 12 (Winter 1960): 457–65.

[7]Important in this regard was passage in 1955 of the New York State Community Mental Health Services Act, which other states quickly copied. The measure offered state aid to localities for the establishment of mental hygiene clinics, which stimulated the construction of such facilities. The state could afford to do that since it derived savings from not having to construct, repair, and operate as many mental hospitals and since it could place ex-patients on categorical assistance—Aid to the Permanently and Totally Disabled—and thereby have the federal government share the cost of their maintenance.

[8]The community mental health program was not in very good shape or standing as late as the 1970s; its performance was dubious and its support was declining. A report by a Ralph Nader study group that undertook to represent the "consumer interest" was very negative, to say the least: "The centers," it declared, "have been neither accountable backwards to the National Institute of Mental Health . . . nor forward to the consumers and citizens in the community they allegedly serve. They have often become . . . windfalls for psychiatrists who have systematically ignored the program's directives to serve poor and . . . blue collar workers."

CRUTCHER, HESTER B. *Foster Home Care for Mental Patients.* New York: Commonwealth Fund, 1944.

DAIN, NORMAN. *Clifford Beers: Advocate for the Insane.* Pittsburgh: University of Pittsburgh Press, 1980.

DAVIES, STANLEY P. *The Mentally Retarded in Society.* New York: Columbia University Press, 1959.

––––––. *Social Control of the Mentally Deficient.* New York: Crowell, 1930.

DEUTSCH, ALBERT. *The Mentally Ill in America.* New York: Doubleday, 1937.

––––––. *One Hundred Years of American Psychiatry.* New York: Columbia University Press, 1944.

DUGDALE, ROBERT. *The Jukes.* New York: Putnam, 1877.

FOX, RICHARD W. *So Far Disordered in Mind: Insanity in California, 1870–1930.* Los Angeles: University of California Press, 1978.

GISH, LOWELL. *Reform at Osawatomie State Hospital: Treatment of the Mentally Ill, 1866–1970.* Lawrence, Kans.: University of Kansas Press, 1972.

GLUECK, BERNARD. "Special Preparation of the Psychiatric Social Worker," *Proceedings* of the National Conference of Social Work (Chicago: Rogers and Hall, 1919): 599–606.

GODDARD, H. H.. *The Kallikak Family.* New York: Macmillan, 1912.

GREENBLATT, MILTON. *From Custodial to Therapeutic Patient Care in Mental Hospitals.* New York: Russell Sage Foundation, 1955.

GROB, GERALD. "Mental Illness, Indigency, and Welfare: The Mental Hospital in Nineteenth-Century America," in Tamara K. Harevan, ed., *Anonymous Americans.* Englewood Cliffs, N.J.: Prentice-Hall, 1971.

––––––. *The State and the Mentally Ill.* Chapel Hill, N.C.: University of North Carolina Press, 1966.

HALLER, MARK H. *Eugenics: Hereditarian Attitudes in American Thought.* New Brunswick, N.J.: Rutgers University Press, 1963.

––––––. "Heredity in Progressive Thought," *Social Service Review* 37 (June 1963): 166–76.

HEALY, WILLIAM. "The Bearings of Psychology on Social Case Work," *Proceedings* of the National Conference of Social Work (Chicago: Hildmann, 1917): 104–12.

JARRET, MARY. "Psychiatric Social Work," *Proceedings* of the National Conference of Social Work (Chicago: University of Chicago Press, 1921): 381–85.

————. "The Psychiatric Thread Running Through All Social Case Work," *Proceedings* of the National Conference of Social Work (Chicago: Rogers and Hall, 1919): 587–93.

LEE, PORTER, AND MARION KENWORTHY. *Mental Hygiene and Social Work*. New York: Commonwealth Fund, 1931.

McCULLOCH, OSCAR C. "The Tribe of Ishmael: A Study in Social Degradation," *Proceedings* of the National Conference of Charities and Correction (Boston: Ellis, 1888): 154–59.

MECHANIC, DAVID. *Mental Health and Social Policy*. Englewood Cliffs, N.J.: Prentice-Hall, 1969.

OWINGS, C. "What Social Hygiene Problems Confront the Social Worker?", *Journal of Social Hygiene* 17 (November 1931): 468–77.

PICKENS, DONALD K. *Eugenics and the Progressives*. Nashville, Tenn.: Vanderbilt University Press, 1969.

POLLACK, HORATIO, ed. *Family Care of Mental Patients: A Review of Family Care in America and Europe*. Utica, N.Y.: State Hospitals' Press, 1936.

PRATT, GEORGE. "Twenty Years of the National Committee for Mental Hygiene," *Mental Hygiene* 14 (April 1930): 399–428.

RIDENOUR, NINA. *Mental Health in the United States*. Cambridge, Mass.: Harvard University Press, 1961.

ROTHMAN, DAVID J. *Conscience and Convenience: The Asylum and Its Alternatives in Progressive America*. Boston: Little, Brown, 1980.

RUSSELL, WILLIAM. *The New York Hospital: A History of the Psychiatric Service, 1771–1936*. New York: Columbia University Press, 1945.

SICHERMAN, BARBARA. "The Paradox of Prudence: Mental Health in the Gilded Age," *Journal of American History* 62 (March 1976): 890–912.

STANTON, ALFRED, AND MORRIS SCHWARTZ. *The Mental Hospital: A Study of Institution Participation in Psychiatric Illness and Treatment*. New York: Basic Books, 1954.

VECOLI, RUDOLPH J. "Sterilization: A Progressive Measure?", *Wisconsin Magazine of History* 43 (Spring 1960): 190–202.

WINTERS, EUNICE. "Adolf Meyer and Clifford Beers, 1907–1910," *Bulletin of the History of Medicine* 43 (September-October 1969): 414–43.

WOODWARD, LUTHER, ed. *Psychiatric Social Workers and Mental Health*. New York: National Association of Social Workers, 1960.

Chapter 10

Renaissance of Public Welfare

FROM THE START, care of the needy in America was a public responsibility. As we have seen, however, over the years, private citizens, either individually or in groups, undertook the administration of aid and services to the dependent. While such assistance became more and more popular, it remained a voluntary assumption by private individuals of a public task; the government's legal responsibility to aid those in need stood unchanged. Nevertheless, by the late nineteenth century, welfare work had become more of a private or voluntary matter than a public one; save for placing the destitute elderly and the permanently disabled in public institutions, public assistance had been substantially curtailed or in many cases even abolished.

In the early years of the twentieth century, however, as the complex of problems associated with rapid industrialization, urbanization, and immigration intensified—especially economic insecurity and deprivation—a growing number of reformers saw the need for more public assistance. The magnitude of the task, they felt, called for greater monetary support than agencies controlled by volunteers could command. Moreover, since poverty was a social rather than an individual matter, more public intervention and aid was not only necessary but just. There was room for public welfare and private charity work. The best results could be obtained by the two working in harmony rather than by one outdoing or assuming superiority over the other. After two decades of activity, the advocates of more public assistance succeeded in redressing the balance, at least to an extent. At the same time, they laid the foundation for many of the important public welfare developments of the 1930s.

201

An early success was the historic White House Conference of 1909. The idea to call a White House conference on dependent children came from James E. West, a Washington lawyer and close friend of President Theodore Roosevelt who later became head of the Boy Scouts of America. An orphan who was reared in an institution, West was interested in the problem of caring for dependent youngsters. He thought that a national conference on the subject would attract attention and be useful, especially if called by the President and held at the White House. Accordingly, West broached the idea to Roosevelt, urging him to "cooperate in an effort to bring the problem of the nation's unfortunate children before the American people." After West got the support of a number of prominent welfare workers—Homer Folks, Lillian Wald, Jane Addams, Florence Kelley, and others—the President agreed, and invited some 200 prominent men and women from all parts of the country to a two-day meeting held late in January 1909.

The conference, which for the first time brought the subject of dependent children before the entire nation, gave to social work, especially child welfare work, a place in the national life that it had never had before. More important, it represented another, and much earlier, about-face from the concept elaborated more than a half-century earlier by President Franklin Pierce—that the federal government had no responsibility in matters of social welfare.

The gathering was designed to perform two functions: to provide an interchange of ideas and experiences among leaders in the work for dependent children, and to recommend a general plan for their care. Through a report adopted unanimously by conference members, the meeting served both of these functions. As its keynote, the report proclaimed: "Home life is the highest and finest product of civilization," and "children should not be deprived of it except for urgent and compelling reasons." For those children "who for sufficient reasons must be removed from their own homes, or who have no homes," the report went on to state, "it is desirable that they should be cared for in families whenever practicable. The carefully selected foster home is for the normal child the best substitute for the natural home."

The meeting had far-reaching practical effects. Its strong recommendation in favor of family care strengthened the movement for home rather than institutional care for dependent and delinquent children. It contributed greatly both to the development of adoption agencies and to the increased use of the boarding-out system for children unsuitable or unavailable for adoption. Increased use of the cottage-type rather than the congregate institution—one of the report's recommendations—was another outcome of the conference.

Other recommendations on the subject of state incorporation and inspection of children's institutions and agencies also resulted in attaining higher standards of child care. Furthermore, the conference set a precedent still followed—every ten years since 1909, there has been a White House conference on child problems and needs, each of which, in turn, has had a far-reaching effect on concepts of child care and progressive child welfare programs.

One of the most immediate and important effects of the first White House Conference was the creation (three years later) of the U.S. Children's Bureau, another and perhaps even more important break with the Pierce doctrine. The idea of creating a federal children's bureau was not new in 1909. As early as 1900, in speeches at colleges across the nation, Florence Kelley had called for the creation of some sort of central agency to collect and exchange ideas and information on child welfare. Four years later, Lillian Wald of the Henry Street Settlement House, incensed over a news item announcing a large-scale federal campaign against the boll weevil (which was damaging the southern cotton crop) at a time when Washington took no notice at all of the decimation of the nation's crop of young children, outlined a plan for a federal children's bureau which she, Miss Kelley, and Edward T. Devine took to the White House. President Roosevelt liked the idea and apparently agreed to support it.

Next, Miss Wald and Miss Kelley, both board members of the National Child Labor Committee, induced that organization to draft a bill for the proposed bureau which was introduced in Congress in 1906. The National Child Labor Committee marshaled support for the measure throughout the nation; prominent citizens, welfare groups, educational associations, newspapers, and others came out in its favor. Opposition to the proposal, however, was violent, especially from business interests fearful that creation of the bureau would lead to the end of child labor, a practice they had a vested interest in preserving. As a result, the bill was never even debated; year after year, it languished in committee.

Then came the 1909 White House Conference, which recommended not only that the bill be passed, but that the President send Congress a special message on its behalf. Roosevelt readily complied. "It is not only discreditable to us as a people that there is no recognized and authoritative source of information upon ... subjects related to child life," the Chief Executive told the nation's lawmakers, "but in the absence of such information as should be supplied by the Federal Government many abuses have gone unchecked...."

The recommendations of the White House Conference and the publicity they received, along with President Roosevelt's support and special message, forced Congress into finally acting. Unable to continue to ignore the matter, lawmakers reluctantly called for public hearings on the bill. Many of those who had attended the White House Conference returned to Washington to appear before Congress and testify on behalf of the measure. The main theme of their testimony was the fact that, through the Bureau of Animal Husbandry within the Department of Agriculture, which had a staff of more than 1000 and an annual appropriation of nearly $1,250,000, the federal government spent far more money each year on animal research than on research into the problems of childhood—and, as a result, the mortality rate of young animals was lower than that of young children.

Still, three more years were to pass before the measure, which called for an appropriation of $50,000 and a staff of fourteen, won approval. In the meantime, numerous individuals, parent-teacher groups, labor unions, and public health, social work, and civic groups continued to support it. Then there were five days of bitter floor debate in which it was charged that those who favored creation of the children's bureau were working under orders from European socialists and communists who intended to use the agency to regulate the nation's youth. Finally, the bill passed the Senate on January 31, 1912. Two months later, it went through the House, and on April 9 it was signed into law by President William Howard Taft.

The U.S. Children's Bureau received an initial appropriation of $25,640 and was placed within the Department of Commerce and Labor from which, a year later, it was transferred to the newly created Department of Labor. (In 1953, it was placed in another newly created federal department, the Department of Health, Education, and Welfare.) Charged with the duty of investigating and reporting upon "all matters pertaining to the welfare of children and child life among all classes of our people," the bureau had no administrative power, nor was it to perform any services, strictly speaking. Rather, it was a research agency. It would establish the facts concerning the condition and treatment of the nation's children, and then call attention to those facts.

Despite its limited function and modest initial appropriation, the Children's Bureau was extremely significant; it soon became the central, and in some cases the sole, source of authoritative information about the welfare of children and their families throughout the United States. More important, its creation marked a significant departure in public policy. It was the first time the federal government recognized not merely the rights of children, but also the need to create a permanent agency at least to study, if not yet protect, them.

President Taft appointed Julia Lathrop, former Hull-House resident and member of the Illinois State Board of Charities, to head the bureau. This was an excellent choice. Miss Lathrop believed fervently in the importance of public welfare and in the need to rejuvenate services set up by the taxpayers to help those in need. She also knew how to use the potent constituency network she had at her disposal and, at the same time, recognized the need to avoid controversy and to divorce politics from social welfare in order to gain and retain congressional support for the new bureau. At the outset, she thus subordinated studies of child labor in favor of less controversial ones, such as the problem of infant mortality. She thereby quickly won confidence in the new agency and additional resources for it; by 1915, for example, its funds had achieved a sixfold increase and its staff had multiplied by a factor of five.

A "baby-saving" campaign had been initiated in America in 1908 when the New York City Department of Health set up a Division of Child Hygiene—the first official admission by a large American city that child health was worthy of special attention from a public health department. Another landmark in the movement to lower the infant mortality rate was a 1909 Conference on the Prevention of Infant Mortality held at Yale University. Called at the request of the American Academy of Medicine, the conference attracted a number of prominent physicians, social workers, sociologists, and educators. The American Association for the Study and Prevention of Infant Mortality, which proved to be instrumental in reducing the infant mortality rate, had its inception at this gathering.

There was, then, some precedent for engaging in infant hygiene work when, in 1913, the newly created Children's Bureau undertook as its initial major project a study to determine, first, how many babies died each year, and second, why. To the dismay of many, the bureau's investigators found not only a shockingly high infant mortality rate, but a high death rate for mothers as well. That more women died unnecessarily each year during childbirth (or lived on afterward in chronic invalidism) than from any other cause except tuberculosis, was a startling revelation. Moreover, the maternal death rate was higher in America than in any other leading nation in the world; hence, the large number of orphans in the nation.

Uncovering this information was not enough for Julia Lathrop, who in 1917 drew up a plan for the "public protection of maternity and infancy" and published it in her *Annual Report* to Congress. Her idea was that the federal government should aid the states to improve their maternal and child health facilities and services, especially in rural areas, where such provisions were especially lacking or poor. The government would offer grants-in-aid, on a matching basis, to those states promising to establish facilities and services such as public health nursing and education, outpatient clinics, hospitals, better inspection of maternity homes, and the like, in accordance with specifications established by the Children's Bureau. State health departments would administer the grants.[1]

---

[1]Two things should be noted in this connection. First, impetus for the proposal came from America's World War I experience as well as from Children's Bureau studies; during the war, thousands of men were rejected for the military draft because of medical problems, many of which could have been averted through suitable health care during infancy and childhood. And second, while rural areas throughout the nation had few such facilities, this was especially true of the South

Julia Lathrop embodied her ideas and program into a bill which, when introduced in Congress in 1918, became known as the Infancy and Maternity or Sheppard-Towner Bill. During the campaign for its enactment, the epithets of socialism, communism, and nationalization of the nation's youth, hurled earlier against the Children's Bureau and other pieces of social legislation, were again heard, this time even more often because of the recent Bolshevik Revolution. Moreover, proponents of the measure had to meet a highly organized and well financed propaganda campaign initiated by leaders of the nation's medical profession, who invoked against it the bugaboos of "state medicine," "interference with private practice," and other such charges.

Typical of the attacks on the bill was a pamphlet entitled *Shall the Children of America Become the Property of the State?*, written and circulated by the Legislative Committee of the Illinois State Medical Society. Attacking both the bill and the Children's Bureau, authors of the pamphlet charged that those who supported the "iniquitous" measures were "masquerading as humanity" while "battening upon the incredulous imagination of the citizens who feel that by this legislation they might evade some of their civic responsibilities." The Children's Bureau, they continued, "will by this bill be the ruling power in the United States. This Bureau, headed by one woman, will become the most despotic influence in the country imposing a yoke that will annually become more unbearable in its crushing burdens."

Such absurd charges reached the floor of the U.S. Senate, where Senator Thomas Reed of Missouri, a staunch opponent of the measure, stated that, if the Sheppard-Towner Bill passed, "female celibates would instruct mothers on how to bring up their babies"; they would "look over the nation's birth lists, check some off, and say 'let's take charge of this or that baby.'" Despite these attacks, after three years of agitation and days of bitter floor debate—and ratification of the Nineteenth Amendment, granting

---

where, because (among other things) of the relatively low per capita income, public services in general were scarce. It should be mentioned that here, perhaps even more than elsewhere, there was a great deal of racial discrimination; thus, the black population in southern rural areas would find it very difficult to reap the benefits of the program.

women the right to vote—the bill emerged successfully from
Congress on November 19, 1921, and was signed into law four
days later by President Warren G. Harding.

As passed, the act authorized an annual appropriation of
$1,252,000 for a five-year period, later extended to seven. Each
year, the Children's Bureau would have $50,000 to administer
the program and to engage in further research on the problems of
maternal and infant care; the remainder was to be divided among
the states participating in the program.

The Sheppard-Towner Act proved to be a great success. Between 1921 and 1929, when, owing to several factors—Herbert
Hoover's opposition to the measure, the collapse of the economy,
and perhaps the weakened clout of female voters—Congress
refused to renew its funds, nearly 3000 child and maternal health
centers were established in forty-five states, chiefly in rural areas.
In addition, the act strengthened state health departments and
helped foster the development of county health units, which in
turn led to the better administration of local services. The nation's infant and maternal mortality rates dropped significantly
during its limited life.

The Sheppard-Towner Act was important for other reasons as
well. It brought the federal government into the field of child welfare through the area of health and was another measure that
aroused the lay public's interest and activity in a subject long considered the exclusive domain of the medical profession. And finally, its influence was long-lasting. On the foundation laid by the
Infancy and Maternity Act—the first statute to provide federal
grants-in-aid to the states for a welfare program other than education—were reared many of the cooperative federal-state programs established under the Social Security Act of 1935. Title V
of the Social Security Act, for example, provided for federal
grants-in-aid to the states (to be administered by the Children's
Bureau) for work in maternal and child health.

The Sheppard-Towner Act resulted in large part from creation
of the Children's Bureau, which, in turn, sprang from the 1909
White House Conference on Dependent Children. From that
conference also came another highly significant development in
public welfare—the widows' pension or mothers' aid movement,
now referred to as Aid to Families with Dependent Children
(A.F.D.C.).

Delegates attending the White House Conference reaffirmed the idea that, whenever possible, needy children should be provided for in their own homes. Still fearing home relief, however, especially public outdoor assistance, administered by untrained personnel, they went on to say that the financial aid necessary to keep families together should be furnished by private rather than by public agencies: the "home should not be broken up for reasons of poverty," the report stated, and added that the aid necessary to keep families intact "should be given by such methods and from such sources as may be determined by the general relief policy of each community, preferably in the form of private charity rather than public relief." Public relief, Frederic Almy, the renowned secretary of the Buffalo C.O.S. declared, is "like undoctored drugs . . . poisonous to the poor."

Unfortunately, private agencies, even when present (and often they were not, especially in rural areas), were poorly equipped or lacked the funds to do this. Moreover, agencies with funds usually refused to help women deemed capable of working. Many widows therefore were forced to give up their children solely because they could not make ends meet.

Some women placed their youngsters in institutions or foster homes; some gave them up for adoption. Others attempted to keep them at home while they went to work in an effort to support themselves and their brood. But low wages forced women to work long hours, which was not only exhausting, but also meant that they could not provide adequate supervision over their young ones. The result, then, of taking jobs while trying to raise a family, of being both breadwinner and homemaker, was that many of the women broke down and many of the children became demoralized and delinquent. In the end, both required further aid—in institutions or hospitals. In 1913, in New York State alone, some 1000 children were committed to public institutions because their widowed mothers had become ill, usually due to overwork and worry (while almost 3000 others were placed in such institutions because their parents could not support them); many of the women were also institutionalized.

For many, widows' pensions, or public aid to women with dependent children, was the answer. Such assistance would end the separation of mother and child for reasons of poverty alone. Furthermore, it would be as much a preventive as an ameliorative device, for it would tend to prevent juvenile delinquency and adult illness by insuring the kind of home surroundings that children needed for proper development and mothers needed for physical well-being. Moreover, to assist dependent mothers so that they could remain at home and care properly for their children would require less expense, it was demonstrated, than to maintain them and their youngsters in public institutions or in foster homes. As a result, social reformers and other interested citizens threw their support behind a campaign to provide public allowances for women with dependent children—persons in need through no fault of their own.[2]

Some people, including a number of social workers, especially those working for private agencies, opposed the idea. They continued to argue that public authorities should maintain public institutions and private agencies should provide home or outdoor relief. Mothers' pensions questioned this informal division of labor; they aimed at returning to public authorities a welfare function that had been assumed voluntarily by private agencies. Proponents of the idea argued that changes in the family and in the economic system required greater government or public intervention. The family's survival was contingent upon uninterrupted earnings, yet because of a variety of impersonal matters—forced unemployment, illness, death of the family breadwinner, and so on—that was not always possible. There was a need, then, for a new mechanism that would assure income flow in the event of a decline in an individual's or a family's earnings. Furthermore, mothers' pensions were based on the idea that the women involved were performing a service to society by raising their children and that they should be rewarded for such service.

These arguments eventually prevailed. In fact, synthesizing the

[2]As Julian Mack, the highly regarded judge who presided over Chicago's juvenile court from 1904 to 1907, phrased it: "If we take a child away from the mother we willingly pay an asylum [or foster home] to care for him; the public funds pay for his support. Why should not the public funds be paid to the mother herself and keep the family together?" It is not surprising that many children's court judges and probation officers also worked hard for the enactment of widows' pension laws. They were as interested in the economic as the emotional well-being of their charges: the former was as likely to be the source of difficulty as the latter. Yet personality problems could be dealt with through counseling, friendship, advice, or psychiatric treatment, while often there was no acceptable agency in the community to deal with economic problems.

era's concerns about children, widows, the home, and just rewards for work well done, mothers' pensions achieved remarkable legislative success. In April 1911, Missouri enacted America's first widows' pension law, a permissive statute allowing the counties to provide cash assistance to mothers who had dependent children. Two months later, Illinois followed suit, and so rapidly did the idea spread that within two years seventeen other states did the same. By 1919, similar statutes had been enacted in thirty-nine states, and by 1935 all but two—South Carolina and Georgia—were extending aid to widows with children.

While the specific provisions of the statutes differed, they were similar in that they were compromise measures. Patterned on the nineteenth-century concept of relief, they were based upon behavioral considerations as well as economic need. All the statutes contained "suitable home" provisions; that is, they applied only to needy widows who, in the opinion of the authorities, were "fit" or worthy parents, exposing them, of course, to administrative discretion and possible abuses. Nevertheless, the statutes represented a major step forward in that they enabled many families to remain intact who otherwise would not have been able to do so.

Moreover, while at the outset, most of the statutes were restrictive in that they were not mandatory, were financed by local or county units, and applied only to dependent widows, before long they were improved. Most became mandatory; they were paid for, in whole or in part, by the state, and their coverage was extended to all needy mothers—women with illegitimate children as well as those whose husbands were sick or incapacitated, in prison, or for any other reason unable to support their families.[3]

Widows' pension laws marked a definite turning point in the welfare policies of many states. In theory at least, they removed the stigma of charity for a large number of welfare recipients. They also broke down the nineteenth-century tradition against public home relief. Their enactment constituted public recognition of the fact that long-time care must be provided for children

---

[3]Also, many widows' pension laws established a new principle in public assistance in that they were not only to provide aid, but *adequate* aid, so that the mother could stay at home and devote herself to housekeeping and the care of her children, a far cry from the nineteenth-century concept of "less eligibility."

whose fathers were dead or incapacitated or who had deserted them, that security at home was an essential part of such care, and that such security could be gained only through public aid.

And finally, like the Sheppard-Towner Act, widows' pension laws laid the foundation for one of the more important parts of the federal Social Security Act of 1935. Title IV of that act, Aid to Dependent Children, established a federal program of cash payments to mothers deprived of their husbands' support. Thus, with federal aid, the widows' pension movement was carried to its logical conclusion and one of the chief recommendations of the 1909 White House Conference—that needy children be cared for in their own homes whenever possible—came close to reality.

The drive for widows' pensions was part of a broader movement, during and after the so-called Progressive era, designed to increase the social and economic security of all citizens living in a modern industrial society. That movement also included efforts to enact workmen's compensation legislation, health and unemployment insurance schemes, and old-age pensions.

As the advocates of mothers' pensions indicated, the traditional methods of insuring against the vicissitudes of life were totally unsuited to the new conditions of an impersonal, wage centered, competitive industrial order. The wage earner was in a precarious position: any interruption of income flow destroyed his or her, and the family's, ability to purchase the goods and services necessary for survival. Yet such interruptions occurred frequently, through no fault of the individual. The only way to restore a measure of security to the working man or woman was by instituting compulsory social insurance—a rational means of minimizing the financial losses from the ordinary contingencies of life in the modern era.

Germany had established a comprehensive system of social insurance as early as 1884 and, by the turn of the century, all the countries of continental Europe had some form of social insurance. In the United States, federal and state labor bureaus had shown interest in these European plans as early as the 1890s. However, it was the American Association for Labor Legislation, founded in 1906 by a group of labor union leaders, economists, political scientists, and social reformers, that led the drive for social insurance.[4] Heading the movement was I. M. Rubinow, chief statistician for the Metropolitan Life Insurance Company, whose 500-page book, *Social Insurance* (1913), became the bible for the cause.

At every turn, the proponents of social insurance were constrained by the ideology of voluntarism, with its credo of self-reliance and the notion that private institutions—"welfare capitalism," industrial establishment funds, trade union benefits, fraternal, mutual, and commercial insurance, and the like—were adequate for the task. However, advocates of social insurance argued that such voluntary programs were full of shortcomings and thus did not preclude the need for government action. In their opinion, welfare capitalism—efforts by astute corporate executives to nurture a pliable work force and check the growth of labor unionism and radicalism by providing employees with a variety of "benefits," including company homes and stores, libraries, recreational facilities, profit-sharing schemes, group life and health insurance policies, and retirement pensions[5]—was particularly reprehensible. Dubbed "industrial feudalism" by its critics, welfare capitalism denied workers vested rights to their benefits; those accused of "unsatisfactory conduct" could be dismissed from their jobs and thus lose all their protection. The scheme, then, was coercive, an obvious effort at social control that failed to provide the protection that industrial wage earners needed.

Other forms of private insurance were very expensive and inefficient and reached only a small percentage of the working population; more often than not, those who most needed protection

[4]The American Association for Labor Legislation was assisted by many settlement house residents, under whose leadership the National Conference of Charities and Correction in 1912 drafted its platform of "minimum standards" for well-being in an industrial society, which included a federal system of accident, old-age, and unemployment insurance.

[5]Recently, the first full-scale history of retirement and pensions in America was published: William Graebner, *A History of Retirement* (New Haven, Conn.: Yale University Press, 1980). Graebner argues that retirement (through pensioning off older workers) developed to serve not the needs of the elderly but rather those of the marketplace; it was designed, in other words, not for the purposes of social justice but for the demands of a capitalist economy for efficiency and social control.

were not covered by such programs. Security and justice, then, could be achieved only by transferring responsibility from the voluntary to the public sector; compulsory social insurance was the only mechanism that could respond predictably and adequately to the needs of all wage earners (and their families) suffering from income deprivation.

Optimism pervaded the social insurance forces as a result of the rapidity with which states passed both mothers' pensions and workmen's compensation laws, which automatically paid injured workers according to a uniform scale of benefits on the assumption that "industrial accidents are not accidents at all, but normal results of modern industry." Between 1909 and 1920, forty-three states enacted workmen's compensation, mainly, however, the record indicates, because such measures had a good deal of appeal to employers, who thus pushed for their enactment. Compensation programs (which avoided the large payments the courts occasionally awarded in injury cases) made it easier for businessmen to insure against losses resulting from industrial accidents, the cost of which easily could be added to the price of production and passed on to the consumer. Furthermore, most compensation statutes omitted many workers, did not include occupational diseases, provided fairly low benefits to disabled laborers, and in other ways were quite weak.

At least they were a start, and social insurance advocates confidently turned next to health insurance. Their confidence, however, was short-lived: the opposition proved overwhelming. The strenuous and costly campaign against health insurance was waged by a strange alliance—the medical profession, insurance companies, employers, Christian Scientists, some labor unions,[6] and a host of superpatriotic groups that during World War I labeled the proposal as "Made in Germany" and later charged that it was "Made in Russia." By 1920, after health insurance

[6]Actually, organized labor, striving for recognition against heavy opposition and generally suspicious of a government that often had helped to crush strikes, was divided on the issue of compulsory social insurance, especially health insurance. Many labor leaders, including Samuel Gompers, opposed the idea, especially since they remembered that Bismark had introduced social insurance in Germany in part to remove issues of contention on which unions might be able to recruit members. Still, others favored health insurance, as did a number of state federations of labor and individual unions.

bills had been defeated in New York and California (the two states that seemed most likely to enact such legislation), the reform forces acknowledged defeat.

The setback in the drive for health insurance seemed to take the remaining steam out of the social insurance movement, although the fight continued in the fields of old-age pensions and unemployment compensation. A number of states passed old-age pension laws in the 1920s, but the statutes were weak and for the most part they remained inoperative. Not until 1929 was an effective statute enacted.

The drive for unemployment compensation moved even more slowly. Although bills were introduced in a number of states between 1916 and 1931, none was enacted during that time. Wisconsin became the first state to place such a law on its books when, in January 1932, in the midst of the nation's most severe depression, it enacted such a statute, to become effective two years later. It was not until passage of the Social Security Act in 1935 that Americans awakened to the problem of unemployment.

Despite the failure to secure some social insurance programs and the faulty provisions of others, American social welfare had come a long way since the late nineteenth century. Beginning with efforts to remove dependent children from institutions and to place them in private homes, reformers had come to see the elemental importance of preserving the family. They had moved to the larger concern for preventive health and other social welfare measures, including the provision of adequate financial resources through state and even federal assistance and the adoption of a comprehensive system of compulsory social insurance, to conserve childhood and the established home. Meanwhile, other important developments included the emergence of a social work profession.

Bibliography

ABBOTT, EDITH. "Grace Abbott: A Sister's Memories," *Social Service Review* 13 (September 1939): 351–408.

ABBOTT, GRACE. "Recent Trends in Mothers' Aid," *Social Service Review* 8 (June 1934): 191–220.

ADDAMS, JANE. *My Friend Julia Lathrop*. New York: Macmillan, 1935.

ALMY, FREDERIC. "Public Pensions to Widows," *Proceedings* of the National Conference of Charities and Correction (Fort Wayne, Ind.: Fort Wayne Printing, 1912): 481–85.

BARKER, SIR ERNEST. *The Development of Public Services in Western Europe, 1660–1930*. New York: Oxford University Press, 1944.

BELL, WINIFRED. *Aid to Dependent Children*. New York: Columbia University Press, 1965.

BRADBURY, DOROTHY E. *Five Decades of Action: A History of the Children's Bureau*. Washington, D.C.: U.S. Children's Bureau, 1962.

BRANDES, STUART D. *American Welfare Capitalism, 1880–1940*. Chicago: University of Chicago Press, 1976.

BRECKENRIDGE, SOPHONISBA. *Public Welfare Administration in the United States*. Chicago: University of Chicago Press, 1938.

CHEPAITIS, JOSEPH B. "Federal Social Welfare Progressivism in the 1920s," *Social Service Review* 46 (June 1972): 213–29.

COHEN, NATHAN E. *Social Work in the American Tradition*. New York: Dryden, 1958.

Conference on the Care of Dependent Children. *Proceedings*. Washington, D.C.: Government Printing Office, 1909.

DAVIS, ADA J. "The Evolution of the Institution of Mothers' Pensions in the United States," *American Journal of Sociology* 35 (January 1930): 573–87.

FRIEDLANDER, WALTER. *Introduction to Social Welfare*. New York: Prentice-Hall, 1955.

GEDDES, ANNE E. *Trends in Relief Expenditures, 1910–1935*. Washington, D.C.: Government Printing Office, 1937.

GOLDMARK, JOSEPHINE. *Impatient Crusader: Florence Kelley's Life Story*. Urbana, Ill.: University of Illinois Press, 1953.

HAMOVITCH, MAURICE B. "History of the Movement for Compulsory Health Insurance in the United States," *Social Service Review* 27 (September 1953): 281–99.

JAMBOR, HAROLD. "Theodore Dreiser, the *Delineator Magazine,* and Dependent Children: A Background Note on the Calling of the 1909 White House Conference," *Social Service Review* 32 (March 1978): 33–40.

JOHNSON, ARLIEN. *Public Policy and Private Charities*. Chicago: University of Chicago Press, 1931.

KELSO, ROBERT. *The Science of Public Welfare*. New York: Holt, 1928.

———. "The Transition from Charities and Correction to Public Welfare," *Annals of the American Academy of Political and Social Science* 105 (January 1923): 21–25.

KLEIN, PHILIP. *From Philanthropy to Social Welfare*. San Francisco: Jossey-Bass, 1968.

LEFF, MARK. "Consensus for Reform: The Mothers' Pension Movement in the Progressive Era," *Social Service Review* 47 (September 1973): 397–417.

LEMMONS, J. STANLEY. "The Sheppard-Towner Act: Progressivism in the 1920's," *Journal of American History* 55 (March 1969): 776–86.

LENROOT, KATHARINE F. "Friend of Children and the Children's Bureau," *Social Service Review* 22 (December 1948): 427–30.

LUBOVE, ROY, "Economic Security and Social Conflict in America," Part I, *Journal of Social History* 1 (Fall 1967): 61–87; Part II, *ibid.* 1 (Summer 1968): 325–50.

———. *The Struggle for Social Security, 1900–1935*. Cambridge, Mass.: Harvard University Press, 1968.

MACDOUGALL, A. W. "Trend Toward Public Social Service," *Survey* 34 (May 15, 1915): 163.

MILES, ARTHUR P. *An Introduction to Public Welfare*. Boston: Heath, 1949.

NELSON, DANIEL. *Unemployment Insurance: The American Experience, 1915–1935*. Madison, Wis.: University of Wisconsin Press, 1969.

NUMBERS, RONALD L. *Almost Persuaded: American Physicians and Compulsory Health Insurance, 1912–1920*. Baltimore: Johns Hopkins Press, 1978.

PARKER, JACQUELINE, AND EDWARD CARPENTER. "Julia Lathrop and the Children's Bureau: The Emergence of an Institution," *Social Service Review* 55 (March 1981): 60–77.

REAGAN, PATRICK D. "The Ideology of Social Harmony and Efficiency: Workmen's Compensation in Ohio, 1904–1919," *Ohio History* 90 (Autumn 1981): 317–31.

ROMANYSHYN, JOHN. *Social Welfare: Charity to Justice*. New York: Random House, 1971.

RUBINOW, ISAAC M. *Social Insurance*. New York: Holt, 1913.

TOBEY, JAMES A. *The Children's Bureau*. Baltimore: Johns Hopkins Press, 1925.

VASEY, WAYNE. *Government and Social Welfare*. New York: Holt, Rinehart, 1958.

WEINSTEIN, JAMES. "Big Business and the Origins of Workmen's Compensation," *Labor History* 8 (Spring 1967): 156–74.

WEISS, NANCY. "Save the Children: A History of the Children's Bureau, 1903–1918," Ph.D. dissertation, University of California, Los Angeles, 1974.

YELLOWITZ, IRWIN. "The Origins of Unemployment Reform in the United States," *Labor History* 9 (Fall 1968): 338–60.

The Quest for Professionalization

At one time, the word "profession" was a generic term that embraced the ministry, law, and medicine. Over the years, especially in the late nineteenth century, as the day of the generalist was beginning to fade before the mounting complexities of modern existence, other groups—teachers, engineers, geologists, chemists, economists, political scientists, and so on—experienced a formative growth toward self-consciousness and efficient organization that resulted in their becoming professions. Before they could do so, they had to have exclusive possession of a systematic body of knowledge, a monopoly of skill obtained from higher education and training, and a subculture whose members shared a group identity and common values.

During the early twentieth century, charity workers also sought professional status. As in so many other areas of American life, the need for professional education and procedures in social service had become clear if some rational control were to be asserted over the drift of life. The complex problems resulting from rapid industrialization (and the shift of most economic activity from the small personal setting of the home to the large impersonal setting of the factory), widespread immigration (from the far reaches of southern and eastern Europe as well as from American farms and small towns), and the crowding together of citizens in ugly, sprawling centers of population, demanded the creation of a group of social experts trained to alleviate, and hopefully resolve, them. As Charles P. Neill, the federal Commissioner of Labor, put it in 1914:

> The need for trained workers is obvious to anyone at all familiar with the many complex, subtle, and baffling problems growing out of the

mere fact of poverty and destitution in all our great congested centers of population. . . . Zeal for the cause of health or devotion is not accepted as a sufficient basis to turn anyone loose as a healer. But too often zeal in the cause is all that is expected of the charity worker. The unintelligent, untrained charity worker can, in spite of disinterested zeal, often cause . . . havoc [with the needy].

The emergence of a profession of social work, then, was related to what Robert Wiebe has called "the search for order" in a "distended society." Ghettos and slums, the white plague, rising rates of crime, juvenile delinquency, the lack of provision for sanitation and public health, the psychological and economic dependency that arose from uncertain employment, low wages, industrial accidents, premature old age—these and other social hazards constituted problems in American life that good intentions alone could not dispel; the creation of schools for the training of social servants, social research and other highly technical skills, and professional discipline were essential.[1]

Charity workers did not have these tools at the turn of the century nor, in the eyes of the public, could they ever develop or acquire them. It was commonly felt that social work consisted of little more than providing aid to people in need, and that no person or group could claim a monopoly on benevolence or could create a profession out of it. To the extent that every person had an obligation to help the suffering, social work was everybody's business. Only when social workers succeeded in convincing the public that not everyone with love in his or her heart could do the job, that social work consisted of more than benevolence and well-wishing, that it had a scientific as well as an ethical component, did they achieve professional recognition. By that time —around the third decade of the twentieth century—social workers had not only founded professional schools that transmitted a systematic body of knowledge rooted in scientific theories, but had demonstrated that they utilized unique skills, and they

---

[1]So, too, according to some (as we have seen), was the enactment of a comprehensive system of social insurance—another effort at "rationalizing" the social and economic order, one that paralleled the professionalization of charity work.

had a self-conscious group of practitioners who belonged to a number of newly created professional organizations.[2]

All this did not occur overnight; the road to professionalism was being paved for some time, at least as far back as the 1870s, when the Conference of Charities was created. The Conference of Charities was the child of the American Social Science Association, an organization founded in 1865 to discuss

> questions relating to the sanitary condition of the people, the relief, the employment, and the education of the poor, the prevention of crime, the amelioration of criminal law, the discipline of persons, the remedial treatment of the insane, and those numerous matters of statistical and philanthropic interest which are included under the general head "Social Science."[3]

Nine years later, members of the existing state boards of charities attending the American Social Science Association's annual meeting decided to get together to discuss common problems and compare methods used to solve them. Later that year, the paid secretaries of those boards got together, in what was no doubt the first meeting of persons making a career of charitable work, to round out a program for another meeting of state board members at the next annual convention of the American Social Science Association. Thus, the Conference of Charities (or Conference of State Boards, as it was sometimes called) came into being. The Conference of Charities continued to meet annually with the American Social Science Association until 1879, when, at the urging of Frederick H. Wines of Illinois and Andrew E. Ellmore of Wisconsin, the group separated from its parent body in order to give more intensive study to its own "practical" work.

From the outset, the group, which (in 1884) changed its name to the National Conference of Charities and Correction, opened

[2]The following analysis of the professionalization of social work is based in part on the excellent work by Harold Wilensky and Charles N. Lebeaux, *Industrial Society and Social Welfare* (New York: Free Press, 1958).

[3]The American Social Science Association was itself the child of the British Association for the Promotion of Social Science, established in 1857 by the heirs of those who had sponsored the poor law "reforms" of 1834 and other social welfare and public health legislation.

its doors to others, including those engaged in private charity, both religious and secular.[4] It published the *Proceedings* of its annual meetings, and later a quarterly bulletin as well, and in general it served as a national clearing house for ideas and experiences in the broad field of social welfare.

Actually, the National Conference served a variety of functions. For the young and inexperienced worker, it provided the first opportunity to witness the relationship between different areas of charitable work. The long-time secretary of the organization saw it as "an occasional or post-graduate school of social work where reformers acquired an education in principles and methods of charitable work—one that reduced the tuition fees of the School of Experience." More important, by creating a certain *esprit de corps* among charity workers and by delimiting a specific occupational area over which they and no others could claim expertise, members of the National Conference established charity work as a distinct field within the social sciences and hence took a major step toward laying the foundation for a professional self-identity and awareness. At the same time, however, by stressing more "practical" concerns over scientific inquiry—especially procedures for operating public and private agencies and techniques of administering assistance—charity workers moved away from social theory and research to a preoccupation with methods and treatment, a development some later leaders would bemoan and seek to rectify.

Meanwhile, another step along the same road was taken by the charity organization societies and their agents who developed what has come to be called casework: "those processes which develop personality through adjustments consciously affected, indi-

---

[4]This open-door membership policy led to important changes in the organization. Shortly after its creation, the organization was taken over by the representatives of private charitable agencies, especially the charity organization societies. During the early twentieth century, the advocates of preventive social work (social reform), especially settlement house residents, dominated its councils. During and after World War I, professional social workers (mainly caseworkers) assumed control of the organization, as witnessed by its name change in 1917 to the National Conference of Social Work. In 1957, it went through another name change, this time to the National Conference on Social Welfare, and once again began to fall under the general influence of the representatives of public welfare, especially at the state and federal levels.

vidual by individual, between men and their social environment," according to one widely used definition. In so doing, friendly visitors realized that to be effective they had to be trained in investigation, diagnosis, preparation of case records, and treatment, all of which required guidance, counsel, supervision, and a knowledge of the principles of scientific philanthropy. By the late nineteenth century, then, social work was beginning to pass beyond mere philanthropy to a vocation based upon the assumption that it required specific knowledge, skills, and techniques, as well as good intentions, and that such capabilities could be transmitted from teachers to students. As one C.O.S. agent put it, charity work must become scientific "by the development of professional skill, professional schools, and authoritative standards of entrance and excellence" in the field.

In the meantime, the settlement house movement had appeared on the scene. And, while it stressed social reform rather than individual treatment, residents were keenly aware of the need to acquire more knowledge, especially in the fields of economics, political science, sociology, and the other social sciences, and to develop more skill in research and what has come to be called community organization, some of the very areas and techniques their immediate predecessors had shunned. Both groups—friendly visitors and settlement house residents—however, were concerned with the problem of education and training for social work and both identified with the National Conference.

Both groups knew that formal education was an inherent part of every profession, and that the more highly developed the profession, the stronger, clearer, and closer the relationship between the school and the field, between advanced education and actual practice. Since the concepts, values, standards, and techniques of the profession are rooted in education, vitality in the field depends upon a reciprocal flow of knowledge between the teacher and the practitioner, between theory and practice, between the training school and the agencies in the community. Social work, then, could not become a profession, and practitioners could not enter the field, without professional training, nor could it remain a profession if it broke its ties with educational institutions.

At first, a form of apprenticeship or "on-the-job training" was all that social agencies offered recruits, salaried workers and volunteers alike. By watching older members, by talking to executives, and by attending staff meetings and the National Conference, new workers learned something of the art and science of helping those in need. Then a number of private agencies, beginning in Brooklyn in 1891 and in Boston a year later, started what amounted to training programs for their workers—if they could be called that—by arranging informal lectures and distributing reading lists.

Some of those people who had entered the field after receiving a higher education, especially those going into settlement house work, had taken some courses in sociology, which in the 1890s was beginning to be taught at American colleges and universities. The emergence of sociology at this time as an academic discipline resulted from a variety of factors, including the needs of a rapidly changing society. More important, however, although related, was the decline of social Darwinism. The belief that the evolution of society was a mechanical process determined by fixed natural, or scientific, laws that should not be tampered with came under attack by a number of people in the late nineteenth century. The most important of these critics was Lester Frank Ward, who argued that society's development could and should be studied and even guided, thus formulating what came to be referred to as reform Darwinism.

The philosophical groundwork for Ward's position—the scientific study of society for the sake of guiding its evolution, thus replacing aimless drift with purposive change—was laid with the publication in 1883 of his important two-volume book, *Dynamic Sociology*. That work provided the first elaborate argument for the development of a science of society, or sociology, for the purpose of "artificially" improving its development, especially by abolishing poverty and providing all citizens with a sound education—a far cry from the social Darwinists' laissez-faire and "survival of the fittest."

Whether one agreed with Ward or not, sociology became a popular course of study at colleges and universities throughout America, and many pioneer instructors in the field, including such well known scholars as Franklin Giddings of Columbia University, Albion Small of the University of Chicago, Charles Cooley of the University of Michigan, and E. A. Ross of Stanford and the

University of Wisconsin, emphasized the relationship between sociology and social work.

They pointed out that, while each subject was in a field of its own, they dealt largely with the same material—human beings and their social relationships. Each had a contribution to make to the other, sociology to discover the general laws and principles governing human intercourse, and social work to furnish the data necessary for the formulation and testing of those laws and principles. During the 1890s the two disciplines were wed, and it appeared as though the marriage between the teaching of sociology and the practice of social work would be a lasting and happy one.[5]

Yet, before long, the honeymoon came to an end. While no divorce or complete separation occurred, the two disciplines began to part. Sociologists felt a need to disassociate themselves and their research from social workers who, they felt, were too value oriented and thus not objective enough, while social workers felt that sociology was too theoretical or scientifically oriented and not practical enough. More important was the fact that many social workers were beginning to feel that their work was related to many disciplines, not just one; that to be effective they had to know as much about such diverse subjects as biology and economics, psychology and law, as about sociology. Hence the need for broader training.

In the meantime, the quest for professionalism continued, and a number of social workers began to plead for the establishment of some sort of special social work education. In 1893, Anna L. Dawes of Pittsfield, Massachusetts, read a paper before the National Conference on "The Need for Training Schools for a New Profession"—the first public plea for the founding of formal schools for the education and training of social workers. After lamenting the want of suitable people in charity work, which, she was convinced, was due not to an unwillingness to serve but to a

---

[5]In 1892, Albion Small, head of the newly created Sociology Department at the University of Chicago, offered a job to Homer Folks, the well known New York social worker. When Folks declined the offer, Small turned to Charles R. Henderson, a Baptist minister who was known primarily for his work with various charitable organizations. Similarly, Franklin Giddings, the first professor of sociology at Columbia University, was head of the New York Charity Organization Society's Committee on Statistics.

lack of opportunity for training, she raised the question of why those retiring from the field could not be allowed to transmit to their successors much of what they had learned during their years of service. New workers thus schooled could take up where their predecessors left off without repeating all their mistakes. Miss Dawes strongly felt that there was much to be taught and to be learned in the practice of charity work, and that such knowledge could be passed on to those who wished to absorb it.

Not many years later, Mary Richmond of the Baltimore Charity Organization Society read what turned out to be a more important paper on the same subject: "The Need of a Training School in Applied Philanthropy." Miss Richmond also argued that only through some sort of educational opportunity could college graduates and any others of talent be drawn into social work. She went on to define the conditions under which such a school should be established, the sort of curriculum it should have, the personnel needed to staff it, and its probable cost. All this went much farther than Miss Dawes's appeal.

According to Miss Richmond, the training school in applied philanthropy should be located in a large city, possibly affiliated with some institution of higher learning. While classroom instruction was important, the curriculum should emphasize "practical work," especially experience in the field. The school should be in close touch with the public and private charities of the community so that its students could observe and engage in social work practice under the supervision of experienced people.

In 1898, one year after Miss Richmond delivered her widely discussed paper, the New York Charity Organization Society founded the first "school" of social work when it organized an annual six-week summer program designed to increase the knowledge and efficiency of those already in the field. Twenty-seven social workers attended the first session of the Summer School of Philanthropy, which was comprised of lectures, visits to public and private agencies and institutions, and field work.

Some years later, when Edward T. Devine, secretary of the Charity Organization Society, replaced his assistant, Philip W. Ayres, as director of the school, the program was expanded to an academic year. Redesigned primarily for students without experience in social work, it was renamed the New York School of

Philanthropy. In the fall of 1910, the program was further expanded, this time to two years, and nine years later it underwent still another name change to the New York School of Social Work. Later, it became the Columbia University Graduate School of Social Work.

In the meantime, other such schools had come into existence. In 1901, Graham Taylor's Chicago Commons settlement house and the University of Chicago cooperated in offering a special extension course taught by Taylor and Julia Lathrop of Hull-House, which in 1907 led to the founding of an independent institution, the Chicago School of Civics and Philanthropy; in 1920, it became the University of Chicago School of Social Work (now the University of Chicago School of Social Service Administration). In 1904, under the prodding of Zilpha Smith, General Superintendent of Boston's Associated Charities, Simmons College and Harvard University joined in founding the Boston School of Social Work. Similar developments occurred elsewhere, and by 1910 America's five largest cities had schools of social work, all of which, with the exception of Chicago's, were established by charity organization personnel.[6]

The creation of these and other schools of social work hardly solved all of the budding profession's educational problems; indeed, they raised many important ones. The real question was the nature of those schools and their curricula. What kind of schools were they to be, educational institutions or training centers? Were they to provide prospective social workers with knowledge (theory) or experience (field work)? If they concentrated on theory, should it be in subject matter or methods; if they concentrated on field work, under whose supervision should it be carried out, an educator or a practitioner? Was there a need for research at such schools? Should they be autonomous institu-

---

[6]These early institutions, especially the eastern ones, were in effect graduate schools, although, when it was established in 1915, the Bryn Mawr School of Social Work was the first to limit admission to students with college degrees. Beginning in the same year, first at Ohio State University, then at Indiana University and the University of Minnesota, social work programs were designed for students pursuing the bachelor's degree. Later, post-master's degree study leading to certificates in advanced practice or to the doctorate were added. Now, technical and vocational training at less than the baccalaureate level is in the stage of preliminary development and experimentation.

tions, or should they be attached to or affiliated with a college or a university? Answers to these and other questions did not come overnight.

At first, most schools of social work were like the New York School of Philanthropy; that is, adjuncts of private social agencies which supplied the instructors and the opportunities for field work, and which for the most part subordinated theory and research to field work. They produced practitioners to staff their own agencies rather than administrators, scholars, social theorists, and the like.

Eventually, an attempt was made to change the situation. People like Julia Lathrop, Grace and Edith Abbott, and other midwesterners who had come out of the settlement house movement and were interested in social policy and public welfare (and who referred to psychiatric social work as "sick-y-atric" social work and, from the start, made the University of Chicago School of Social Work an exception to the rule by stressing research, social policy, and public administration) began a movement to broaden the curricula and bring schools of social work within the mainstream of American higher education. In an influential book, *Social Welfare and Professional Education,* published in 1931 during the Great Depression when it was becoming increasingly obvious that individual treatment and private charity had to give way to social reform and public welfare, Edith Abbott outlined the case for an expanded curriculum and university affiliation. The following paragraph (from a chapter entitled "The University and Social Welfare") sets forth the gist of her argument:

The academic curriculum of most of the professional schools [of social work] is now poor and slight and covers . . . only the various aspects of a single field—casework. None of us will deny the importance of casework. It is as necessary to the social worker as, for example, the study of contracts is to the law student. But casework is very far from being the whole story. There are great reaches of territory, some of them yet unexplored and stretching out to a kind of no man's land—the great fields of public charitable organization, of law and government in relation to social work, of social economics, of social insurance, of modern social politics—all of which are required if the social worker is to be an efficient servant of the state. In these fields the independent schools will always be limited. It is in the university where there is well-organized graduate work not merely in one, but in all, of the social sciences and where there are cooperative relations with the law and medical schools that the great schools of social welfare will ultimately be developed. At the present time, particularly in the non-university schools, the student too often becomes a routine technician—sometimes a clever technician—but still a technician and not a scientific person with the love of knowledge and the use of the tools of learning.

So if the profession was to be more than a mere technique, if it was to have social workers rather than just caseworkers, training for the field had to have a foundation in many of the social and biological sciences. A knowledge of the structure and functioning of society was as indispensable to social workers as physiology was to physicians; therefore, they had to study sociology and anthropology. The same was true of economics, for society's economic institutions and resources vitally affected the very nature and scope of social work, as people living through the depression all too readily knew. Psychology, biology, and other sciences were also essential to social workers, as was law. Aside from having to know law to be able to recognize legal problems and advise clients, social workers involved in public assistance had to digest legislative details and judicial rulings and, when necessary, even draft new legislation. For these and other reasons, schools of social work had to become integral parts of universities, according to the reformers.

Then there was the question of research which, in one form or another, became an essential part of the curriculum at all schools of social work. While settlement house residents and others had for a long time engaged in research and seen its value for social work and reform, a 1908 Supreme Court decision highlighted its importance. The case, *Muller* v. *Oregon,* involved a law prohibiting the employment of women in factories and laundries for more than ten hours in any one day. The statute was challenged by some employers, who argued that it impaired women's freedom of contract and thus violated their rights under the Fourteenth Amendment of the U.S. Constitution. When the question eventually reached the U.S. Supreme Court, the state hired Louis Brandeis, the able Massachusetts lawyer known as the "people's counsel," to argue its case.

Brandeis, in preparing his brief, departed from standard practice—the arguing of cases on the basis of abstract logic and legal precedents; in fact, he presented only two pages of conventional legal reasoning and citation of past cases. Instead, he offered the court more than one hundred pages of facts amassed for him by a group of social workers, including Florence Kelley and Josephine Goldmark of the National Consumers' League, engaged for the purpose. By citing the evidence they had gathered from a variety of sources, including case studies and reports of government bureaus, legislative committees, commissions on hygiene, and factory inspectors, Brandeis showed that long hours of work were dangerous to women's health, safety, and morals, and that a shorter workday had practical benefits. When he declared that there "is no logic that is properly applicable to these laws except the logic of facts," the justices, to the surprise of many, agreed unanimously.

Their decision not only upheld the Oregon statute but, in effect, sanctioned what came to be known as "sociological jurisprudence"—the presentation of factual data to establish the reasonableness (or unreasonableness) of social legislation, which quickly became ordinary legal practice. Thus, research was important not only for the development and analysis of new social service programs and policies, but also for all campaigns involving social legislation. Therein lay another reason for social workers to have training in research, and for schools of social work to become integral parts of American universities, primarily research institutions.[7] The proliferation of Ph.D. programs in social welfare indicates continued interest in research among those in the field today.

Finally, in regard to field work, it was customary for students to get their practical experience by working in an agency while attending school. However, it came to be felt, and this was eventually so stated by the professional accrediting agency, that practice as well as theory should be directed by college faculty members—clinical or field work instructors rather than agency per-

[7]Other developments have helped to foster social research, especially the spread of social science research facilities at colleges and universities and the growth of foundations, independent research organizations, and federal and state government agencies (many of which have research divisions) devoted to the study of social problems.

sonnel—who would presumably perfect educational methods in field practice, a major step forward in distinguishing professional social work education from apprenticeship training. Thus emerged the curriculum pattern common to all schools of social work—a substantial number of courses in theory (both in subject matter and in methods), some training in social research, plus field work instruction.[8]

In the meantime, as more schools of social work appeared, their directors met annually at the National Conference to discuss common problems, including the maintenance of standards. When it became clear that some accrediting agency was necessary, Porter R. Lee, director of the New York School of Social Work, invited the heads of the seventeen existing schools to discuss the matter. Thus, in 1920, was established the Association of Training Schools of Professional Social Work, which, after undergoing a number of name changes (National Association of Professional Schools of Social Work, American Association of Schools of Social Work), in 1952 became the Council on Social Work Education, an organization that has continued to set the standards of social work education in the United States and Canada.

This accrediting body gave enormous impetus to the movement to bring schools of social work under the aegis of a university —and make a reality of Edith Abbott's model of social work education based largely on social science theory and research— when, in 1935, it decreed that any school desiring membership had to be part of an institution approved by the Association of American Universities. Interestingly, the New York School of Social Work, the nation's first such school, was the last to give up its independent status when it affiliated with Columbia University in 1940. By the early 1980s there were approximately ninety

[8]This helped to overcome long-standing opposition to university affiliation by leaders of the private charities, who feared that such institutions would not place enough value on field work for students. In any case, at the outset, especially during the period of social reform, most schools offered such courses as political science, sociology, labor, economics, child welfare, and, above all, "charities and corrections." As we shall see, however, after World War I, almost all schools became obsessed with the teaching of casework, especially as practiced in private agencies—medical and psychiatric casework. More recently, courses in group work, community organization, and social policy have become quite popular.

accredited schools of social work in the United States and Canada.

Another important, although much more informal, development in the emerging profession was the appearance of specialized magazines and journals. In the late nineteenth century, there were no means of providing continuity for persons engaged in health and welfare work between the meetings of the National Conference, whose official *Proceedings* contained the best of the papers and addresses delivered each year. In response to this need, concerned persons caught up in charitable and reform work in Boston, New York, and Chicago founded journals to carry news of welfare activities to the executives and board members of agencies which provided services, to volunteers and paid employees in the field, and to others interested in the work.

In Boston, the journal *Lend-A-Hand* was established in 1886 under the editorship of Edward Everett Hale. Five years later, the New York Charity Organization Society began publishing *Charities Review* which, according to Edward T. Devine, its editor and one of the most prominent men in the field, was a "dignified, scholarly, educational, and provocative journal," one that for the next ten years spoke for the social work of the day. Then a review for settlement house workers, which quickly became the national organ for that movement, *The Commons,* was launched in 1896 by Graham Taylor, founder of Chicago Commons.

To meet the demand for a more practical journal, in December 1897, the New York C.O.S. launched a second official publication, *Charities,* a kind of house organ which promoted the work of the agency. In March 1901, in the first of a series of mergers, *Charities* absorbed its predecessor, *Charities Review.* Then, in 1905, the journal (which went by its original name) was joined by Graham Taylor's *The Commons,* and a year later by *Jewish Charity,* the official paper of the United Hebrew Charities of New York, becoming *Charities and The Commons.* After four years of publication, *Charities and The Commons* became *Survey,* taking its name from the monumental study of Pittsburgh initiated in 1907.

During all these years, the publications had been under the wing of the New York C.O.S., but in 1912 *Survey* was incorporated separately and placed under the editorship of Paul Kellogg.

From that time until it ceased publication in 1952, *Survey* (and its child, *Survey Graphic,* created as an independent journal in 1923 to reach a broader audience than its parent), under Kellogg's command, was unequaled in the field of social work publications; not only did it stand at the heart of the evolution of social work as a profession, but it also had a profound influence in the shaping of social welfare policy, both public and private.

Meanwhile, numerous other specialized and general practice journals appeared—*Social Casework* in 1920, *Child Welfare* in 1922, *Social Service Review* in 1927, *Social Work Today* and *Public Welfare* in the mid-1930s, and so on—all of which were exceedingly important; not only did they provide an outlet for the publication of the results of research, but they allowed students and practitioners to keep abreast of such research and of other technical and nontechnical professional developments, in general providing education, guidance, and a means of communication for those in and out of the field.

Before it could be considered a profession, however, social work needed some other things, including agencies of control other than schools—professional associations. Professional associations are important, for they help to raise standards and to determine the relationship between the profession and the society they serve. Also, if paid professionals could be linked to their colleagues through a network of such organizations, it would be easier to view amateurs, volunteers who could not join such bodies, as nonprofessionals or "outsiders." Perhaps more important is the fact that professional organizations serve as the main channel of reciprocity between schools and practitioners. While there are other channels of communication, it is at meetings of professional associations (and through their journals) that faculty members and practitioners get together regularly and exchange views. Through these experiences, the nature and "character" of the profession is created and progress is achieved.

Traditionally, there have been two types of national associations in social work—groups concerned with extending and improving the quality of work of member agencies (such as the National Federation of Settlements, the Family Welfare Association, the Council on Social Work Education), and associations of individual social workers which seek to further professional development and improve working conditions (such as the American Association of Medical Social Workers and the American Association of Psychiatric Social Workers). Since space does not permit discussion of all such associations, perhaps it would be useful to look at one of the earliest and most important of these—the National Association of Social Workers.

The National Conference offered the first opportunity for charity workers across the country to meet together to exchange ideas and experiences. It was not composed exclusively of paid workers, nor did it have vocational criteria for selection of membership. As a result, it largely ignored vocational questions, considering, instead, social ones. As schools of social work emerged, faculty members and graduates felt the need for a new kind of organization, one that brought together paid personnel in the field for the discussion of "bread-and-butter" issues.

The so-called Monday Club of Boston was the first such group, and by the second decade of the twentieth century, New York, Detroit, Pittsburgh, Minneapolis, San Francisco, and other cities had similar gatherings with such revealing names as the Hungry Club, the S.O.S. Club, and so on. Social workers employed by different agencies met to try to understand each other's work better and to discuss mutual problems. However, since there was no formal communication betwen these clubs, they were not the direct precursors of the national professional association, although their members did influence its development, especially the organization of local chapters, something that, when founded in 1921, the professional association had not anticipated doing.

The unwitting parent of the first national professional association was the Intercollegiate Bureau of Occupations, organized in 1911 by the New York City alumnae of several eastern women's colleges to serve as an employment agency. Soon after the bureau began to operate, its members discovered that the demand for social work positions was so great, and that the field was so loosely defined, that a special department was needed for social work applicants. Such a department was established, but it soon ceased functioning solely as an employment agency; among other things, it maintained a registry of all social workers who wished to affiliate with it, laying the foundation for a national organization.

In 1917, the department separated from its parent body, the Intercollegiate Bureau of Occupations, and established the National Social Workers' Exchange which, although basically an employment bureau, from the outset assumed supervision over a variety of other areas, including recruitment, working conditions, salaries, ethics, standards, and means of better communication between various branches of the field. Members of the exchange obviously felt a need for a national organization with a wider scope of activities than mere job placement.

The matter of defining requirements for membership proved difficult. After a year of study, the exchange, with branches in several cities, decided not to restrict membership to employed workers, but to open its ranks to anyone engaged in social work either on a paid or on a volunteer basis, and to others interested in the work. Thus, it took in all those who felt, or wanted themselves, included under the term social worker.

On June 27, 1921, at a meeting held in Milwaukee, Wisconsin in conjunction with the National Conference, members of the exchange voted to change its name to the American Association of Social Workers, a name retained for the next quarter-century. After merging with a number of other bodies in 1955 and deciding that graduation from an accredited school of social work was necessary for membership, the organization again changed its name, this time to the National Association of Social Workers. N.A.S.W. is currently the social workers' major professional association with some 92,000 members.[9] Through it all, its purpose, as outlined in its constitution, has remained the same:

> To serve as an organization whose members, acting together, shall endeavor through investigation and conference 1) to develop professional standards in social work; 2) to encourage adequate preparation and professional training; 3) to recruit new workers; and 4) to develop a better adjustment between workers and positions in social work.

In the meantime, social workers in hospitals and clinics, aware of a professional society's advantages for doctors and its con-

[9] A degree from an accredited school of social work (or welfare) meant graduate education; recently, however, that was changed. Now, one can gain membership after securing a bachelor's degree in social work, and there is talk of extending membership to people with a bachelor's degree in other areas who have some experience in the field of social welfare.

tribution to medical progress, organized, in 1918, the American Association of Hospital Social Workers, which later became the American Association of Medical Social Workers. In 1926 the American Association of Psychiatric Social Workers was launched, and other organizations were created similarly. While all of these groups grappled with such questions as professional education and job analysis, prerequisites for admission, financing, and effective practice, they tended to raise the level of professional worth and to promote the delivery of more adequate and efficient social services.

By the time of World War I, then, charity workers were making rapid headway in becoming professional "social workers," as indicated by the change in name, in 1917, from National Conference of Charities and Correction to National Conference of Social Work. Schools of social work abounded, in and out of universities. The volunteer friendly visitor had yielded to the paid, trained caseworker. The pragmatic, reform-oriented settlement house resident was beginning to decline in importance and prestige. And new professional groups were forming. All that remained for professionalization was popular acceptance of the fact that social work had a well defined body of knowledge and unique techniques capable of transmission through a formal educational process.

Bibliography

ABBOTT, EDITH. *Social Welfare and Professional Education*. Chicago: University of Chicago Press, 1931.

———. "Twenty Years of University Education for the Social Services," *Social Service Review* 15 (December 1941): 670–705.

American Association of Social Workers. *Vocational Aspects of Family Social Work*. New York: American Association of Social Workers, 1925.

———. *Vocational Aspects of Medical Social Work*. New York: American Association of Social Workers, 1927.

———. *Vocational Aspects of Psychiatric Social Work*. New York: American Association of Social Workers, 1925.

BRECKINRIDGE, SOPHONISBA. "The New Horizons of Professional Education for Social Work," *Social Service Review* 10 (September 1936): 437–49.

BROWN, ESTHER L. *Social Work as a Profession.* New York: Russell Sage Foundation, 1935.

BRUNO, FRANK J. *Trends in Social Work, 1874–1956.* New York: Columbia University Press, 1957.

———. "Twenty-Five Years of Schools of Social Work," *Social Service Review* 18 (June 1944): 152–64.

CABOT, RICHARD C. *Social Service and the Art of Healing.* New York: Dodd, Mead, 1928.

COSTIN, LELA B. "Edith Abbott and the Chicago Influence on Social Work Education," *Social Service Review* 57 (March 1983): 94–111.

DAWES, ANNA. "The Need of Training Schools for a New Profession," *Lend-A-Hand* 11 (1893): 90–97.

DINER, STEVEN J. "Department and Discipline: The Department of Sociology at the University of Chicago, 1892–1920," *Minerva* 13 (Winter 1975): 514–53.

GETTLEMAN, MARVIN. "John H. Finley and the Academic Origins of American Social Work, 1887–1892," *Studies in History and Society* 2 (Fall 1969 and Spring 1970): 13–26.

GLASSER, MELVIN A. "The Story of the Movement for a Single Professional Association," *Social Work Journal* 36 (July 1955): 115–22.

GREENWOOD, ERNEST. "Attributes of a Profession," *Social Work* 2 (July 1957): 45–55.

HARRISON, FRANCIS N. *The Growth of a Professional Association.* New York: American Association of Social Workers, 1935.

HENDERSON, CHARLES R. *Modern Methods of Charity.* New York: Macmillan, 1904.

HILLMAN, ARTHUR. *Sociology and Social Work.* Washington, D.C.: Public Affairs Press, 1956.

JOHNSON, ARLIEN. *School Social Work: Its Contribution to Professional Education.* New York: National Association of Social Workers, 1962.

LUBOVE, ROY. *The Professional Altruist: The Emergence of Social Work as a Career, 1880–1930.* Cambridge, Mass.: Harvard University Press, 1965.

MEIER, ELIZABETH G. *A History of the New York School of Social Work.* New York: Columbia University Press, 1954.

PIVEN, FRANCES F., AND RICHARD A. CLOWARD. "Notes Toward a

Radical Social Work," in Roy Bailey and Mike Brake, eds., *Radical Social Work*. New York: Pantheon Books, 1976.

RICHMOND, MARY. "The Need of a Training School in Applied Philanthropy," *Proceedings* of the National Conference of Charities and Correction (Boston: Ellis, 1897): 181–86.

STEINER, JESSE. *Education for Social Work*. Chicago: University of Chicago Press, 1921.

STITES, MARY A. *History of the American Association of Medical Social Workers*. Washington, D.C.: American Association of Medical Social Workers, 1955.

TUFTS, JAMES H. *Education and Training for Social Work*. New York: Holt, 1923.

TYLER, RALPH W. "Distinctive Attributes of Education for the Professions," *Social Work Journal* 33 (April 1952):55–62.

WALKER, SYDNOR H. *Social Work and the Training of Social Workers*. Chapel Hill, N.C.: University of North Carolina Press, 1928.

WARD, LESTER FRANK. *Dynamic Sociology*, 2 Vols. New York: Appleton, 1883.

WIEBE, ROBERT H. *The Search for Order, 1877–1920*. New York: Hill and Wang, 1967.

WITTE, ERNEST F. "Social Work Education in the United States: A Review," *Child Welfare* 31 (June 1952): 6–9.

WRIGHT, HELEN R. "Research and the Social Services," *Social Service Review* 15 (December 1941): 625–35.

Chapter 12

Social Work and Welfare in the 1920s

IN THEIR DRIVE toward professionalization, social workers underwent changes in outlook and in practice. To paraphrase two students of the subject, in outlook, from viewing the needy person as largely a product of impersonal social and economic forces, social workers came to see him or her as primarily a product of personal impulses. In practice, they went from concern with social reform and preventive legislation to preoccupation with individuals and with methods and techniques to help them become adjusted to their environment.[1] Thus, at the turn of the century, the spirit of social work had been described in this way: "Other tasks for other ages. This be the glory of ours, that the social causes of dependency shall be destroyed." Two decades later, with the push for professionalism and the evolution of social and psychiatric casework, it was described otherwise: "The concern of social work is the individual, ... the understanding of his needs, ... and his adjustment to his environment."

Absorbed in the technical aspects of their work (such as more competent use of their new skills and training so that they could be deemed worthy of professional recognition), most social workers in the 1920s no longer had the time or inclination for social reform. Instead, they operated on the premise that an individual in need had the strength and inner resources which, if freed from the shackles of fear, inhibition, and other psychological impediments, could overcome his or her difficulty. They frequently discussed ego strengths and weaknesses and tried to help clients

---

[1]The author wishes once again to acknowledge his debt to Harold L. Wilensky and Charles N. Lebeaux, *Industrial Society and Social Welfare* (New York: Free Press, 1958) as a source of many of his ideas on the professionalization of social work, including the developments in the 1920s.

help themselves by clarifying their problems. Men out of work were no longer regarded as able, healthy people willing to work if given a chance; rather, they were viewed as abnormal or maladjusted individuals whose mental or emotional deficiencies were the causes of their unemployment. Hence, they were not supplied with jobs; instead, they were helped to understand why they had lost their jobs or why they were having difficulty finding new ones.

This method of dealing with needy people on a personal basis in an attempt to reconstruct their lives, rather than the social and economic conditions under which they lived and worked, was not novel. The charity organization societies and their friendly visitors had a personalized approach to social welfare. But because they knew little of the human personality—psychology was still in its infancy and there was a paucity of knowledge about emotional problems—and because they had a moralistic approach to the needy—they made decisions on the basis of judgmental attitudes and middle-class values and sought to distinguish between the "worthy" and "unworthy" poor—friendly visitors provided little or no real treatment. They merely investigated the needy and on occasion attempted to manipulate them, to get them to change their way of life or rid themselves of "bad" influences (especially alcohol or bad associates), in the long run relying upon the shaping power of the environment. In their hands, "casework," as it came to be called, was basically a device for snooping, refusing appeals for help, or attempting to control the needy. No wonder it came under heavy attack.

Despite the attacks, casework did not disappear; it was utilized in a number of institutional settings—in the court (probation work), in the school (truancy work), in the hospital (medical social work), and in the mental facility (aftercare work). As a way of dealing with poverty, however, it was pushed into the background. Settlement house residents focused on social and economic problems rather than on needy people, being more interested in reform and preventive legislation than in individual treatment. By the early 1920s, however, thanks largely to Mary Richmond, publication of her classic book, *Social Diagnosis,* and a number of other factors, casework once again became dominant.

Miss Richmond, a frail woman who spent most of her life over-coming chronic invalidism in order to help others, was born in Belleville, Illinois, in 1861. Orphaned when young and frequently ill, she spent a lonely, unhappy childhood in Baltimore. Starting in 1878, she held a variety of jobs, but in 1889 she began her life's work by becoming assistant treasurer of Baltimore's Charity Organization Society. Two years later, she became its general secretary, a position she held until 1899 when, after moving to Philadelphia, she headed the Society for Organizing Charity. In 1909, she became director of the Charity Organization Department of the newly formed Russell Sage Foundation in New York City.

Influenced by the organized charity movement at home and abroad and by such European figures as Thomas Chalmers and Octavia Hill, both of whom believed in the individual causes of poverty and the self-help concept, Mary Richmond came natural-ly to the casework approach. Unhappy, however, because it had no logically conceived theoretical base, she spent years on the tedious and sometimes painful task of systematically probing the entire procedure. Eventually, she conceived of investigation, diagnosis, prognosis, and treatment as entities in a chain-like series; the treatment of individuals, then, was an extended, logical process, the techniques of which could be ordered, described, analyzed, and transmitted from one generation of social workers to another. She embodied her ideas in *Social Diagnosis* (which of course implied a pathology), the first definitive treatise in book form of social casework theory and method. The work not only won immediate widespread acclaim, but almost overnight helped raise casework from one of several instruments of the charity worker to a method and philosophy that was preeminent in the profession.

Three things are worth noting. First, Mary Richmond's book, originally published in 1917, was not influenced by the writings or thought of Sigmund Freud, the brilliant psychoanalyst. Freud had paid a visit to the United States—his only one—in 1909 to deliver a significant series of lectures at Clark University in Worcester, Massachusetts. At the time, he was still a relatively obscure Viennese neurologist. And although his progress as a ce-lebrity was fairly rapid thereafter, and Freudianism and psychoanalysis became more and more popular between 1909 and 1917, as Nathan Hale, Jr., has shown, most of the literature on the man and the subject was confined to periodicals read mainly by physicians, psychologists, and a few young intellectuals. Freud was still not widely known to the general public. In any event, *Social Diagnosis* bore the impress of the preceding sociological rather than the oncoming psychoanalytical era; it described the caseworker as an artificer in social relations and emphasized the social environment and financial distress rather than psychological factors and intrapsychic conflict. As a result, it would soon be outdated.

Second, while Miss Richmond was not enthusiastic about social reform, she was not hostile toward it or toward other social work methods. In fact, she deplored the "socially mischievous" antagonism between the social worker and social reformer, and tried desperately to show her associates how casework was related to other forms of social work, including research and reform: "This topic of the interplay of different forms of social work deserves fuller treatment than I have been able to give it," she pointed out, "but that all forms are inextricably woven in the great task of furthering social advance should be evident." On another occasion she exclaimed in exasperation: "I have spent twenty-five years of my life in an attempt to get social casework accepted as a valid process in social work" and now "I shall spend the rest of my life trying to demonstrate to social caseworkers that there is more to social work than . . . casework."

Still, in her opinion, social reform had failed. Despite the rise of preventive social work and the enactment of a great deal of social legislation, poverty and need had not been eliminated—nor could they be. The need for individual treatment would always persist. As one of her colleagues put it, social action and reform dealt with need in wholesale, casework dealt with need in retail; both were essential. Mary Richmond employed the retail method. Handling individuals in need, she used the step-by-step process of helping them, a process that once again became widely accepted by social workers.

Third, casework, for Mary Richmond, consisted of both diagnosis and treatment, and she was as concerned with the latter as with the former. *Social Diagnosis,* however, dealt only with the first of these matters—the investigation of clients' problems. She intended to deal with the second at a later date, something she never did.

In any event, one reason for the enormous enthusiasm casework received after publication of *Social Diagnosis,* was the negative approach that had been taken in a widely publicized paper read at the 1915 National Conference by Dr. Abraham Flexner, then America's foremost authority on graduate professional education. In his paper, "Is Social Work a Profession?," Flexner, to the dismay of his audience, concluded that social work was not a profession since it had no unique method. Rather, it was a function of conscripting the resources of the community and placing them at the disposal of the needy. Social workers, he said, were kindhearted, resourceful people engaged in good work—work, he contended, that almost anyone could do. They were mediators rather than originators of action; the "very variety of the situations the social worker encounters compels him to be not a professional agent so much as the mediator invoking this or that professional agency." Hence, if a man is sick, the social worker gets a doctor; he does not utilize any technical skill of his own. Lacking its own "technique which is communicable by an educational process," social work was no profession!

Flexner's paper had a profound effect upon the social worker and his or her world. While not all social workers accepted his criteria, or his analysis, most did. Accepting the verdict as pronounced by this expert on the subject, they desperately began trying to define and perfect techniques they could call their own.[2]

Then came Mary Richmond's *Social Diagnosis,* a 500-page work that guided the reader—the beginning caseworker —through every conceivable circumstance to be found in the

[2]They did so with such a singleness of purpose that they virtually blinded themselves to the fact that method was only *one* test of a profession. And while method is important, indeed essential, for a profession, the practitioner whose sole objective is facility in a method becomes a technician and fails to realize to the fullest his or her professional responsibilities; that is, to examine his and the profession's place in society and continuously interpret to himself and to his contemporaries the social problems he and his colleagues are attempting to solve, something most social workers failed to do in the 1920s.

lives and attitudes of prospective clients, and described in minute detail how to secure the necessary data in each instance, why such data were basic, what weight should be given each item in determining the final diagnosis, and the like.[3] Acclaimed as meeting the most exacting requirements of professional and scholarly standards, the very criteria specified by Flexner, the effect of the work was dramatic. Almost overnight, social diagnosis or casework became the method of social work and the badge of professionalism, overshadowing even to this day all other techniques in the field.

This trend toward casework was reinforced by America's entrance into World War I. First of all, shortly after the United States entered the war, the American Red Cross set up a Home Service Division to provide casework services to uprooted soldiers and their families—of all classes. Existing schools and well-known social workers collaborated with the agency in developing training "sessions" to prepare people for such work. In fact, the American Red Cross provided funds to fifteen colleges and universities, some of which came from the United States Public Health Service, to finance the creation and teaching of such courses, and Mary Richmond prepared a special casework manual for use in them. Welcoming the opportunity to expand their practice and theory in casework, social workers eagerly registered for those courses and then worked with the Red Cross in providing such services.

More important, dealing with people "above the poverty line" demonstrated that successful casework did not have to depend on relief funds to hold its clients and made it easier to construe casework as a technical service analogous to that performed by a lawyer or even a doctor. At the same time, however, it raised challenging problems for the social worker. Since much casework dealt with maladies formerly outside the social worker's experience—war neuroses, for example—the necessity of linking hands with psychologists and psychiatrists in order to become well versed in their revelations of the human psyche was seen. Psy-

---

[3]Unfortunately, *Social Diagnosis,* the first edition of which sold out in a month, was more concerned with process than with person, with means rather than with ends, and continued to blind many social workers to the fact that methods were not the raison d'être of social work.

chologists and psychiatrists, for their part, encouraged such an alliance.

Psychologists, psychiatrists, and physicians who examined the men called into military service, or who treated those rejected or dismissed because of mental or emotional problems, saw in caseworkers, specialists in the field of social adjustment, just the assisting personnel they needed. Enamored by the opportunity to work with doctors and flattered by the offer, many social workers seized the opportunity. World War I thus helped facilitate the social workers' shift from a social-economic to an individual-psychological base. Then, in 1918, Smith College established its School of Psychiatric Social Work—the first of its kind in America which, interestingly, began by offering a six-month course for psychiatric aides attached to the Army Medical Service. This not only symbolized the growing importance of psychiatric theory for social work, but by training psychiatric social workers the school furthered its use as well.

The need for new knowledge, which wartime social workers had felt, was further satisfied in the 1920s by the mental hygiene movement and the work of the National Committee for Mental Hygiene, and especially by psychoanalytic thought, which by that time had become almost a national mania. The casework emphasis upon the individual and upon an introspective view of problems made social workers naturally receptive to Freud. More important, enthusiastic acceptance of his ideas resulted from the fact that much of what Freud said found responsive echoes in caseworkers' experience and at the same time provided them with both a theoretical base and a scientific method of treatment that until that time had been lacking.

Social workers already knew that some individual afflictions (of the flesh as well as of the spirit) were not amenable to programs of social betterment; they remained untouched by social engineering. They could not predict which persons would respond successfully to such an approach and which would not. Moreover, they did not have a systematic way to proceed when personality *was* the resistant factor. They acted intuitively and used "common sense"; success depended more on chance than on any logically conceived process. Therefore, they were ready to accept and utilize the new concept of psychoanalysis, with its relatively coherent theory of personality, focusing upon the importance of childhood experiences and emotions in shaping personality and behavior.[4]

In other words, Freud's ideas placed caseworkers' relationships with clients in a new light; psychoanalytic theory was a body of knowledge that provided them with a scientific understanding and a way of dealing with psychological factors in human behavior that they had long observed but could not explain—facets of human behavior hitherto ignored as irrelevant or dismissed as irrational. It was obvious that a close relationship existed between the method of evaluating social data, as developed by the caseworker, and the psychiatrist's method of probing the inner recesses of the mentally ill. Each dealt with people in difficult situations but only the latter had developed a method designed to explain the nature of the trouble and how to aid the patients or clients to overcome it by themselves. It was inevitable, or certainly likely, that an intellectual mating of the two would occur, and that they would work together to achieve their respective goals.

Elated, many social workers set about adapting Freud's major discoveries in the language and practice of psychoanalysis to the language and practice of casework. They naturally identified themselves with the psychiatric clinical team rather than with social reformers or even social caseworkers, who seemed old fashioned if not passé. (Once alerted to the effect of the unconscious on motivation, psychiatric caseworkers felt that environmentalism, based upon the assumption that people are rational, had no relation to the dynamic factors in human behavior.) They developed a fresh concept of casework, based on Freud, the mysteries of the psyche, personality, and the emotions. As one historian has written, "The psychiatric social worker emerged as the queen of the caseworkers," for if her point of view was relevant to all casework, no group was better qualified by training and experience to speak for the profession.

Most important, psychiatry promised to eliminate one of the

[4]Psychoanalysis is both a systematic structure of theories concerning the relation of conscious and unconscious psychological processes to human behavior and a technical procedure for investigating those processes and treating psychoneuroses.

most serious obstacles to the attainment of professional status by the social worker—the historic link with charity and humanitarianism, the belief that social work required nothing more than a warm heart and a cheerful outlook. The new preoccupation with psychological rather than with economic factors allowed social workers to see and portray themselves in a new light. No longer were they dispensers of charity interested primarily in the poor. Rather, shorn of old-time moralism and armed with a vocabulary strewn with psychological and medical terms, they were social physicians concerned with problems of emotional maladjustment—problems that occurred as frequently among the upper classes as among the lower—and this was worthy of professional status.

The new professionalism, however, may not have been as far removed from the old moralism as many social workers would have liked to believe. As David and Sheila Rothman have pointed out, the net result of the new approach "was to couch in modern terminology some very traditional ideas." Once again, the poor were responsible for their difficulties, only now rationalized in updated language. The unworthy poor had become the emotionally disturbed or deprived poor. Or, as an equally perceptive person put it: "Substituting expertise for moral superiority as the basis of the relationship, social workers [in the 1920s] perpetuated the charity organization ideal of personal contact and influence in place of material relief, but avoided the fiction that such contact was one of friends and peers bound in neighborhood association."

Nevertheless, this surrender to Freud and the clinical orientation contributed further to the shift already taking place in social workers' orientation from the social environment to the individual emotional environment, from poverty and economic problems to personality and emotional problems, from social reform to individual adjustment. Other forces within the field—forces not peculiar to social work but typical features of an urban-industrial society that affected most aspects of American life at the time—tended further to reinforce this development. The growing size of agency operations and the demand for specialization, for example, meant that social workers were caught up in bureaucratic routines that usually afforded little opportunity for observing or dealing with anything more than their clients; limited by regulations, procedures, and systems of hierarchical structure and forced to abide by various agency as well as professional standards, practitioners did not have the time or the incentive to become involved in social policy, theory, or reform. Increasingly, policies were determined by executives and committees (often comprised of conservative lay men and women) over which the practitioner had little or no control.

With this growth in the size of operations, social work leaders became administrators rather than professional colleagues. Gertrude Vaile, in her presidential address before the National Conference in 1926, lamented the decreasing zeal in the field, attributing it in large part to the decline in crusading leadership and the emergence of a new kind of institutional head, more an organizer and an executive absorbed in administrative duties than someone likely to possess the penetrating insight, broad social vision, or humanity of the great social work leaders of the Progressive era.

Related was the problem of money raising. With more and more and larger and larger agencies, raising funds became a greater problem, not only for organizations but for potential donors as well. Many causes and appeals compelled a degree of selectivity that givers often found difficult to make. Eventually, united giving, or the community chest, the ultimate in bureaucracy—an anonymous public supporting anonymous machinery supporting anonymous clients—was utilized.

Federated fund raising began much earlier, like so many other developments in American social welfare, in England, where it was tried for the first time in Liverpool in 1873. Its inception in America came in 1887 with the creation of the Associated Charities of Denver. While a few other localities followed suit, most community chests were not created until during, and especially after, World War I. During the conflict, "war chests" sprang up almost overnight and thousands of people who never before had known what it was to give to charity, gave generously. After the war, the war chests were converted into community chests. So rapidly did the idea grow, that by the mid-1920s about 200 cities had adopted the plan and the movement was still spreading.

While in theory federated fund raising offered innovative programs and agencies with little popular support an opportunity to get started, in practice just the opposite occurred. Community chests proved to be conservative forces in social welfare, formalizing the somewhat uneasy but long-standing alliance between private agencies and wealthy donors. A throwback to C.O.S. days, in that they sought to streamline and coordinate the financing and administration of private charity (and a reflection of the consolidation of big business that took place in the 1920s, just as the organized charities reflected the monopolization of big business in the late nineteenth century), the chests requested support not for individual agencies but for an organized pattern of welfare services that was tied to the social structure of the community. This, in turn, contested the independence and distinctiveness (and even the leadership of the heads) of the participating agencies, for the power of their purses, and thus their very existence, was in the hands of outsiders—usually the community's business and financial leaders—to whom they had to be accountable.[5] To be funded, agencies were forced to play it safe, to stress service to the community, to refurbish established practice rather than to encourage social reform and change from the existing order.

Thus, Judith Trolander, in a recent study on *Settlement Houses and the Great Depression,* found that the programs of various settlement houses, especially the degree to which they sought to alter prevailing social and economic conditions, were related directly to whether or not those institutions were financed by community chests: "Although settlement boards retained control over personnel, the ultimate decisions as to the programs of the individual houses [in any given city] were made by the chests which controlled their finances." And, she wrote, the "more dependent a settlement house was on a community chest, the more conservative it was on social issues," whatever they happened to be. "Those settlements that functioned meaningfully as community organizers [in the 1920s and 1930s] were those which remained relatively independent of the business-dominated chests." This would help explain the loss of reformist zeal among those settlement houses that managed to survive the so-called prosperity decade.

---

[5]This was especially true since in most cases member agencies were required to give up their own fund raising efforts (in order, theoretically, to avoid duplication of appeal), thus making them almost totally dependent on the community chest, now usually known as the United Way.

There were still other external factors that help to explain the shift in social work away from reform and back toward individual service. As Mary Richmond and others had pointed out, despite the reforms of the early twentieth century, many of the problems that had plagued the organized charities and the settlement houses persisted. In some ways, the entire Progressive movement had been a failure. In many respects, American society in the 1920s was no different than it had been two or three decades earlier; big business dominated society, racism and bigotry were growing, political corruption was widespread, mass conformity prevailed, and, with the suppression of civil liberties during the war and the enactment of Prohibition after it, even the federal government had become an instrument of repression and social control. Many Americans, not just social workers, were disillusioned with the progressive crusade and with social reform in general.

Then, too, there was the widespread belief that social reform was unnecessary, for this was the "prosperity decade," or so it was believed. There was no need to improve the social environment, to eliminate poverty, to raise the standard of living; for all practical purposes, those tasks had already been accomplished, as Herbert Hoover told Americans in October 1928. Congratulating his countrymen on being born into a land from which poverty had been banished, the G.O.P. presidential candidate declared: "Our American experiment in human welfare has yielded a degree of wellbeing unparalleled in all the world. It has come nearer to the abolition of poverty, to the abolition of fear of want, than humanity has ever reached before." And it got there, Hoover and many others believed, not through state intervention (or social reform) but through individualism and voluntarism—through science and technology, big business, industrial relations, welfare capitalism, and the like. So, emphasis upon the individual and the consequent refusal to face harsh social and economic facts reflected not only the social worker's preoccupation with the three "Ps"—professionalism, psychiatry, and psychoanalysis—but also the conservative social and economic climate of the postwar years.

This is not to say, however, that psychoanalytic theory completely dominated social work thought and practice in the

1920s—that there was a "Freudian deluge" during the prosperity decade.[6] Casework clearly became the nuclear skill of the emerging profession and "counseling," especially family counseling provided by private agencies, often to middle and upper class families for a fee, certainly became the major professional function. However, the psychiatric caseworker remained a member of an elite (although growing) minority, and psychodynamic formulations did not come to pervade agency practice until later.[7] Actually, most social workers and welfare agencies at this time sought to bring the insights of the new psychology into line with the older practice, based upon rational assumptions and environmental manipulation. If the two could be combined, the best efforts of both approaches could be achieved.

Nor is it correct to suggest that the development of casework as the professional method and of family counseling as the professional function brought an end to all relief giving. Some caseworkers and family service agencies still provided clients with financial aid but reconciled doing so with psychiatry and professionalism. They argued that they had to deal with the reality of clients' obsession with money, the key to both their physical and their emotional survival. Financial dependency in America—a competitive capitalistic society that equated wealth with status—implied personal inadequacy and unworthiness. Needy clients, therefore, carried the burdens of guilt and inferiority, psychological liabilities that financial relief could help rectify. The social worker could not permit clients' concerns with money to go unattended. Moreover, the skilled caseworker could use financial relief to promote therapeutic objectives: such assistance provided an excellent entrée into the confidence and good will of clients

[6]To social reformers, though, it may have seemed like such a deluge; social reform, one activist bitterly declared, had given way to "individual psychology, social psychology, psychiatry, and social psychiatry, psychometry, mental testing, mental hygiene, psychoanalysis, child guidance, and what not."

[7]Particularly important in that regard was the publication, in 1930, of Virginia Robinson's *A Changing Psychology in Social Case Work,* a book that sharply contrasted with Mary Richmond's *Social Diagnosis.* To use Roy Lubove's words, Robinson "abstracted casework almost entirely from its roots in the client's social environment and cultural milieu and placed it squarely in the camp of the psychiatrists and psychologists." In other words, she made casework synonymous with psychotherapy, and publication of her work opened the gates much further to the teachings of Freud in the schools of social work.

and, by insuring physical survival, permitted them to divert their attention to nonmaterial matters.

Finally, it also would be incorrect to say that the 1920s were totally devoid of social reform. Clarke Chambers and others have amply demonstrated that, thanks to the efforts of social workers and others, the decade was not a complete wasteland for constructive social change. In Chambers' words, although they at times suffered from confusion and disunity and were often frustrated and rebuffed, "social workers kept alive and vital the crusade for social action, and thus formed a viable link between prewar progressivism and the New Deal; they sparked many social action crusades that anticipated the reform programs of the following decade." However, while some social workers remained reformers and worked for important social changes, including the abolition of child labor and the improvement of public and mental health services and facilities, most did not. Those who continued the reform tradition were not professional social workers, graduates of training schools, but basically the same people who had led the progressive crusade earlier in the century, including some aging settlement house residents. On the whole, the profession, including its schools and organizations, embodied the spirit herein described.

By the time of the Great Depression, then, social work had undergone or was undergoing a profound change, from "cause" to "function," to use Porter Lee's terms, from advocating reform to efficiently rendering technical services. "I am inclined to think," Lee told his colleagues at the National Conference in 1929, "that in the capacity of the social worker . . . to administer routine functional responsibility in the spirit of the servant in the cause lies the explanation of the great service of social work."

Most social workers attended training schools which had already adopted or were in the process of adopting as their main requirement some sort of course on "Human Growth and Development." Designed to present an integrated theory of human personality, it concentrated on such Freudian concepts as defense mechanisms, transference, ego strengths and weaknesses, libidinal attachment, the Oedipus complex, and so on. After graduation, the students became practitioners—a growing number, psychiatric caseworkers—who helped clients to become adjusted to their environment. They saw themselves as technicians with a responsibility to their cases, not as crusaders bent upon curing the maladies of society.

This, however, did not solve all of social work's problems. On the contrary, it left the young profession with some serious ones. As noted earlier, the changes that occurred in the 1920s seriously affected the profession's leadership and zeal, and thus its effectiveness. Instead of broad-minded, charismatic leaders motivated by a true sense of neighborliness, such as Jane Addams, Florence Kelley, and Julia Lathrop, leadership was assumed by uninspiring and uninspired bureaucrats and executives who merely conducted the business of running various agencies. Then there was the virtual demise of the settlement house movement, which, in turn, had a detrimental effect on the profession.

More significant, was the fact that psychiatry—which at first seemed to be a blessing that would elevate social work to its deeply cherished professional status—created a serious long-range problem for the field. Aside from undermining the capacity and desire for social workers to promote change and deal with mass deprivation in an urban society, psychiatry threatened the very professional identity which social workers were so anxious to attain, for if psychiatric knowledge was fundamental to the profession, what distinguished psychiatric casework from psychotherapy, except for the social worker's inferior education and training? Were psychiatric social workers mere handmaidens to psychiatrists? As Roy Lubove has pointed out, it was one thing to reject social reform, but quite another to fail to substitute some specific alternative that really differentiated the social worker from others in the helping professions. For this and other reasons, some critics have argued that social work was, and remains, an "incomplete profession," or "semi-profession."

And finally, while social workers' efforts to increase scientific understanding of personality were legitimate, they swung the pendulum too far. Despite all their professions, the social and economic causes of poverty—illness, injury, low wages, involuntary unemployment, old age, death of the family breadwinner—had not disappeared. And dependency caused by these factors demanded social and economic solutions, not casework. A handful of social workers and reformers such as Jane Addams,

Florence Kelley, Karl de Schweinitz, and Isaac Rubinow not only saw this but also warned of the danger of neglecting these matters. So, too, did the National Federation of Settlements, which in 1928 was so worried about growing unemployment that it launched a study on the subject, one that clearly dispelled the myth of "full employment"—the belief that anyone who really wanted to work could find a job. Meanwhile, the stock market crashed and the Great Depression followed and the reformers' worst fears proved to be true; the nation's social welfare institutions and agencies were unprepared to meet the crisis.

Bibliography

ALEXANDER, LESLIE B. "Social Work's Freudian Deluge: Myth or Reality?", *Social Service Review* 46 (December 1972): 517–38.

BERLEMAN, WILLIAM C. "Mary Richmond's *Social Diagnosis* in Retrospect," *Social Casework* 49 (July 1968): 395–402.

BORENZWEIG, HERMAN. "Social Work and Psychoanalytic Theory: A Historical Analysis," *Social Work* 16 (January 1971): 7–16.

CHAMBERS, CLARKE A. *Seedtime of Reform: American Social Service and Social Action, 1918–1933*. Minneapolis: University of Minnesota Press, 1963.

CHEPAITIS, JOSEPH B. "Federal Social Welfare Progressivism in the 1920s," *Social Service Review* 46 (June 1972): 213–29.

DAVIS, ALLEN. "Welfare Reform and World War I," *American Quarterly* 19 (Fall 1967): 516–33.

FIELD, MARTHA H. "Social Casework Practice During the Psychiatric Deluge," *Social Service Review* 54 (December 1980): 482–507.

FLEXNER, ABRAHAM. "Is Social Work a Profession?", *Proceedings* of the National Conference of Charities and Correction (Chicago: Hildmann, 1915): 576–90.

FRENCH, LOIS. *Psychiatric Social Work*. New York: Commonwealth Fund, 1940.

FRIEND, MAURICE R. "The Historical Development of Family Diagnosis," *Social Service Review* 34 (March 1960): 2–16.

GARRET, ANNETTE. "Historical Survey of the Evolution of Casework," *Social Casework* 30 (June 1949): 219–29.

GILBERT, NEIL, AND HARRY SPECHT. "The Incomplete Profession," in *The Emergence of Social Welfare and Social Work*. Itasca, Ill.: Peacock, 1976.

GLENN, MARY W. "The Growth of Social Casework in the United States," *The Family* 9 (December 1928): 270–77.

GREEN, A. D. "The Professional Worker in the Bureaucracy," *Social Service Review* 40 (March 1966): 71–83.

GRINKER, R. R. et al. "The Early Years of Psychiatric Social Work," *Social Service Review* 35 (June 1961): 111–26.

HALE, NATHAN G., JR. *Freud and the Americans*. New York: Oxford University Press, 1971.

HEIMAN, MARCEL, ed. *Psychoanalysis and Social Work*. New York: International Universities Press, 1953.

HODSON, WILLIAM. "Is Social Work Professional? A Re-examination," *Proceedings* of the National Conference of Social Work (Chicago: University of Chicago Press, 1925): 629–36.

KASIUS, CORA. *New Directions in Social Work*. New York: Harper, 1954.

LEE, PORTER. "Social Work as Cause and Function," *Proceedings* of the National Conference of Social Work (Chicago: University of Chicago Press, 1929): 3–20.

LEEBRON, HARVEY. *The Financial Federation Movement*. Chicago: American Association for Community Organization, 1924.

LURIE, H. L. "Private Philanthropy and Federated Fund-Raising," *Social Service Review* 29 (March 1955): 64–74.

MESS, HENRY A. *Voluntary Social Service Since 1918*. London: Paul, Trench, Tubner, 1948.

NEUSTAEDTER, ELEANOR. "The Integration of Economic and Psychological Factors in Family Case Work," *Proceedings* of the National Conference of Social Work (Chicago: University of Chicago Press, 1930): 198–216.

ODENCRANTZ, LOUISE C. *The Social Worker in Family, Medical and Psychiatric Social Work*. New York: Harper, 1929.

ORME, JOHN G, AND PAUL STUART. "The Habit Clinics: Behavioral Social Work and Prevention in the 1920s," *Social Service Review* 55 (June 1981): 242–56.

PERLMAN, HELEN HARRIS. "Freud's Contribution to Social Welfare," *Social Service Review* 31 (June 1957): 192–202.

PUMPHREY, MURIEL. "The 'First Step'—Mary Richmond's Earliest

Professional Reading, 1889–91," *Social Service Review* 31 (June 1957): 144–63.

RICH, MARGARET. *A Belief in People: A History of Family Social Work.* New York: Family Service Association of America, 1956.

———. "Mary Richmond: Social Worker 1861–1928," *Social Casework* 33 (October 1952): 363–70.

RICHMOND, MARY. *The Good Neighbor in the Modern City.* Philadelphia: Lippincott, 1907.

———. *Social Diagnosis.* New York: Russell Sage Foundation, 1917.

———. *What Is Social Case Work?* New York: Russell Sage Foundation, 1922.

ROBINSON, VIRGINIA P. *A Changing Psychology in Social Case Work.* Chapel Hill, N.C.: University of North Carolina Press, 1930.

ROSS, AILEEN D. "The Social Control of Philanthropy," *American Journal of Sociology* 58 (March 1953): 451–60.

RUBINOW, I. M. "Can Private Philanthropy Do It?", *Social Service Review* 3 (September 1929): 361–94.

SCHLESINGER, ARTHUR, JR. *The Crisis of the Old Order, 1919–1933.* Boston: Houghton Mifflin, 1957.

SEELEY, JOHN R. et al. *Community Chest: A Case Study in Philanthropy.* Toronto: University of Toronto Press, 1957.

TOREN, NINA. *Social Work: The Case of a Semi-Profession.* Beverly Hills: Sage Publications, 1972.

TROLANDER, JUDITH. *Settlement Houses and the Great Depression.* Detroit: Wayne State University Press, 1975.

VAILE, GERTRUDE. "Some Significant Trends Since Cleveland, 1912," *The Family* 7 (July 1926): 127–33.

WATTS, PHYLLIS A. "Casework Above the Poverty Line: The Influence of Home Service in World War I on Social Work," *Social Service Review* 38 (September 1964): 303–15.

WILENSKY, HAROLD L., AND CHARLES N. LEBEAUX. *Industrial Society and Social Welfare.* New York: Free Press, 1965.

WOODROOFE, KATHLEEN. *From Charity to Social Work in England and America.* Toronto: University of Toronto Press, 1962.

Chapter 13

Depression and a New Deal

THE STOCK MARKET CRASH in the fall of 1929, and the long, deep depression that followed, hit the nation with a jarring impact. Some thirteen to fifteen million workers lost their jobs. Banks were closed, some permanently. Many citizens lost their life's savings. Factories lay idle. Stores had few customers. Hundreds of thousands of farmers were forced off their land. Numerous others lost their homes. Huddled figures shuffling despondently in bread lines or at soup kitchens testified to destitution and suffering to an extent unknown in American history.

The task of relieving the jobless and their families was first undertaken by private local agencies. It quickly became evident, however, that they were unprepared to meet the crisis. To begin with, they were ill suited to the task because the "services" they performed would not feed the hungry or shelter the homeless. Furthermore, the financial needs of so many people—not only the aged, the sick, the disabled, and other members of the lower classes but also the plain, ordinary, middle class people who had worked all their lives but who were now unemployed, penniless, and hungry, the so-called new poor—were clearly beyond their meager means. As one observer aptly remarked, "Trying to turn back this tide of distress through private philanthropic contributions is about as useless as trying to put out a forest fire with a garden hose." For many, then, the depression answered, once and for all, the vexing question of whether private or public agencies should be responsible for relief-giving. Voluntary charity simply could not cope with the situation; only public agencies could deal with the collapse of the economy, mass unemployment, and widespread destitution.

Despite the suffering, public action to meet the emergency did not make itself felt for some time, especially since so many locali-

257

ties had abolished public home relief. Public officials made some effort to encourage reemployment. A few committees were organized by state and federal personnel, but they were advisory in nature, and for the most part they confined themselves to continued encouragement of local enterprise. Other than certain municipal and state public works projects, no public action of consequence was taken until September 1931—almost two years after the crash. Then, under the prodding of Governor Franklin D. Roosevelt, the New York State Legislature acted to provide unemployment relief to jobless citizens of that state.

In the meantime, many social workers saw—were forced to see—that destitution usually resulted from social and economic factors which the needy could not control. As a result, they urged their colleagues to return to social action. Grace Coyle, for example, lashed out at those in the field who "continued to pick up the pieces without ever attempting to stop the breakage." Or as another social worker put it: "The futility of the case by case method of dealing with the problem is increasingly obvious. The flood must be stopped at its source, not mopped up by the bucketful, however scientifically modelled the bucket." Even Bertha Reynolds, associate director of the Smith College School of Psychiatric Social Work, agreed. It would be absurd to deal with emotional problems when there were millions of hungry people to feed; other methods were needed to handle the crisis.

Most social workers responded accordingly. Aware of the inadequacy of private and even local public resources, as well as the desperate straits to which many Americans were being driven—and perhaps feeling a bit guilty for spending too much time on the perfection of techniques and not enough on social reform in the 1920s—they called for public action, even federal aid. Thus, in October 1931, William Hodson, of the New York City Welfare Council, addressed an open letter to President Herbert Hoover urging federal unemployment relief—not as a matter of charity but as a matter of right. Over the next few months, Hodson and others, including the American Association of Social Workers, took an active part in organizing a series of historic U.S. Senate committee hearings on unemployment relief.

Testifying before the LaFollette-Costigan Committee, which held those hearings, a social worker described how families in

Philadelphia were forced to manage under the circumstances:

> One woman went along the docks and picked up vegetables that fell from wagons. Sometimes fish vendors gave her fish at the end of the day. On two different occasions the family was without food for a day and a half. Another family did not have food for two days. Then the husband went out and gathered dandelions and the family ate them.

Another social worker appearing before the committee presented an account of a family of ten that had just moved into a three-room apartment that was already occupied by a family of five. "However shocking that may be to members of this Committee," the witness stated, "it is almost an everyday occurrence." Walter West, executive secretary of the American Association of Social Workers, summed up the situation best when he said, "The relief problem has ceased to be a local one. It is national in origin [and] . . . national in scope." It needed a national response!

Despite the gravity of the situation, the pleas of social workers and others, and the LaFollette-Costigan Committee's evidence that federal aid was needed, there was still a great deal of opposition to such action, especially from President Herbert Hoover. Over the past decade or so, a number of historians—for instance, Joan Hoff Wilson and David Burner—have reassessed Hoover and his career, including his presidency, and have argued that he was a complex, thoughtful, intelligent, and able leader who led the way into the policies and programs of the New Deal. It is true that in 1921, as Secretary of Commerce, Hoover had convened a conference on unemployment relief to deal with the problems of the postwar recession and in 1927 he had organized a major flood relief effort in the Mississippi Valley. It also is true that as a result of these and other things, including his successful experiences as a relief administrator in Europe during and after World War I and as a food administrator in America after the United States entered the conflict, Hoover had a good deal of support among social workers throughout the nation when he ran for President in 1928. Nevertheless, when he was in the White House and the economy collapsed, Hoover's response to America's deep depression was less than adequate—and most of the social work community turned away from him.

To begin with, Hoover refused to recognize or admit the seriousness of the problem. He was convinced that the economy was sound and that prosperity was just around the corner—all that was necessary was a restoration of confidence. Thus, the public was reminded time after time that "the fundamental business of the country . . . is on a sound and prosperous basis," that "we now have passed the worst," that "the crisis will be over within sixty days," and so on.

Hoover's miscalculated optimism or blindness was aggravated by his loyalty to the American folklore of self-help. For him, relief was a moral, not merely an economic, matter; private charity (such as he had distributed in war ravaged Europe) was fine, but public aid, especially from the national government, was a "dole." Thus, while Hoover approved of relief distributed by the American Red Cross, for example, he rejected all proposals for federal aid.

Hoover opposed federal aid for a wide variety of reasons. In his opinion, it would delay the natural forces at work to restore prosperity, it impaired the credit and solvency of the government, it stifled voluntary giving, it was inflexible and thus could not respond to local needs, it established politicized bureaucracies, it undermined free enterprise, it was illegal—a violation of local responsibility and states' rights—and it ultimately endangered democratic government: "You cannot extend the mastery of government over the daily lives of the people without at the same time making it the master of their souls and thoughts," Hoover declared. Why federal aid for the unemployed and needy necessarily meant government mastery over their lives—or whether neglect and starvation were better—he did not say.

The belief that public assistance would demoralize and enslave its recipients while private charity would not—that somehow private was democratic and public undemocratic—was, of course, an old idea that long since had been outmoded. Among other things, this notion failed to recognize that the imperatives of a modern society had rendered many of the distinctions between private organizations and public agencies meaningless (if they ever had existed), so that the American Red Cross was far from immune to the bureaucratic rigidities, arbitrary methods, and other alleged evils Hoover attributed to large public organizations. Far more important, however, was the fact that by 1930 and 1931 the country's economy had collapsed, millions of citizens were unemployed through no fault of their own, *and* the nation's private charitable resources had dried up. The jobless and the hungry wanted and needed to eat! It made little difference to them who supplied the food.

Hoover's attitude toward public relief was exemplified in December 1930, when he approved a congressional appropriation of $45 million to feed stricken livestock of Arkansas farmers but opposed an additional $25 million to feed the starving farmers and their families; chickens, obviously, could not get demoralized. A year later, when House Speaker John Garner and Senator Robert F. Wagner of New York jointly sponsored a measure calling for a $2.6 billion federal public works program, arguing that such a project would put people back to work and stimulate the economy, Hoover vetoed the measure, declaring that "never before in the nation's entire history has anyone made so dangerous a suggestion."[1]

Elsewhere, however, bold action was taken. "The country needs, and unless I mistake its temper, the country demands bold, persistent experimentation," New York Governor Franklin D. Roosevelt would declare in accepting the Democratic Party's presidential nomination in 1932. "It is common sense to take a

---

[1]Hoover was obviously not a good student of history—the only subject he failed while attending college. The idea of federal public works projects during times of involuntary unemployment was an old one, going at least as far back in England to the Poor Laws of 1536 and 1601 and in America to the depression of the 1890s, when "General" Jacob Coxey of Ohio led an army of unemployed on a march to Washington demanding, among other things, a federal public works program. In any event, despite presidential reassurances, prosperity was not around the corner; in fact, conditions continued to grow worse. Finally, after three winters of depression so severe that it had depleted even state, let alone private and local, resources, Hoover consented to some federal action. In the summer of 1932, he signed the Emergency Relief and Construction Act, a measure that authorized the Reconstruction Finance Corporation (a federal agency created six months earlier to extend government aid to large corporations and banks) to lend to the states up to $300 million "to be used in furnishing relief and work relief to needy and distressed people and in relieving the hardships resulting from unemployment." Since they were loans rather than grants, however, many states, already heavily in debt, refused to borrow such funds, and by the end of 1932 only one-tenth of the appropriated sum, or $30 million, was sent to the states for relief purposes, while Congress had sent more than three times that amount to a single Chicago bank, the head of which was former Vice President and R.F.C. chairman Charles G. Dawes. Many of the nation's hungry were incensed.

method and try it. If it fails try another. But above all, try something."

Roosevelt had indeed tried something. Less bound by tradition than Hoover and aware (from studies conducted for him by the Joint Committee on Unemployment Relief of the State Board of Welfare and the New York State Charities Aid Association) that unemployment was not only severe but getting worse, in August 1931 he called a special session of the legislature to consider the emergency. Placing unemployment in the same category as old age, widowhood, and industrial accidents—hazards over which the individual had no control, certainly not in the current crisis—the Chief Executive asked the state's lawmakers for funds to help local authorities meet the needs of the unemployed. "Modern society acting through its government owes the definite obligation to prevent the starvation or dire waste of any of its fellow men and women who try to maintain themselves but cannot," Roosevelt told them. Aid to jobless citizens, he declared, "must be extended by government, not as a matter of charity, but as a matter of social duty."

Inasmuch as relief funds came from taxation, which was borne by the entire community, most of those who received aid, Roosevelt argued, had contributed to relief costs during their days of self-support; they were not receiving something for nothing. Since relief was financed on the same basis as all other public services, accepting such aid, the Governor maintained, should be no different than sending children to public school or calling the fire department.

In any event, the State Unemployment Relief Act—better known as the Wicks Act—emerged from the special legislative session, making the Empire State the nation's first to provide unemployment relief to its needy citizens. Enacted on September 23, 1931, the measure provided for an emergency period, during which time millions of dollars in aid were extended to localities throughout the state, on a matching basis, for work and for home relief under the direction of a new, independent agency, T.E.R.A.—the Temporary Emergency Relief Administration. Harry Hopkins, an energetic young social worker employed by the New York Tuberculosis and Public Health Association, was made executive director of the program.

The act was of major significance. Among other things, it helped establish the constructive social value of adequate public relief, and thus helped to break down the notion that such aid tended to pauperize and demoralize its recipients. In addition, by treating unemployment as a statewide social problem, the measure went far toward changing the setting within which social work operated. The army of unemployed had to be dealt with en masse, not individually. Social workers, once again, were forced to visualize themselves as something more than the custodians of the individual; they had to deal with the welfare of many people. Furthermore, by bringing many trained social workers into government service, quite a few of whom were borrowed from private agencies, the T.E.R.A. forged significant links between private charity and public welfare.

Equally important, the Wicks Act was widely copied. By the end of the year, twenty-four states had followed New York's example of providing unemployment relief and setting up a new state agency to administer the funds. And finally, it served as a forerunner and prototype for later federal practices, providing not only a model but also personnel for New Deal programs and agencies.

As the name of its administrative agency (T.E.R.A.) indicated, the Wicks Act was conceived of as a temporary device intended to bring the state into the business of providing unemployment relief merely for the duration of the crisis. Still, New York and the states that followed its lead were acting, while, for the most part, Washington did nothing. Instead, one member of the President's cabinet suggested that restaurant owners be urged to collect plate scraps and leftovers and place them in containers to be distributed to the "worthy" unemployed, perhaps a superfluous suggestion, as an item in a Chicago newspaper indicated: "Around the truck which was unloading garbage and other refuse were about thirty-five men, women, and children. As soon as the truck pulled away from the pile, all of them started digging with sticks, some with their hands, grabbing bits of food and vegetables."

As a result of federal inaction, by the spring of 1933, the nation faced a serious threat. Disorder spread and talk of revolution was heard; many destitute and starving citizens had only contempt for the government and the system that was responsible for their plight but that did little to alleviate their distress. Then came the inauguration of Franklin D. Roosevelt as the thirty-second President of the United States.

Roosevelt had been an excellent governor of New York. While in principle he was rather conservative—he favored small government, local responsibility, and balanced budgets, and he did not like public home relief—as an heir to the progressive social justice movement he was more concerned about the suffering of the unemployed and other needy than about adhering to certain beliefs. He also knew (as Boss Plunkitt had known) that appealing welfare policies were good politics. Thus, he was especially strong in matters of social justice, and during his two terms in office the state's Public Welfare Law was vastly improved, a progressive Old Age Pension Law passed, and the Wicks Act and other social legislation enacted. Under his leadership, New York became the most progressive state in America with regard to taking practical steps to prevent and relieve distress.

As President, Roosevelt acted on the same ideas that had guided his actions as governor—the belief that mankind had a responsibility for the well-being of all human beings, that an impersonal and uncontrolled economic system, not the unemployed themselves, usually caused unemployment, that public assistance was not a matter of charity but a matter of justice that rested upon the individual's right to a minimum standard of living in a civilized society, and that liberty and security were synonymous; thus, the very existence of a democratic state depended upon the health and welfare of its citizens. So, although he came into office with a pledge for retrenchment and economy, it was plain he would do what was necessary in order to aid the needy, even if it meant spending federal funds and incurring large deficits—at least for a while. By instituting a large federal relief program and by reviving the economy, however slowly, Roosevelt succeeded in restoring confidence in the nation's basic institutions, thereby preventing further catastrophe.

This, of course, is not to say that Roosevelt was a saint. He certainly had some shortcomings, particularly in the area of civil rights, especially for blacks, where he moved very slowly. Despite having a favorable image among black people and despite his success in weaning most of them away from the Republican Party, Roosevelt's actual commitment to the Negro was slim; he was more a symbol than an activist for the oppressed minority, at least prior to America's entrance into World War II.

Roosevelt sympathized with the black citizen's plight, but his compassion was tempered by the enormity of the decisions which came before him and by the political considerations he had to face. An astute politician, he generally used political weights and measures on a scale to judge the evidence, and blacks were often found wanting. Thus, when Walter White, executive secretary of the N.A.A.C.P., obtained an audience (through the good graces of Eleanor Roosevelt) with the President to plead for public support of a federal antilynching bill, F.D.R. demurred because he needed southern votes in Congress on other matters. Likewise, the progress of many federal relief measures was dogged by racial discrimination.

Thus, the Civilian Conservation Corps (C.C.C.) not only restricted the enrollment of blacks to 10 percent of the total but also in many instances placed blacks in segregated areas. In addition, black tenant farmers and sharecroppers suffered greatly from government-induced crop reductions under the provisions of the Agricultural Adjustment Act (A.A.A.).[2] So many others suffered the loss of jobs from the closing of small businesses as a result of the National Recovery Administration's (N.R.A.) "codes of fair competition" that blacks referred to the measure that had created the new federal agency as the "Negro Removal Act." Under the Federal Emergency Relief Act (F.E.R.A.), the design of work projects and the allocation of funds were left to local officials, who often discriminated against blacks, especially in southern rural areas, but elsewhere as well. One could cite numerous other examples of racial discrimination during the so-called New Deal. Consequently, blacks and other minority group members,

[2]Perhaps it should be mentioned that the most deprived members of American society at this time were small farmers and farm laborers, especially sharecroppers and tenants living in the South, white as well as black. Their bleak living and working conditions and their grievous suffering are movingly described by James Patterson in *America's Struggle Against Poverty, 1900–1980* (Cambridge, Mass.: Harvard University Press, 1981), pp. 38–39.

who usually were the first to lose their jobs, felt the crush of the depression even more than their white counterparts did.

In any event, soon after entering the White House, surrounded by signs of despair and social unrest and convinced that the need for federal assistance was so overwhelming that it could no longer be postponed, President Roosevelt plunged the national government into the business of relief. The Civilian Conservation Corps (C.C.C.) took thousands of unemployed young men off the streets and out of rural slums and put them to work on reforestation and flood and fire control. The Public Works Administration (P.W.A.) provided employment for millions of citizens in vast public works programs created to stimulate depressed industries, especially construction. The National Youth Administration (N.Y.A.) provided part-time jobs for high school and college students so that they could earn enough money to complete their education. The Works Progress Administration (W.P.A., later known as the Works Projects Administration) provided jobs for the unemployed, including artists, musicians, and scholars, suited to their skills and experience. These and a host of other measures—the Wagner National Labor Relations Act, which finally gave unions effective guarantees of their right to organize; the Farm Security Administration, which, in a variety of ways, aided small farmers and migratory workers; slum clearance and public housing programs, and so on—indicated Roosevelt's willingness to mobilize the resources of the nation to battle hard times and to assist those in need through no fault of their own.

This is not to say that all these and other alphabet agencies and programs were ideal or that they worked perfectly. On the contrary, as Bonnie Fox Schwartz has amply demonstrated, "politics" was not entirely lacking in their design or implementation. Many party regulars—Democrats and Republicans alike—found it difficult to separate opportunities to aid the unfortunate from opportunities to aid themselves through the bountiful flow of dollars and jobs from Washington to their localities and state.[3]

Moreover, federal work relief programs, which were aimed at patching up rather than significantly changing the system, were

[3]Bonnie Fox Schwartz, "Social Workers and New Deal Politicians in Conflict," *Pacific Historical Review* 42 (February 1973): 53–73.

not designed to put all the unemployed to work or to pay wages that competed with those of private enterprise. At least partial unemployment was considered desirable in order to keep down the salaries of those who were fortunate enough to be at work. Likewise, while the income of those on work relief was greater than that of welfare recipients, their wages were considerably lower than those paid to employees doing comparable work in the private sector and their "hours" far fewer—a source of encouragement not only to continue working but to take a job in private industry as soon as one became available. In short, these programs were clearly constructed so as not to threaten private profits: the welfare of the lower classes remained secondary to the welfare of the business classes. Still, given the conservative nature of American society and what had, or had not, preceded them, these measures were a significant advance. Moreover, whatever their shortcomings, work relief programs were looked upon favorably by most Americans, chiefly because they made public assistance something earned rather than merely granted, whether it be as a right or as a charity. Not only did millions of citizens who otherwise would have had no income receive at least some assistance thanks to these programs, but also they did so in a way that permitted them to retain their dignity and respectability.

One of the earliest and most important of the new federal relief measures was the Federal Emergency Relief Act, signed into law in May 1933. A tradition-shattering statute that opened up an era of federal aid that had momentous consequences for social welfare, the measure made available at the outset $500 million of federal funds to be distributed as grants-in-aid to the states to be used for emergency unemployment relief, transferring responsibility for the relief of a large number of citizens from the county (and, in part, state) to the federal government.

The Federal Emergency Relief Act was closely patterned after New York State's Wicks Act and, like its model, was conceived of as a temporary emergency measure. It set up the nation's first national relief agency (the Freedmen's Bureau excepted), the Federal Emergency Relief Administration (F.E.R.A.), and the social-minded Harry Hopkins, executive director of New York's T.E.R.A., was appointed its head.

While the authority for determining the extent of the grants-in-aid to the states was vested in the head of F.E.R.A., the responsibility for administering funds remained with the states and localities. Although from the outset the main emphasis was on emergency work programs, federal aid covered all forms of unemployment relief, including home relief, to be paid in cash, and a surplus commodities program to help distressed rural families.

Furthermore, provisions of the statute stipulated that each local relief administrator was to employ at least one experienced social worker on his or her staff, with at least one qualified supervisor for every twenty employees. This not only helped further bridge the gap between social work and public welfare (a process started earlier by Hopkins in New York under the T.E.R.A.) but also had a profound constructive effect on both—it brought social workers and their methods into every county and township in America and, by assuring the public that welfare would be administered by skillful, professional social workers (rather than politicians or appointive officers), it helped to dissipate further the fears of public assistance.

Also important was a directive by Harry Hopkins that all federal grants were to be handled by public agencies. Thus, state bodies were prohibited from turning over federal funds to private agencies, an important matter in light of the widespread use of the subsidy system and the many abuses that resulted from it.

The federal statute did the job assigned to it and did it well. It was one of the largest public relief programs in the world, eventually touching some twenty million lives and expending some $4 billion. Its policies were uniform throughout the nation, it functioned with speed and dispatch, and its program was carried out with little waste or corruption.

Clearly the best of the New Deal welfare measures, however, was the Civil Works Administration (C.W.A.), created by an executive order of the President in November 1933. This crash program was designed to put lots of people to work quickly, not to provide them with "relief." Thus, whereas to qualify for aid under the F.E.R.A. (and the other welfare programs) potential recipients had to appear at a relief station, certify that they were needy, and then undergo a "means test," no such stigmatizing strings were attached to the C.W.A. Furthermore, it offered "regular" hours of work and paid "going" wages, which averaged two and a half times F.E.R.A. benefits. As a result, no New Deal creation was more well received than the C.W.A.—or created more dismay when it was terminated in March 1934, throwing some four million people out of work or forcing them on to the rolls of the much less desirable F.E.R.A., which itself was phased out a year and a half later, again placing the unemployed and the unemployable at the mercy of the states and localities, neither of which had the financial resources to care adequately for them.

Actually, the C.W.A. debacle, as it was viewed by some, brought to a head some social work discontent with Roosevelt and the New Deal. Whereas most social workers had few reservations about capitalism, even in the midst of the depression, and hence supported the administration and its reform efforts, a radical minority did not. Seeking a fundamental reorganization of society—a planned socialist economy—members of this group, led by Mary van Kleeck of the Russell Sage Foundation and Harry Lurie of the Council of Jewish Federations and Welfare Funds, were unhappy with both the aims and the accomplishments of the New Deal—and their colleagues who supported it. Known as "Rank-and-Filers" (to distinguish themselves from the majority, which was centered in the American Association of Social Workers), they were upset at the administration not only for abruptly terminating the C.W.A. but also for its racism, its political expediency, its emphasis on work relief, and a number of other things. They would be very unhappy with the Social Security act because of its emphasis on contributory social insurance rather than on general relief and because it lacked provision for medical care; the decision to end the F.E.R.A. (in December 1935, several months after passage of the S.S.A.) would further infuriate them. In short, to them, Roosevelt's do-something program was not much better than Hoover's do-nothing approach; it merely stabilized poverty and strengthened the structure of a faulty economic order. An absorbing account of these dissidents, whose chief accomplishment was the forging of some ties between professional social work and organized labor, can be found in Jacob Fisher's *The Response of Social Work to the Depression* or in the pages of their journal, *Social Work Today*.

Whatever the merits or demerits of the New Deal or of the left-wingers' evaluation of it, Roosevelt was intent on getting the federal government out of "this business of relief." Surely, he was anxious to save money, but he also never really liked direct federal assistance or envisioned it as a permanent feature of the American welfare system; indeed, he was anxious to prevent it from becoming what he called a "habit with this country." (Roosevelt's decision to discontinue the F.E.R.A. and replace it with the W.P.A., a work relief program, reflected that desire.) He also knew, however, that relief alone, especially on a temporary basis, was not enough to assuage the economic insecurity that grew out of the depression. Something more was needed, something of a lasting nature that would not only include a rescue operation to relieve distress during emergencies, but would comprise a long-range plan for preventing dependency, especially for the nation's aged, many of whom were hard hit by the depression.[4] Aside from humanitarian considerations, a system of security that would help prevent destitution was essential for social and economic stability: "Democracy has disappeared in several other great nations," the President declared on one occasion, "because the people of those nations had grown tired of unemployment and insecurity. . . . In desperation they chose to sacrifice liberty in the hope of getting something to eat. We, in America, know that our democatic institutions can be preserved and made to work," only, however, by proving that "the practical operation of democratic government is equal to the task of protecting the security of the people"—a far cry from Hoover's fears of government "mastery."

---

[4]From 1920 to 1934, the American population increased by 20 percent, while the number of industrial jobs declined by about 25 percent. In addition, the death rate declined considerably. This meant that more and more people, with fewer jobs, were living longer lives. This was reflected in the estimate that three out of every four people in America over the age of sixty-five were dependent, in whole or in part, upon others for their means of support. It is not surprising, then, that there was a great deal of pressure on the administration for some sort of old-age assistance, especially by advocates of the so-called Townsend Plan, a scheme concocted by Dr. Francis Townsend of California. Townsend, who claimed to have more than a million followers, advocated monthly payments of $200 to all persons over sixty years of age on the sole proviso that they retire from work and spend the money.

With these things in mind, on June 8, 1934, President Roosevelt sent to Congress a special message calling for "some safeguards against misfortunes which cannot be wholly eliminated in this man-made world of ours." He urged creation of a system that would "provide at once security against several of the great disturbing factors of life," and advised the Congress that when it reconvened in January 1935, he would place before it such a program.

Three weeks later, by executive order, Roosevelt created a Committee on Economic Security and charged it with the responsibility of developing a workable social security program, one that he could submit to Congress for action. The committee, which consisted of four cabinet members and Harry Hopkins, and which was headed by Secretary of Labor Frances Perkins, hired a University of Wisconsin economist and expert in the field, Edwin E. Witte, to be its executive director. An excellent choice for the position, Witte was not only knowledgeable, but patient, statesmanlike, and a tireless worker. He received able help from one of his former students, Wilbur J. Cohen, who came with him to Washington as his research assistant. They, in turn, relied upon the services of numerous others (including another former Witte student who would become the first Social Security Board chairman—Assistant Secretary of Labor Arthur J. Altmeyer), anyone who, in Witte's words, "in one way or another . . . had ever written anything touching on social security problems or who claimed to have any special knowledge of any phase of the subject."

By January 17, 1935, the committee and its staff had finished their work. After much study, the hearing of a great deal of testimony, and wrestling with many technical and policy questions, they supplied a set of recommendations for a social security program which Roosevelt then transmitted to Congress. The program was embodied in a federal bill sponsored in the U.S. Senate by Robert F. Wagner of New York, and in the House by David Lewis of Maryland, two legislators who had known firsthand the problems of social insecurity. The bill, which was passed in Congress by a vote of 371 to 33 in the House and 77 to 6 in the Senate, became law on August 14, 1935.

As finally adopted, the Social Security Act was an omnibus

measure, which through two lines of defense—contributory social insurance and public assistance—aimed at preventing destitution. It provided for old-age insurance (or pensions) and public assistance for the needy aged, unemployment insurance (or compensation), public assistance to dependent mothers with children, to crippled children, and to the blind, and federal monies for state and local public health work.

First, and most important, the act created a national system of Old-Age Insurance (O.A.I.) in which most employers were compelled to participate. At age sixty-five, workers would receive retirement annuities financed by taxes on their wages and on their employers' payroll; the benefits would vary in proportion to how much they had earned and contributed. In addition, the measure created a program of Old-Age Assistance (O.A.A.) in which the U.S. government would share with the states the cost of the care of persons over sixty-five who were not able to take part in the Old-Age Insurance system or who, after receiving O.A.I., still "needed" such assistance.

It has been argued by William Graebner and others that these old-age provisions of the Social Security Act were included less out of humane considerations than out of concern about the marketplace: corporate leaders and businessmen wanted to encourage (force?) older workers to leave the labor force in order to provide jobs to younger, more productive employees. No doubt there is an element of truth to that view. But there are other elements as well, which cannot be ignored, including the aging of the population and the growing organization among older citizens who wanted such pensions and indeed had been working for them for a long time. As Edwin Witte later put it, without pressure from the elderly "I doubt whether anything . . . would have gone through at all." In addition, these measures were politically advantageous to the administration. In the end, then, Old-Age Insurance and Old-Age Assistance served the interests of many —and were very popular.

The act also set up a federal-state system of Unemployment Insurance designed to encourage the states to carry the administrative burden. The law required employers to contribute to the federal treasury a certain percentage of their payroll for insurance purposes, but it also stipulated that 90 percent of that levy would be returned to those states that set up their own unemployment insurance plans in accordance with standards approved by a federal Social Security Board created to administer the program. (Within two years, every state had set up an unemployment insurance system that met the requirements fixed by the board.)

In addition, the act provided federal aid to the states, on a matching basis, to help dependent women with children ("to assist, broaden, and supervise existing mothers' aid programs"), crippled youngsters, and the blind. While these "categorical relief" programs would come under severe attack later on, especially in the 1960s and 1970s, when the Aid to Dependent Children (A.D.C.) rolls increased dramatically and contained many unmarried black women (as opposed to "worthy" white widows), at the time they were included with very little discussion and no controversy. As we have seen, the act also provided federal funds for state and local public health work.

With the exception of unemployment insurance, which by 1934 had been enacted only in the state of Wisconsin, the provisions of the Social Security Act were not novel. They were influenced by or based upon previous or existing federal and state statutes, such as the Sheppard-Towner and Federal Emergency Relief Acts, and numerous state widows' aid and old-age pension laws.[5] The new statute merely strengthened, expanded, and in some cases revived these practices. Furthermore, based primarily on the insurance principle rather than on the public assistance model, it provided "relief" only to the needy blind, aged, and young—the unemployable, or "deserving poor."

Nevertheless, the Social Security Act became the target of a good deal of criticism—from all sides. There were those, of course, who liked it, such as Secretary of Labor Frances Perkins, chair of the Committee on Economic Security and the first woman to hold a cabinet position, who no doubt spoke for the majority when she said that it constituted "a very significant step in grounding a well-rounded, unified, long-range plan for social se-

---

[5]By 1934, twenty-seven states had old-age pension systems as well as laws providing cash assistance to the blind, and forty-five had widows' pension laws.

curity." For others, however, the measure went too far to the left, was too radical—a violation of the traditional American concepts of self-help and individual responsibility—and therefore was a threat to individual liberty and the American way of life.

Then there were those who attacked the act for not going far enough, not just "Rank-and-Filers" but more moderate people, too, including Isaac Rubinow, Abraham Epstein, another long-time crusader for social insurance, Solomon Lowenstein, executive director of the New York Federation of Jewish Philanthropies, and Frank J. Bruno, a noted social work educator. Bruno considered it "a series of miscellaneous provisions in the field of public welfare which altogether do not furnish a logical plan for social security." It can "only be called a measure to furnish such means as do not arouse opposition," he stated.

Actually, the critics were right. At best, the Social Security Act was a compromise framed within the political and fiscal realities of the day. At worst, it was a conservative measure that fell far short of its title. In large part financed through individual contributions, it not only tied benefits to stable long-term labor force participation, but it was a deflationary and regressive measure that siphoned off billions of dollars in taxes from the purchasing power of those it was supposed to protect.

Insofar as workers were taxed for the various benefits, the act was like a sales tax, making the poor pay for the poor. And, insofar as employers were taxed (for old-age pensions and unemployment compensation), the cost was passed on to the consumer in the form of higher prices—in both cases, lowering the standard of living. The measure did nothing about fundamental social and economic problems, including the question of income redistribution. And it established the only welfare system in the world in which the state did not bear full responsibility for the care of its senior citizens (through general tax revenues raised, for the most part, from the more well-to-do); only in America did workers contribute directly to a program of old-age security.

There were other shortcomings. The system paid benefits on the basis of past earnings and contributions, not on current needs. Moreover, the payments were minimal. Also, unemployment compensation was limited to a relatively short period, with no provision for coverage beyond that period. It neglected the question of permanent disability. More important, the law, as originally enacted, left millions of people unprotected, covering only "regular workers"; it excluded from its provisions numerous classes of people, including many of those who needed protection most, especially farm laborers, seasonal and migrant workers, domestic servants, and workers' dependents.

The most serious criticism of the act, however, was its omission of health insurance, perhaps the most pressing need in the field of social security, the oldest form of compulsory social insurance in the world, and one that was almost universally included in the social insurance programs of other nations.

When the Committee on Economic Security began its work, health insurance was designated as the principal topic for inquiry. Thus, the matter was not only discussed, but committee members concluded that sickness was the major cause of insecurity and that its prevention and treatment was the most humane and least expensive way of dealing with the problem. In their report to the President, they advocated a national health insurance program and even included detailed recommendations for its implementation. But there was a great deal of well-organized opposition to health insurance, especially from the medical profession, and, rather than jeopardize the entire Social Security Bill, its sponsors decided to eliminate it from the measure—with the understanding that a separate national health insurance proposal would be introduced in Congress shortly after passage of the first measure. (In later defending that position, Wilbur Cohen put it this way: it was better "to digest one meal at a time rather than eat breakfast, lunch, and dinner all at once and get indigestion.") The failure to enact such a measure is one of the unwritten chapters in American social welfare history.

Still, the Social Security Act—upheld by the U.S. Supreme Court on May 24, 1937, in two separate decisions, *Steward Machine Co.* v. *Davis* (301 U.S. 548) and *Helvering* v. *Davis* (301 U.S. 619)—was a landmark in American history. Without minimizing its shortcomings, one can say that it brought expanded and improved standards of welfare activities throughout the nation and marked a substantial advance in the nation's treatment of its poor.[6] By giving people cash payments in cases of unemployment, old age, and widowhood—some of the leading causes of poverty—it not only helped prevent destitution and dependency but also did so in a way that preserved individual freedom and human dignity.

As a result of the statute, destitution (as least in theory) was no longer regarded as a question of individual weakness. It was recognized as a fundamental social and economic problem, one that needed to be attacked by society as a whole; hence, the need for a national system of social security. For the first time in the modern period, the American people as a whole accepted the assumption that a large number of people had a right (which could be legally enforced) to public benefits, or at least that failure to provide such benefits was socially and economically shortsighted. In either case, the charitable and the temporary gave way to the just and the permanent, and the dominance of private charity over public welfare came to an end. Public welfare emerged from relatively small and often inadequate programs associated with the poor—a gratuity to be given or withheld at the discretion of an administrator—to a great network of activities providing a variety of services to a broad spectrum of society, services protected by the right to equal treatment and a "fair hearing" when so denied.

The Social Security Act established a new alignment of responsibility in the field of public welfare. It marked the beginning of a policy of federal aid to the states upon a permanent basis for regular, recurring social work, closing the door on three centuries of the poor law and its principle of local responsibility. For the first time in American history, funds to finance all or part of the needs of selected groups in the population became a major permanent item in the federal budget, one that has continued to grow each

---

[6]One of the more important advances in that regard was the establishment of public welfare departments in just about every county in America, virtually made mandatory under the public assistance and child health and welfare titles of the act. While mandating such units and requiring approved plans of operation for receipt of federal monies, which had to be administered on the basis of need ("means-tested" programs), the act, however, left to the states many other specifics regarding eligibility, which allowed for great variation from state to state and encouraged a number of other shortcomings, including administrative discretion and discrimination.

year. With the Social Security Act (and other New Deal programs), the federal government assumed responsibility for the economic security of all its citizens; hence, the American welfare state was born.[7]

The seed planted by the S.S.A. sprouted in other ways as well. Not only did subsequent legislation widen the law's coverage and increase its benefits but also, from the agency created to implement the act, the Social Security Board, a new cabinet-level department grew—the Department of Health, Education, and Welfare, established in 1953.[8] Thus, 100 years after President Pierce rejected Dorothea Dix's plea to make provision for the indigent insane, the federal government established an agency responsible for the health, education, and social welfare of all its citizens, one that spawned its own bureaucracy whose momentum would be difficult to stop.

Such changes did not escape most social workers. To be sure, as already mentioned, some were unhappy with the President and his administration. To them, the New Deal was too timid or conservative, more interested in bolstering the status quo than in bringing about a just society. They were further embittered by the so-called Roosevelt recession of 1937, when approximately four million workers returned to the unemployment rolls because the President, encouraged by the business advance, called

[7]It consisted, largely of (1) social insurance (financed by workers and their employers), which provided pensions to retired workers and unemployment compensation to the jobless, (2) categorical public assistance (financed by the federal government and the states) for the needy aged not entitled to "pensions," the blind, and dependent children, (3) work relief (funded by the federal government) for jobless employables, and (4) general assistance (funded by the states and counties) for the needy who did not fall into the other categories.

[8]In 1939, the Social Security Board was transferred to the newly created Federal Security Agency; seven years later, that agency was strengthened and partially reorganized, and in 1953 it was succeeded by the Department of Health, Education, and Welfare. Actually, the idea to create a federal cabinet-level Department of Public Welfare predated enactment of the Social Security Act; a bill to that effect was introduced in Congress as early as 1921. With regard to improvement in the S.S.A., payments were increased and unemployment compensation benefits extended. In addition, the act was amended to include dependents or survivors as beneficiaries (S.I.), to cover most of the self-employed (including some farmers), to provide benefits to the crippled and to disabled wage-earners (D.I.), to include needy children of unemployed (along with dead, disabled, or absent from home) fathers (A.F.D.C.-UP), and to provide hospitalization and limited medical services to the aged (Medicare).

for additional reductions in federal expenditures, especially on relief programs. The critics, however, remained in the minority. Most social workers were quite pleased with the administration's actions, which they felt had had a constructive impact not only on society as a whole but on their own particular activities.

The Great Depression and the New Deal did have a profound effect on social workers and their profession. First of all, many new jobs were created, especially for women, in the public social services. However widespread unemployment was for others during the crisis, qualified social workers were in constant demand; their number—approximately 40,000 in 1930—just about doubled during the decade. This, in turn, made unprecedented demands on training schools, especially on their curricula and resources for field experience, expediting the changes in social work education that people like Julia Lathrop, the Abbott sisters, and others interested in social policy and public welfare had been urging for some time.[9]

The depression also prompted a resurgence of interest among many social workers in social reform and even old-fashioned relief. What good was psychiatric treatment when millions of citizens were unemployed and whole families were starving? As Paul Kellogg put it: "You cannot deal effectively with an inferiority complex on an empty stomach." The immediate task was to meet material needs—food, clothing, and shelter. The searing experience was proof, at least for the time being, that economic forces were at the root of the problems with which social work dealt. As Grace Coyle stated in her presidential address before the National Conference at the end of the depression decade: "There is no reasonable doubt that poverty itself is responsible for increased illness [physical and mental], that unemployment breeds unemployability, that crowded housing undermines family life, that undernourished children will grow into incompetent" adults. The message was clear: Social workers could best make their contributions by allying themselves with those groups in society working for political, social, and economic change. This, in

[9]On the other hand, the mushrooming demand for social workers in public agencies tended to drain many social work schools and private agencies of their (few) social reform-oriented personnel, leaving behind psychiatrically oriented faculty and staffs, which would have an important effect on the postdepression years.

turn, of course, tended to politicize social workers once again, a sharp contrast to their nonpartisanship of the prior decade.

For others, however, the experiences of the decade had no such effect. By bringing the federal government into the field of social welfare and by getting public agencies to take over the job of maintaining incomes and providing financial aid to the needy, the New Deal seemed to free some social workers and private agencies from feeling an obligation to concern themselves with such matters, giving them the opportunity to return to their work with problems of emotional adjustment and individual development—problems, it was argued, that were compounded by the depression. So, "direct services" and private social work—concern for the individual and the superego, child and family counseling, and the like—did not give way entirely to the economic deluge and concern for the trade cycle in the 1930s.[10]

Perhaps more important, social work assumed a new prestige in American life as a result of the depression and the New Deal. Social workers, such as Harry Hopkins, Frances Perkins, "Molly" Dewson (of the Women's Division of the Democratic National Committee), Aubrey Williams (director of N.Y.A.), and numerous others were listened to, in Washington and elsewhere, as never before. They were no longer on the outside crying in the wilderness; now they were on the inside, in high positions, shaping policy and making all sorts of other basic decisions.

There was good reason for this. The New Deal drew heavily upon the knowledge, assistance, and heritage of social workers. Without minimizing their significance, many New Deal measures were, in Robert Bremner's words, "largely implementations, amplifications, and—in some instances—but partial fulfillments of the program of preventive social work formulated before World War I." No less an authority than Senator Robert F.

---

[10]In 1935 Grace Marcus protested the low esteem into which casework had fallen among social workers, who, in her opinion, had become obsessed with economic matters. She referred caustically to those who had "retreated entirely from any acknowledgment of personal factors in maladjustment . . . into economic dogmas that caricature Marxian theory." She must have had some listeners because whereas earlier in the decade members of the National Conference had confined their discussions to such things as unemployment, health insurance, and social legislation, by 1936 and 1937 such topics as social work education and methodology and agency administration again were on the agenda.

Wagner, perhaps the New Deal's leading architect, stated that "one could not overestimate the central importance played by social workers" in laying the legislative groundwork for, and then administering, the statutes designed to meet the crisis of the 1930s.

Finally, by the end of the decade, social work was not only an acknowledged obligation of the federal government and every city, village, and hamlet in the nation, but its scope had greatly expanded. It no longer meant providing financial relief to the destitute, or even casework to the emotionally disturbed, but both of these and much more. Social workers were now involved in social insurance schemes, park and recreational programs, agricultural resettlement projects, slum clearance and relocation plans, and numerous other activities; all efforts to make America a better and more secure place in which to live. Social work was no longer viewed as an emergency profession, but as an accepted part of the machinery of the state, an important everyday function in a modern urban industrial society.

Still, the developments of the 1930s left social workers with many problems. They had to face the question of how to forge links between the fields of private and public welfare—a difficult task, for private social work remained local and was concerned mainly with the problems of individuals and families, relying upon the use of casework, while public welfare was largely a state and federal matter in which the problem of maintaining the economic and social security of the American people demanded the use of such skills as group work, community organization, and social reform. Also, social workers had to face the related issue of how much of their attention should be devoted to the welfare of society and how much to the welfare of the individual—in other words, whether or not to continue to take an active part in politics and, if so, in which field and by what means.

Bibliography

ABBOTT, EDITH. *Public Assistance*. Chicago: University of Chicago Press, 1940.

———. "Social Insurance and Social Security," *Social Service Review* 8 (September 1934): 537–40.

ALTMEYER, ARTHUR J. *The Formative Years of Social Security.* Madison, Wis.: University of Wisconsin Press, 1966.

———. "The Future of Social Security in America," *Social Service Review* 27 (September 1953): 251–68.

———. "The Wisconsin Idea and Social Security," *Wisconsin Magazine of History* 42 (Autumn 1958): 19–25.

ARMSTRONG, BARBARA N. *Insuring the Essentials.* New York: Macmillan, 1932.

BELLUSH, BERNARD. *Franklin D. Roosevelt as Governor of New York.* New York: Columbia University Press, 1955.

BIRD, CAROLINE. *The Invisible Scar.* New York: McKay, 1966.

BRANDT, LILIAN et al. *The Impressionistic View of the Winter of 1930–31 in New York City.* New York: Welfare Council, 1932.

BREMER, WILLIAM W. "Along the Way: The New Deal's Work Relief Programs for the Unemployed," *Journal of American History* 62 (December 1975): 636–52.

BROWN, JOSEPHINE C. *Public Relief, 1929–1939.* New York: Holt, 1940.

BURNER, DAVID. *Herbert Hoover: A Public Life.* New York: Knopf, 1979.

BURNS, EVELINE M. *The American Social Security System.* Boston: Houghton Mifflin, 1949.

———. *Social Security and Public Policy.* New York: McGraw-Hill, 1956.

CHARLES, SEARLE F. *Minister of Relief, Harry Hopkins and the Depression.* Syracuse, N.Y.: Syracuse University Press, 1963.

CLARKE, HELEN. *Social Legislation.* New York: Appleton-Century, 1940.

CLEMENT, PRISCILLA F. "The Works Progress Administration in Pennsylvania, 1935–1940," *Pennysylvania Magazine of History and Biography* 95 (April 1971): 244–60.

COHEN, WILBUR J. "The First Twenty-Five Years of the Social Security Act, 1935–1960," *Social Work Year Book* (New York: National Association of Social Workers, 1960): 49–61.

CORSON, JOHN T. "Social Security and the Welfare State," *Social Service Review* 24 (March 1954): 8–12.

EPSTEIN, ABRAHAM. *Insecurity: A Challenge to America.* New York: Smith and Haas, 1933.

FEDER, LEAH. *Unemployment Relief in Periods of Depression*. New York: Russell Sage Foundation, 1936.

FISHEL, LESLIE H. "The Negro in the New Deal Era," *Wisconsin Magazine of History* 48 (Winter 1964–65): 111–26.

FISHER, JACOB. *The Response of Social Work to the Depression*. Boston: Hall, 1980.

FOX, BONNIE. "Umployment Relief in Philadelphia, 1930–32: A Study of the Depression's Impact on Voluntarism," *Pennsylvania Magazine of History and Biography* 93 (January 1963): 86–108.

GALBRAITH, JOHN KENNETH. *The Great Crash*. Boston: Houghton Mifflin, 1954.

GRAEBNER, WILLIAM. *A History of Retirement: The Meaning and Function of an American Institution*. New Haven, Conn.: Yale University Press, 1980.

HALL, HELEN. *Unfinished Business: in Neighborhood and Nation*. New York: Macmillan, 1971.

HANLAN, ARCHIE. "From Social Reform to Social Security: The Separation of ADC and Child Welfare," *Child Welfare* 45 (November 1966): 493–500.

HARRIS, JOSEPH P. "Federal Financial Participation in Social Work as a Permanent Policy," *Social Service Review* 9 (September 1935): 445–57.

HENDRIKSON, KENNETH E. "Relief for Youth: The Civilian Conservation Corps and the National Youth Administration in North Dakota," *North Dakota History* 48 (Fall 1981): 17–27.

HIRSHFELD, DANIEL S. *Last Reform: Campaign for Compulsory Health Insurance from 1932–1943*. Cambridge, Mass.: Harvard University Press, 1970.

HOFSTADTER, RICHARD. *The American Political Tradition*. New York: Knopf, 1958.

HOGAN, JOHN. *American Social Legislation*. New York: Harper, 1956.

HOPKINS, HARRY L. *Spending to Save*. New York: Norton, 1936.

KIMBERLY, CHARLES M. "The Depression in Maryland: The Failure of Voluntarism," *Maryland Historical Magazine* 70 (Summer 1975): 189–202.

KRAMER, RALPH. *Voluntary Agencies in the Welfare State*. Berkeley, Calif.: University of California Press, 1981.

KRIEGER, LEONARD. "The Idea of the Welfare State in Europe and in the United States," *Journal of the History of Ideas* 24 (October-December 1963): 553–68.

KURZMAN, PAUL. *Harry Hopkins and the New Deal*. Fairlawn, N.J.: Burdick, 1974.

LEUCHTENBURG, WILLIAM E. *Franklin D. Roosevelt and the New Deal, 1932–1940*. New York: Harper, 1963.

MERIAM, LEWIS. *Relief and Social Security*. Washington, D.C.: Brookings Institute, 1946.

MERTZ, PAUL E. *New Deal Policy and Southern Rural Poverty*. Baton Rouge, La.: Louisiana State University Press, 1978.

NELSON, DANIEL. *Unemployment Insurance: The American Experience, 1915–1935*. Madison, Wis.: University of Wisconsin Press, 1969.

RAMSDELL, LEROY A. "The New Deal in Social Work," *The Family* 14 (October 1933): 191–92.

ROMASCO, ALBERT. *The Poverty of Abundance: Hoover, the Nation, the Depression*. New York: Oxford University Press, 1965.

ROPER, ARTHUR F. "The Southern Negro and the NRA," *Georgia Historical Quarterly* 64 (Summer 1980): 128–45.

RUBINOW, ISAAC. *The Quest for Security*. New York: Holt, 1934.

SCHLABACH, THERON F. *Edwin E. Witte, Cautious Reformer*. Madison, Wis.: State Historical Society, 1969.

———. "Rationality and Welfare: Public Discussion of Poverty and Social Insurance in the United States, 1875–1934," Report on a research project entitled "Ideas on Economic Security in America, 1874–1935" (1969).

SCHNEIDER, DAVID M., AND ALBERT DEUTSCH. *The History of Public Welfare in New York State, 1876–1940*. Chicago: University of Chicago Press, 1941.

SCHWARTZ, BONNIE FOX. "Social Workers and New Deal Politicians in Conflict," *Pacific Historical Review* 42 (February 1973): 53–73.

SHANNON, DAVID. *The Great Depression*. Englewood Cliffs, N.J.: Prentice-Hall, 1960.

SYDENSTRICKER, EDGAR. "Health Under the Social Security Act," *Social Service Review* 10 (March 1936): 12–22.

WILSON, JOAN HOFF. *Herbert Hoover: Forgotten Progressive*. Boston: Little, Brown, 1975.

WITTE, EDWIN E. *The Development of the Social Security Act*. Madison, Wis.: University of Wisconsin Press, 1962.

Chapter 14

From World War to Great Society

WHILE THE UNITED STATES still had a long way to go to provide adequately for its impoverished and handicapped citizens, it had taken giant strides in that direction in the half-century from 1890 to 1940, summed up in the title of Grace Abbott's book, *From Relief to Social Security,* published in 1941.

In the late nineteenth century, public assistance, still referred to as poor relief, was the responsibility of the locality. For the most part, it was confined to institutional care for the young, the old, and the physically or mentally infirm. Outdoor relief, or cash assistance to the needy in their own homes, if provided at all, was usually given by private agencies, and then only sparingly. The obligation to provide care for the mentally ill, the defective, and the delinquent had been accepted by the states, but they had undertaken almost no preventive work. The juvenile court and probation movements, as well as widespread use of home placement for dependent children, were just beginning. The public health movement was in its infancy, and the mental health movement had not even been thought of as yet. A partnership of federal, state, and local governments in anything resembling a national system of social welfare was unknown.

By 1940, the situation had greatly changed. As a result of certain developments, including passage of the Social Security Act and other legislation, the states and the federal government were linked in their public assistance to the aged, the blind, and crippled and dependent children, in the expansion of public (and soon mental) health programs, and in the administration of unemployment compensation. In addition, the federal government had instituted a national system of old-age and survivors' insurance and such other programs as low-cost housing, public works, and agricultural resettlement—advances that social workers helped bring about.[1]

Still, all was not clear sailing, especially since many social workers were beginning to revert to individual service. While the depression and destitution of the 1930s had returned many members of the profession to social action and reform, by the end of the crisis, and then in the 1940s and 1950s, most social workers again became concerned with casework and technique rather than with the further expansion of public social services and the improvement of living conditions; once again, they lost touch with the larger social problems of which maladjustment of the individual was only a small part.

How can one account for this rapid flight from reform and return to casework? As indicated, some social workers felt that, as a result of the many reforms of the 1930s, "living conditions" were being improved by those in political office. This was especially true with the enactment of the Social Security Act, which, despite its limitations, many people felt provided most citizens with a foundation of income maintenance, thus protecting them from poverty and want. There was no need for social workers to concern themselves with all that; instead, they could return to providing aid to individuals in need of psychological assistance.

Then there was World War II, which brought full employment and rising incomes for most Americans, blacks and members of other oppressed groups included. The wartime gains in jobs and incomes were not achieved easily. There was a great deal of opposition to the employment of blacks in the nation's factories and shops, resulting in numerous race riots throughout 1940 and

---

[1]These changes can readily be seen in a few simple statistics. Annual expenditures for public welfare went from $40 million and less than one-tenth of 1 percent of the national income in 1890, to more than $6 billion and 8 percent of the national income in 1940. Another important trend was the marked centralization of such expenditures. In 1890, 65 percent of the total expenditures for public welfare came from local revenues and the rest came from the states; the federal government made no significant contribution. In 1940, local contributions had declined to 20 percent of the total, state funds had increased to 39 percent, and federal funds had jumped to 41 percent. Also, outdoor relief declined from 85 percent of total expenditures for public welfare in 1890 to 10 percent in 1940.

1941. Still, the administration realized that in time of dire need blacks (and women, too) were a source of untapped and underutilized labor. Moreover, the administration was alarmed by the prospect of a march on the nation's capital by 100,000 blacks, designed primarily to open up opportunities for Negro labor in the burgeoning defense industries, which was planned for July 1941, under the leadership of A. Philip Randolph, president of the Brotherhood of Sleeping Car Porters. Such a demonstration would be a major embarrassment to a government about to enter a war for the defense of democracy and human equality. As a result, on June 25, 1941, President Roosevelt issued his famous Executive Order 8802, which forbade "discrimination in the employment of workers in defense industries or Government because of race, creed, or national origin" and established a Fair Employment Practices Committee (F.E.P.C.) to administer the measure. And although the committee lacked the necessary power effectively to punish offenders of the directive, and there was some defiance of its provisions, blacks and members of other disadvantaged groups did make gains unprecedented in any other period in American history.[2]

Also during the war years, social workers again helped meet the needs of families, often middle and upper class families, troubled by the absence of husbands and fathers who were in the military and of mothers who were in the labor force.[3] This trend continued into the postwar years, as more and more self-supporting individuals and families turned to social workers for help. Social workers quickly exchanged their low salaries in agencies for the far more lucrative rewards of private practice, built largely

[2]Thus, thanks to F.E.P.C.'s activities and the critical labor shortage, blacks' share of wartime jobs in the defense industries increased from 3 to 8 percent, and the number of black employees in the federal government jumped from approximately 40,000 to more than 300,000.

[3]Perhaps it should be mentioned that World War II and military conscription again provided a rough yardstick for measuring the health of the nation or, rather, of its healthiest and most vigorous citizens, those between the ages of eighteen and forty—with the same shocking results as previously. Although the government adopted the most minimal physical and mental requirements for military service, the overall rejection rate was exceedingly high—above 50 percent (and as high as 70 percent in some areas)—largely due to malnutrition and an acute shortage of basic medical care. The military draft demonstrated a critical national health problem.

on referrals from doctors and other professional personnel and shared with various other counselors. Ironically, social workers seemed to receive a better reception from many of these clients than from those of the poorer classes whom they had helped in the past. Perhaps casework was most appealing to clients more or less like social workers themselves. Whatever the reason, this "better" clientele enamored many social workers, made their work more financially rewarding, and helped divert their attention from social issues.

"Benign neglect" of the poor was furthered after World War II by the enhanced power of corporate groups, the military, and a conservative coalition in Congress determined to scuttle New Deal relief agencies. Then there was the Cold War, the brandishing of atomic weapons, and the other anxieties of the postwar era. Sheer survival of the human race became a real concern, before which advances in the field of social welfare seemed insignificant.

Related was the problem of McCarthyism. A nation shaken by fears and suspicions, by vague rumors and charges of disloyalty and Communist conspiracies, by government campaigns to ferret out radicals and to impose tests of loyalty based not upon people's actions but upon their intentions, ideas, associations, and other criteria so vague as to guarantee confusion and error, hardly offered a climate hospitable to social criticism and reform.

Then there was the demise of *Survey* magazine, for nearly a half-century the major organ in the field of social policy and reform. When *Survey* ceased publication in 1952 it left a void that no other journal could fill and, in the words of its official biographer, Clarke Chambers, "the attachment of the profession as a whole to broad social action was irrevocably weakened."

Of importance, too, was the fact that many of the poor—those who had not shared in the war-born prosperity or who suffered during the postwar years, in part because of increased longevity and mobility, which left many older citizens without the help of friends and relatives who used to live nearby—were scattered and, as the social critic Michael Harrington would say, "invisible"; they were isolated in dark pockets of Appalachia and Harlem, and in other rural and urban ghettos where the nonpoor rarely ventured. Moreover, the poor comprised those who were least articulate, and who were unable to make their plight known or their power felt—the young, the old, the unskilled, and members of minority and culturally distinct groups.

Concern with poverty seemed remote and almost antiquarian during the war and postwar years, which leads to the most important factor responsible for the decline of social reform during the period—widespread belief in mass prosperity. Just as in the 1920s, most Americans thought that prosperity existed and that there was little or no poverty. Despite a series of recessions (in 1948–49, 1953–54, and 1957–58), the general image of the nation, once again, was that of an affluent society with the highest standard of living in the world, which gave everyone its fair share. Why engage in reform? For all practical purposes, the task had already been accomplished. Almost everyone had a television set and a car, didn't they?

While the theme of prosperity, and the idea that poverty and insecurity no longer existed, affected virtually every aspect of American life—from President Eisenhower's news conferences to publication of David Potter's *People of Plenty* (1954)—it was given its fullest statement by the liberal economist, John Kenneth Galbraith, whose influential book, *The Affluent Society,* led the best-seller list in the late 1950s. In this work, Galbraith stated that American civilization had essentially solved the age-old problems of scarcity and poverty. He did not say there was absolutely no poverty in America. In fact, he said there was some, and that its survival in so affluent a society was "remarkable" and a "disgrace." Still, he stressed affluence, and defined poverty as a uniquely "minority problem." Poverty in America, the well known and highly regarded economist concluded, was "no longer a massive affliction [but] more nearly an afterthought."

Galbraith's statement, although highly inaccurate, was widely accepted—so much so that Walter Lippmann, the syndicated journalist, scornfully observed: "We talk about ourselves as if we were a completed society, one which has achieved its purposes and has no further business to transact." It was an era of complacency: contain the Communists, balance the budget, cut taxes, and don't rock the boat were the goals.

One of the ways to achieve those goals, or at least some of them, was to get the needy off the welfare rolls, which, despite the claims of Galbraith and others, actually were increasing at this time. Thus, in the late 1950s state after state began instituting punitive administrative policies designed to reduce the number of welfare recipients and to deter new applicants. State residency requirements were strictly enforced so that migrants (especially blacks moving from the South to the North) would not receive assistance, and all sorts of new eligibility investigations were initiated, including "suitable home" and "man-in-the-house" policies.[4]

The best publicized of such efforts—one that was symbolic of all others—occurred in Newburgh, New York, where Joseph Mitchell, the reactionary city manager, promulgated a thirteen-point code of regulations intended to uncover alleged welfare fraud, reduce the assistance rolls, encourage the work ethnic, and cut public expenditures. Since the new rules—including the loss of benefits for all able-bodied adult males who refused municipal work, the denial of relief to anyone who voluntarily left a job, the substitution of vouchers for cash payments, and the termination of relief to unwed mothers who had another illegitimate child— did not comply with federal grant-in-aid regulations and thus jeopardized New York's receipt of federal welfare funds, the state's Social Welfare Board ordered Newburgh officials to refrain from administering the regulations and they never were implemented.

Meanwhile, however, the flight from social reform in the 1940s and 1950s and the attack on public welfare and its recipients did not proceed without uneasy words of warning from some people inside as well as outside the social work profession—scholars, reporters, politicians, and others. Ernest Hollis and Alice Taylor, the authors of *Social Work Education in the United States*

---

[4]Under these policies, widely adopted at the time, the presence of a man automatically made a home "unsuitable" and was considered evidence that financial need did not exist, regardless of who the man was, his economic situation, or his relationship to the family. "Midnight raids" by welfare department personnel to uncover men in the homes of A.D.C. recipients were common until March 1967, when the California Supreme Court in effect ruled that they were illegal invasions of privacy. A year later, man-in-the-house rules were held unconstitutional by the U.S. Supreme Court in *King v. Smith,* 329 U.S. 309 (1968). As mentioned earlier, the following year the U.S. Supreme Court also invalidated residency requirements.

(1951), a widely discussed study prepared for the Council on Social Work Education, maintained that for the last quarter-century "the profession has accepted too little of a unified responsibility for appraising and improving social welfare institutions" and urged readers to take a stand on the major social issues of the day.

Whitney Young, the social worker who later headed the National Urban League, told the National Conference on Social Welfare that "social work was born in an atmosphere of righteous indignation," but that "somewhere along the line 'the urge to become professional' had overcome the initial crusading impulse." He called upon the profession to reclaim the "lost heritage" of its founders. So did Marion Craine, who, speaking at a University of Chicago symposium on "Pioneers and Professionals" in social welfare, chastised her collegues for being "too timid" to engage in reform, blaming it on the fear of being labeled "unprofessional."

Benjamin Youngdahl, when retiring as president of the American Association of Social Workers in 1953, concluded his farewell address with the rhetorical question: "Is our function as social workers limited to the treatment of pathologies, or do we have a positive or preventive function to perform as well?" There was little doubt where he stood on the issue.

The 1956 Alumni Day address at the Columbia University Graduate School of Social Work, given by Agnes E. Meyer, was another forthright and militant plea for a return to social action. She exhorted social workers as, in her words, "the conscience of American society," to assume the task of "community reorganization." Observing that the older professions—law, medicine, and teaching—"have become encrusted in bureaucracy, respectability, and economic rewards," she argued that social work "is still free—to some extent—from this lock-step towards success which most Americans worship." Now was the time to act, before it was too late!

In addition, throughout the 1950s, Saul Alinsky, the well known community organizer who stressed conflict and giving the poor the power to speak for themselves, talked about the existence of poverty and the need to abolish it. Also, Senators Paul Douglas (Dem.-Ill.) and John Sparkman (Dem.-Ala.) chaired congressional committees during the decade that conducted studies and hearings on the health of the economy. Many low-income families "had been left behind in the progress of America," they concluded, and only a "vigorous attack" on poverty would overcome their distress. In 1956, Adlai E. Stevenson, the Democratic presidential candidate, echoed that theme.

These critics were not totally ignored; some positive consideration was being given to the subject. As Edward Berkowitz, Kim McQuaid, and others have pointed out, neither welfare expansion nor welfare reform disappeared in the 1950s, at least not completely. To begin with, thanks in part to the pressure of labor unions, which had grown quite strong during the war, many private businesses either began to provide or increased their provision of employee benefits—life insurance, health insurance, retirement programs, and the like. Such private measures constituted an important secondary layer of assistance above the benefits offered by Social Security and other public programs.

Moreover, many public programs, including Social Security, were broadened during the "affluent decade." Thus, in 1950, Congress amended the S.S.A. to provide "caretaker" grants to mothers of dependent children and added a new category of public assistance—Aid to the Permanently and Totally Disabled. In 1956, Disability Insurance was added to the system, and shortly thereafter several groups omitted from the original legislation were brought into the program, including farm workers and the self-employed. Meanwhile, "social services" were added to the A.D.C. program, child welfare services were extended from rural to urban areas, and a partial sliding scale for assistance grants to the states was adopted in an effort to equalize welfare payments in poor and wealthy states, at least in part.

Finally, some new welfare programs were enacted during these years, including the Servicemen's Readjustment Act, or the so-called G.I. Bill of Rights (1944), the National Mental Health Act (1946), the National School Lunch Program (1946), the Housing Act (1949), the School Milk Program (1954), and the Vocational Rehabilitation Act (1954). The postwar era, then, was not a complete wasteland for welfare reform.

Despite these advances, many Americans continued to suffer throughout this period, especially those who were marginally employed or who were not in the labor force at all—the old, the sick, the disabled, women with children whose husbands had deserted them or who had no husbands, and so on. For the most part, they were ignored; most Americans knew little and cared less about them and the other needy. The prevailing belief was that prosperity and economic growth had conquered or soon would conquer the remaining poverty problem, that it would "wither away," to use James Patterson's words, or that it was "more nearly an afterthought," to use Galbraith's.

Before long, however, the situation would change. Indeed, by the early 1960s, when some of the optimism of the postwar years had begun to fade, a change already was evident. Before long, few subjects would be as fashionable—at least to talk about. President Johnson's declaration of war on on poverty in 1964 only put the highest official sanction on what had already become a vogue.

This rather sudden turnabout resulted from a variety of factors. The running debate in the 1950s on American foreign policy, especially the question of foreign aid, may have had some effect; no doubt it awakened many Americans to the discrepancies between the affluent and the poorer nations of the world and this, in turn, may have awakened some citizens to the existence of similar discrepancies at home. Also, poverty was an embarrassment that gave the Soviet Union ammunition to use against the United States in the Cold War.

More important was the coming into office of President John F. Kennedy, who not only made poverty, unemployment, and hunger major themes in the bid for his party's nomination but also was elected to the presidency after a campaign that was highly critical of the 1950s, one that conveyed a sense of vitality and urgency in the approach to social problems neglected by his predecessor. Setting the tone in his inaugural address of 1961, Kennedy asked the nation to "bear the burden of a long twilight struggle against the common enemies of man: tyranny, poverty, disease, and war. . . . " "The hand of hope," he said, "must be extended to the poor and the depressed." Such statements aroused many citizens, especially the nation's young people, and helped to revive faith in purposeful social action.

Even more important was the staggering relief explosion that accompanied the mass migration to the nation's cities of people who belonged to groups for whom poverty was endemic but who, for the most part, had been left out of the mainstream of American life: displaced and unemployed southern blacks and mountain whites, Mexican Americans and American Indians leaving their hovels and reservations in the West and Southwest, and Puerto Ricans moving to the mainland in search of a better life. While this massive urban movement by members of these "fringe" groups resulted from a variety of factors, the major cause was the agricultural revolution that occurred between the 1940s and 1960s, especially modernization and mechanization, which lessened the need for farm labor. Thus, a Presidential Commission on Rural Poverty found that between 1950 and 1965 new machines and new agricultural methods increased farm output in the United States by 45 percent, and at the same time reduced farm employment by the same percentage. Between 1940 and 1970, well over twenty million people (a great many of whom were black) were forced off the land, especially in the South, where these forces had their greatest impact.

This tremendous upheaval caused a good deal of suffering, especially since, as these displaced citizens migrated to the nation's cities, mainly in the North and West, the need for unskilled labor was declining. They were unable to secure adequate employment (or employment at all) and were forced to live in wretched, crowded ghettos, swelling the relief rolls. The number of persons receiving public assistance more than doubled from 1960 to 1970, from approximately six to twelve million, as did the amount of money distributed to them, which increased from about $3.1 billion to well over $6 billion.[5]

Was this relief explosion mainly the result of the migration of large numbers of displaced farm workers and others to the nation's cities where, in numerous instances, relief was available to them for the first time, as many maintain? Or did it result from other (although related) factors? Frances Piven and Richard Cloward, in their widely read book *Regulating the Poor,* take

[5]Two other things should be noted in this connection: (1) The enormous increase in the number of recipients during the 1960s was in marked contrast to the previous decade, when about 800,000 citizens were added to the welfare rolls; and (2) of the six million new recipients between 1960 and 1970, about five million were in various Aid to Families with Dependent Children (A.F.D.C.) programs.

issue with the premise that relief rolls automatically grow when the pool of people eligible for assistance increases, arguing that the outpouring of relief payments at that time was not solely, or even principally, the result of the urban migration and an increase in poverty. The expansion of the relief rolls in the 1960s, they contend, "was a political response to political disorder," a response to both the urban violence of the decade and the increased political power of the mass of black poor, who now had to be contended with in the nation's voting booths as well as on its city streets. Rather than deal with the real poverty-producing factors—racial discrimination and structural unemployment—the administration chose to give these people money in an effort to pacify them.[6] Whether Piven and Cloward or their critics are correct, the staggering increase in the number of people applying for and receiving public assistance and the enormous growth of welfare expenditures during these years helped make the problem a major topic of public concern rather than merely a marginal affair.

The civil rights movement also made the nation aware of its poor and played a prominent role in the changes that occurred during the decade. Again, Americans who had regarded poverty as somehow an exception in an otherwise affluent nation were confronted with a militant reform movement that arose precisely because this was not the case. It was demonstrated that social

[6]Those who differ with Piven and Cloward argue that, in addition to the movement of many needy Americans from poor rural areas to the nation's cities, other factors responsible for the relief explosion of the 1960s were: a rapidly increasing divorce rate; a growing feeling that low-paying jobs are demeaning and exploitive, which encouraged many marginally employed citizens to stop working and "go on welfare"; increasing "advocacy" by social workers—that is, efforts to encourage and mobilize the poor to exercise their right to public assistance; and the invalidation by the courts of restrictive administrative and investigative features of the welfare system, including "man-in-the-house" rules and "midnight raids," arbitrary terminations without hearings, residency laws, and the like. But it is precisely this relaxation of regulations for the receipt of public assistance that Piven and Cloward argue was the political response to the urban disorder and new political realities of the decade. For an extended criticism of *Regulating the Poor* and the authors' response to it, see Eugene Durman, "Have the Poor Been Regulated? Toward a Multivariate Understanding of Welfare Growth," *Social Service Review* 47 (September 1973): 339–59, and Frances F. Piven and Richard A. Cloward, "Reaffirming the Regulation of the Poor," *Ibid.* 48 (June 1974): 147–69. Also see Walter I. Trattner, ed., *Social Welfare or Social Control?* (Knoxville, Tenn.: University of Tennessee Press, 1983), pp. 152–57.

and legal discrimination against black Americans—the last to be hired, the first to be fired, the lowest paid, and so on—had induced and prolonged their poverty. It was clear that American Negroes were both class and race, for whatever criteria were used—income, employment, education, skill, health, dependency—they constituted a disproportionate number at the bottom of society.

There was, then, an obvious relationship between civil rights, or the lack of them, and poverty; to be made aware of the injustice of racial discrimination was inevitably to be made aware of want, and this could no longer be ignored when blacks and then other minority groups became demonstrative and began to press their claims for equality and the full rights of citizenship. Those who had overlooked the unskilled, the migrant laborer, the tenant farmer, the victim of regional depression, black and white alike, were forced to come to grips with a blight that they had tried to forget, or pretend did not exist; they were forced to describe American society more accurately—to "tell it as it was."

The 1960 census figures provided scholars and writers with the raw material to do just that, to factually discover or rediscover what the civil rights movement and the rising relief rolls already were beginning to indicate—that the New Deal and World War II had not eradicated poverty and it had not withered away—and they took great advantage of the opportunity. The literature on poverty grew large as it was demonstrated that, beneath the layers of American affluence, there were strata of deprivation, and that the deprived were not merely those who lived in Harlem or other black ghettos, or even those who lived in the depressed areas of the rural South. Rather, the poor were ubiquitous; they could be found in all sections of the country, in all parts of the population, in all age groups.

Gabriel Kolko, the historian, in his *Wealth and Power in America,* showed that income statistics failed to tell all there was to say about the poor. James Morgan and his team of University of Michigan social scientists provided further data exposing the poverty syndrome in *Income and Welfare in the United States.* Dwight Macdonald, the social critic, summed it up well in a *New Yorker* article entitled "Our Invisible Poor."

Above all, Michael Harrington, the journalist and social activist—whose book, *The Other America: Poverty in the United States,* which challenged complacent assumptions about American affluence and focused movingly on poverty, quickly became a classic—successfully evoked the peculiar state of being poor and analyzed the reasons for the persistence of mass poverty amidst abundance. Harrington demonstrated that the poor, black and white alike, were subjected to a chronic suppression of their living standards, something that escaped most citizens. The average American could not view the rundown company towns from the highways he traveled, and there were no shacks in the national parks where he roamed. Nor did he really see the urban slums as he commuted to and from his suburban home and downtown office on new freeways or rapid transit. Therefore, the poor continued as a hidden subculture, one that was beyond the reach of the contemporary welfare state, one that perpetuated itself in an endless cycle.[7]

The poor were unemployed laborers haunting employment agencies; displaced miners, loitering on street corners or in bars; former midwestern meat-packers shoved aside by automation; misfits on New York's Bowery; the aged stored away to die in institutions and roominghouses. All were not necessarily unemployed; some were poorly paid dishwashers whose small earnings had to be supplemented by public aid; some were farmers unable to subsist off their poor land; many were blacks, at work (if lucky enough to be employed) in the worst-paying jobs.

Then there were other longtime residents of the poverty subculture, such as Mexican Americans, or Chicanos, whose plight

---

[7]Many (including Harrington) argued that the American welfare system created and perpetuated the poverty it was intended to prevent and alleviate. According to Richard Elman, author of *The Poorhouse State,* just as the nineteenth-century county almshouse collected the dependent of that era, current public assistance programs collected the poor "into stagnant pools of dependent people who become increasingly separated from the mainstream of economic life." The system eroded the poor's psychic energy and self-image so that they became "steadily more crystallized as a residue from the normal economic and social life of the nation." Until we "vest dependency itself with decency, and provide assistance without the implication that the recipient of such assistance is maladjusted or sick," wrote Kermit Wiltse in reviewing that book, "we will perpetuate the Poorhouse State." The cure for poverty, according to these critics, is income without strings attached, not more imposed poverty.

was as bad and who now were being spurred to action by black activism and other forces encouraging increased racial and ethnic pride. The nation's second largest disadvantaged minority, most of the four million persons of Mexican ancestry were still gathered in various barrios throughout the Southwest and West. Handicapped by lack of job skills, inadequate schooling, language problems, and discrimination, they had been generally ignored, even by those seeking to improve the lot of the other impoverished. Similarly, efforts to help those in need had failed to reach the American Indian, perhaps the nation's most desperate and deprived minority group—the poorest of the poor. Some 450,000 Indians lived in squalor in twenty-five states, not always in obscure rural areas.[8] As Harrington and others demonstrated, poverty was one of the nation's gravest social problems, one that was not disappearing but growing worse, a way of life that had become permanent for some forty to fifty million Americans.

As if to bear out what these writers were saying, America's cities exploded in the mid-sixties. Riots erupted not only in the slums of New York, Los Angeles, Detroit, and Newark, but also in hundreds of other black communities around the nation. And while the various outbreaks differed in their origin and development, all resulted from long-festering wounds—unemployment, poverty, poor housing, crowded living conditions, economic exploitation, widespread desperation, frustration, and hope-

[8]During the 1960s both of these groups, affected by the black revolt and the various nationalist movements of the decade, took on a new militancy; "Uncle Taco," the stereotype of the servile Mexican American, gave way to the "Sons of Zapata," while the Indians bid farewell to "Uncle Tom-Tom" and joined movements for "Red Power." Their increased aggressiveness and sense of unity began to create an awareness in the nation of their organizations, their leaders, and their demands: civil and legal rights, better educational opportunities, dignified treatment, and a voice in their own and the nation's affairs. The best known Mexican-American movement was led by Cesar Chavez and the National Farm Workers Association, whose successful strike and boycott of the grape growers in Delano, California, demonstrated the benefits of organization. Other new and dynamic alliances included the Political Association of Spanish-Speaking Organizations (P.A.S.O.) and the Mexican-American Political Association (M.A.P.A.). Perhaps the largest and best-known Indian groups were the National Congress of American Indians (N.C.A.I.) and the National Indian Youth Council (N.I.Y.C.), although more recently the militant American Indian Movement, under the leadership of Russell Means, had emerged as an important organization, especially for the young urban Indian.

lessness, and a profound disillusionment with urban life; clearly, the city was not the promised land full of economic opportunity and free of institutionalized oppression, as many Americans had been led to believe. Feeling that the power structure mitigated against them and that the channels of social redress were closed, the have-nots in society expressed themselves by bombing, sniping, burning, looting, harassing, and striking against the symbols of the establishment—namely, the police and the businessmen who had long exploited them. Once again, the issue was joined; the blacks of America's urban slums were no longer "invisible." Their violent expressions of bitterness and frustration forced all Americans to confront unpleasant realities they had largely managed to avoid until the "troubled decade."[9]

Following the 1967 riots, President Lyndon B. Johnson created a National Advisory Commission on Civil Disorders, the so-called Kerner Commission, to determine the cause of the disturbances and to recommend ways to prevent their future occurrence. After intensive study, the commission placed most of the blame for the riots on "white racism." Its report stated that the civil rights gains of the previous fifteen years had done very little to improve the quality of life in the black ghetto, where millions of citizens continued to be denied an equal chance in American society. The commission made a series of modest proposals for social change, few of which were implemented; the principal response to the riots was greater expenditures for police and weaponry.

Still, the urban violence and wide variety of other developments throughout the decade—social, political, economic, and demographic—led to a new look at poverty and new attempts to prevent it or at least to alleviate its effects. Those attempts began early in the Kennedy administration, long before the eruptions in the nation's ghettos. Among the more important of the early measures was the extension, in 1961, of A.F.D.C. to needy two-parent families whose heads of household were out of work and had exhausted their unemployment benefits. Not only would such

---

[9]Adding to the turmoil of the period and at the same time arousing concern for the underprivileged was the anti-Vietnam War movement. Among many other things, the antiwar movement was a protest against the nation's draft policies, which clearly militated against the poor and especially against black Americans.

a change help families in need but also it would keep them together by discouraging desertion by unemployed fathers in order to get dependents off general relief and onto the more generous federally aided categorical assistance program. Although the change was not made mandatory and many states, especially poorer rural ones, refused to participate in it, Aid to Families with Dependent Children–Unemployed Parent (A.F.D.C.-UP) was an important step forward.

The Kennedy administration also turned to the areas of juvenile delinquency and mental health. Shortly after taking office in the spring of 1961, Kennedy created the President's Committee on Juvenile Delinquency and Youth Crime, which led to the passage, that same year, of the Juvenile Delinquency and Youth Offenses Control Act, a measure that, among other things, helped fund and operate Mobilization for Youth. Two years later, after receiving a message from the President on the subject, Congress enacted the Mental Retardation Facilities and Mental Health Centers Control Act, which provided federal funds for research, training, and the construction and staffing of community mental health centers throughout the United States.

The most widely heralded of the Kennedy administration's responses to the growing welfare crisis, however, were the 1962 Public Welfare Amendments to the Social Security Act, signed into law by the President on July 25, 1962.[10] These measures, more familiarly known as the Social Service Amendments, greatly increased federal support (75 percent of the cost) to the states to provide casework, job training, job placement, and other direct services to public assistance recipients. The amendments grew out of lengthy study and extensive advice from social workers and other experts who promised the President, the Congress, and the nation that their new approach would rehabilitate and bring financial independence to the needy and, hence, a reduction in the relief rolls and in public welfare expenditures.

Actually, the amendments were the product of several forces, including the fact that "social services" were added to the

---

[10]Earlier, on February 1, 1962, President Kennedy had delivered a message to Congress on "Public Welfare," the first presidential message in American history devoted entirely to the subject.

A.D.C. program in 1956 but, for various reasons, went un-funded. Basically they reflected social workers' renewed con-cern with casework—the belief that the poor needed not just, or even primarily, financial aid but rather psychological assistance and other forms of counseling; they had to "adjust" to being single parents or to life in the city; they needed instruction on how to keep house and manage their meager resources in order to make ends meet; they needed to learn how to make friend-ships and develop self-esteem; above all, of course, they had to be taught how to secure and retain jobs. In reality, then, the new approach was an old one: attributing the needy's problems to personal shortcomings and providing "counseling," or advice, in order to promote participation in the labor force. (Moreover, by once again linking relief granting to the provision of "services" and placing both functions in the hands of the same person, it was a further throwback to charity organization society days.)

Nevertheless, Kennedy clearly put the power of the White House and the federal bureaucracy behind a drive for welfare reform and his successor, Lyndon B. Johnson, followed suit. Under their administrations, dubbed the New Frontier and the Great Society, respectively, the poor obviously were moved from a state of benign neglect to a prominent place on the public agenda. Most of the measures enacted at the time, however, were designed to do the same thing as the Social Service Amend-ments—to reinforce commitment to the work ethic by those who were economically marginal, a clear shift away from the many cash (and public works) programs of the New Deal. Thus, the Area Redevelopment Act of 1961 and the Economic Develop-ment Act of 1965 were designed to focus on regional unemploy-ment by inducing new industries to move into depressed areas of the nation; the 1962 Manpower Development and Training Act was intended to provide training or retraining for workers displaced by economic or technological change; Title VII of the 1964 Civil Rights Act prohibited racial, sexual, or ethnic dis-crimination in employment and established an enforcement mechanism—the Equal Employment Opportunity Commission —to implement the provision; and, above all, there was the so-called War on Poverty, conceived by Kennedy before his death but carried out by his successor.

In his State of the Union Message in January 1964—a time when the President's Council on Economic Advisors concluded that about one-fifth of the American people, including nearly half of the nation's blacks, were poor—Lyndon Johnson, a Roosevelt protegé, called upon Congress to enact a thirteen-point program that would declare "unconditional war on poverty," a "domestic enemy which threatens the strength of our Nation and the welfare of our people." Seven months later, the Economic Opportunity Act (E.O.A.), or the antipoverty bill, was passed, establishing the Office of Economic Opportunity (O.E.O.), an independent federal agency headed by a director (Sargent Shriver, a man of "infectious energy") responsible to the President. The measure also called for the creation of Volunteers in Service to America or V.I.S.T.A., a domestic peace corps; a Job Corps for school dropouts; an Upward Bound program to encourage bright slum children to go to college; a Neighborhood Youth Corps for jobless teenagers; Operation Head Start, a project to give preschool training to children; special programs of grants and loans to low-income rural families and migrant workers; a comprehensive Community Action Program to permit "maximum feasible participation" of the residents of the areas to be served in mobilizing the resources of their communities to combat poverty; and a number of other programs designed to "pursue victory over the most ancient of mankind's enemies."

The Economic Opportunity Act, planned by a task force of experts, including some of the nation's leading academics and social scientists, was a make-do, crash program that left a good deal to be desired. However well intentioned, it was badly conceived and, in the opinion of many, bound to fail, primarily because it was designed not to change society but to change its victims. Like the Public Welfare Amendments of 1962 and most of the other legislation of the period, it emphasized not adequate income and job creation but education, manpower training, and various social services that were supposed to enhance the productive ability of the needy and facilitate their transition from welfare to work. (In that sense, it was perfectly in tune with the widely held, but misguided, notion that economic growth would continue and that it would lead to the elimination of poverty.) Even on its own terms, however, the statute did not live up to expectations. Less a war on poverty than a minor skirmish or, as one scholar called it, "a sitzkrieg—a phony war of stalemate and standstill," it was scantily financed. In fact, Congress appropriated less money each year to combat poverty across the country than was necessary to finance an adequate welfare program in any one of the nation's leading cities. During the first year of the act's operation, when Mayor John Lindsay said that New York City needed $10 billion annually for five years to solve its welfare problems, Congress allocated around $750 million for the entire nation. (The act also did virtually nothing to alleviate destitution in the countryside, where a sizable proportion of the nation's poor still resided at the time.)

Moreover, much of what was appropriated was squandered or caught in bureaucratic red tape, delaying tactics, and political imbroglios. Throughout the United States, power struggles occurred in deciding who was to control the programs—and reap the rewards. For the most part, mayors came out on top. By keeping the funds in City Hall, they were able to create high-paying jobs for faithful political supporters and thus strengthen their hold on office, at the same time preventing meaningful political and social action by the needy, who might otherwise have jeopardized the status quo. No wonder radicals like Saul Alinsky attacked the program as a "huge political pork barrel" and a "macabre masquerade," while conservatives called it a "Madison Avenue deal" and a "poverty grab bag." In the meantime, those who were supposed to be helped by the measure continued their miserable existence in urban and rural slums.[11] Then, late in 1966,

[11]As June Axinn and Herman Levin, to whom I am indebted for some of the ideas in this chapter, have indicated in their book on *Social Welfare,* perhaps the most important feature of the E.O.A. was the development of community legal services. Such services were not specifically mentioned in the original act. Once they began, their importance for testing older rights and securing new ones for the poor (through various class action suits) became so obvious that later amendments to the statute spelled out their inclusion. Ironically, these services then helped to terminate the whole program, for the President and members of Congress were not pleased by having legal actions against various public programs supported by government-funded legal services. Another contribution of the program, however, was its tendency to move at least some social workers, once again, from a therapeutic to a reform approach; as social workers were brought into community action programs, some of them began to reevaluate their views regarding the profession and its function in society, even going so far as to become "advocates" of the poor.

by which time President Johnson had become increasingly disenchanted with the program, as well as obsessed with the Vietnam War, dismemberment of the O.E.O. began, a process continued by the next administration as soon as Richard M. Nixon came into office in 1969.

Meanwhile, however, some unintended and rather unfortunate results occurred. The disastrous affair, especially the cruel contrast between promise and performance, infuriated the poor and punctured their inflated aspirations, which, in turn, contributed (ironically) to the urban rioting of the period, Piven and Cloward notwithstanding. And, as James Patterson has pointed out, the war's failure also "chastened theorists," congressional activists, and others, who began to question the potential of "social engineering." "More than any other program of Johnson's so-called Great Society," Patterson wrote, "the war on poverty accentuated doubts about the capacity of social science to plan, and government to deliver, ambitious programs for social betterment"—and no doubt helped provoke the surge of neo-conservative developments that would follow.

Before that, however, there were some exceptions to the rule, including passage by Congress in 1964 of the Food Stamp Act, a considerable improvement over an existing food distribution program. At the time the nation had a commodity scheme that was designed primarily to promote the interests of farmers rather than those of poor consumers; economic, rather than social welfare, policy determined its operation. Under its provisions, which were embodied in the Agriculture Act of 1949, the Secretary of Agriculture, in order to prevent waste, was directed to distribute commodities acquired through federal price supports to low-income families. The level of program activity, then, as well as the type of items provided, depended entirely on the availability of surplus foods rather than on the nutritional needs or desires of those participating in the program.

The Food Stamp Program was aimed at overcoming these deficiencies, largely by expanding the purchasing power of the needy and by separating operation of the program from the concerns of agricultural producers and the condition of their markets. Certified low-income families could purchase stamps at substantial savings—a family of four with a monthly income of $100, for example, could buy $78 worth of stamps for

$44—which in effect replaced cash in food stores, allowing their users the freedom to purchase what they wished and needed. And while the scheme was by no means perfect—it was optional rather than mandatory, and many communities chose not to participate in it; each state set its own eligibility requirements and hence there was a good deal of variation within the program; the cost of the stamps was too high for some, who could not take advantage of the arrangement—it was an important welfare-oriented program that served the needs of many low-income families, one that would be improved later.

An advance for the nation's aged was also scored at this time with the adoption of the "medicare" amendments to the Social Security Act, approved by President Johnson on July 30, 1965. A victory over the American Medical Association and its allies, who relentlessly lobbied against it, the measure represented the nation's first long stride toward an adequate health scheme, at least for more than twenty million of its older citizens.

In brief, the statute provided hospital and medical insurance (as well as coverage for some posthospital care) for virtually all Americans on reaching age sixty-five. The hospital insurance was compulsory and financed by an increase in social security taxes, while enrollment in the medical plan was voluntary and paid for by a monthly premium of three dollars. While the measure had its shortcomings—it covered only the aged, it was relatively costly, it did not cover all medical and hospital expenses, it was curative rather than preventive, and so on—the fact is that a large number of older people received medical and hospital care that previously they could not have obtained, or that otherwise would have exhausted their savings.

A mixed blessing, too, were the "medicaid" amendments to the Social Security Act, also signed into law by President Johnson on July 30, 1965. Under their provisions, the federal government provided grants to the states to assist them in helping medically indigent citizens receive improved medical and hospital services. While the plan was established primarily for recipients of federally aided public assistance programs, if funds were available coverage could be extended to citizens who were not on welfare but who otherwise could not afford medical treatment. The program was designed to end "charity medical care" by giving the needy the money and, presumably, access to the entire health care system: whereas previously most of the poor were forced to depend on overcrowded and sometimes distant public hospitals and clinics, where they frequently received inadequate care, medicaid recipients could now visit any doctor or hospital willing to treat them.

While an excellent idea in theory, in practice the program proved to be full of shortcomings. To begin with, many doctors and hospitals refused to treat such patients, often citing excessive paperwork, inadequate compensation, and government interference in medicine as their reasons. In the early 1970s, only 17 percent of New York's physicians accepted such patients, and the situation was similar elsewhere. In addition, the care given to those who were treated by private physicians and hospitals frequently tended to be less than ideal; all too often they were run through offices and wards as if through a mill, given unnecessary treatment and drugs, overcharged, and forced to put up with a number of other abuses that the system was devised to eliminate. Again, however, despite these and other shortcomings, the program grew—to the point, in fact, where now many feel it has gotten out of hand—and delivered health care over the years to millions who otherwise would not have been able to afford it.

Meanwhile, the welfare crisis continued. Neither the Public Welfare Amendments of 1962 nor the Economic Opportunity Act of 1964—or the spate of other measures enacted during the Kennedy-Johnson administrations, including a rent supplement program (1965), the Elementary and Secondary Education Act of 1965, the Higher Education Act of the same year, and the 1966 Demonstration (Model) Cities and Metropolitan Development Act—succeeded in getting people off the relief rolls and onto the tax rolls, as had been hoped. Indeed, the number of recipients and total expenditures continued to climb: despite the fact that between 1963 and 1966 federal grants to the states for social services more than doubled, approximately one million new public assistance cases were added to the welfare rolls, especially in A.F.D.C. programs—and another 3.3. million would be added before the end of the decade. While the poor had become a major topic of public concern, instead of a marginal affair, poverty certainly had not disappeared. As one student of the subject put it, the New Frontier and the Great Society had promised the moon and had gotten it; they had not solved the welfare problem, however. As a result, social workers and their services became increasingly subject to scrutiny, and in 1967 Congress responded with further amendments to the Social Security Act, which tended to denigrate or downplay casework and other "soft" social services in favor of such "hard" or more tangible programs as day care, housing, vocational rehabilitation, and drug treatment centers.

More important, using January 1967 as a base, Congress imposed a freeze on the number of children under age twenty-one who would be allowed to receive A.F.D.C. payments because of the absence of a parent from the home. Since the measure was aimed at pressuring the states to crack down on welfare payments due to desertion and illegitimacy, it exempted cases resulting from either the death of a father or a parent's unemployment.[12] Next, it established a Work Incentive Program, or W.I.P., a carefully chosen acronym that would later be changed to W.I.N. The Work Incentive Program—which was based on the old and once again popular notion that welfare spawned laziness and immorality, that it was the *cause* of the problem rather than a solution to it—disqualified adults and older out-of-school children from A.F.D.C. payments if they refused to accept employment or participate in training programs—females and males alike, mothers as well as fathers, even in single-parent, female-headed families. This was a far cry from the approach to public assistance and child welfare that had been taken throughout the twentieth century. Whereas mothers' pensions and the Social Security Act had stressed the needy child's right to public support and to a mother's care, this measure affirmed the right to remove that child from the welfare rolls and to force his or her mother to work outside the home for such support. Here again, however, the states had some discretion in requiring recipient participation in the program, and since some excluded mothers with young children, the full effects of the program were delayed. Still, the punitive nature of the measure (which affected primarily weak and abandoned women and helpless children and was referred to by one observer

[12]It should be noted that the measure was hotly resisted by some, especially officials in hard-pressed states. As a result, President Johnson, and then Nixon after him, delayed implementation of the freeze, which Congress repealed in 1969. Its spirit lived on, however, as we shall see in the next chapter.

as the "first [piece of] purposively punitive welfare legislation" in American history), which was a dismal failure, was clear and signaled what was to come.[13]

As the welfare explosion continued and the stereotype of the "reliefer" hardened into the image of the black woman with hordes of illegitimate children—adding racism to the traditional prejudice against the poor, a potent combination—the reaction progressed. A growing number of citizens and leading politicians denounced the "welfare mess," including the newly elected governor of California, Ronald Reagan, who in his first inaugural address in 1967 asserted. "We are not going to perpetuate poverty by substituting a permanent dole for a paycheck." Meanwhile, the riots in the black ghettos, the civil rights demonstrations, the anti-war protests, the student upheavals, and other developments—women's liberation, new lifestyles, the drug culture, inflation and high taxes, etc.—were also causing a great deal of resentment, especially among members of the working class, or the so-called Silent Majority, who in 1968 turned to Richard Nixon to end the social turmoil and, in the words of the new President, make sure that "social workers would be looking for honest work."

Bibliography

ABBOTT, GRACE. *From Relief to Social Security.* Chicago: University of Chicago Press, 1941.

ALINSKY, SAUL. *Reveille for Radicals.* New York: Random House, 1946.

---

[13]W.I.N. was a simplistic device that failed to get at the real problem—poverty itself, caused not by welfare but by a variety of deep social and economic causes, including the lack of decent paying, steady jobs for all able-bodied workers and the need for adequate income for the unemployable poor. It was especially inappropriate for A.F.D.C. recipients, mothers who were ill, untrainable, without access to day care for their young children, or already working at menial, low-paying jobs. As a result, only a small percentage were enrolled in the program and, of those, only about one-fourth completed the training; only a handful of the latter could find or were placed in jobs, almost always low-wage work with little or no opportunity for advancement. All studies indicate that the program cost more to operate than it saved in reduced welfare expenditures.

AXINN, JUNE, AND HERMAN LEVIN. *Social Welfare: A History of the American Response to Need,* 2d Edition. New York: Harper and Row, 1982.

BALL, ROBERT M. "Is Poverty Necessary?", *Social Security Bulletin* 28 (August 1965): 18–24.

BERKOWITZ, EDWARD, AND KIM MCQUAID. *Creating the Welfare State: The Political Economy of Twentieth-Century Reform.* New York: Praeger, 1980.

———. "Welfare Reform in the 1950s," *Social Service Review* 54 (March 1980): 45–58.

BRAUER, CARL M. "Kennedy, Johnson, and the War on Poverty," *Journal of American History* 69 (June 1982): 98–119.

BRIAR, SCOTT. "Welfare from Below: Recipients' Views of the Welfare System," *California Law Review* 54 (May 1966): 370–85.

BURNS, EVELINE M., ed. *Children's Allowances and the Economic Welfare of Children.* New York: Citizens' Committee for the Children of New York, 1968.

———. "Further Needs in Social Security Legislation in the Field of the Social Insurances," *Social Service Review* 25 (September 1951): 283–88.

CHAMBERS, CLARKE A. "Social Service and Social Reform: A Historical Essay," *Social Service Review* 37 (March 1963): 76–90.

COHEN, HENRY. "Poverty and Welfare: A Review Essay," *Political Science Quarterly* 87 (December 1972): 631–52.

COHEN, WILBUR J. "A Ten-Point Program to Abolish Poverty," *Social Security Bulletin* 31 (December 1968): 3–13.

Council on Social Work Education. *Current Issues in Social Work Seen in Historical Perspective.* New York: Council on Social Work Education, 1962.

DONOVAN, JOHN C. *The Politics of Poverty.* New York: Pegasus, 1967.

DURMAN, EUGENE. "Have the Poor Been Regulated? Toward a Multivariate Understanding of Welfare Growth," *Social Service Review* 47 (September 1973): 339–59.

ELMAN, RICHARD M. *The Poorhouse State.* New York: Pantheon Books, 1966.

FISHMAN, LEO, ed. *Poverty amid Affluence.* New Haven, Conn.: Yale University Press, 1966.

FRIEDMAN, MILTON. *Capitalism and Freedom.* Chicago: University of Chicago Press, 1962.

GALBRAITH, JOHN KENNETH. *The Affluent Society*. Boston: Houghton Mifflin, 1958.

GARVIN, CHARLES D., AUDREY D. SMITH, AND WILLIAM J. REID, eds. *The Work Incentive Experience*. Montclair, N.J.: Allanheld, Osmun, 1979.

GILBERT, CHARLES E. "Policy-Making in Public Welfare: The 1962 Amendments," *Political Science Quarterly* 81 (June 1966): 196–224.

GORDON, MARGARET, ed. *Poverty in America*. San Francisco: Chandler, 1965.

HARRINGTON, MICHAEL. *The Other America: Poverty in the United States*. New York: Penguin Books, 1962.

HOLLIS, ERNEST, AND ALICE TAYLOR. *Social Work Education in the United States*. New York: Columbia University Press, 1951.

KAHN, ALFRED. *Issues in American Social Work*. New York: Columbia University Press, 1959.

———. "Social Services in Relation to Income Security," *Social Service Review* 39 (December 1965): 381–89.

KEYSERLING, LEON. *Progress or Poverty: The United States at the Crossroads*. Washington, D.C.: Conference on Economic Progress, 1964.

KLARMAN, HERBERT. *The Economics of Health*. New York: Columbia University Press, 1965.

KOLKO, GABRIEL. *Wealth and Power in America*. London: Thames and Hudson, 1962.

LEVITAN, SAR A. *The Great Society's Poor Law: A New Approach to Poverty*. Baltimore: Johns Hopkins Press, 1969.

———, AND ROBERT TAGGART. *The Promise of Greatness*. Cambridge, Mass.: Harvard University Press, 1975.

LEWIS, MICHAEL. "The Negro Protest in Urban America," in J. R. Gusfield, ed., *Protest, Reform, and Revolt*. New York: Wiley, 1970.

LOVE, JOSEPH L. "La Raza: Mexican-Americans in Rebellion," *Transaction* 6 (February 1969): 35–41.

LUBOVE, ROY. "The Welfare Industry: Social Work and the Life of the Poor," *The Nation* 202 (May 23, 1966): 609–11.

MACDONALD, DWIGHT. "Our Invisible Poor," *New Yorker Magazine* 38 (January 19, 1963): 82–132.

MACDONALD, MAURICE. "Food Stamps: An Analytical History," *Social Service Review* 51 (December 1977): 642–58.

MAY, EDGAR. *The Wasted Americans*. New York: Harper and Row, 1964.

MENCHER, SAMUEL. "Perspectives on Recent Welfare Legislation, Fore and Aft," *Social Work* 8 (July 1963): 59–65.

MERIAM, IDA C. "Social Welfare in the United States, 1934–1954," *Social Security Bulletin* 18 (October 1955): 3–14.

MERRIFIELD, ALEANOR. "Implications of the Poverty Program: The Caseworker's View," *Social Service Review* 39 (September 1965): 294–99.

MILES, RUFUS E. *The Department of Health, Education, and Welfare*. New York: Praeger, 1974.

MILLER, HERMAN P. *Rich Man, Poor Man*. New York: Crowell, 1964.

MORGAN, JAMES et al. *Income and Welfare in the United States*. New York: McGraw-Hill, 1962.

MOYNIHAN, DANIEL P. "The Crisis in Welfare," *Public Interest* 10 (Winter 1968): 3–29.

———. *Maximum Feasible Misunderstanding: Community Action in the War on Poverty*. New York: Free Press, 1969.

———. *The Negro Family: The Case for National Action*. Washington D.C.: Government Printing Office, 1965.

———. "The Professionalization of Reform," *Public Interest* 1 (Fall 1965): 6–16.

NEWCOMER, MABEL. "Fifty Years of Public Support of Welfare Functions in the United States," *Social Service Review* 15 (December 1941): 651–60.

PATTERSON, JAMES T. *America's Struggle Against Poverty, 1900–1980*. Cambridge, Mass.: Harvard University Press, 1981.

PECHMAN, JOSEPH A. et al. *Social Security: Perspectives for Reform*. Washington, D.C.: Brookings Institute, 1968.

PERLMAN, HELEN HARRIS. "Social Work Method—A Review of the Past Decade," *Social Work* 10 (October 1965): 166–78.

PIOUS, RICHARD M. "The Phony War on Poverty in the Great Society," *Current History* 61 (November 1971): 266–72.

PIVEN, FRANCES F., AND RICHARD A. CLOWARD. "Reaffirming the Regulation of the Poor," *Social Service Review* 48 (June 1974): 147–69.

———. *Regulating the Poor: The Functions of Public Welfare*. New York: Random House, 1971.

President's National Advisory Commission on Rural Poverty. *The Peo-*

ple Left Behind. Washington, D.C.: Government Printing Office, 1967.

RAINWATER, LEE, AND WILLIAM L. YANCY. *The Moynihan Report: The Politics of Controversy*. Cambridge, Mass.: Massachusetts Institute of Technology Press, 1967.

RAPPAPORT, LYDIA. "In Defense of Social Work: An Examination of Stress in the Profession," *Social Service Review* 34 (March 1960): 62–74.

Report of the National Advisory Commission on Civil Disorders. Washington, D.C.: Government Printing Office, 1968.

RITZ, JOSEPH P. *The Despised Poor: Newburgh's War on Welfare*. Boston: Beacon Press, 1966.

ROHRLICH, GEORGE. "Guaranteed Minimum Income Proposals and the Unfinished Business of Social Security." *Social Service Review* 41 (June 1967): 166–78.

SELIGMAN, BEN B., ed. *Poverty as a Public Issue*. New York: Free Press, 1965.

STEINER, STANLEY. *La Raza: The Mexican Americans*. New York: Harper and Row, 1970.

STEVENS, ROBERT AND ROSEMARY. *Welfare Medicine in America: A Case Study of Medicaid*. New York: Free Press, 1974.

STEWART, PAUL. "United States Indian Policy: From the Dawes Act to the American Indian Policy Review Commission," *Social Service Review* 51 (September 1951): 451–63.

THEOBALD, ROBERT. *The Challenge of Abundance*. New York: Mentor Books, 1962.

———, ed. *The Guaranteed Income: Next Step in Economic Evolution?* Garden City, N.Y.: Doubleday, 1966.

TOBIN, JAMES. "The Case for an Income Guarantee," *Public Interest* 4 (Summer 1966): 31–41.

TRATTNER, WALTER I., ed. *Social Welfare or Social Control?* Knoxville, Tenn.: University of Tennessee Press, 1983.

VISWANTHAN, NARAYAN. "The Role of American Public Welfare Policies in the United States, 1930–1960," Ph.D. dissertation, Columbia University, 1961.

WEEKS, PHILIP, AND JAMES B. GIDNEY. *Subjugation and Dishonor: A Brief History of the Travail of the Native Americans*. New York: Krueger, 1981.

WICKENDEN, ELIZABETH. "The '67 Amendments: A Giant Step Backward for Child Welfare," *Child Welfare* 48 (July 1969): 388–94.

WILL, R. E., AND H. G. VATTER, eds. *Poverty and Affluence*. New York: Harcourt, Brace, and World, 1965.

YOUNGDAHL, BENJAMIN E. *Social Action and Social Work*. New York: Association Press, 1966.

Chapter 15

A New Era: Disenchantment and Retreat

RICHARD NIXON'S ELECTION in 1968 was the result of many factors, including the growing unpopularity of Johnson's Vietnam policies and the divisions within the Democratic Party over the war and other matters. In large part, however, it was the product of a changing national mood—a distinct turn to the right. After four decades of activity, the yearning for social change and increased federal involvement in social welfare (and other areas) had faded; a new era had commenced.

By the late 1960s, an increasing number of Americans were tired of the decade's social turmoil and resentful of the attention directed toward minorities and the poor. In their view, the middle class values of thrift, hard work, and self-reliance had been assaulted. Federal social programs had funneled billions of dollars into the inner cities to help the poor and unemployed, at the expense of "hard-working citizens" and of local and state government, all in vain, no less, as the "welfare mess" continued. In their opinion, it was time for a change.[1]

In Richard Nixon, these unhappy, middle class Americans

---

[1]As James Leiby has pointed out in his excellent *History of Social Welfare and Social Work in the United States,* it was not only conservatives who were affirming solicitude for state and local government; so, too, were members of the New Left and other radicals, who were preaching "participatory democracy" and community control and criticizing bureaucrats, "experts," and other managers of society. Even Common Cause, a liberal consumer organization, stated that the "reason the United States cannot solve the urgent problems that are plaguing our country, is because *the government is the problem,*" a sentiment President Reagan would repeat.

found a person who mirrored their mood. A product of an industrious, middle class family, Nixon had risen to prominence as a result of his own efforts. He was sternly dedicated to traditional values and the conservative approach. He constantly spoke about the need for "law and order" and for the reestablishment of authority over young people and the turbulent masses in the nation's cities. He disapproved of federal involvement in services to individuals and communities, preferring self-help, individual responsibility, and private action or local and state efforts. He was suspicious of "welfare fraud" and tended to be moralistic and punitive toward recipients of public assistance. He disliked government bureaucrats (especially since most tended to be Democrats who favored social welfare) and what he referred to as the elitist, liberal intellectual establishment. No wonder *Newsweek* called Nixon "the champion of the good God-fearing burghers of Heartland, U.S.A."

In fact, the Nixon presidency was full of surprises. He initiated a series of programs, dubbed the "New Federalism," to "reverse the flow of power and resources from the states and communities to Washington and start power and resources flowing back . . . to the people all across America." That effort, designed to make the national government smaller, to stop it from meddling in social reform, and to liberate capitalism from the alleged restraints imposed by prior administrations, was to be accomplished primarily through "revenue sharing"—the return of funds from the federal government to the states and localities for their use with virtually no conditions attached.[2]

In the area of social welfare, Nixon began by advocating a

---

[2]Actually, there were two parts to revenue sharing: (1) general revenue sharing, whereby monies were distributed to the states without any strings attached, and (2) special revenue sharing, which was used by the federal government to consolidate 130 conditional grants-in-aid to the states into six areas to deal with urban community development, rural community development, education, law enforcement, transportation, and manpower training. The latter program was embodied in the Comprehensive Employment and Training Act of 1973, or CETA, which consolidated the many New Frontier and Great Society manpower and job programs, substituting a single federal grant to local governments with populations over 100,000 and to states, which were to distribute the funds to less populated areas. The aim of the measure was to replace the previous panoply of separately funded, federally designed and administered manpower and job programs with a single, flexible, locally run system. Later on, the Reagan administration terminated the program, throwing some 400,000 people out of work and thus exacerbating an already staggering unemployment problem.

major alteration in the nation's welfare system—a bold plan, ironically, for shifting the burden of payments *from* the states and localities *to* the federal government and equalizing such payments throughout the country. However, the plan's key feature, establishment of a federally guaranteed minimum annual income, was coupled with an elaborate system of penalties and incentives designed to force recipients to work.

Nixon's Family Assistance Plan (F.A.P.)—conceived largely by Daniel Moynihan (a liberal carry-over from the Kennedy-Johnson years) and announced in August 1969—was motivated, in part at least, by a desire to destroy the network of bureaucrats and social workers established by the E.O.A. and other welfare programs of the decade. Under the F.A.P., limited to families with children, every unemployed family of four would receive at least $1600 (subsequently raised to $2400) a year from the federal government. Since the program was designed, in part, to provide the difference between marginal wages and the money needed to live above the poverty line, the working poor would receive the $1600 minimum and would be allowed to keep their pay until their earned income reached close to $4000, at which time the benefits would be discontinued.[3] To be eligible for such assis-

---

[3] A family of four with no regular income would be permitted to retain the first $720 of earned income without any reduction in the proposed minimum grant of $1600. Thereafter, it could keep one-half of all additional income, with the cutoff point for a family of four at $3920 (or $5720 for a family of seven). It was assumed that the application of this 50 percent marginal tax on nonexempt earnings, instead of the 100 percent tax which for the most part prevailed in public assistance, would provide the incentive to work.

Proposed Family Assistance Plan Payment Schedule for Family of Four (Assuming $720 Income Exemption and 50 Percent "Tax" on Nonexempt Income)

Earnings	Nonexempt Earnings	"Tax" at 50 Percent	Net Payment	Net Income
$0	$0	$0	$1600	$1600
720	0	0	1600	2320
1000	280	140	1460	2460
1500	780	390	1210	2710
2000	1280	640	960	2960
2500	1780	890	710	3210
3000	2280	1140	460	3460
3500	2780	1390	210	3710
3920	3200	1600	—	3920

tance, the able-bodied—including women with children over three years of age—would be required to work (or be placed in a job training program). The administration of the program would eventually be turned over to the states under a principle that Nixon labeled the "new federalism."

The President's welfare recommendations provoked immediate controversy. While some people hailed them as a great step forward in helping the poor, most experts denounced the proposals as inadequate and even retrogressive. To begin with, the minimum figure was approximately $2000 less than the federal government's own official poverty line and some $4500 below the Bureau of Labor Statistics' adequate income level for a family of four. Also, while the program would have increased welfare payments in some parts of the country, especially in the rural South where approximately 10 percent of the nation's welfare recipients lived, it would have added little or nothing elsewhere, where the remaining 90 percent of the nation's public dependents resided. Indeed, there were fears that it would lead the more progressive areas to cut back their welfare payments in order to conform to the federal standard.

In addition, the notion that women with young dependent children should leave home and go to work—at any type of job, often at substandard wages—was anathema to many, which led to the proposal's most glaring shortcoming: its emphasis on job training and work when a majority of the poor were "either too young, too old, or too sick to work," were "already employed at below subsistence wages," or were women with young children. Moreover, the plan was work oriented at a time when absorption of all Americans into the labor market (even those with normally marketable skills) was hardly possible. Despite tax cuts, the war in Vietnam, general prosperity, and other factors making for increased job opportunities, unemployment hovered at about 6 percent of the labor force and was rising. Jobs were not available for many Americans, especially for semiskilled and unskilled workers. The administration, however, bound by old stereotypes and myths, continued to set up complex and costly work and training programs for a client population unable to utilize them.

Still, the proposed F.A.P. had virtues, especially in theory. The principle of a federal welfare system and what amounted to a guaranteed annual income, however inadequate to begin with, constituted a major step forward in meeting current and especially future needs. As a result, at least some social workers and welfare groups supported it, as did some local and state officials, who welcomed the financial relief the program would provide their welfare budgets. Most of those concerned, however, did not, including the National Welfare Rights Organization and its leader, George Wiley, who set out to "zap F.A.P."—the "Family Annihilation Plan," which, in Wiley's opinion, would "fuck America's poor." Meanwhile, Nixon had tired of the struggle and never really exerted much pressure to secure the plan's passage. Thus, several years after it was proposed, the F.A.P. was still bogged down in committee, where it eventually expired.

Meanwhile, the welfare problem grew. Apparently, two distinct economies had developed in America. One, the economy of affluence, included most Americans—well trained, holding steady jobs, in relatively good health, living in reasonably comfortable homes. The other, the economy of poverty, was inhabited by the poorly trained, unable to find or hold jobs, suffering from low incomes, bad health, and poor housing. Born to the wrong parents, in the wrong part of town, or in the wrong racial group, they were trapped in a cycle of poverty and degradation.

Despite various welfare programs and expenditures, it appeared as though poverty, even in an affluent society, had congealed and hardened into a kind of subculture that represented a social syndrome, an ineradicable condition. Perhaps Ben Seligman, the author of *Permanent Poverty*, was right when he stated that America would always have its outcasts:

> In an industrial society where large segments of the population must suffer joblessness because they are unskilled, low wages when they are employed, a distorted family structure and inadequate services in such areas as education and health, there are many who [always] will find themselves rejected.

Yet, few Americans were willing to concede this point—or deal with its implications. Most echoed the sentiments of Senator Russell Long of Louisiana, chairperson of the influential Finance Committee, who charged that the "welfare system ... is being manipulated and abused by malingerers, cheaters, and ... frauds."

Still, all was not bleak; there were a few rays of hope. Notwith-standing the lack of significant social welfare reform and a novel attack on the problem, some progress toward conquering poverty had been made. In 1960, the number of poor—not of welfare recipients—was officially estimated to be around 40 million, or 20 percent of the population; in 1969, the number had declined to about 25 million, or 12 percent of the population (thanks largely to urban migration, to increased welfare expenditures— Medicare, Medicaid, food stamps, rent subsidies, etc.—and especially to vast increases in old-age insurance). While not the total victory L.B.J. had talked about in 1964, nevertheless it was a large step in the right direction. Then, too, the war in Vietnam was winding down and even showed signs of coming to an end, and when it did, presumably more funds would be available for badly needed domestic social services.

Also, more Americans were beginning to accept the idea that since automation had broken the traditional link between jobs and income—some citizens could not work, or find jobs, or earn living wages in the labor market—there was a need to set up a truly sound system of social security, including some sort of federal in-come maintenance program, especially a guaranteed annual in-come. Only in this way, they argued, by meeting immediate need with the instrument best designed to overcome that need— money—would the rejects of society, most of whom were not maladjusted or ill, be brought into the mainstream of American life. Even Milton Friedman, the famed conservative University of Chicago economist, favored such a plan, although for different reasons. Believing that it would abolish the welfare bureaucracy and cut welfare costs, he had worked out such a plan—in this case a "negative income tax"—and explained it as early as 1962 in his widely read *Capitalism and Freedom*.

It was not totally surprising, therefore, that when President Johnson's Commission on Income Maintenance Programs, better known as the Heineman Commission, appointed in January 1968 and comprised of leading economists, businessmen, and political activists, released its report in November 1969, it recommended a negative income tax, one far more generous than that proposed by Nixon four months earlier. The commission's report stated that unemployment and underemployment "were basic facts of

American life" and that the nation's social and economic structure "virtually guaranteed" poverty for millions of citizens. "The simple fact is," members of the commission concluded, "that most of the poor remain poor because access to income through work is currently beyond their reach." As a result, while Nixon's F.A.P. stressed work—indeed, required it as a condition for receiving aid—the commission's proposal discounted it entirely; only a negative income tax without any strings attached could deal with the situation, in its opinion.

Meanwhile, the expectations of the poor had been aroused, and it appeared that they no longer were willing to return to their urban and rural slums and sit by in quiet desperation. Influenced by the mass protest programs and techniques of the civil rights movement and faulting the system rather than themselves for their condition, they demanded adequate assistance as a right not as a privilege.

Mass welfare rights demonstrations began in June 1966, with thousands of people in sixteen cities across the nation participating. Then, in August 1966, 100 representatives from twenty-three cities met in Chicago to form the National Coordinating Committee of Welfare Rights Groups and to formulate goals and strategies for a nationwide organizing campaign. By February 1967, the movement had expanded to 173 identifiable groups in twenty-three states, and it was still growing. Among the movement's chief aims were: an adequate guaranteed annual income; curtailed investigatory practices, especially with regard to "man-in-the-house" rules, violations of privacy, and "midnight raids"; the right to earn additional income without reduction in assistance payments until an adequate minimum was reached; more respect for recipients' legal rights; improved day care for children of working mothers; higher clothing and furniture allowances; more adequate medical care; and elimination of all residency requirements. The demonstrations, with their picket lines, protest marches and meetings, sit-ins, and school and rent boycotts, promised to end only when these demands were met, when the stigma of poverty was gone and the promise of American life was fulfilled for all citizens.

And finally, by the start of the 1970s, there was considerable evidence that social work was again beginning to carry the banner of reform, that it was identifying once more with the "cause" (rather than the "function" or service) aspects of its historic tradition. While most social workers still trod a narrow path, acknowledging the importance of social reform but seeing themselves primarily as clinicians whose first responsibility was to their clients, the profession was changing.

A growing number of social workers declared that casework was not effective, that it had little impact on those it was supposed to help, that, in fact, it was often more harmful than helpful, and that social workers should be "advocates" for the poor, or "social brokers," not therapists. These critics aided the organizing efforts of the new welfare rights groups. Also, schools of social work were recruiting students from among traditionally disadvantaged segments of society and revising their curricula, placing more emphasis on such things as group work and community organization, public administration, and social policy. The Council on Social Work Education had demanded that its members shape their curricula on the assumption that their graduates would be called upon to participate in the making of social policy. Even Helen Harris Perlman, the well known educator and author of several casework textbooks, forthrightly enjoined her fellow social workers to become more interested in social reform: "The great federal programs for poverty prevention and for education and training call for versatile social workers," she wrote. "Our present-day articulated repertoire of actions is a limited one. It needs expansion, experiment, ranging. . . ."

Professional associations began placing social problems on the public agenda and pressing to keep them there until the American people and their political leaders grappled creatively and effectively with them. The National Association of Social Workers (which changed its bylaws to state that the profession had a dual obligation to use "both social work methods and . . . social action" to prevent and alleviate "deprivation, distress, and strain") stationed a paid lobbyist in Washington, D.C., for the purpose. It also appointed a committee to devise a method of translating data from practice into social policy, and began stressing its members' responsibility for social action.

Then there was the announcement by the Community Service Society of New York (the forerunner of the Association for

Improving the Condition of the Poor and the nation's oldest, largest, and wealthiest family service agency) that it was discontinuing casework. "If you don't deal with the pathology of the ghetto, all the individual counseling you do with a person is not going to help," said Dr. James G. Emerson, the agency's executive secretary. "The situation," he added,

> is not just a matter of persons with problems, but rather of whole areas afflicted with social ills. If the individual is to be helped, someone has to deal with the complex of social ills that bears on the individual, not just on the individual himself. We are convinced that an approach that focuses primarily on individuals may help some people, but will not really alleviate the basic problem of a sick community. Instead of starting out by saying that the individual is the client, we're going to say the community is the client.

The rays of hope occasioned by these developments, however, quickly dimmed. Poverty did not disappear, nor was the welfare problem legislated out of existence—and the plight of many of its victims became increasingly worse. The darkening situation resulted from a variety of factors. First of all, various income maintenance proposals continued to be ignored, including those recommended by President Johnson's Commission on Income Maintenance Programs. If anything, the enactment of these and other pieces of social legislation appeared less likely than a half-decade earlier; a more conservative Congress and other developments did not bode well for the future.

One such development, which seemed to foreshadow what was to follow, was a measure Congress enacted into law in December 1971. Rather than pass legislation designed to deal with the causes of the problem or meet the needs of the poor, Congress strengthened the more coercive features of the Work Incentive Program (and the now dead Family Assistance Plan). The measure, known as the Talmadge Amendments, or W.I.N. II, repealed that section of the 1967 Public Welfare Amendments that allowed the states to determine who was to be referred to job and training programs. Now all A.F.D.C. recipients had to register for work or training programs, with the exception of mothers with children under six years of age, and those states which did not somehow place at least 15 percent of those so registered faced the loss of federal funds. The administration and Congress continued to reject the idea that the poor always would be with us and that some sort of guaranteed minimum income therefore was essential; few wanted to spend time or money on the "undeserving poor." Instead, they ignored the "facts"—including the severe job shortage and other factors that rendered most welfare recipients either unable to find work or unsuitable for it—and thus the obvious failure of the original program, continuing to fantasize about "workfare" as the cure for dependency.[4]

Interestingly, in October 1972, the federal government assumed responsibility for all aid to the aged, the blind, and the disabled. Adoption of the Supplemental Security Income Program (S.S.I.), as it was called, which was to become effective on January 1, 1974, and which combined and federalized all public assistance for the adult poor who clearly were unemployable —thereby establishing the nation's first guaranteed income program, of sorts, for this group—further demonstrated the lasting strength of America's work ethic. While the unemployable, or "deserving poor," would be relatively well treated, some 11 million other people on welfare, mainly A.F.D.C. recipients and the unemployed receiving general assistance at the county level, remained under an inadequate and punitive system. The states and localities continued to avoid federal regulations aimed at humanizing their welfare systems, equalizing the amount of aid they provided recipients, and improving administration. Thus, administrators attempted to keep eligible people off the rolls and to stigmatize and humiliate those receiving assistance, and variations from state to state and from county to county continued to plague the system. Above all, payments remained low, falling further and further below the inflation rate and making the plight of these people increasingly dire.

Meanwhile, American troops were withdrawn from Vietnam early in 1973, but little money was diverted to badly needed domestic programs, as had been promised. Indeed, after his landslide victory in 1972, Nixon moved vigorously to cut back many

[4]The results of W.I.N. II were about the same as those of W.I.N. I: the program put few people to work, those who did go to work were employed in unskilled, low-paying jobs, and the real problem of welfare dependency remained unresolved.

of the social programs enacted during the 1960s, especially as many members of the working class, plagued by their own problems of inadequate wages, soaring prices, and rising taxes, called for reductions in government services and expenditures.[5]

At the same time, the Nixon administration had become mired in the gravest political scandal in American history—Watergate—which by March 1974 had led to the resignation or firing of more than a dozen men from high national office and the indictment or conviction of thirty-five people for criminal acts of one kind or another. In August of that year, faced by almost certain removal from office through impeachment, Nixon became the only Chief Executive in American history to resign from the presidency. Many began to question sharply the ability of elected officials to govern fairly and control the course of events, especially in a humane and rational way, and further urged that government involvement in social programs be curtailed. This liberal opposition to the nature of the federal role in social welfare intersected with conservative opposition to *any* federal role and, under Nixon's successors, led the nation further from the expansive path of the 1960s.

First to succeed Nixon was Gerald Ford, the longtime Michigan congressman and short-term Vice-President, who took the oath of office on August 9, 1974, while the former President and his family were flying to their home in California. Amiable, even-tempered, open, hard-working, and, above all, honest, Ford was, for the most part, well liked and respected. He destroyed some of his good will, however, when shortly after entering the White House he granted Nixon an unconditional pardon for all federal crimes, known or unknown, he had committed while in office—an act that would come back to haunt Ford when he sought election in 1976.

While thought to be a moderate, in reality Ford was quite con-

---

[5]With regard to rising taxes, the Social Security tax, one of the most regressive of all, was a major case in point. It rose from 4.8 percent of the first $7800 earned in 1970 to 5.85 percent of $15,300 in 1976 (and 5.85 percent of $16,500 a year later), hitting hardest the lowest paid in the working class. Today it stands at 6.7 percent of the first $35,700 in wages, and is scheduled to increase to 7 percent on January 1, 1984.

servative, even more so than his predecessor. At no time while in the White House did he express any concern for the needy or mention welfare reform as one of his, or the nation's, legislative priorities. On the contrary, Ford was committed to restricting welfare funds, as his vetoes of a wide range of important welfare measures—among them a federal public works bill, federal aid to education, health care, a school lunch program—indicate. In addition, he repeatedly cut H.E.W.'s budget, fulminated against proposed compulsory health insurance schemes, and proved indifferent to civil rights (especially busing) legislation.

Inflation, which Ford called Public Enemy Number 1, and the ailing economy were the President's top priorities, but he approached these matters in a very conservative way. His obsession with inflation at a time of rising unemployment and declining productivity (ills inherited from the Nixon administration) made conditions bad, or worse, for many Americans. Under Ford's efforts to fight inflation with unemployment, joblessness in America had climbed to 9 percent by the spring of 1975, the highest rate since 1941, while the real gross national product had fallen more sharply than at any time since the collapse of the economy in 1929. Meanwhile, the inflation rate remained high, creating a condition termed "stagflation," which continued to baffle the experts and plague the nation. Symptomatic of the situation were the poverty figures; not only had they ceased to decline, but the number of poverty-stricken citizens in the nation increased significantly once again. Whereas at the start of 1975 the number of poor in America was close to twenty-five million, about the same as six years earlier (although, owing to the growth in population, the percentage had dropped from 12 to 11.5), a dramatic reversal occurred that year. Primarily because of long-term unemployment, spiraling inflation, and a decline in purchasing power, some 2.5 million more citizens dropped below the official poverty level—the largest increase in a single year since the federal government began keeping such figures in 1959,[6] and the figure

[6]While the overall unemployment rate in 1975 was around 9 percent, it was approximately twice that for the nation's blacks and three times that for its youth. Not only had the problem increased significantly, but a total of 4.3 million individuals were out of work for so long in 1975 that they exhausted their unemployment compensation benefits, while two million others had done the

would continue to rise each year, so that by 1980 the total number of people below the poverty line would be greater than in 1969. Proportionally speaking, the greatest gain occurred among those who did not ordinarily dominate such statistics—members of white, male-headed families; as in the 1930s, the "new" joined the "old" poor. Still, the distribution of poverty remained, as always, structured by race, ethnicity, sex, family situation, and employment status—lowest for whites, higher for Hispanics, and highest for blacks; higher for women than for men; higher for single-parent, as opposed to two-parent, families; and so on.

About the only exception to the rule was the aged, whose numbers among the poor declined throughout this period. Senior citizens' exit from poverty, at least to a degree, was due to a number of related causes, especially the expansion and increased effectiveness of income transfer programs, particularly Old-Age Insurance, for which older Americans deserve much of the credit. By the 1960s, the aged were not only greater in number but also increasingly well organized; in 1972, the "gray lobby" helped secure a 20 percent increase in O.A.I. benefits; that was followed by an 11 percent increase in 1974; and a year later all such income was tied to increases in prices and wages. Similarly, S.S.I. payments to the elderly poor (the program that went into effect in January 1974) were "indexed" to keep pace with (or stay slightly ahead of) inflation. (The same was not true, it might be added, of benefits received by A.F.D.C. clients and others on welfare.) Thus, the aged were not as vulnerable to poverty as they had been previously or as were others less powerful and considered less worthy.

Meanwhile, memories of Watergate and his pardon of Nixon, lingering suspicions of those in power, and his inability to solve the nation's economic problems contributed to Ford's loss to Jimmy Carter, "the outsider," in the 1976 presidential contest. Carter, a little-known former governor of Georgia, exploited the public's continued discontent with professional politicians and

---

same the year before. Furthermore, owing to inflation, there was a decline in real wages for those who were fortunate enough to be working; consumer prices, especially for food, were rising from 10 to 15 percent a year, much more rapidly than wages. As a result, the real purchasing power of the typical American family dropped by about 2.6 percent in 1975.

bureaucrats and their same old programs. Insisting that the American people were searching for "new voices, new ideas, [and] new leaders" and promising that he would control inflation, redress the unemployment situation, and thereby lower the "misery rate"—the sum of the inflation and unemployment rates—to eight, Carter won the presidency and carried into office with him a huge Democratic majority in Congress. Once in the White House, however, he would have to surmount persistent doubts about his ability to govern effectively and to solve the nation's pressing social and economic (as well as diplomatic) problems.

In some ways, Carter was an old-fashioned populist who felt for the common folk; he also possessed a human rights dominated ideology. Yet he was aware of the conservative popular mood and he shared one of the major themes of public discourse during the 1976 bicentennial celebration—the idea that the nation had to accept a sense of limits to its power, its resources, and its potential for economic growth. Carter proceeded, therefore, with fiscal restraint, prompting one writer to call him "the most conservative Democrat since Grover Cleveland." And in the spring of 1977, Senator George McGovern, the previous Democratic presidential candidate, accused Carter of being addicted to "republican economics" and stated that it was difficult to remember which party had won the election.

It was both inaccurate and unfair to label Carter a "warmed-over Gerald Ford," for among other things he signed into law a strip mining control bill that Ford had vetoed, he waged many battles on behalf of the environment, he persuaded Congress to create a cabinet-level Department of Energy and then one of education (turning H.E.W. into the Department of Health and Human Services), and he appointed an unprecedented number of women and members of minority groups to judgeships and other government positions. In addition, he fostered a national youth employment bill, asked Congress to enact a costly measure to make mental health facilities and treatment available to many more people, elaborated a national urban policy designed mainly to aid inner cities with problems of chronic high unemployment, and pushed for a whole series of other important measures, including major welfare reform. Thus, on January 26, 1977, only six days after his inauguration, the President appointed a study group to conduct a detailed analysis of the nation's welfare policy and come forward with proposals for reform of what he referred to as the "complicated and often inequitable system."

Several months later, the President told the American people that the nation's welfare program was even worse than he thought, and that it "should be scrapped and a totally new system implemented." And he promised to reveal, within three months, plans for such a new system, one that would cost no more than the present scheme.

True to his promise, Carter publicly unveiled his welfare reform proposal at a news conference in Plains, Georgia, on August 6, 1977. The plan, introduced in Congress several weeks later, was known as the "Better Jobs and Income Program" (B.J.I.P.). To become effective in October 1980, if enacted into law, the sweeping program would abolish the existing welfare system with its patchwork of benefits, including A.F.D.C., S.S.I., and food stamps, and replace it with a new two-tier system—a job program for those who could work, and an income maintenance program for those who could not.

In brief, the proposal called for the creation of 1.4 million full- and part-time jobs and job-training slots designed to allow every able-bodied head of a household on relief who could not find a job in the private sector to work at one that would pay the minimum wage or higher. The benefits received by those working full time, whether in the private or in the public sector—two-parent families, single adults, childless couples, and single parents with no children under age fourteen—depended on the size of their families and the amount of their earnings. Thus, while a single individual who earned up to $3800 a year would receive $1100, a family of four earning that amount would get an additional $2300 from the federal government, bringing its total annual income up to $6100. For each additional dollar earned (beyond $3800) up to $8400, the benefits would be reduced by only fifty cents. In addition, an earned-income tax-credit program, which increases the take home pay of low-wage workers, would be expanded to provide further benefits in the form of tax relief for the working poor in private or nonsubsidized public employment.

Those unable or unexpected to work full time, or at all, because

, blindness, or disability, or because they were single
ιs with children under fourteen years of age, would receive
⌐ ∩thly cash benefit that, in most instances, was more generous
than what they were already receiving. Hence a family of four in
which no adult could work would receive a basic benefit of $4200
a year (in 1978 dollars), an elderly couple $3750, and a single per-
son $2500. Here, too, when possible, there were incentives to
supplement this guaranteed annual income. Those who secured
part-time employment, including mothers with children between
the ages of seven and fourteen who were expected to work while
their youngsters were in school, would have their benefits
reduced by only fifty cents for each additional dollar of outside income, up to $8400, when the payments would cease. And the ex-
panded earned-income tax credit would provide added tax relief
to these people as well.

The program, which would affect some thirty-two million
Americans, would cost the federal government approximately
$30.7 billion a year, or $2.8 billion more than the existing system.
However, it would bring some $2 billion in financial relief to state
and local governments during the first year and substantially
more thereafter.

Carter's proposal, then, in many ways was similar to Nixon's
proposed F.A.P.: both provided a federal guarantee of minimum
income, both used a negative income tax mechanism, and both
had monetary work incentives. On the other hand, there were
very important differences between the two: the Carter plan
provided universal coverage while Nixon's proposal had concerned only families with children, the benefits were considerably
higher in the Carter proposals, as were the exemptions from work
for women with young children, and, perhaps most important,
Carter's proposal, unlike Nixon's, included the provision of jobs.
By so doing, the Carter plan, in contrast to the F.A.P.—or the
E.O.A., for that matter—would have shifted the onus of poverty
from the unemployed to the malfunctioning of the labor market.

On the whole, initial reaction to Carter's proposal was quite favorable, but Congress adjourned without taking action on the
measure and, not surprisingly, a year later it was pronounced
dead by congressional leaders. Conservatives opposed the plan's
cost and the creation of public service jobs, which they feared

would compete with private industry, while liberals complained that the payments (both the guaranteed annual income and the proposed wages) were too low and that the plan smacked of "workfare." Perhaps the real reason for the proposal's expiration was its comprehensive nature; incremental reform seems more suited to the American political process, especially in this very touchy area.

Meanwhile, in May 1977, Carter had proposed publicly the use of substantial amounts of general tax revenues and greater employer contributions to shore up the financially troubled Social Security System. Unfortunately, that proposal, too, was rejected; instead, Congress passed, and the President approved, large increases in the payroll tax for employees and employers alike, a costly band-aid solution, at best, that failed to get at the causes of the problem—rampant inflation, growing unemployment, and the aging of the population.

Carter also was "committed to the phasing in of a workable health insurance system" and in July 1978 he unveiled the broad outlines of such a plan, one that placed as much emphasis on curbing rising medical costs as on assuring health care for all citizens. Because the plan—to be called Health Care—was to be phased in slowly and piecemeal and because it had many budgetary (and hence service) restraints, supporters of a more immediate and a more comprehensive scheme opposed it, including Senator Edward Kennedy, A.F.L.-C.I.O. President George Meany, and other longtime supporters of compulsory health insurance. To no one's surprise, this measure, too, died shortly.

So, while proposing many significant reforms, Carter was unable to get most of them through Congress, a Congress controlled by his own party. Rather than the "strong, independent, and aggressive President" he had promised to be, he appeared to be weak, indecisive, and ineffectual. In fact, his failure to exert effective presidential leadership led the *New York Times* to refer to Carter as "President Wobble."

Carter's failure to inspire confidence was highlighted by the Iranian hostage crisis—the languishing of fifty-two American citizens in the American embassy in Teheran, where they were held captive for well over a year while Carter and the nation were unable to secure their release. Then came the Soviet Union's invasion of Afghanistan, which also left many Americans feeling angry, frustrated, impotent, and disillusioned with the government's ability to resolve important problems—and with Carter's leadership or lack of it.

Even more costly to Carter's political future and reputation, however, was his handling of the economy. In 1980, the nation witnessed the second consecutive year of double-digit inflation, the first such instance since World War I. When, with Carter's approval, the Federal Reserve Board drove up interest rates in an attempt to curb inflation, a severe recession ensued, with rising unemployment and continuing high prices. The "misery rate" stood not at eight, as Carter had promised four years earlier, but at 18.7 (7.8 percent unemployment and 10.9 percent inflation). As a result, in the summer of 1980 Carter received the lowest approval rating ever recorded for an American president, 21 percent. Not surprisingly, that fall he was swept out of office in an electoral landslide that returned the Republicans to power behind Ronald Reagan, the former movie actor who had served two terms as governor of California.

Relying on folksy and nostalgic rhetoric and his training as an actor, Reagan, the darling of the nation's conservatives, managed to capture the confidence that Carter had been unable to inspire. Promising an "era of national renewal" through a restoration of the nation's older values and institutions, its military might, and its role in world affairs, Reagan won an overwhelming victory. Not only did he capture the White House but his party also gained control of the Senate for the first time in more than a quarter of a century and added thirty-five seats in the House, with almost all of the changes involving the dislodging of liberals by conservatives. While, in fact, the outcome of the election represented less a right-wing realignment than a dissatisfaction with Carter's leadership and a concern about the nation's economic woes, especially growing unemployment and skyrocketing inflation, Reagan interpreted the vote as a mandate to move the nation in a new direction—or to continue moving it further in the direction in which it had been moving since Nixon's election in 1968. He chose a cabinet dominated by conservative businessmen who shared his philosophy and immediately turned to what he called "the worst economic mess since the Great Depression."[7]

Reagan's positions on public issues, which he had been espousing for some time, were very clear. He detested big government, regarded free enterprise and a healthy business world as the source of prosperity for all Americans, and took a hard line on military preparedness and strength. In the area of welfare, he had long demonstrated a dislike for welfare recipients and was convinced that the relief rolls were swollen with "cheats" and "free loaders" who should be forced back into the labor market.

These positions, of course, and their proposed solutions, "supply-side economics," or "Reaganomics," as they were called—a combination of reduced government spending on social programs, a heavy dose of military expenditures, the termination of government regulations, tax cuts, and a balanced budget—were not new. Carter had advocated tax cuts, reduced federal spending, and even increased defense appropriations relative to social welfare.[8] In fact, these proposals differed little from Herbert Hoover's "trickle down" theory. And Reagan's director of the Office of Management and Budget, David Stockman, created a sensation, within and without the administration, when he confided to a journalist that the administration's policies were a "Trojan horse" full of benefits for the rich and that supply-side economics was nothing but "trickle down" economic theory in disguise.

In the area of social welfare, Reagan's thinking also was "Hooverian" or, rather, classic nineteenth century. (The President's chief advisor on these matters, Martin Anderson, was a

---

[7] Throughout the presidential campaign, Reagan had likened himself to Franklin D. Roosevelt, implying that when in office he, too, would be forced to take bold economic action. Reagan's legislative proposals and executive decisions, however, unlike Roosevelt's, curtailed the functions and responsibilities of the federal government. In fact, many of the New Deal programs were among the first to go, along with those of the New Frontier and the Great Society.

[8] Also, Carter recommended that Congress repeal some earlier amendments to the Social Security Act that extended benefits (S.I.) to full-time students, eighteen to twenty-one years of age. He thereby was the first President to recommend a reduction in Social Security benefits. Congress refused, but Reagan secured these and other cutbacks in the program.

senior fellow at Stanford University's Hoover Institution. Anderson's 1978 book, *Welfare,* was largely a critique of the Great Society from a conservative perspective.) Reagan believed that it was essential to reverse the historical trend that had gotten Washington heavily involved in the area of welfare—that the key, in other words, to solving the welfare problem was not only cutting back on assistance but also removing responsibility for the needy from the vast federal bureaucracy, where, in his opinion, waste and inefficiency abounded, and returning it to the states and localities. Lost necessary revenues, he argued, would and should be provided by private foundations, churches, fraternal groups, businesses, and charitable organizations—an assumption or hope that rested on questionable economic and historical premises. Aside from the inability of the private sector to provide the necessary financial resources—as the Hoover years and the Great Depression seemingly had proven—federal welfare had grown for compelling reasons: Washington had taken on responsibilities in this area when, and only when, it was clear that problems that were national in scope had arisen and that existing institutional arrangements could not or would not cope with the situation. Moreover, while waste and inefficiency (and perhaps even corruption) exist in the federal bureaucracy, they are present at lower governmental levels and in private agencies as well. In addition, one might argue, and in fact studies demonstrate, that there is more fraud and abuse in the nation's tax system, or in its defense industry, or in the health care professions than in the welfare system—fraud and abuse that is far more costly to the nation's taxpayers.[9]

The Reagan administration provided few surprises, with

[9]In 1980–81, there were approximately 11 million recipients of welfare in America, 7 million of whom were children. Of the 4 million adults receiving assistance, most were mothers of those children, many of whom were under six years of age; others were working (usually for inadequate wages) or had been working and were unemployed but looking for other jobs. Furthermore, studies of these people have shown that the overwhelming majority of them remain on welfare for short periods of time, usually to cope with temporary unemployment, illness, or some other crisis, and that they prefer work to public assistance. So, contrary to the administration's assumption—and the prevailing belief—the number of welfare "cheats" or "malingerers" appears to be very small.

perhaps the exception of the speed, tenacity, and skill with which it pursued its goals. Demonstrating remarkable political adroitness, Reagan within a matter of months managed to increase greatly the defense budget, significantly reduce taxes (for three years, in a way that clearly favored the upper classes), and slash government spending, by billions, mainly on social programs designed to help the poor and the elderly ill—A.F.D.C., S.S.I., Medicare and Medicaid, food stamps, subsidized housing, energy assistance, school lunch programs, legal aid, and the like. At the same time, the President announced that additional reductions in social programs (of $95 billion and $30 billion, respectively) would be proposed in 1983 and 1984 in order to help defray the cost of the tax cuts and increased military expenditures and achieve a balanced budget.

Then, to implement his desire to tranfer government functions from Washington to the state capitals, Reagan (in his 1982 State of the Union Message) called for a "New Federalism," a "great leap backwards," as one critic put it, involving forty-six programs, most notably, however, the three that have the greatest effect on the lives of the poor and dependent—A.F.D.C., food stamps, and Medicaid.[10] Under the plan, to begin in 1984 and be phased in over the following three years, the states would assume all the costs of the first two programs, while the federal government would completely finance the latter. State and local governments would have the option to abandon, or reduce the scope of, the programs if they so desired, as would the federal government, and given their economic plight and the prevailing ideological climate, that was a very real possibility, something the Reagan administration no doubt had in mind.[11]

Again, however, the so-called New Federalism really was not

[10]The remaining 43 programs, which cost about $30 billion to maintain, would go to the states and would virtually take the federal government out of the fields of special education, youth employment, job training, and mass transportation.

[11]For an excellent discussion of the administration's intentions and the likely effects of the "New Federalism" had it been enacted, see Frances F. Piven and Richard A. Cloward, *The New Class War* (New York: Pantheon Books, 1982), pp. 125–34.

very new at all. Nixon had proposed a similar approach and had used that very term in initiating his revenue sharing scheme. In some ways, however, as Henry Steele Commager, the well known American historian, pointed out, it really was "a throwback to the Confederacy (1781–89) when the thirteen states . . . [claimed] to be sovereign and the national government was all but impotent." Some even went further back in history, labeling it the "New Feudalism." The plan, however, won little support, among Republicans as well as Democrats, and it died stillborn.

Reagan also wanted to make substantial cuts in Social Security, particularly in Old-Age Insurance, but he backed off when influential organizations of the aged and others protested. As it turned out, however, by raising the issue and the anxiety of many Americans, the administration did the nation a service, at least in the long run, for even Social Security's most loyal advocates conceded that changes in the system were essential in order to maintain its solvency and preserve the funds of more than 35 million beneficiaries.

The system had been strained for some time. An increase in the number of people living to old age and their growing political clout meant a rapidly increasing amount of retirement benefits and medical costs, especially due to inflation and the "indexing" of payments. The cash flow crisis was exacerbated by rising unemployment and the declining birth rate, which not only put a severe burden on the unemployment insurance reserves but also meant that there were (and would continue to be) fewer workers contributing funds to assist the larger and larger non-working segment of the population; bankruptcy or ever-increasing taxes for the working class faced the administration, neither of which prospect was very appealing.

Seeking a solution, Reagan created a bipartisan commission and charged it with making recommendations to prevent the system's defaulting. Despite a great deal of public skepticism, the fifteen-member National Commission on Social Security Reform, under the leadership of economist Alan Greenspan, a member of Reagan's Economic Policy Advisory Board and a former chair of the President's Council of Economic Advisers, eventually came up with a compromise plan that received widespread support not only in Congress but also throughout the nation.[12]

Briefly, the "rescue plan," which was projected to save $168 billion over the next seven years and thereby guarantee the system's solvency over the next seventy-five years, consisted of the following: a delay, for six months, of an impending 5 percent cost-of-living increase in benefits; the taxing of half the benefits, starting in 1984, of higher income retirees (single people with adjusted gross incomes, exclusive of Social Security, of more than $25,000 and couples with incomes in excess of $32,000); the bringing of new federal employees and workers in non-profit organizations into the system; the acceleration of scheduled future payroll tax increases; and the gradual raising of the retirement age from sixty-five to sixty-seven (between the years 2000 and 2027). Thomas "Tip" O'Neill, the Democratic Speaker of the House of Representatives and one of the moving forces behind the changes, referred to them as "landmark measures," while President Reagan, when signing them into law on April 20, 1983 (before eight hundred people, friend and foe alike, invited to the White House for the occasion), declared, "Older Americans no longer need worry that their check will be stopped. These amendments reaffirm our government's commitment to Social Security."

Meanwhile, many Americans continued to suffer; indeed, their number grew. By the end of 1982, Reaganomics did not appear to be working; if anything, the President's economic program seemed to have worsened the situation. The gross national product continued to decline, interest rates remained high, and the nation was mired in the worst recession since the Great Depression. Unemployment was approaching, and soon would exceed, 10 percent of the work force. Many major industries—steel, automobiles, and others—were faced with virtual collapse. Entire

---

[12]Representative Barber Conable (R.-N.Y.), who served on the commission, perhaps best summed up the popular reaction to the proposed changes when he said of the plan: "It may not be a work of art, but it is artful work.... It will do what it was supposed to do: ... save the nation's basic insurance system from imminent disaster."

regions of the nation, especially the industrial Midwest, had descended into depressionlike conditions. Business failures were occurring in unprecedented numbers and thousands of people across the nation were being thrown onto the streets, where soup kitchens and temporary shelters could not keep up with their needs. Furthermore, the administration, which had pledged a balanced budget, ran the highest deficits in American history—with no end in sight. Only a lower inflation rate brightened the otherwise dark economic picture.

Much of the President's initial popularity had vanished. Wall Street financiers, once his biggest supporters, called upon Reagan to reverse his course, as did many of his own advisors, who urged him to reduce military spending, delay additional scheduled tax cuts, and show more compassion for the poor by restoring some of the funds slashed from numerous welfare programs. Reagan, however, remained firm. In fact, he not only insisted on going ahead as planned but even demanded additional monies for defense and proposed further reductions in social spending, prompting a group of religious leaders representing all faiths and denominations to state that the President's budget revealed a "nation intent on a selfish and dangerous course of social stinginess and military overkill," a "real moral failure," according to the President of the United Church of Christ.[13]

As 1983 began, Reagan appeared somewhat sobered by the deep recession, by the 12 million unemployed wage earners, by the record-breaking federal deficits, and perhaps by his rapidly tarnishing image as well. In his State of the Union Message he expressed a willingness to consider cuts in defense spending—or at least a slight reduction in the proposed increases, to be balanced by additional cutbacks in welfare spending, including a temporary freeze on the indexing of Social Security and S.S.I. payments. He also indicated a readiness to support federal aid to the states

---

[13]Reagan's fiscal 1983 budget, which included another tax cut that favored the well-to-do and projected a $99 billion deficit, called for a $34 billion increase in defense outlays (over 1982 levels) and, at the same time, a $27 billion reduction in spending on social programs. No wonder he was accused of callousness toward society's less fortunate members.

for an extension of unemployment compensation to those who had exhausted their benefits. And in what clearly elicited the warmest response from his audience, the President declared, "We who are in government must take the lead in restoring the [nation's] economy"—a statement that stood in sharp contrast to one made when he had assumed the presidency two years earlier, namely that "government is not the solution to the problem; government is the problem."

True to his word, Reagan quickly signed into law a measure that Congress had long debated, one that earlier he had threatened to veto—a $9.6 billion relief package, with $4.6 billion earmarked for the creation of 300,000–600,000 public service jobs and $5 billion designated to go to twenty-seven financially distressed states to subsidize the extension of their unemployment compensation programs.

Meanwhile, there were growing signs that economic recovery was on the way. Inflation continued to drop, interest rates began to fall, and the G.N.P. was growing. Most encouraging, however, was the report in March that the Index of Leading Economic Indicators, the administration's main economic forecasting gauge, had increased for the fifth consecutive month and that its 3.6 jump in January, the last month for which figures were available, was the largest monthly increase since July 1950. Unfortunately, however, the unemployment situation had not yet changed; it remained at 10.4 percent of the work force, leading a number of economists to warn that "the euphoria of a sharply improved economic outlook ... need[s] tempering." Still, conditions continued to improve and in July, for the first time in fifteen months, public opinion polls indicated that more Americans approved of Reagan's handling of the economy than disapproved of it.

The economic situation, of course, is crucial, both to the President's popularity and likely political future and to the well-being of all Americans, especially those near the bottom of society. A healthy economy would enable many of them—the unemployed and underemployed—to secure steady, full-time jobs at adequate wages. Yet, it now appears certain that even under the best of circumstances America will not achieve full employment; there always will be some, perhaps many, who will be unable to participate in the economic fruits of society, at least directly. The question is, what will happen to these people?

It is doubtful that the nation will ever return to the policy assumptions that fueled the New Frontier and the Great Society —and most of American history, for that matter—the notion that nothing was impossible if Americans but wished to achieve it. However much the Reagan administration repeats the simple verities of the past and denigrates the so-called prophets of doom, the days when all (or even most) Americans believed that they could control their own destiny—that they could be the world's guardian of freedom, develop the world's most impressive technology, control the universe, conquer injustice, eliminate poverty—are gone. The nation's first military defeat, in Vietnam, the unprecedented sight of a President resigning from office in disgrace, the painful experience of an energy crisis that plainly highlighted the extent to which the nation is dependent on others for its well-being (and perhaps even survival), the frustration of not being able to secure the release of the American hostages in Iran—these and other developments, including the inability of the "experts" to heal an ailing economy and to abate the threat of nuclear holocaust, have forced Americans, or at least many of them, to lose their sense of infallibility, and even confidence, and to accept the idea that there are limitations to their power and their capabilities. These developments also have led many Americans to turn inward, to replace social concerns with personal ones. None of these changes augers well for the nation's less fortunate citizens, nor does the fact that the critics of the current administration—those who bemoan the conservative counterrevolution that has occurred in the past ten or fifteen years, politicians and others—do not seem to have devised any workable alternatives to the more recent policies.

If one wished to close on a more optimistic note, it could be argued, or at least hoped, that "adversity makes us wise" or that it sometimes brings success. In the midst of the Civil War, Abraham Lincoln asserted that "the dogmas of the quiet past are inadequate for the stormy present. As our case is new, so we must think and act anew." As our case once again is new—as we now are faced with a realization of our limitations and can look back at many lost wars against poverty—perhaps we will think and act anew. Perhaps the time has come, or is coming, when most Americans will acknowledge (or be forced to acknowledge) that the poor will be with us, always, through no fault of their own, and that they, too, have a right to a healthy, happy, and secure life.

Bibliography

ANDERSON, MARTIN. *Welfare*. Stanford, Calif.: Hoover Institution, 1978.

ATHERTON, CHARLES A. "The Social Assignment of Social Work," *Social Service Review* 43 (December 1969): 421–29.

BURKE, VINCENT AND VEE. *Nixon's Good Deed: Welfare Reform*. New York: Columbia University Press, 1974.

CLOWARD, RICHARD A., AND FRANCES F. PIVEN. "The Weight of the Poor: A Strategy to End Poverty," *The Nation* 202 (May 2, 1966): 510–17.

DANZIGER, SHELDON, AND ROBERT PLOTNICK. "Can Welfare Reform Eliminate Poverty?", *Social Service Review* 53 (June 1979): 244–60.

DERTHICK, MARTHA. *Policymaking for Social Security*. Washington, D.C.: Brookings Institute, 1979.

FEAGIN, JOE R. *Subordinating the Poor: Welfare and American Beliefs*. Englewood Cliffs, N.J.: Prentice-Hall, 1975.

FRIEDMAN, MILTON. *Capitalism and Freedom*. Chicago: University of Chicago Press, 1962.

GOLDBERG, GERTRUDE S. "New Directions for the Community Service Society of New York: A Study of Organizational Change," *Social Service Review* 54 (June 1980): 184–219.

GRØNBJERG, KIRSTEN. *Mass Society and the Extension of Welfare, 1960–1970*. Chicago: University of Chicago Press, 1977.

HOFFMAN, WAYNE, AND TED MARMOR. "The Politics of Public Assistance Reform: An Essay Review," *Social Service Review* 50 (March 1976): 11–22.

LEVIN, HERMAN. "Conservatism of Social Work," *Social Service Review* 56 (December 1982): 605–615.

LYNN, LAWRENCE E., AND DAVID DEF. WHITMAN. *The President as Policymaker: Jimmy Carter and Welfare Reform*. Philadelphia: Temple University Press, 1981.

MacDonald, Maurice. *Food Stamps and Income Maintenance*. New York: Academic Press, 1977.

Moynihan, Daniel P. *The Politics of a Guaranteed Income: The Nixon Administration and the Family Assistance Plan*. New York: Vintage Books, 1973.

Owen, Henry, and Charles L. Schultze, eds. *Setting National Priorities: The Next Ten Years*. Washington, D.C.: Brookings Institute, 1976.

Ozawa, Martha. "S.S.I.: Progress or Retreat?", *Public Welfare* 32 (Spring 1974): 33–40.

Paull, Joseph E. "Recipients Aroused: The New Welfare Rights Movement," *Social Work* 12 (April 1967): 101–106.

Piven, Frances F., and Richard A. Cloward. *The New Class War: Reagan's Attack on the Welfare State and Its Consequences*. New York: Pantheon Books, 1982.

Plotnick, Robert, and Felicity Skidmore. *Progress Against Poverty: A Review of the 1964–1974 Decade*. New York: Academic Press, 1975.

President's Commission on Income Maintenance Programs. *Poverty amid Plenty: The American Paradox*. Washington, D.C.: Government Printing Office, 1969.

Rangel, Charles B. "Making the Political Process Respond to Human Needs," in *The Social Welfare Forum*. New York: Columbia University Press, 1971.

Richan, Willard C., and Allan R. Mendelsohn. *Social Work: The Unloved Profession*. New York: New Viewpoints, 1973.

Seligman, Ben B. *Permanent Poverty*. Chicago: Quadrangle Books, 1968.

Index

New York Association for Improving
the Condition of the Poor,
67–71, 93, 320–21

New York Charity Organization
Society, 95, 100, 171, 172, 226
and antituberculosis work, 102, 143
Committee on Statistics, 225n5
and first school of social work,
226
and publications, 232

New York Children's Aid Society,
114–17: *see also* Charles Loring
Brace; Child welfare movement
opposition to, 117–18

New York City Department of
Health, and Division of Child
Hygiene, 205

New York City Welfare Council, 258

New York Federation of Jewish
Philanthropies, 274

New York Humane Society, 54

New York Metropolitan Health Law,
138

New York School of Philanthropy,
183, 226–27, 228: *see also*
Columbia University Graduate
School of Social Work; New
York School of Social Work

New York School of Social Work,
227, 231: *see also* Columbia
University Graduate School of
Social Work; New York School
of Philanthropy

New York Society for the Prevention
of Pauperism, 54, 55

New York State Care Act, 182,
182n1

New York State Charities Aid
Association, 79, 118, 262
and aftercare work, 183–84
and antituberculosis work, 144–48
Committee on Mental Hygiene,
194–95

New York State Community Mental
Health Services Act, 198n7

New York State County Poorhouse
Act, 58

New York State Department of
Health, 150–51

New York State Probation
Commission, 128

New York State Public Health
Council, 150–51, 150n6

New York State Public Health Law,
150

New York State Reformatory at
Elmira, 122

New York State Social Welfare
Board, 289

New York Times, on Carter, 329

New York Tuberculosis and Public
Health Association, 262

Nixon, Richard, 313–16, 319, 322,
323
and Family Assistance Plan,
315–17, 315n3
on social workers, 307
and welfare recipients, 314

Northwest Ordinance, 62

Office of Economic Opportunity
(O.E.O.): *see* Economic
Opportunity Act

Of Plimouth Plantation (Bradford), 17

Ohio State University, 227n6

Ohlin, Lloyd, 128

Old-Age Assistance (O.A.A.), 272

Old-Age Insurance (O.A.I.), 272,
284–85, 325, 334

Old-age pensions, 212, 215

Olds, Victoria, 84

Old Testament, and social welfare, 2

Olmsted, Frederick Law, 78n1

O'Neill, Thomas "Tip," on Social
Security "rescue plan," 335

O'Neill, William, on women and the
Civil War, 80

*One Thousand Delinquents: Their
Treatment by Court and Clinic*
(Glueck and Glueck), 129

Operation Head Start: *see* Economic
Opportunity Act

O'Reilley, John Boyle, on charity
organization socieites, 96